THE SON ALSO RISES

THE PRINCETON ECONOMIC HISTORY
OF THE WESTERN WORLD

Joel Mokyr, Series Editor

A list of titles in this series appears at the back of the book.

THE SON ALSO RISES

SURNAMES AND THE HISTORY OF SOCIAL MOBILITY

GREGORY CLARK

with Neil Cummins,
Yu Hao, *and*
Daniel Diaz Vidal

and *Tatsuya Ishii,*
Zach Landes,
Daniel Marcin,
Firas Abu-Sneneh,
Wilfred Chow,
Kuk Mo Jung,
Ariel M. Marek, and
Kevin M. Williams

PRINCETON UNIVERSITY PRESS
Princeton and Oxford

Published by Princeton University Press, 41 William Street, Princeton, New Jersey 08540
In the United Kingdom: Princeton University Press, 6 Oxford Street, Woodstock,
Oxfordshire OX20 1TW

press.princeton.edu

Jacket design by Faceout Studio.

Library of Congress Cataloging-in-Publication Data

Clark, Gregory, 1957–
    The son also rises : surnames and the history of social mobility / Gregory Clark.
        pages   cm.—(The Princeton economic history of the Western world)
    Includes bibliographical references and index.
    ISBN 978-0-691-16254-6 (hardcover : alk. paper)
    1. Social mobility—History.   I. Title.
    HT612.C53   2014
    305.5′1309—dc23   2013042815

British Library Cataloging-in-Publication Data is available

This book has been composed in Minion Pro with Maestrale display
by Princeton Editorial Associates, Inc., Scottsdale, Arizona.

Printed on acid-free paper. ∞

Printed in the United States of America

10 9 8 7 6 5 4 3 2 1

To Mary

CONTENTS

THIS BOOK WILL BE CONTROVERSIAL. So the first task of this preface is to establish that while those listed on the title page collaborated on estimates of social mobility rates in various societies, the text itself was written by me. The interpretation of the evidence from these studies, and the proposed theory of mobility presented in the book, all represent my opinion alone. Also, none of the people I thank below should be taken as endorsing the conclusions of the book.

My second task is to note that the spirit and style of this book follow those of my earlier book, *A Farewell to Alms: A Brief Economic History of the World*. It tries to show that extraordinarily simple models of social mobility can successfully predict outcomes across a whole range of societies and institutions. This is a claim based on incomplete evidence. It may be wrong. But even if it is wrong in aspects, I hope it will point the way to a better and more complete theory of the mechanisms of social mobility. Even in an area as freighted with aspirations and disappointments as social mobility, there should still be room for exploration and conjecture.

The work discussed in this volume was undertaken with several collaborators. The most extensive collaboration was with Neil Cummins, who is jointly responsible for most of the material in chapters 4 and 5 on England. The chapter on China and Taiwan reports on the work Yu Hao completed for his graduate dissertation here at the University of California, Davis, where he devised the methods needed to deal with the small numbers of Han Chinese surnames. The chapter on Chile is a summary of just some of the ongoing dissertation research of Daniel Diaz Vidal, also at the University of California, Davis. The chapter on

Japan is based on an exploration Tatsuya Ishii did for his senior thesis at UC Davis. Zack Landes assisted in getting the estimates for Bengal, including figuring out how to download the 2.2 million names of people in the Kolkata electoral register, the task itself being performed admirably by Lincoln Atkinson. Daniel Marcin of the University of Michigan alerted me to the existence of the tax lists for the United States published in newspapers in 1824 and 1825 and was able to supply us with several such lists. Firas Abu-Sneneh, Wilfred Chow, Kuk Mo Jung, Ariel Marek, and Kevin Williams, students in my graduate history class, worked on the social mobility of Ivy League students from 1850 and earlier as a class project. To all these collaborators I owe a debt of gratitude. This book would not have been possible without their contributions.

This has not been an easy book to complete. A major obstacle was the limited abilities of the principal author. Patterns that seem blindingly obvious in retrospect were initially missed or dismissed. The original intent of the project was just to extend conventional mobility estimates from the modern world into the distant past in countries like England and India. Thus, in the early stages of the research, I gave sunnily optimistic talks about the speed and completeness of social mobility. Only when confronted with evidence of the persistence of status over five hundred years that was too glaring to ignore was I forced to abandon my cheery assurance that one of the joys of the capitalist economy was its pervasive and rapid social mobility. Having for years poured scorn on my colleagues in sociology for their obsessions with such illusory categories as class, I now had evidence that individuals' life chances were predictable not just from the status of their parents but from that of their great-great-great grandparents. Indeed there seems to be an inescapable inherited substrate, looking suspiciously like social class, that underlies the outcomes for all individuals. This book is the product not of acute intelligence but of muddling through to a conclusion that should have been obvious to anyone who looked.

A second obstacle was the extent of the data collection needed to expand the scope of the original study to a wider range of countries and time periods. I am grateful for the grant I received from the NSF (SES-0962351), which was crucial to financing this effort. I am grateful also to the various research assistants who were employed with these funds: Douglas Campbell, Yu Hao, Xi He, Natalie Ho, Tatsuya Ishii, Max McComb, Claire Phan, Richard Scriven, Stephen Sun, and Daniel Diaz Vidal at UC Davis, and Joseph Patrick Burke and Raphaelle Schwarzberg in London. Grants from the All-UC Group in Economic History to Yu Hao and Daniel Diaz Vidal to aid their dissertation research, and a fellowship from the Economic History Association to Yu Hao, were also enormously helpful. John Daniels and Jean Stratford of the Social Science Data Service at Davis were generous with their help on many issues of organizing data collection. Ancestry.com was generous in allowing Neil Cummins and me special access to its wonderful online data sources for the purposes of research.

This whole project was actually sparked by a suggestion of Nicholas Wade, a science writer for the *New York Times,* that surnames could be used to test a hypothesis from the earlier book, of higher reproductive success among upper social classes in preindustrial England. I am happy to report that they confirm that hypothesis. But in exploring surnames, I came to realize that they say a lot more about the nature of the social world.

As before, I owe a huge debt to Princeton University Press. Joel Mokyr, the series editor, and two reviewers of the manuscript, Joe Ferrie and Cormac Ó Gráda, were extraordinarily generous with their time and expertise. Peter Dougherty managed to take time from his more-than-full-time job directing the press to cajole the manuscript to completion, including spending a whole day with me in Los Angeles trying to wrestle an early, inchoate draft into a functioning shape.

Peter Strupp and his team at Princeton Editorial Associates did a stellar job in designing the book and marching it, and its author, through a tightly compressed production schedule.

As always, I owe a great debt to my colleagues in the economics department at UC Davis, first for providing a congenial and intellectually stimulating environment and next for listening over lunch to endless accounts of the arcana of surname practices and to a variety of half-baked theories of the nature of the social world we inhabit. Colin Cameron contributed the insight that led to the simple model that underlies the book. Pontus Rendahl, my former colleague, was pressed into service for his knowledge of Swedish institutions.

I also owe a debt to Sam Bowles and Herb Gintis. It was through interacting with them at the Santa Fe Institute that I came to understand the issues in social mobility. For me these two scholars represent an intellectual ideal: inquisitive, adventurous, independent of academic fashion, always open to new ideas and challenges, laughing at the march of years. Another expert on social mobility, Gary Solon, was generous with his comments and suggestions. This, of course, does not imply that they would endorse any of the conclusions of this book.

The final content of the book has benefited enormously from the comments and criticisms of lecture and seminar audiences at the American Economic Association Annual meetings (San Diego); Autónoma University, Madrid; Bilbao University; California State University, East Bay; Cliometric Society meetings (Boulder); the Colombian Economic History Congress (Bogotá); Cornell University; City University of New York, Queens; Economic History Society meetings (Cambridge); Edinburgh University; the European Historical Economics Society (London); FRESH conference (Pisa); George Mason University; Glasgow University; Harvard University; the INET Conference on Social Mobility (University of Chicago); the International Congress on Medieval Studies; Kalamazoo; the London School of Economics; the Murphy Institute of Tulane University; Northwestern University; the PSID Conference on Multigenerational Social Mobility (Ann Arbor); the Scottish Economic Society; the Sound Economic History Workshop (Lund); State University of New York, Binghamton; the Tsinghua Summer Workshop for Quantitative History (Tsinghua University); University of California, Berkeley; University of California, Davis; the Anderson School of Management at UCLA; University of California, Riverside; the Booth School of Business at the University of Chicago; the economics department at the University of Chicago; University of Copenhagen; University of Michigan; Warwick University; and Yale University.

The one advantage of studying social mobility is that—unlike much of the dry, convoluted, and useless arcana of academic economics—it is a topic on which everyone is informed by her or his own history and experience. So I also benefited from discussions outside the bounds of economics with Anthony Clark, Gerry McCann, Felicity McCann (née Pakenham-Walsh), Patrick Kerr, and Anna and Ernie Spencer.

My last and greatest debt is to Mary McComb, for reasons too numerous to list here.

Mishka's Café, Davis, October 2013

THE SON ALSO RISES

ONE

Introduction

Of Ruling Classes and Underclasses:
The Laws of Social Mobility

FIGURE 1.1 SHOWS A BOY IN GOVAN, a grim, deprived district of my home-town, Glasgow, in my youth in the 1970s. Will his children, grandchildren, and great-grandchildren be found in similar circumstances? To what extent would the chances of a middle-class child of equal ability, placed in the same family in Govan, be reduced by the poverty of his parents? Figure 1.2, in contrast, shows the pleasant suburban Glaswegian street I grew up in, appropriately named Richmond Drive. To what extent is the status of the children raised in that street predictable just from that picture? To what extent would their fortunes have changed had they been raised in Govan?

These questions have, of course, been the subject of extensive enquiry by sociologists and economists.[1] Most people believe that high rates of social mobility are fundamental to the good society. How can we justify the inequalities of income, wealth, health, and longevity so characteristic of the capitalist economy unless any citizen, with sufficient courage and application, has a chance of attaining the grand prizes? Why wouldn't those in the bottom half of the income distribution in a democracy punitively extract resources from the top half if they have no prospect of ever obtaining these goods through the market system?

A convenient summary measure we can use for intergenerational mobility is the correlation of the income, wealth, education, occupational status, and even longevity, of parents and children. This correlation varies from zero to one. Zero represents complete intergenerational social mobility, with no correlation

---

[1] An online search of books and articles containing the phrase *social mobility* yields 244,000 items.

FIGURE 1.1. Boy playing football in Govan, Glasgow, Scotland, 2008.

FIGURE 1.2. Richmond Drive, Cambuslang, Glasgow.

between generations: under these conditions, we can predict nothing about children's outcomes from the circumstances of their birth. A correlation of one represents complete immobility, with a perfect correlation between the status of children and parents: we can predict at birth the entire outcome for any child.[2]

This intergenerational correlation is closely related to another important concept, that of the rate of *regression to the mean* (calculated as one minus the correlation). This is the average rate at which families or social groups that diverge from the mean circumstances of the society move toward that mean in each generation. Thus we refer to the intergenerational correlation as the *persistence rate* of characteristics. The intergenerational correlation can be interpreted as a measure of *social entropy*. The lower this correlation, the greater the degree of social entropy, and the quicker a particular structure of advantage and disadvantage in any society is dissolved.

The intergenerational correlation also has a convenient intuitive interpretation. The square of the correlation is the share of the variation in social status that is explained by inheritance. That share will also be between zero and one. For practical purposes, if the correlation is less than 0.3, then the square is 0.09 or less, suggesting that almost none of the outcomes for the current generation are predictable from parents' circumstances. In such a society, each generation is born anew. The past has little effect on the present. The intergenerational correlation thus indicates the degree to which the accidents of our birth, or, more precisely, our conception, determine our fate.

Most people believe, from their own experience of families, friends, and acquaintances, that we live in a world of slow social mobility. The rich beget the rich, the poor beget the poor. Between the Old Etonian and the slum dweller, between Govan and Richmond Drive, lies a gulf of generations. But a hundred years of research by psychologists, sociologists, and economists seems to suggest that this belief is fictional. Conventional estimates imply that social mobility is rapid and pervasive. The Old Etonian and the slum dweller are cousins.

Standard estimates suggest high modern intergenerational mobility rates. Figure 1.3, for example, shows estimated intergenerational correlations of earnings across a variety of countries. That correlation ranges between 0.15 and 0.65. But these rates imply that inheritance explains only 2 percent to 40 percent of the variation in individual incomes in any generation. Figure 1.4 shows the

[2] Appendix 1 explains these concepts in more detail.

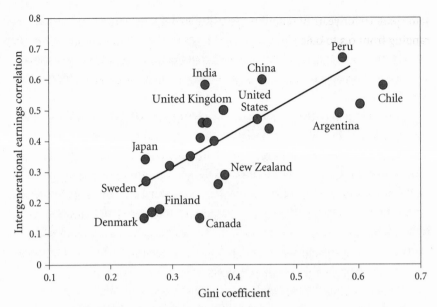

FIGURE 1.3. Intergenerational earnings correlation and inequality.

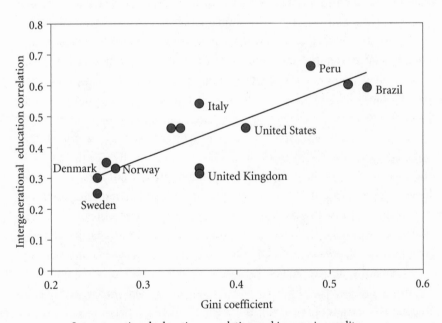

FIGURE 1.4. Intergenerational education correlation and income inequality.

same pattern for years of schooling, with implied intergenerational correlations ranging from 0.3 to 0.65. Only 9 percent to 40 percent of the variation in years of schooling is explained by inheritance. Regression to the mean appears very strong, and human societies seemingly display a high degree of entropy in their social structure.

If all the factors that determine people's life chances are summarized by their parents' status, then these persistence rates imply that all initial advantages and disadvantages for families should be wiped out within three to five generations. In this case the correlation in any measure of social status, such as income, between generations n steps apart is the intergenerational correlation raised to the power n. If the intergenerational correlation for income is 0.3, for example, then the correlation between grandparents and grandchildren is 0.3^2, or 0.09. Between great-grandparents and great-grandchildren, it is 0.3^3, or 0.027. Thus with intergenerational correlations in the range 0.15 to 0.65, correlations for subsequent generations quickly approach zero.

In the standard picture portrayed in figures 1.3 and 1.4, intergenerational mobility rates vary substantially across societies. They are high in the Nordic countries, which have lower income inequality. The degree of income inequality is represented by the Gini coefficient, which is zero with complete equality and one when a single person in society has everything and everyone else nothing. If much of the inequality in modern society is driven by inequality in access to capital, education, and social networks, then the good society would have a low rate of inheritance of social status and correspondingly low variations in income and wealth.

On the conventional picture of social mobility rates, the lower mobility rates observed in countries such as Britain or the United States represent a social failure. The life chances of the descendants of high- and low-status ancestors can be equalized at low social cost. The Nordic countries, after all, constitute one of the richest regions of the world, attractive in many other ways beyond the material: they enjoy high life expectancy, low crime rates, near gender equality, lack of corruption, and political transparency.

Within many societies, particular populations experience much slower rates of social mobility than others. In the United States, for example, blacks, Latinos, Native Americans, and Jewish Americans are all experiencing much slower movement upward or downward toward the mean than is predicted by the intergenerational correlation of 0.5 for income and education. This fact reinforces the idea that on conventional estimates, social mobility rates are suboptimal. Members of poorer minority groups, for example, seem to face greater barriers to mobility than do individuals of the majority population. Richer ethnic groups are able to entrench their social advantages through connections, networks, or access to wealth.

The association in figures 1.3 and 1.4 of greater social mobility rates in higher-income societies also suggests that one of the gains of the Industrial Revolution has been an increase in social mobility rates. The world has been on the march from a preindustrial society of great inequality, where fates were determined by the accidents of birth, to one where lineage and inheritance are of minor significance in an individual's destiny.

Again under conventional mobility estimates, genetic transmission of talent must be unimportant in the determination of social success. Nurture dominates nature. Suppose genetic inheritance matters a lot. Suppose also that mating is assortative across all societies: high-status men marry high-status women. Under these conditions, there is a lower bound to the intergenerational correlation observed in well-functioning market economies. The very low correlations observed in Nordic countries imply that the importance of families and inheritance in determining socioeconomic success must be purely a feature of the social institutions of societies.

These conclusions from conventional scholarly estimates of social mobility rates, however, sit poorly with popular perceptions of social mobility. People looking back to their own grandparents, or forward to their grandchildren, do not generally see the kind of disconnect in status that these estimates imply. People looking at their siblings or cousins see a much greater correlation in status than is implied by the intergenerational correlations reported above.

Consider, for example, the case of the English family the *Pepyses*, made famous by Samuel Pepys, 1633–1703, first secretary of the English Admiralty, member of Parliament, and noted diarist (figure 1.5). *Pepys* has always been a rare surname, flirting with extinction. In 1881 there were only thirty-seven *Pepyses* in England, and by 2002 they were down to eighteen. Seventeenth-century parish records of baptisms and marriages suggest there were only about forty *Pepyses* living at one time even then. The *Pepyses* emerged from obscurity in 1496 when one of them enrolled at Cambridge University, and they have prospered ever since. Since 1496, at least fifty-eight *Pepyses* have enrolled at Oxford or Cambridge, most recently in 1995. For an average surname of this population size, the expected number of enrollees would be two or three. Of the eighteen *Pepyses* alive in 2012, four are medical doctors. The nine *Pepyses*

FIGURE 1.5. John Hayls, *Samuel Pepys*, 1666.

who died between 2000 and 2012 have left estates with an average value of £416,000, more than five times the average estate value in England in this period. If the standard mobility estimates are correct, the chance that a family like this could maintain a high social status over seventeen generations is vanishingly small.[3]

Pepys is not the only rare surname to maintain a surprising presence and persistence at the upper reaches of English society. The phenomenon is remarkably common. Sir Timothy Berners-Lee, OM, KBE, FRS, FREng, FRSA, the creator of the World Wide Web, is a descendant of a family that was rich and prominent in early-nineteenth-century England. But, further, the name *Berners* is descended from a Norman grandee whose holdings are listed in the Domesday Book of 1086. Sir Peter Lytton Bazalgette, the producer of the TV show *Big Brother* and chair of the Arts Council England, is a descendant of

[3] The most famous *Pepys*, Samuel, did not contribute himself to this distinguished lineage, as he has no known descendants.

Louis Bazalgette, an eighteenth-century immigrant and tailor to the prince regent—the Ralph Lauren of his age—who died, leaving considerable wealth, in 1830.[4]

Alan Rusbridger, editor of the *Guardian* newspaper, that scourge of class privilege and inherited advantage, is himself the descendant of a family that achieved significant wealth and social position in Queen Victoria's time. Rusbridger's great-great-grandfather was land steward to His Grace the Duke of Richmond. The value of his personal estate at his death in 1850 was £12,000, a considerable sum at a time when four of every five people died with an estate worth less than £5.

Using surnames to track the rich and poor through many generations in various societies—England, the United States, Sweden, India, Japan, Korea, China, Taiwan, and Chile—this book argues that our commonsense intuition of a much slower rate of intergenerational mobility is correct. Surnames turn out to be a surprisingly powerful instrument for measuring social mobility.[5] And they reveal that there is a clear, striking, and consistent social physics of intergenerational mobility that is not reflected in most modern studies of the topic.

The problem is not with the studies and estimates themselves. What they measure, they measure correctly. The problem arises when we try to use these estimates of mobility rates for individual characteristics to predict what happens over long periods to the general social status of families. Families turn out to have a general social competence or ability that underlies partial measures of status such as income, education, and occupation. These partial measures are linked to this underlying, not directly observed, social competence only with substantial random components. The randomness with which underlying status produces particular observed aspects of status creates the illusion of rapid social mobility using conventional measures.

Underlying or overall social mobility rates are much lower than those typically estimated by sociologists or economists. The intergenerational correlation

---

[4] Ironically, given *Big Brother*'s reputation, Sir Peter is also the descendant of Louis's son Sir Joseph Bazalgette, the nineteenth-century designer of the London sewer system.

[5] Given the power of the results shown in this book, it is surprising that the systematic use of surnames to trace social mobility has been so little used in the past. The only author to pursue this line of inquiry was Nathaniel Weyl, whose *Geography of American Achievement* (1989) uses surnames to measure the status of groups of different ethnic origin. Weyl was a racist and was seeking by these means to show the presumed permanent superiority of those of Jewish and northern European descent.

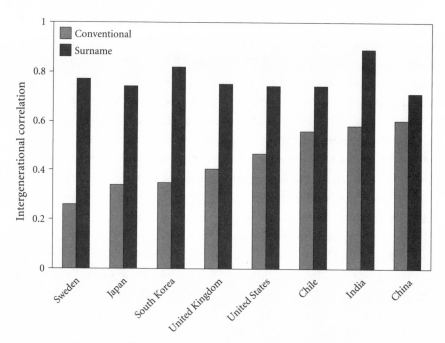

FIGURE 1.6. Conventional versus surname estimates of status persistence.

in all the societies for which we construct surname estimates—medieval England, modern England, the United States, India, Japan, Korea, China, Taiwan, Chile, and even egalitarian Sweden—is between 0.7 and 0.9, much higher than conventionally estimated. Social status is inherited as strongly as any biological trait, such as height. Figure 1.6 compares conventional estimates of mobility (for income and years of education) with those yielded by surname measures.

Even though these rates of intergenerational mobility are low, they have been enough to preclude the formation of any permanent ruling and lower classes. Mobility is consistent across generations. Although it may take ten or fifteen generations, social mobility will eventually erase most echoes of initial advantage or want.

Counterintuitively, the arrival of free public education in the late nineteenth century and the reduction of nepotism in government, education, and private firms have not increased social mobility. Nor is there any sign that modern economic growth has done so. The expansion of the franchise to ever-larger groups in the nineteenth and twentieth centuries similarly has had no effect. Even the redistributive taxation introduced in the twentieth century in countries like the United States, the United Kingdom, and Sweden seemingly has had no impact. In particular, once we measure generalized social mobility, there is no sign that inequality is linked to social mobility rates. Instead social mobility seems to be a constant, independent of inequality.

Groups that seem to persist in low or high status, such as the black and the Jewish populations in the United States, are not exceptions to a general rule of high intergenerational mobility. They are experiencing the same universal rates of slow intergenerational mobility as the rest of the population. Their visibility, combined with a mistaken impression of rapid social mobility in the majority population, makes them seem like exceptions to a rule. They are instead the exemplars of the rule of low rates of social mobility.

Some groups do seem to defy the general rule of slow regression to the mean: the Brahmins of India, the Jews for much of their earlier history, and the Copts of Egypt are longstanding elites of a millennium or more. By contrast, the Gypsies or Travellers in England (now numbering as many as three hundred thousand people) have been at the bottom of the economic scale for more than four hundred years. But these cases are only apparent violations of the rule of regression to the mean: their status can be explained either by an absence of intermarriage or by selective in- and out-migration from the group.

These high estimates of underlying intergenerational correlation imply that 50 to 70 percent of the variation in general social status within any generation is predictable at conception. This assertion will be troubling to some people. If so much is predictable, is not the individual trapped inside the social system? Does this state of affairs imply that the boy from Govan might as well give up any attempt to get educated, become financially secure, or find an occupation that is challenging and satisfying?

The answer is that these data do not imply that outcomes happen to people solely because of their family background. Those who achieve high status in any society do so because of their abilities, their efforts, and their resilience in the face of obstacles and failures. Our findings do suggest, however, that we can predict strongly, based on family background, who is likely to have the compulsion to strive and the talent to prosper.

Though parents at the top of the economic ladder in any generation in pre-industrial England did not secure any lasting advantage for their progeny, there was one odd, enduring effect. Surname frequencies show that the rich were a growing share of the population in the years before 1800. Their genes, consequently, are found more widely in the English population in the nineteenth century than would be expected. But after 1880, the process operated in reverse. Surname frequencies show that the rich families of 1880 have produced surprisingly few descendants living now. Their genes have been disappearing from the modern population until recently.

These effects are likely common in Western Europe. The different demographic correlates of social status before 1800 and after 1880 show that in the modern world, social mobility tends to be predominantly upward, whereas in the preindustrial world it was mainly downward.

Why do the results of our surname measures differ so much from those of conventional mobility studies? Current one-generation studies suffer from a key limitation. Suppose we assume that the various aspects of social status in each generation—income, wealth, education, occupation—are all linked to some fundamental social competence or status of families, with some random deviation. The random component for any aspect of status exists for two reasons. First, there is an element of luck in the status attained by individuals. People happen to choose a successful field to work in or firm to work for. They just succeed in being admitted to Harvard, as opposed to just failing. Second, people make tradeoffs between income and other aspects of status. They may choose to be philosophy professors instead of finance executives. Bill Gates, for example, is a college dropout, a fact that would conventionally mark him as being of relatively low status. Yet the reason he decided to abandon his Harvard education was to further his wealth—an aspiration at which he succeeded spectacularly.

Because current studies are all measures of just one aspect of status, they overestimate overall mobility. Further, they overestimate mobility in later generations even for single aspects of mobility, such as income. They also overestimate even single aspects of mobility for social, ethnic, and religious groups such as Jews, Muslims, black Americans, and Latinos. The rate of regression to mean social status for these groups is much slower than conventional estimates would imply. So, for almost all the issues of social mobility we care about, these estimates are not useful. Further, for families that have not only low income but also low education, no capital, poor health, and a history of unemployment, the general intergenerational correlation for income greatly overstates the likely income of the next generation. Surname estimates are an appropriate tool for reevaluating these predictions.

These differences can also be explained using the biological concepts of *genotype* and *phenotype*, which were introduced to deal with very similar issues of regression to the mean in biological characteristics across generations. The genotype is the set of genes carried by a single organism. Its phenotype comprises all of its observable characteristics, influenced by both by its genotype and its environment. Conventional studies of social mobility measure just the inheritance of particular aspects of the status phenotype. But families also have an underlying status genotype, which is inherited much more faithfully. Surname mobility estimates reflect this status genotype.[6]

Estimated through surnames, social mobility turns out to have a surprisingly simple structure. The same intergenerational correlation applies to the top and the bottom of the status distribution. Upward mobility occurs at the same rate as downward mobility. The same correlation applies to all aspects of mobility, as reflected by income, wealth, education, and longevity. And the process is indeed Markov, meaning that all the information useful to predict the status of the next generation is contained in the current generation.[7] If b is the persistence rate over one generation, then the persistence rate over n generations is given by b^n. Indeed, this book suggests, based on these characteristics, a social law: there is a universal constant of intergenerational correlation of 0.75, from which deviations are rare and predictable.

What is the meaning and explanation of these surname results, which suggest persistent but slow social mobility? This is a much more contentious and difficult question. Studies of social mobility are plagued by a reflexive assumption that more social mobility is good. The last section of the book considers the likely sources of mobility and whether improving the rate of intergenerational mobility would indeed produce a better society.

To know whether an intergenerational correlation of 0.75 represents a social problem or the best of all possible worlds requires a theory of the source of this persistence. If it is created mainly by the social environment in which people spend their childhoods, then any society will produce a mismatch between individuals' talents and their social position. But if persistence is created mainly by an unchangeable familial inheritance of ability, we must conclude that, whatever their institutional structure, societies consistently produce matches of innate talents and social positions.

How important is genetics in determining people's education, income, occupation, wealth, health, and longevity? The data presented in this book cannot

---

[6] The term *status genotype* does not imply here that genes do in fact transmit status, just that the process looks similar in character to genetic transmission.

[7] Strictly speaking, the process is first-order Markov.

answer that question. We can, however, ask whether we can rule out genetics as the primary source of persistence of status across generations. A genetic explanation has a number of empirical implications that we can test with the data assembled here.

If genetics dominates, then the persistence rate should be the same at the top and at the bottom of the social hierarchy. Moreover, endogamous social groups—groups whose members do not marry outside the group—will be completely persistent in their status, high or low. Groups that are on average high or low on the social scale will not succeed or fail socially because of any distinctive culture that they adopted. Instead their success or failure will be the result purely of their positive or negative selection from a larger population. The more distinctive they are now in social status, the smaller a share they will be of the descendants of their parent population.

If genetics matters most, then the outcomes for adopted children will be largely uncorrelated with those of their adoptive parents but highly correlated with those of their biological parents. And if genetics matters, then the only factor that determines social status is one's parents. Grandparents, great-grandparents, uncles, aunts, and cousins play no role. In particular, if we can measure without bias the underlying social competence of the parents, that will predict an individual's social outcomes. If two people have parents of equivalent social competence, but in one case these parents come from a distinguished lineage, with a rich background of helpful social connections, and in the other the parents are nouveau riche, with no such networks, those differences will make no difference in the outcomes for the children.

Another implication of a genetic explanation of status persistence is that family size does not matter in determining social outcomes for children. The idea of a tradeoff between quantity and quality in family life is one of the sacred doctrines of neoclassical economics, one that lies at the heart of attempts to explain the long-delayed arrival of modern economic growth. But if genetics dominates in the transmission of status, by implication this tradeoff is insignificant or nonexistent.

By and large, social mobility has characteristics that do not rule out genetics as the dominant connection between the generations. Ascribing an important role to genetics helps to explain one puzzle of social mobility, which is the inability of ruling classes in places like England, Sweden, and the United States to defend themselves forever against downward mobility. If the main determinants of economic and social success are wealth, education, and connections, then there is no explanation for the consistent tendency of the rich to regress to the society mean even at the slow rates we observe. We see, for example, that in the years 1880–1990, the rich in England consistently had fewer children than the poor. This should have enabled them to invest more time and resources in their children and preserve their wealth by dividing it among fewer descendants. With this behavior, why have they not persisted at the top of society, or even moved further above the mean? In contrast, in the years 1500–1800, the rich consistently had many more children than the poor, dividing their attention and wealth among many surviving offspring. Yet these very different demographic regimes had no effect on social mobility rates in England. They were the same before the Industrial Revolution as after.

Only if genetics is the main element in determining economic success, if nature trumps nurture, is there a built-in mechanism that explains the observed regression. That mechanism is the intermarriage of the children of rich and educated lineages with successful, upwardly mobile children of poor and uneducated lineages. Even though there is strong assortative mating—because this is based on the social phenotype created in part by luck—those of higher-than-average innate talent tend to mate with those of lesser ability and regress to the mean. Similarly, those of lower-than-average innate talent tend to marry unlucky offspring of higher average innate talent.

If nature does indeed dominate nurture, this has a number of implications. First, it means the world is a much fairer place than we intuit. Innate talent, not inherited privilege, is the main source of economic success. Second, it suggests that the large investment made by the upper classes in the care and raising of their children is of no avail in preventing long-run downward mobility: the wealthy Manhattan attorneys who hire coaches for their toddlers to ensure placement in elite kindergartens cannot prevent the eventual regression of their descendants to the mean. Third, government interventions to increase social mobility are unlikely to have much impact unless they affect the rate of intermarriage between levels of the social hierarchy and between ethnic groups. Fourth, emphasis on racial, ethnic, and religious differences allows persistent social stratification through the barriers they create to this intermarriage. In order for a society to increase social mobility over the long run, it must achieve the cultural homogeneity that maximizes intermarriage rates between social groups.

What is the significance of these results for parents socially ambitious for their children? The practical implication is that if you want to maximize your children's chances, you need to pay attention not to the social phenotype of your marriage partner but instead to his or her status genotype. That genotype is indicated by the social group your potential partner belongs to, as well as the social phenotype of their siblings, parents, grandparents, cousins, and so on to the nth degree of relatedness. Once you have selected your mate, your work is largely done. You can safely neglect your offspring, confident that the innate talents you secured for them will shine through regardless. If, that is, the theory on the source of status persistence conjectured here is correct.

I want to emphasize that this book is not a jeremiad. Despite the low reported rates of social mobility, despite the importance of lineage in determining current outcomes, and despite our inability to significantly influence underlying rates of social mobility, this book takes cheer from the completeness of social mobility. Thus the title *The Son Also Rises*. For the evidence of the book is that social position is likely determined by innate inherited abilities. The social world is much fairer than many would expect. And the evidence is that in the end, the descendants of today's rich and poor will achieve complete equality in their expected social position. This equality may require three hundred years to come about. Yet why, in the grand scheme of societies, is three hundred years for convergence any more significant an interval than thirty years?

But an important corollary to the finding that social outcomes are the product of a lineage lottery is that we should not create social structures that magnify the rewards of a high social position. The justification for the great inequalities we observe is often that reward is the required stimulus for achievement. But we see in the various settings studied in this book, as in figure 1.6, no correlation between inequality and underlying rates of social mobility. If social position is largely a product of the blind inheritance of talent, combined with a dose of pure chance, why would we want to multiply the rewards to the lottery winners? Nordic societies seem to offer a good model of how to minimize the disparities in life outcomes stemming from inherited social position without major economic costs.

It should also be emphasized that the concentration in the book on the patrilineal line of inheritance, which is only one of many lines of descent once we look across many generations, is driven purely by the fact that in the societies studied here, surnames until recently were overwhelmingly inherited from fathers. It does not reflect any belief that women are unimportant: it merely results from the fact that until the last few generations, women's status largely reflected that of their husbands. But there is no indication that were we to measure status persistence rates through the matrilineal line, we would observe more mobility. In the modest number of cases where we observe, for example, the correlation between fathers and sons-in-law, it is just as high as between fathers and sons.[8] It is notable, however, that the emancipation of women in recent generations has had no influence on social mobility rates. Emancipated women mate as assortatively as before and transmit their status to children as faithfully as in the patriarchal societies of the past.

[8] See, for example, Olivetti and Paserman 2013.

PART ONE

SOCIAL MOBILITY

BY TIME AND PLACE

TWO

Sweden

Mobility Achieved?

IN EXPLORING SOCIAL MOBILITY USING SURNAMES, we begin with Sweden for two reasons. First, by conventional measures, modern Sweden has social and economic mobility more rapid than that of either the United Kingdom or the United States. And Sweden is representative of a group of Nordic countries —Denmark, Finland, Iceland, Norway, and Sweden—believed to have achieved low inequality, widespread educational attainment, and fast social mobility. In recent years these societies have been cited as a reproach to the economic model of the United Kingdom and the United States. Both have greater inequality in outcomes and lower apparent rates of social mobility. These contrasts are evident in figures 1.3 and 1.4 above. The rapid measured social-mobility rates of Nordic countries imply that very little of their citizens' current income and educational attainment can be predicted from parental income or education. The Nordic social world is made anew each generation. These societies seem to offer profound equality in life chances for the children of rich and poor, educated and uneducated.

A recent study of four generations of families in Malmö suggests that intergenerational earnings and education correlations in Sweden have been at the modern level for at least three to four generations. The initial generation in the Malmö study was born between 1865 and 1912.[1]

Such mobility would suggest that Swedish institutional arrangements—the support for public education, for example, and the progressive taxation of wealth —play a vital role in determining rates of social mobility. The implication, as

[1] Lindahl et al. 2012, table 5.

discussed in chapter 1, is that the lower rates of social mobility observed in countries such as England and the United States represent a social failure. The life chances of the descendants of high- and low-status ancestors can be equalized at low social cost. Sweden is, after all, one of the richest economies in the world.

However, this chapter shows that the persistence rates reported for these countries, unless carefully interpreted, lead to a false interpretation of Nordic social reality. Estimated using surnames, the intergenerational correlations for measures of status such as occupation or education are much higher.[2] And in the modern era they are as high as the rates of the eighteenth century. Whatever the short-run mobility shown by earnings or education, there is considerable persistence of status—measured through earnings, wealth, education, and occupation—over as many as ten generations in Sweden.

The finding that social mobility is much slower than conventional estimates comes from the study of the frequency of two historically elite sets of surnames among modern high-status groups compared to their frequency in the general population. If this ratio, the relative representation, is greater than one, the surname group still constitutes an elite. If it is less than one, it forms an underclass. The speed with which the relative representation approaches one for any group reveals the social mobility rate of the society.[3] The first set of names comprises uncommon surnames associated with the Swedish nobility. The second is the surnames of the educated elite of the seventeenth and eighteenth centuries. Both sets of names are still overrepresented among modern Swedish elites—physicians, attorneys, university students, and members of the Royal Academies—showing that true social mobility rates in Sweden have been low. By looking at the rate at which their overrepresentation in these groups has declined over the last two or three generations, we can measure mobility rates up to 2012. The results are summarized in table 2.1. They show that current social mobility in Sweden is very slow—no faster, as we shall see, than comparable estimates in the United Kingdom or the United States, and no faster than social mobility in eighteenth-century Sweden under monarchic rule.

[2] When intergenerational mobility is estimated using surnames, the length between generations has to be specified. In this book, for convenience, it is always taken as thirty years.

[3] Appendix 2 provides the technical details of this calculation.

TABLE 2.1. Estimates of status persistence rates by occupations, Sweden, 1700–2012

	1700–1900	1890–1979	1950–2012
Attorneys	—	—	0.73
Physicians	—	0.71	0.80
University students	0.80	—	0.67
Royal Academy members	0.88	0.75	0.83

Swedish Surnames

Surprisingly, despite Sweden's reputation as a model social democracy, a class of nobles is very much alive and functioning. The country has a formal guild of noble families, the Riddarhuset (House of Nobility) (figure 2.1). Though noble families have existed since medieval times, the modern Riddarhuset was created in 1626. From 1668 to 1865, it functioned as one of the four governing estates of the kingdom, analogous to the House of Lords in England. Since 2003 the Riddarhuset has been a private institution that maintains the records of the Swedish noble families, and lobbies on their behalf. In spite of Sweden's advances in gender equality, only men vote in the Riddarhuset, and only sons transmit titles to their offspring.

FIGURE 2.1. The Riddarhuset, headquarters of the Swedish nobility, in downtown Stockholm.

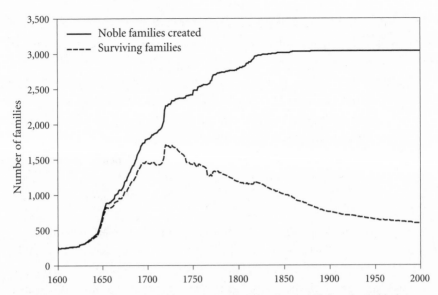

FIGURE 2.2. The history of ennoblement in Sweden: families enrolled in the Riddarhuset.

The families enrolled in the Riddarhuset occupy three hierarchical ranks: in descending order, these are counts, barons, and "untitled" nobility. More than two thousand families have been enrolled, though only about seven hundred have living representatives.[4] The timing of these ennoblements is summarized in figure 2.2. As the figure shows, almost all extant noble families were enrolled before 1815: indeed, a large fraction of all noble families was created in the period 1658–1721, when Sweden's territories encompassed Finland, Estonia, and some north German states. From 1680 onward the nobility gradually lost its privileges, starting with the reclamation by the crown in 1680 of much of the land granted to nobles in previous years. By 1866 the nobles had no economically significant privileges.

When Swedish families were enrolled in the Riddarhuset, they typically adopted a new surname embodying status elements such as *gyllen* (gold), *silfver* (silver), *adler* (eagle), *leijon* (lion), *stjerna* (star), *creutz* (cross), and *ehren* (honor). Thus we get names like *Leijonhufvud, Gyllenstjerna, Ehrensvärd,* and *Adlercreutz*. Rosencrantz and Guildenstern, the two unfortunate Danish nobles in Shakespeare's *Hamlet* (written around 1600) have forms of two com-

[4] Riddarhuset 2012.

mon noble Danish and Swedish surnames. One-tenth of the aristocrats participating in the Danish coronation of 1596 supposedly bore one or the other of these names.[5]

Many Swedish noble surnames, however, are German in origin, reflecting the number of German military commanders rewarded with ennoblement for their service to the Swedish crown in the seventeenth century: hence names such as *von Buddenbrock* and *von Köningsmarck*. Scottish, English, French, and other foreign surnames also appear: *Douglas, Maclean, Bennet, de la Gardie.* Some noble surnames are, however, quite common and held by many people probably not descended from these noble families, such as *Björnberg* or *Hamilton.* The analysis below is therefore restricted to noble surnames now held by four hundred or fewer people, of whom a large fraction of current holders likely descended from an original ennobled family.

One privilege that the nobility obtained through the Names Adoption Act of 1901 was a ban on anyone else's adopting their surnames.[6] Thus, apart from foreign imports and name changes before 1901, the surnames of the enrolled nobles in the Riddarhuset uniquely identify the lineage of these noble families. Such surnames constitute a small Swedish elite. Only sixteen thousand individuals currently hold the surnames of count and baronial families (defined according to the criterion specified above). A further forty thousand people hold rarer surnames associated with the untitled nobility.

Signs that these surnames are mostly derived by descent from those ennobled many years ago come from the stock of these names as a share of the population. Figure 2.3 shows the incidence of a sample of aristocratic surnames among male deaths from 1901 to 2009, and among male births from 1810 to 1989. From 1810 to the present, these noble surnames have accounted for the same share of surnames.

The second class of surnames of interest are latinized surnames. In the preindustrial era, when most Swedes had impermanent patronyms, clerics, academics, and some merchants adopted surnames sometimes derived from Swedish names but typically ending in *-ius* or *-eus,* which became characteristic of an educated class. These include the names of a number of famous Swedish scientists of the seventeenth and eighteenth centuries: Carolus Linnaeus

[5] Boyce 2005, 154.
[6] There was concern that disreputable people were adopting noble surnames.

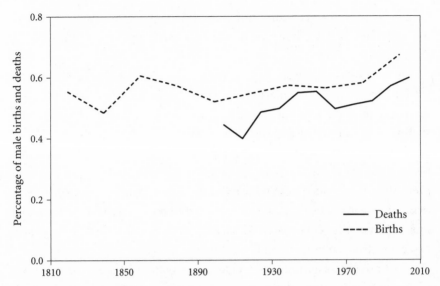

FIGURE 2.3. Percentage of aristocratic surnames at death for men born 1810–2009.

(1707–78), Anders Celsius (1701–44), Jöns Jakob Berzelius (1779–1848), and Olaus Rudbeckius (1630–1702). Typical examples of these surnames now are *Aquilonius, Arrhenius, Berzelius, Boethius,* and *Cnattingius.*

Only a small fraction of the modern population bears such latinized surnames. Of those dying between 2000 and 2009, for example, only 0.5 percent bore a surname ending in either *-ius* or *-eus*. However, in the late nineteenth and early twentieth century, significant numbers of people adopted newly created latinized surnames. Figure 2.4 shows that of men born 1810–1990 the proportion with latinized surnames doubled over time.

To avoid including newly adopted surnames, the latinized surnames employed here are restricted to those that existed before 1800. One quick way to identify such long-established surnames is to consider only latinized surnames held by forty or more people in 2011.[7] They are overwhelmingly held by those who inherited them from their parents as opposed to adopting them, perhaps because of the restrictions imposed on name changes in the Name Regulation Law (*släktnamnsförordningen*) of 1901 and the Naming Law of 1982,

---

[7] Because a new latinized name only recently adopted would not have time to grow to have forty holders by 2011, this criterion narrows names to those in existence much earlier.

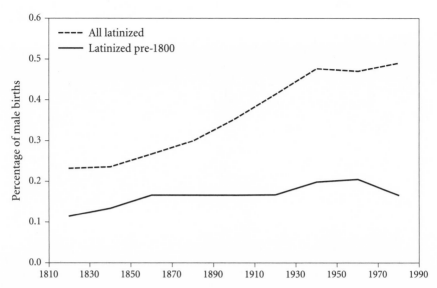

FIGURE 2.4. Percentage of latinized surnames at death for men born 1810–1979.

which now requires the Swedish Tax Agency to approve all surname changes. These surnames constitute 0.2 percent of the current population.[8] The share of these older latinized surnames in the population is close to stable between 1810 and 1989.

The most common Swedish surnames are patronyms, surnames formed from the first name of the father and ending in *-son*. These were the predominant type of surname in preindustrial Sweden. A sample of seventeenth-century parish marriage records, for example, shows that 93 percent of those who married bore such patronyms.[9] In early Sweden, such patronyms changed from generation to generation. In the eighteenth and nineteenth centuries, their use declined, and families adopted more permanent surnames. The 1901 Name Regulation Law called for each family to have a surname that would remain unchanged across generations.

The decline of patronyms has continued to this day. Figure 2.5 shows estimates by twenty-year periods of the number of Swedish men born with and

[8] As Watson and Galton famously demonstrated, rare surnames over many generations tend to either die out or survive at a relatively higher frequency (Watson and Galton 1875).

[9] FamilySearch, n.d.

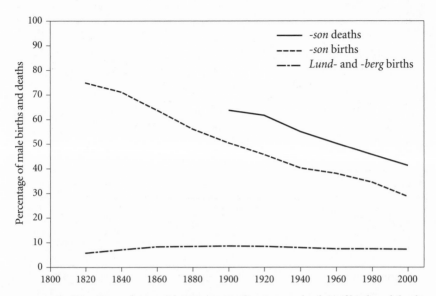

FIGURE 2.5. Percentage of men with surnames ending in *-son,* by date of birth and death.

dying with a patronym as surname. After the year 2000, only 40 percent of males who died in Sweden bore a patronym. But for those dying before age 10, the share was even lower, approximately one-quarter.[10]

We can observe the sources of this decline if we consider the percentage of patronyms occurring among all men born in 1950–51 dying by 2009. Of this cohort, half of those dying before age 10 but only a third of those dying between ages 50 and 59 had a patronym. By implication, nearly one-third of men born with patronyms changed their surnames, with most of the changes occurring by age 30. Thus, although patronyms in Sweden are associated with low social status, we have to be careful when using them to measure social mobility, since such patronyms are only selectively retained by the modern population.

Nina Benner, a reporter for Swedish Radio, tells a nicely illustrative story from her own family of how such surname changes took place. Her grandfather and his four brothers changed their surname from *Andersson* to *Benner* in 1916, when her grandfather was sixteen. His eldest brother was studying to become a physician, and his professor made it clear that *Andersson* wasn't a suitable name

---

[10] This trend is due in part to a substantial increase in children born to immigrants in this period. Of males born in 2000 who died by 2009, one in ten had a Muslim first name, and another one in ten had a name suggesting an immigrant parent.

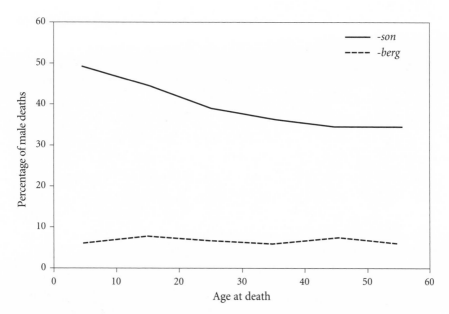

FIGURE 2.6. Percentage of men born in 1950–51 with surnames ending in -berg and -son, by age at death.

in that profession. The name *Benner* stems from the small village of Bennebo, where her great-grandfather grew up.

The incidence of other Swedish names, however, remains constant among men in different age cohorts. As figure 2.6 shows, of men born in 1950–51, the percentage holding surnames ending in -berg (mountain) was the same among those dying before age 10 as among those dying after age 50. These topographical surnames can be used as a standard for measuring social mobility rates.

Surnames and Current Earnings and Wealth

Since the two sets of elite surnames, noble and latinized, were established before 1800, we would expect, given the rapid rates of social mobility reported for Sweden in the current and previous generations, that these surnames would have regressed completely to mean social status. They would not differ in any way from the average surname in Sweden. Their connotation of exalted status would have been totally lost.

One way we can measure the status of different surnames, and also the distribution of status, in modern Sweden is from tax records. This information is publicly available and is even sold commercially under the slogan "Know what your neighbors earn."

Figure 2.7 shows for Stockholm *kommun* (municipality) some of the information for the noble surname *Leijonhufvud*. The publications conveniently give detailed addresses for each taxpayer. The first column of numbers shows earned income in Swedish kroner. The second shows capital income. The tax returns reveal clearly that the expected social entropy in Sweden has not occurred. Individuals with noble and latinized surnames have higher taxable incomes, both earned and capital incomes, than those with the common surname *Andersson*. The differences are not huge, but they are quite clear. Thus for six *kommuns* in the Stockholm region, the average taxable income of people with noble surnames in 2008 was 44 percent greater than for those named *Andersson,* and 27 percent greater for those with latinized surnames than for *Anderssons*.[11]

Analysis of the tax data shows that those with noble and latinized surnames have higher incomes not only because there are more of them at the upper end of the income distribution but also because there are fewer of them at the bottom of the distribution. As figure 2.8 shows, the range of income among individuals with these names is just as great as among *Anderssons,* but the mean of that range is higher in each case.

The income level for the top 1 percent of taxable incomes in these six *kommuns* was two million Swedish kroner or more. Among those with noble surnames, 2.6 percent have incomes in this top 1 percent. Thus the relative representation of noble surnames among the income elite is 2.6: these names are 2.6 times as likely as the average surname to be in the top 1 percent of incomes. Such estimates of relative representation among elite groups for Sweden and throughout the book are used as a convenient measure of the social status of surnames.

As long as the intergenerational correlation of income is less than one, the mean income of those with noble surnames must be approaching the overall mean income. As this happens, the relative representation of noble surnames at the top of the income distribution will decline, and the relative representation of such surnames at the bottom will increase. Appendix 2 details how the speed with which the relative representation of surnames moves toward one at the upper tail of the status distribution gives us a measure of the intergenerational

[11] 2008 tax returns for the *kommuns* of Botkyrka, Huddinge, Haninge, Nacka, Stockholm, and Täby (Kalenderförlaget 2008a,b,c).

Leijonhielm, Anna Örnbacken 26	320,400	10,131
Leijonhielm, Larsson, May Backvindeln 63	283,000	
Leijonhufvud, Cecilia Banérgatan 46 2 tr	481,700	467,543
Leijonhufvud, Madeleine Basaltgrand 10	340,100	
Leijonhufvud, Margareta Bergsmarksvagen 4 1 tr	1,576,800	100,317
Leijonhufvud, Louise Blackebergsbacken 5 tag 144	119,400	1,080,423
Leijonhufvud, Eld Blanchegatan 18 4 tr	336,700	
Leijonhufvud, Margareta E C A Halsingehöyden 11	247,000	2,082,476
Leijonhufvud, Christina Hogbergsgatan 11	279,200	
Leijonhufvud, Elisabeth Kommendorsgatan 28	573,500	
Leijonhufvud, Jenny Krukmakargatan 67 lag 0015	523,000	
Leijonhufvud, Alice Langelandsgatan 10	318,200	289
Leijonhufvud, Susanna Manhernsgatan 13 bv	283,000	
Leijonhufvud, Sven Märdvagen 34	362,100	54,519
Leijonhufvud, Elisabet Märdvagen 34	308,200	1,256
Leijonhufvud, Eric Mybrogatan 64	648,000	40,340
Leijonhufvud, Gustaf Mybrogatan 68 t tr	239,500	152,518
Leijonhufvud, Titti Odengatan 23 5 tr	322,700	
Leijonhufvud, Ewa K S Ragvaldsgatan 21 4 tr	534,300	123,020
Leijonhufvud, Ruth Sigrid G Rindogatan 42	289,300	
Leijonhufvud, Fredrik Rälambsvägen 10 A	1,224,800	23,100
Leijonhufvud, Elizabeth Rälambsvägen 10 A 3 tr	667,800	

FIGURE 2.7. Sample of published tax returns for Stockholm, 2008.

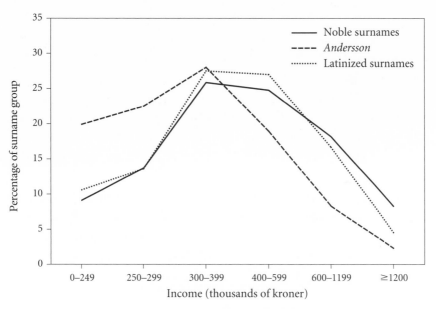

FIGURE 2.8. Distribution of taxable income within surname groups, 2008.

correlation of status. Below are shown these calculations for four elite groups in Sweden: attorneys, physicians, university students, and members of the Royal Academies. These estimates present a unified picture of very slow social mobility in Sweden, now and earlier.

ATTORNEYS

The Swedish Bar Association maintains a register of seven thousand member attorneys that records each member's date of birth. A comparison of the frequency of surname types in this register with the frequency of surname types in the general population reveals significant mismatches. As figure 2.9 shows, the surnames held by titled nobles—counts and barons—appear in the register at nearly six times the rate they occur in the general population.[12] Other over-represented surnames include those associated with untitled nobles and latinized surnames, both appearing at about three times the expected rate (their share in the population). Surnames beginning with *Lund-* appear at the expected rate. In contrast, surnames ending in *-son* appear at half the expected rate.

These results again imply that the distant past has a surprising effect on the present even in Sweden. Surnames that were differentiated socially in the eighteenth century remain so even ten generations later. Noble surnames have retained their ranking in the social hierarchy: the surnames of counts and barons carry still higher status than those of the untitled nobles.

Members of the bar can be divided into two generations, those born between 1930 and 1959 and those born between 1960 and later. Figure 2.10 shows the relative representation of each surname type in these two cohorts. It reveals, first, that each of the surname types has been regressing toward the expected mean representation of one. Second, however, it shows that the rate of regression to the mean is slow. Even among attorneys born in 1960 and later, those qualifying within the past thirty years, there are substantial differences in the relative representation of surnames.

The implied intergenerational correlation of occupational status from the attorney data by surname group is as follows: titled nobles, 0.79; untitled nobles, 0.72; latinized surnames, 0.71; and patronyms, 0.69. (Note, however, that interpreting intergenerational correlations for patronyms requires caution because significant numbers of people switched from the patronyms of their birth to other types of surnames. If it was mainly the more socially successful who

---

[12] For details of how these data were treated, see Clark 2013.

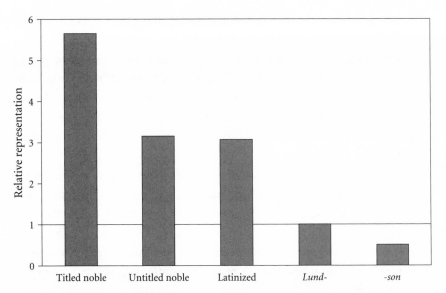

FIGURE 2.9. Relative representation of surname types among attorneys, 2012.

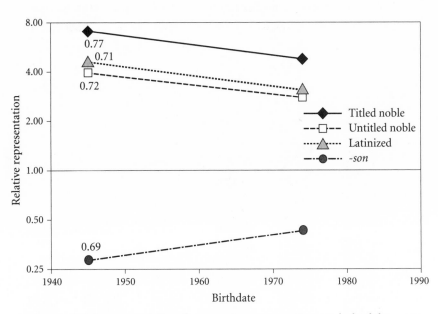

FIGURE 2.10. Relative representation of surname types among attorneys, by birthdate, 2012.

changed their names in this way, the estimated correlation could be significantly higher than the true correlation.) The average intergenerational correlation reported for attorneys in table 2.1 is 0.73 for the three elite surname groups. The estimated correlations do differ by surname group, but because the numbers of attorneys in each surname group are typically less than fifty, these variations in estimated correlations could easily stem from chance alone.

PHYSICIANS

A second source for measuring social mobility rates is the list of physicians in Sweden registering first between 1890 and 2011, which covers four generations. Starting with currently registered physicians, we see in figure 2.11 the same differences in relative representation of surnames that we see among attorneys. The surnames of the three elite groups of the eighteenth century are overrepresented relative to their share of the population. Patronyms are greatly underrepresented.

Analyzing surname types for Swedish physicians is complicated by the fact that a substantial proportion of currently registered physicians in Sweden are of foreign origin. Physicians with a medical license from any other European

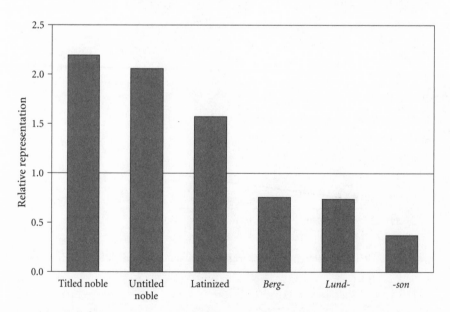

FIGURE 2.11. Relative representation of surname types among registered Swedish physicians, 2011.

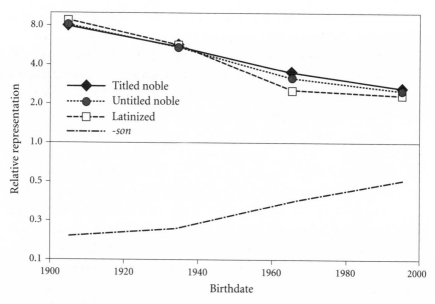

FIGURE 2.12. Relative representation of surname types among Swedish physicians, 1890–2011.

Union country can register in Sweden without further required training. Thus in 2007, almost one in five of all physicians registered in Sweden were trained abroad, including Swedes who attended foreign medical schools. But of those registering first in 2007, excluding Swedes trained in foreign medical schools, two of every five were foreign.[13] One consequence is that even surnames such as *Lund-,* which have an average representation among attorneys, are underrepresented among physicians.

To correct for this complication and calculate the relative representation of Swedish surname types among Swedish-born physicians in Sweden, it is assumed that all foreign physicians were registered in 1980 or later, and that the relative representation of the surnames *Lund-* and *Berg-* averaged one between 1980 and 2011. These assumptions imply that in this cohort, only 70 percent of all physicians are Swedish born—a reasonable estimate. The overall domestic physician population for these years is calculated accordingly. For the years before 1980, it is assumed that all registered physicians in Sweden were Swedish born.

Figure 2.12 shows relative representation of the four surname types—titled noble, untitled noble, latinized, and patronyms—among physicians in thirty-

[13] "Every Other Doctor in Sweden from Abroad" 2009.

year cohorts, by registration date, beginning in 1890. To make clearer what is happening with the patronyms, a logarithmic scale is used in figure 2.12. All three groups regress toward the mean, but their rate of regression is again very slow among all cohorts. Figure 2.13 shows the best-fitting relative representation for all those in the three high-status groups across the four generations. The estimated persistence rate in this case is 0.74, and the fit, as can be seen, is good. The rate of regression to the mean was no faster in the past thirty years than in earlier years. To a first approximation, it was the same as in the years before 1980.

The corresponding persistence rate for the patronyms is similarly high, at 0.74. Again, however, we must be cautious about the estimate for patronyms. Because of the abandonment of patronyms, which was likely more common among the upwardly mobile, the intergenerational correlation estimated here may overestimate the persistence of status among those with patronym surnames. However, the persistence rate estimated for this group is the same as for the three elite surname groups.

Thus the representation of surnames among both attorneys and physicians in Sweden suggests a similar pattern: social mobility in Sweden is much slower than the conventional estimates suggest, even for very recent generations. A

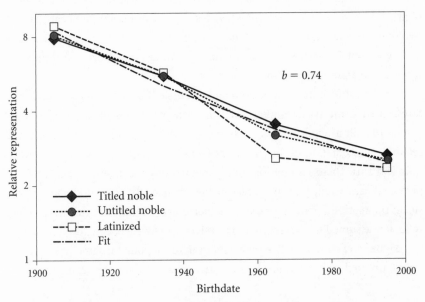

FIGURE 2.13. Estimated persistence rate for Swedish physicians with elite surnames.

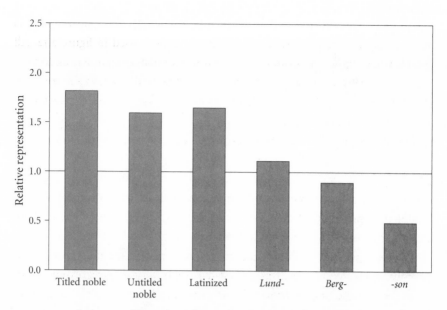

FIGURE 2.14. Surnames of Uppsala students submitting master's theses, 2000–2012.

second surprising finding from the surname distribution of Swedish physicians is that not only are true social mobility rates slower than conventionally estimated, but they are no faster now than they were in the early twentieth century. The enlargement of the political franchise and the institutions of the extensive welfare state of modern Sweden, including free university education and maintenance subsidies to students, have done nothing to increase rates of social mobility.

Educational Mobility, 1948–2012

The ineffectiveness of free university education in increasing social mobility is borne out by patterns of surname distribution among university graduates, even in recent decades. Figure 2.14, for example, shows the relative representation of the surname groups among those completing master's theses at Uppsala University from 2000 through 2012. Taking surnames of the form *Lund-* or *Berg-* as having an average representation, the noble and latinized surnames, largely originating before 1800, are again overrepresented by 60 to 80 percent. The most common patronyms appear at half their expected representation.[14]

[14] See again Clark 2013 for details of these calculations.

The differences between the elite surnames and patronyms among university graduates are less pronounced than among attorneys and physicians. But master's degree programs, even at elite universities such as Uppsala, are less exclusive than the professions of attorney and physician. Indeed, based on the numbers of master's theses submitted annually at Sweden's most selective universities—Gothenburg, Lund, Stockholm, and Uppsala—we can predict that 8 percent of Swedes born in 1990 will complete a master's thesis at one of these universities.[15]

If a surname type, such as a latinized name, is at a relative representation of two for the top 8 percent of the population, then its relative representation among the top 1 percent (approximating the selectivity of the legal and medical professions) would be 2.8.[16] Thus the information for university students is consistent with the evidence for physicians and attorneys in the most recent generations and suggests again that there is currently very slow regression to the mean for elite and underrepresented surnames.

These data imply that if 8 percent of all twenty-two-year-olds in Sweden now get a master's degree from one of these four elite universities, the rate for those with elite surnames is 13–14 percent. The status differences signaled by Swedish surnames will not end soon.

There are extensive records of those enrolled at the only two Swedish universities established before 1954: Uppsala (founded in 1477) and Lund (founded in 1666). These records include the surnames of more than two thousand members of three student "nations" (dining and residence associations) at Uppsala between 1942 and 1966. These records show the relative representation of different surname types at Uppsala circa 1948 and circa 2008 (two generations later). Figure 2.15 shows, again, a clear convergence of all four groups toward the mean across these two generations.

To calculate the intergenerational correlation for education implied by the data in figure 2.15, we need to take into account that Uppsala and Lund were much more elite institutions in the 1940s than in 2000–2012. The fraction of Swedes attending Uppsala and Lund in the late 1940s can be roughly estimated as still only 1 percent of the population, compared to an estimate for master's theses of 8 percent of the population today. The estimated persistence rate for each of the three elite groups, allowing for this shift in the upper proportion of the popu-

[15] For details of this calculation, see Clark 2013.
[16] Clark 2013.

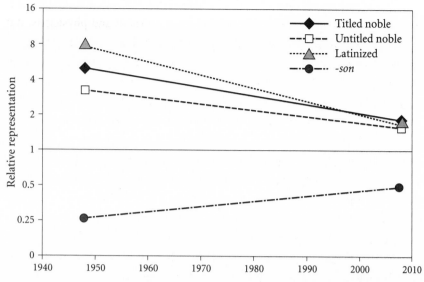

FIGURE 2.15. Relative representation of surnames at Uppsala University, 1948–2012.

lation being observed at universities, is 0.72 for the titled noble surnames, 0.75 for the untitled noble surnames, and 0.57 for the latinized surnames.

However, because the sample size for these surnames at Uppsala in the years 1942–66 is small, there is significant sampling error in these estimates. Combining these groups into one elite implies an overall intergenerational correlation across these two generations of 0.66. Yet the two subsequent generations of students matriculated after major reforms in 1977 that greatly expanded access to universities. Tuition is now free, and grants and loans are available to students to cover living costs.

For the patronym surname group, here estimated on the basis of the surnames *Andersson, Johansson, Karlson,* and *Nilsson,* the implied intergenerational correlation, 0.87, is even lower. The caveats detailed above for such estimates apply here also.

Educational Mobility, 1700–1908

There are good data available on the surnames of Lund attendees for the period 1666–1908: sources include a register of all students for 1732 through 1830 and detailed biographies from a number of the student nations that all students had to enroll in. For Uppsala there is complete registry data for the period 1477–1817, but data from only one student nation for the period 1817–1902.

Figure 2.16 shows the relative representation of latinized surnames at Lund by thirty-year cohorts, starting in 1700. In the first generation observed, 14 percent of Lund students had latinized surnames, compared with an estimated 0.13 percent of the general population. Such names were thus 122 times more common among students than in the general population. The share of latinized surnames among students fell to 1.1 percent by 1880–1909. They were 5.3 times as frequent among Lund students as among the general population. The pace of this decline in representation implies a high persistence of this group, however. The persistence rate estimated for 1700–1909 is 0.78, assuming that university students represented the top 0.5 percent of the status distribution.

One complication in calculating persistence is surname changing. If students born with the surname *Andersson* were changing this to *Wigonius* as they entered the university elite, then persistence would be exaggerated. The biographical sources for some of the student nations at Lund and Uppsala, which list the parents' surnames for most students, allow us to estimate the fraction of latinized surnames newly adopted in each generation. Figure 2.17 shows what

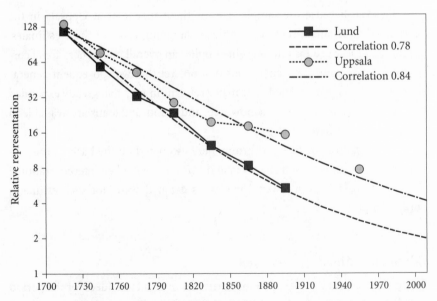

FIGURE 2.16. Relative representation of latinized surnames, Lund and Uppsala university students, 1700–2012.

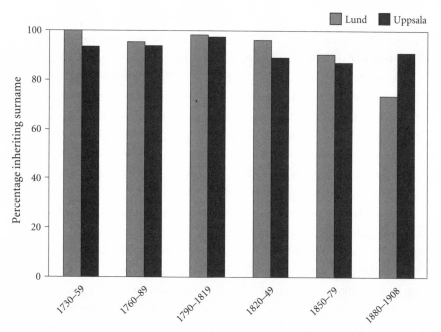

FIGURE 2.17. Percentage of latinized surnames inherited, 1730–1908.

percentage of students in each generation inherited rather than adopted a latinized surname.[17] Between 1730 and 1819, 96 percent of students acquired latinized names by inheritance. However, in the period 1820–1909, that proportion fell to 88 percent (even though, by design, these are all surnames that existed before 1800).[18] The tendency of new members of the university-educated elite in nineteenth century Sweden to switch to such latinized surnames means that the persistence rate estimates for these years represent an upper bound. The true persistence rate is likely lower. Thus there is no good evidence of any decline in the persistence rate for status between preindustrial and modern Sweden, despite the enormous institutional changes that have taken place.

A more elite group of academics than Lund and Uppsala students is the members of the various Royal Academies of Sweden. There are nine such academies. Comprehensive membership lists are available for the Swedish Academy

[17] In the first thirty-year period, 1700–1729, a larger fraction of students adopted latinized surnames, but this trend does not affect the calculated intergenerational correlation, which is affected only by the fraction of students who changed their surnames later.

[18] Some acquired latinized names from their mothers.

of Sciences, founded in 1739; the Swedish Academy of Music, founded in 1771; and the Royal Academy, founded in 1786. Together these three have had nearly three thousand domestic members.

Figure 2.18 shows the relative representation of latinized and noble surnames among the members of these three academies by thirty-year cohorts, starting in 1740 and ending in 2012. In the earliest period, such surnames were held by half of the members of the academies. By the last generation, this figure had declined to 4 percent. But these surnames in 2011 were held by only 0.7 percent of the general Swedish population, so they were still strongly over-represented among academy members.

The small size of this group compared to other groups examined above raises the possibility of significant sampling error. Taking these academies to represent the top 0.1 percent of Swedish society, the implied persistence parameter over these 273 years is 0.87. There is little sign of an increased rate of regression to the mean for the entrants to the academies for the period 1980–2012 compared to 1950–79. The estimated persistence for elite surnames is still 0.83 for this last generation.

Figure 2.18 also shows the relative representation of patronyms among academy members. Such surnames are still strongly underrepresented, but they

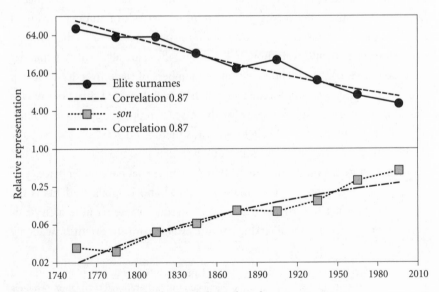

FIGURE 2.18. Elite surnames in the Swedish royal academies, 1740–2012.

have shown a slow but steady convergence toward proportional representation. However, the implied persistence rate for this group is 0.87, close to that for the elite surnames. The caveats above on such estimates apply here also.

Interpretation

Despite conventional estimates, our analyses suggest that Sweden appears to be a society with low rates of intergenerational mobility for income, occupation, and education. Moreover, rates of social mobility seem no higher now, in the modern inclusive, social-democratic Swedish state, than in the preindustrial era. Why do the results presented here differ so much from those of conventional mobility studies?

One possible explanation is that the surname evidence presented here relates to the top 0.1 percent to 8 percent of the status distribution, whereas conventional studies look at mobility across the entire population. Could there be high persistence of status at the upper extreme of the distribution, but greater social mobility for 99 percent or more of families in Sweden? Björklund, Roine, and Waldenström (2012), for example, find an expected overall income intergenerational correlation for Swedish men of only 0.26. But for the top 0.1 percent of the income distribution, their estimate is 0.9.

Assuming such a large disparity in status persistence rates to exist, consider what would happen to families with the surnames of the eighteenth-century elite—the noble and latinized surnames. Once descendants of such families fell out of the top 1 percent, the rapid social mobility in the bottom 99 percent of the distribution would cause their status to quickly fall to the social mean. Distribution of elite surnames across measures of status such as income would no longer be normal and might even be bimodal, with a cluster at the top and then a near-normal distribution around the mean (as in figure 2.19). In particular, there would be no marked deficiency of originally elite surnames at the bottom of the distribution.

But, as is evident from the tax data, noble and latinized names are as underrepresented at the bottom of the income and wealth distribution as they are overrepresented at the top. Even when they fall out of the top 1 percent in various measures of status, they are still experiencing markedly slower rates of downward mobility than would be expected. Noble and latinized surnames are conspicuously absent from the bottom of the distribution of income, for example.

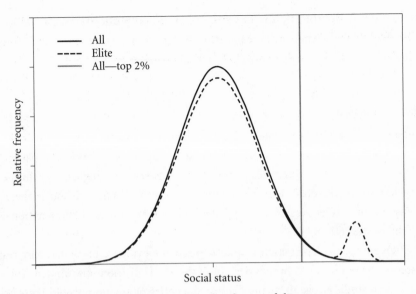

FIGURE 2.19. Hypothetical bimodal status distribution of elite surnames.

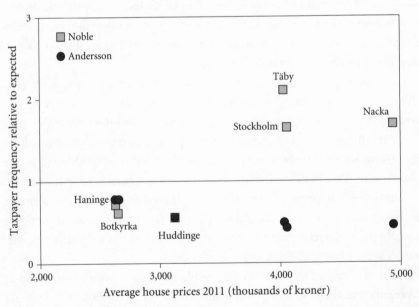

FIGURE 2.20. Frequency of noble surnames and the name *Andersson* relative to expected frequency, by *kommun* average house price, 2011.

Another illustration of the absence of elite surnames in the bottom parts of the income and wealth distribution comes from evidence from the published tax returns on where people are living. The horizontal axis of figure 2.20 shows average house prices for six *kommuns* in the Stockholm region in 2008. Prices in Nacka are double those of Haninge and Botkyrka. Also shown for each *kommun* is the frequency of noble surnames relative to their frequency in the population of Swedish ancestral origin, and the same for the name *Andersson*.[19] Taxpayers with noble surnames are found at half the expected frequency in poorer *kommuns* such as Botkyrka and at twice the expected frequency in rich *kommuns* such as Täby. Thus the relative frequency of noble surnames is four times higher in the highest-income than in the lowest-income *kommuns*. Along with the occupational segregation of surname types in Sweden, there is a social segregation.

Figure 2.20 also shows, however, that taxpayers named *Andersson* are not underrepresented only in rich areas such as Täby; they are also underrepresented in poorer *kommuns*. There are only about half as many *Anderssons* filing tax returns as would be expected from their population share, and half as many more of the noble surnames in returns than would be expected from the population share. The differences in reported taxable incomes understate average income differences between these surname groups.

Conclusions

Generalized and long-term social mobility rates in Sweden in recent years are much lower than the rates reported in standard two-generation studies of the intergenerational correlation of income or education. Indeed, rates of long-run social mobility are so low that the eighteenth-century elite in Sweden have persisted to the present day as a relatively privileged group. There is little evidence that intergenerational mobility rates have increased within the last two or three generations compared to rates in the preindustrial era. The persistence rate for underlying social status is as high as 0.70–0.80. The implied social mobility rates are as low as those of modern England or the United States (see chapters 3 and 5).

Nearly one hundred years of Swedish social democracy has created a more economically equal society, but it has been unable to change the underlying rate

---

[19] Clark 2013 details how this calculation was performed.

of social mobility. The strong intergenerational persistence of status in a country after many years of generous public provision of opportunities and funding for education, at a level similar to that of other countries without such equalizing expenditures, suggests that the forces that determine intergenerational mobility must be fundamental to the formation and functioning of families. These may be forces that are impossible to alter.

THREE

The United States

Land of Opportunity

THIS CHAPTER EXAMINES SOCIAL MOBILITY RATES in the United States using the same methods as those applied to Sweden, again using surnames as the diagnostic. Measured by surname distributions, U.S. social mobility rates are also low. But, importantly in light of recent political debates, they are no lower than Sweden's, and they show no sign of a decline in recent years.

Using surnames, we identify a variety of elite and underclass groups whose mobility can be tracked across three generations. The elite groups are the descendants of Ashkenazi and Sephardic Jews, the descendants of the wealthy individuals as of 1923–24 who had rare surnames, the descendants of individuals with rare surnames who graduated from Ivy League universities in or before 1850, and people of Japanese descent. The underclass groups are Native Americans, black Africans whose ancestors came to the United States before the Civil War, and, surprisingly, the U.S. descendants of the French settlers who came to the French colonies of North America between 1604 and 1759.

This chapter examines mobility rates across three generations—1920–1949, 1950–1979, and 1980–2012—using two sources. The first is the American Medical Association's *Directory of Physicians in the United States.* This lists more than a million licensed physicians in the United States. About a quarter of them are of foreign origin. But because the AMA directory records the medical school attended by each physician, it can identify physicians who are likely of domestic birth. Here Caribbean and some Central American medical schools are counted as domestic.

As a guard against the fraudulent impersonation of retired and deceased physicians, the current directory lists many physicians who completed medical school as early as the 1920s. The directory thus presents a view of the surname composition of the U.S. medical profession from the 1920s to the present, though with small numbers of observations in the earliest decades.

The second source is lists of licensed attorneys, with year of licensure. Attorneys are licensed by state agencies, with no central register, so this information is contained in fifty state websites. Using a selection of twenty-five more populous states allows similar measures of social mobility rates for attorneys as for physicians. Attorneys are a less exclusive elite than physicians.

As in Sweden, the measure of average social status used for each surname group, and for birth cohorts of each group, is their relative representation among physicians and attorneys. That is just the frequency of these names among physicians or attorneys in relation to their frequency in the general population. If this ratio is greater than one, this surname group constitutes an elite. If it is less than one, it forms an underclass.

Elite and Underclass Surnames

To measure social mobility using surnames requires estimates of the frequency of surnames in the United States by cohort. The main source for this information is a file produced by the U.S. Census Bureau giving the frequency of all surnames that appear at least one hundred times in the 2000 census. This source also records the fraction of holders of each surname declaring themselves members of the census categories white, black, Asian/Pacific Islander, Native American, and Hispanic.[1]

To infer the frequency of surnames that appear less than a hundred times in the U.S. census in 2000, the Social Security Administration's Death Index is employed.[2] This lists those who have died in the United States in 1962 and later by name and year of birth. To estimate surname frequencies by birth cohorts, earlier surname frequencies are estimated using the Death Index or information on the size of ethnic groups over time from the U.S. censuses. The Death Index correction, however, is biased by the differential death rates of social groups at each age.

The analysis below uses the following surname groups.

[1] See Ward et al. 2012.
[2] Social Security Death Index, n.d.

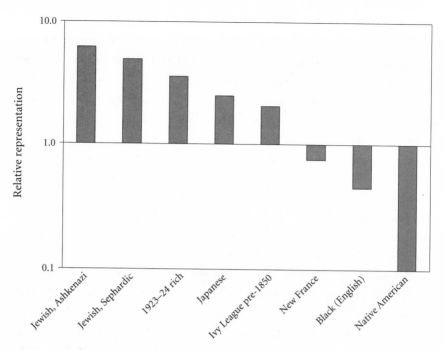

FIGURE 3.1. Relative representation of surname types among physicians.

ASHKENAZI JEWS

This group consists of individuals with the surnames *Cohen, Goldberg, Gold-man, Goldstein, Katz, Lewin, Levin, Rabinowitz,* and variants, who numbered nearly three hundred thousand in 2000. These surnames are common in New York City, the area of the greatest Jewish population share in the United States. However, in the 2000 census, nearly 4 percent of people bearing these surnames declared themselves black (5.5 percent for *Cohen*). This mostly stems not from intermarriage but from black Americans' independently adopting these surnames because of their Biblical resonance. These names appear among physicians at a rate nearly six times higher than in the general population, the highest frequency of any domestic surname group, as shown in figure 3.1.[3]

[3] The average surname incidence for the 2000 population for domestically trained physicians is 2.85 per thousand. We show below that some recent immigrant groups are even more elite according to this measure than the Jewish population, especially once foreign-trained physicians are included. The Jewish population is losing its distinction as the highest-status ethnic group in the United States to such newcomers as Egyptian Copts, Hindus, and Iranian Muslims.

SEPHARDIC JEWS

Certain surnames are associated with the Sephardic Jewish community: *Abecassis, Baruch, Saltiel, Salomone, Sarfaty, Sasson,* and variants. These are much less common than the Ashkenazi surnames, being held by only five thousand people in 2000—not enough to measure social mobility rates. But Sephardic Jewish names appear among physicians at a rate more than four times higher than among the general population, making them the second most elite group among long-established populations in the United States (see figure 3.1).

1923–24 RICH

These surnames were chosen from those appearing in the *New York Times* lists of federal taxpayers in New York in 1923 and 1924. Congress passed a provision for public inspection of income-tax returns in 1924. Before the effective repeal of that provision in 1926, major newspapers across the country printed thousands of names and tax payments for the tax years 1923 and 1924. The *Times* alone reported the tax payments of more than thirty thousand people.

The sample was formed of rarer surnames held by at least one taxpayer reported per ten births recorded prior to 1900 in the Death Index. The modal such surname was held by less than one hundred people in 2000. The ten most common of these names were *Vanderbilt* (1,717), *Roosevelt* (961), *Winthrop* (727), *Colgate* (616), *Guggenheim* (512), *Sonn* (480), *Bloomingdale* (467), *Plaut* (455), *Kempner* (436), and *Pruyn* (421). This group thus includes descendants of the Puritan settlers of New England, the colonial Dutch, and the Jewish populations.

The number of people with these surnames in 2000 is more than one hundred thousand. These surnames appear among physicians at a rate nearly three times higher than among the general population.

JAPANESE AMERICANS

As figure 3.1 shows, Japanese surnames also signal an elite group, appearing at a higher than expected frequency among domestically trained physicians. The overrepresentation seems to apply to all Japanese surnames, since the thirty most common Japanese surnames all have an above-average representation among physicians. The surnames used here are the most common Japanese surnames in the United States, representing 145,000 people in 2000. They appear at more than double the expected frequency. But because the mobility behavior of this group is unusual, the discussion of it is deferred until the end of the chapter.

These surnames are the rare surnames of graduates of Brown University, Columbia University, Dartmouth College, Harvard University, Princeton University, Rutgers University, the University of Pennsylvania, the College of William and Mary, and Yale University from 1850 or earlier.[4] The bulk of the sample graduated in the early nineteenth century, a period when university education expanded and the population grew. The surnames selected from this group were those held by fewer than three hundred people in the 2000 census and fewer than two hundred in the 1850 census.[5] This set consists of a thousand surnames, with an average estimated frequency in 2000 of only 83.

Of these surnames only a very few are familiar, for example, *Rutgers* and *Rensselaer.* The rest are obscure surnames of largely English, Dutch, German, and Irish origin. These surnames still appear among physicians at more than twice the expected rate.

NEW FRANCE SETTLERS

These are surnames derived mainly from the descendants of the colonists of New France. They arrived in the United States through the takeover of parts of Acadia by the English, the expulsion of Acadians to Louisiana, and the movement of French Canadians to New England in the years 1865–1920 to take up employment in factories. The surnames chosen were those more common in Canada than in France. A further restriction was that at least 90 percent of holders of these names in 2000 declared themselves as white and fewer than 5 percent declared themselves black.

Examples include *Gagnon,* whose distribution across Canada and the United States is shown in figure 3.2. The highest incidence of *Gagnon* is in New Brunswick, Canada (part of the old French colony of Acadia), and in New Hampshire and Maine in the United States, where it accounts for 0.2 percent of surnames. While its frequency in Canada overall is 633 per million, in France it is a rare surname, with a frequency of 15 per million. These surnames in the United States represent an underclass, occurring among physicians at less than three-

---

[4] Rutgers and William and Mary are, of course, not members of the Ivy League but are of similar antiquity.

[5] It was also required for the chosen surnames with a hundred or more holders in the 2000 census that the holders of the name be at least 80 percent white and less than 10 percent black. This restriction was specified because of the aim of identifying just elite surnames from the early history of the United States.

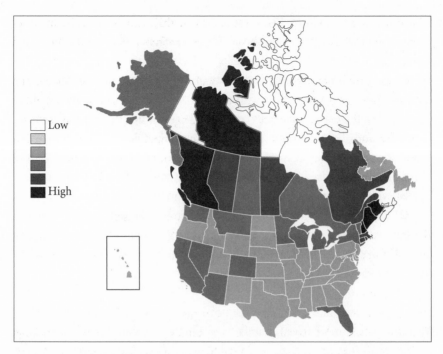

FIGURE 3.2. Map of the distribution in North America of the surname *Gagnon*, 2012.

fifths of the expected rate. There are nearly seven hundred thousand people in this sample. The most common of these names, each with between forty and sixteen thousand holders in 2000, are *Hebert, Cote, Gagnon, Bergeron, Boucher, Delong,* and *Pelletier.*

BLACK AMERICANS

This group is identified as surnames of English or German origin of which 87 percent of more of the holders identified as black in the 2000 census. The English-or-German criterion enabled us to exclude surnames belonging to more recent immigrant groups of black African origin who are actually social elites within the United States.[6] Of the four hundred thousand people in this group, about two-fifths have one name, *Washington,* presumably because it was widely adopted by emancipated slaves lacking surnames after the Civil War.[7]

---

[6] Barack Obama is the most visible member of this elite. Chapter 13 shows that black Africans, for example, have substantially more physicians per 1,000 members than the general white population in the United States.

[7] *Jefferson* is another surname that is predominantly black. It presumably arose in the same way as *Washington.* But only about two-thirds of *Jeffersons* are black.

The other predominantly black surnames in this sample include, in order of frequency, *Smalls, Cooks, Gadson, Merriweather, Broadnax, Boykins,* and *Pettaway.*

Many of the other surnames in this group sound classically English and presumably were adopted in the slavery era from masters whose own families died out or left few descendants. One such surname is *Doyley,* which is recorded in the Domesday Book of 1088 as that of a substantial Norman landlord in England. Another is *Rockingham,* a high-status locative surname from medieval England. Others are more whimsical, such as *Idlebird.*

On average, 91 percent of people with these surnames declared themselves black in the 2000 census, and 4 percent declared themselves white, with the majority of the rest identifying as mixed race. These surnames appear among physicians at one-third of their frequency in the population in 2000.

NATIVE AMERICANS

These are surnames of which 90 percent or more of the holders in 2000 identified themselves as Native American. Two names, *Begay(e)* and *Yazzie,* account for about two-fifths of this population. Many of the less common Native American surnames are quite distinctive: *Manygoats, Roanhorse, Goldtooth, Fasthorse, Yellowman, Twobulls, Bitsilly,* and *Smallcanyon* all had more than two hundred holders in 2000. These surnames are concentrated in the southwest of the United States. The sample includes nearly eighty thousand such surnames. They occur at an extremely low rate among physicians, about 6 percent of the expected rate.

The remarkable differences in the representation of these groups of surnames among physicians imply low social mobility rates in the United States. The rich 1923–24 taxpayers, for example, are at least two generations removed from the majority of the physicians recorded in the current AMA directory, and those who attended Ivy League universities in or before 1850 are four generations removed; yet their names remain more common than expected among physicians.

As figure 3.3 shows, other surnames associated with national origins also show significant variations in relative representation among physicians. Names of Japanese origin, as noted above, are heavily overrepresented. Next in frequency come German, Scottish, Irish, Italian, Scandinavian, and Dutch surnames (in all cases, no more than 5 percent of the holders of these names in the sample are black). French names are markedly underrepresented, creating another puzzle whose consideration is deferred for the moment.

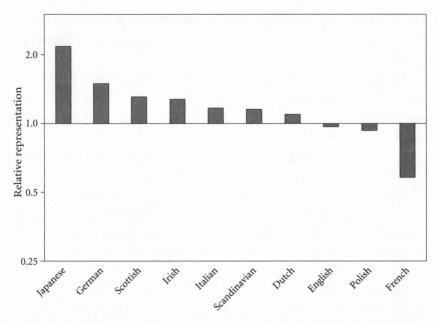

FIGURE 3.3. Differences in ethnic surname representation among U.S.-trained physicians.

Social Mobility, 1920–2012

The rate of change of over- or underrepresentation of the surname groups identified above among physicians and attorneys across generations of thirty years
can be used to estimate the underlying persistence rate of social status, as explained in appendix 2.

The AMA directory reveals how many physicians of each surname group
graduated in each of three thirty-year generations. To estimate the relative representation of the surnames among physicians requires just dividing the share
of each surname group among physicians with its population share among
those age 25 in the same generation.[8]

The relative representation of each surname group in three generations
completing medical school is shown in table 3.1 and graphed in figure 3.4. All
five surname groups exhibit a general convergence toward a relative representation of one in the later two generations observed. But, as the graph shows and

[8] Because the numbers of Native American physicians are so small, their intergenerational status correlation cannot be meaningfully estimated, and this group is therefore omitted from the discussion below.

TABLE 3.1. Relative representation by surname groups among doctors, by generation

	1920–49	1950–79	1980–2011
Ashkenazi Jews	4.76	6.95	5.63
1923–24 rich	4.12	3.48	2.88
Ivy League graduates, 1650–1850	2.47	2.07	1.62
New France settlers	0.44	0.52	0.65
Black (English)	0.31	0.25	0.40

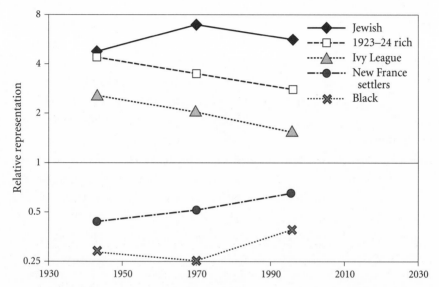

FIGURE 3.4. Relative representation of surname types among physicians, by generation.

as the estimates of the underlying persistence rate for each group confirm, this is a slow process that, for a number of these groups, will not be complete for many generations.

In the earlier generations, both the Jewish and black surname groups diverge from the mean in their representation.[9] For the Jewish surnames, the likely cause was the policy of many medical schools between 1918 and the 1950s to limit admissions of Jewish students. The tightening of these quotas in the

---

[9] Using the method adopted here, this would imply a persistence parameter for these groups greater than one. In this case, such a parameter cannot be an intergenerational correlation, since it would imply that the distribution of status is not constant over time.

1930s led to a decline in the number of Jewish students in AMA-approved medical schools: there were 794 in the class of 1937 but only 477 in the class of 1940.[10]

The lifting of anti-Jewish quotas in the 1950s is reflected in the directory data. Data for the 1930s and the 1940s show a substantial decline in Jewish surname overrepresentation for physicians completing medical school. In figure 3.8 below, which shows relative representation by decade, there is a rise in Jewish relative representation among medical school graduates from the 1950s to the 1970s.

For the black surnames, there was a decline in relative representation in the 1940s and 1950s, though the numbers of black medical graduates in these decades is so small that this may just be a random fluctuation. The AMA in these years recognized only two medical schools catering primarily to black students, Howard University's College of Medicine and Meharry Medical College. Its reluctance to accredit more such schools in an age when many other institutions discriminated against blacks could explain why there is no increase of black surnames in the AMA directory for the 1950s and 1960s.

The maintenance even now of a relative representation among physicians well above one for the Jewish surnames, the 1923–24 rich surnames, and the pre-1850 Ivy League surnames implies slow long-run social mobility. Those completing medical school in 1980 and later would be typically three generations removed from the rich taxpayers of 1923–24 (their great-grandchildren). Similarly, those completing medical school in 1980 and later are at least four or five generations removed from the early Ivy League graduates. At the intergenerational correlation of 0.3–0.5 conventionally believed to apply to educational and occupational mobility in the United States, these more recent graduates should show little trace of any advantage enjoyed by their forebears.

The estimate of the underlying rate of persistence in status using these data makes two assumptions, analogous to those made for Sweden. The first is that physicians represent the upper 0.5 percent of the occupational status distribution.[11] The second is that occupational status within each surname group has a normal distribution, with the same dispersion for all groups. The difference for

---

[10] Borst 2002, 210. These quotas were progressively tightened during the 1920s and 1930s. Thus, in the most dramatic case, Jewish enrollment at Boston University Medical School was cut from 48 percent in 1929 to 13 percent by 1934 (Borst 2002, 208).

[11] Estimated persistence rates change little if this assumed cutoff is changed.

elite surnames and lower-class surnames is just that the distribution is shifted upward or downward.

The highest-status group among the surname samples, those of Jewish origin, certainly exhibits a distribution of educational attainment that appears higher than the average for the United States (see figure 3.5). There are plenty of Jews with modest educational attainments: they just constitute a smaller share of the Jewish population than those with limited education do of the general population. The converse holds for the lower-status group, blacks (see figure 3.6). Black educational attainment in figure 3.6 looks as though it is shifted downward compared to the average.

Given the assumptions that physicians represent the top 0.5 percent of the status distribution and that every group has a normal distribution of status, the numbers in table 3.1 allow us to fix the mean for social status of each group at any time. Figure 3.7, for example, shows the implied mean occupational status for Jews and blacks in the United States in 1980 and later. The heavy overrepresentation of Jews, and heavy underrepresentation of blacks, at the top of the status distribution does not require that means for these groups be far from the social mean. There is plenty of overlap in these distributions, but at the bottom or the top of the status distribution, one or the other group will heavily predominate.

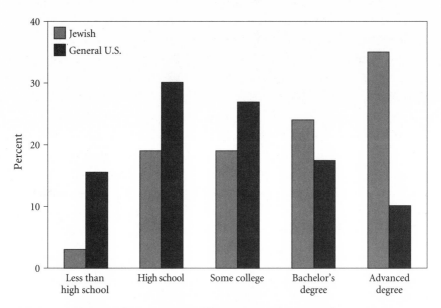

FIGURE 3.5. Educational attainment, Jewish versus general U.S. population, 2007.

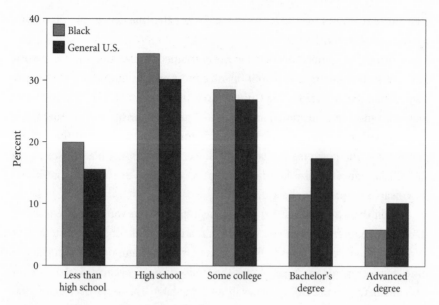

FIGURE 3.6. Educational attainment, black versus general U.S. population, 2007.

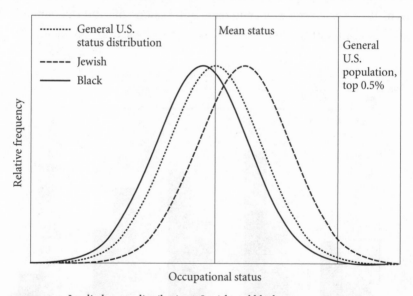

FIGURE 3.7. Implied status distributions, Jewish and black names, 1980–2011.

Table 3.2 shows the calculated persistence rates by generation. These rates for occupational status are remarkably high compared to conventional estimates. In the most recent generation (column 2), the persistence rate for the five groups averaged 0.74, ranging from 0.65 for the New French and Ivy League groups to 0.88 for Ashkenazi Jews. For the earlier generation in the three cases less affected by racial quotas for medical schools, the average rate of persistence is even higher, at 0.80. In the table persistence rates are not calculated for the groups affected by quotas in earlier years.

Table 3.2 also shows calculations of the average persistence rate for a generation of thirty years calculated for the 1970s and later. These calculations are included because estimated social mobility rates for Jews were clearly still being influenced by medical school quotas as late as the 1960s.

Figure 3.8 thus shows the relative representation of each of the five surname groups for each decade from the 1940s onward. The peak frequency of Jewish surnames among physicians qualifying from domestic medical schools, at 7.6 times the expected rate, occurs in the 1970s. In the 1970s, blacks graduated from medical schools at a rate nearly three times higher than in earlier decades, in part as a result of affirmative action policies that have continued to this day.

Figure 3.8 immediately suggests that these relatively high black mobility rates are likely partly a result of the dramatic institutional changes arising from the civil rights movement of the 1960s and have not been sustained. Similarly the regression to the mean of the Jewish population is underestimated by these generational estimates because the number of Jewish physicians was still being limited by racial quotas even in the 1950s.

TABLE 3.2. Calculated intergenerational persistence for surname groups among doctors

	1920–49 to 1950–79	1950–79 to 1980–2011	Average, 1970–2011
Ashkenazi Jews	—	0.88	0.75
1923–24 rich	0.78	0.84	0.94
Ivy League graduates, 1650–1850	0.80	0.65	0.23
New France settlers	0.81	0.65	0.78
Black (English)	—	0.69	0.96
Average, all groups	0.80	0.74	0.73

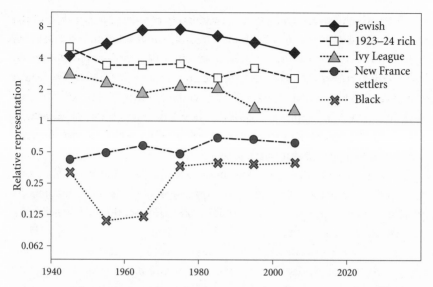

FIGURE 3.8. Relative representation of surname types among physicians, by decade.

Table 3.2 also shows the estimated persistence rates for 1970 and later. The estimated social mobility of the Ashkenazi Jewish group increases, as expected, to a rate of 0.75 per generation. But this still implies remarkably slow mobility compared to conventional measures. For example, at this rate of mobility it will be three hundred years before the Ashkenazi Jewish population of the United States ceases to be overrepresented among physicians.[12]

For the black population, the estimated recent rate of convergence toward the mean is even slower. The persistence rate per generation is 0.96. This implies that even in 2240, the black population will be represented among physicians at only half the rate of the general population. However, since the 1970s, rates of relative representation of blacks among physicians have likely been significantly influenced by affirmative-action policies at U.S. medical schools. The measured black persistence rate in this interval may thus also reflect a decline in the effects of such policies over time.

Among descendants of the New France settlers, representation among physicians is also slowly approaching the mean for the general population. The persistence rate for this group is 0.78, again implying several generations before full convergence.

[12] We define convergence as being within 10 percent of the expected representation.

The two elite white groups, the descendants of the 1923–24 rich and the descendants of pre-1950 Ivy League graduates, show very different rates of social mobility. The descendants of the rich show very high persistence rates, with no convergence on the average predicted even by 2316. But the Ivy League descendants exhibit rapid social mobility, with a persistence rate of only 0.23. However, under this approach, random error has a big effect on persistence rates for groups that deviate only by small amounts from the social average, as in the case of the Ivy League descendants.

But as table 3.2 shows, even taking into account sampling errors, the overall rate of social mobility implied by surname persistence among physicians is very low. The persistence parameter averages 0.73 across these five groups for the last four decades.

Attorneys

We observe significant status differences and slow intergenerational social mobility using physicians as an indicator of social status. The pattern observed is indicative of a general one found across all high- and low-status occupations. Its broader applicability can be demonstrated in part by carrying out a similar analysis among attorneys.

Surnames are more difficult to track among attorneys. Like physicians, attorneys are licensed at the state level. But unlike the AMA, the American Bar Association, the main national association for attorneys, maintains no national directory of attorneys. The records of surname distributions among attorneys are contained in fifty different sources. To make the task feasible, the surname frequencies were checked in only the larger states. Also a smaller set of surnames for each group was used, and the surnames *Olson* and *Olsen* were taken as representative of the average frequency of names in the domestic population among attorneys by decade.[13]

Bar associations and court systems in different states employ different practices with respect to recording inactive attorneys. Some, such as Illinois, record even attorneys first licensed in the nineteenth century. Others, such as Michigan, maintain records only of currently active attorneys. Because surname types are distributed differently across states, these different practices introduce

[13] *Olson/Olsen* also shows an average representation among physicians.

potential error into the process. Attorneys can be licensed in multiple states, and there was no attempt to eliminate multiple listings.

Using the records of just half the states, it is possible, based on the distribution of physicians with these surnames, to observe 88 percent of the expected attorney stock of a major Jewish surname, *Katz*; 86 percent of the most common surnames of the 1923–24 rich; 71 percent of *Olson/Olsen*; 82 percent of the most common New France surnames; and 72 percent of the common black surname *Washington*. The lower representation of *Olson/Olsen* comes from the fact that it is more evenly distributed across states than many of the other surnames examined, such as *Katz*, which is heavily concentrated in a few states.

With the limitations noted, the same patterns found among physicians are seen for attorneys. Attorneys were assigned to generations by their first licensing date in each state. Usable attorney data actually goes back further than that for physicians, with reasonable numbers of observations even in the 1920s. As figure 3.9 shows, surnames are over- and underrepresented among attorneys in close proportion to their over- or underrepresentation among physicians for the most recent generation.

There is perhaps a slight tendency among the descendants of the 1923–24 rich to prefer law to medicine, but otherwise the pattern is very similar. This finding suggests that there is nothing special about the occupations of physi-

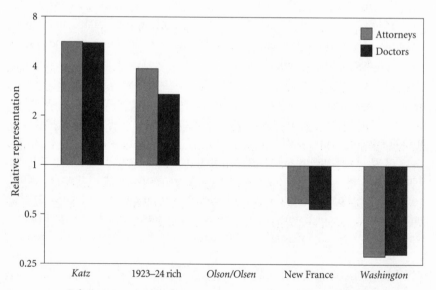

FIGURE 3.9. Relative representation by surname types among attorneys and physicians, 2012.

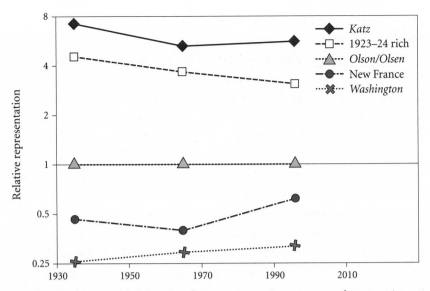

FIGURE 3.10. Relative representation of surname type among attorneys, by generation.

cian and attorney as measures of status. High-status groups are equally disproportionately overrepresented in all elite occupations of equivalent social status. Low-status groups are equally underrepresented.

To measure social mobility rates among attorneys, relative representations for surname types were calculated across three generations, as for physicians. The results are shown in figure 3.10. There is again a pattern of persistent but very slow regression to the mean for all groups.

Table 3.3 shows the persistence rate implied for each surname type and period in figure 3.10.[14] For the most recent generations of attorneys, the average implied intergenerational correlation is greater than for physicians, averaging 0.84. For the two earlier generations, the average implied correlation is even higher, at 0.94. The earlier estimates, however, are subject to substantial margins of error because of the small numbers of observations.

Moving to the most recent measurement, which compares the 1990–2012 cohort to that of 1970–89, there is little sign of any improvement in mobility rates. The average persistence rate in this period is still 0.83.

[14] This assumes that attorneys represent the top 1 percent of the occupational status distribution, whereas physicians were assumed to represent the top 0.5 percent.

TABLE 3.3. Calculated intergenerational persistence for surname groups among attorneys

	1920–49 to 1950–79	1950–79 to 1980–2011	Average, 1970–2012
Katz	0.82	1.04	0.95
1923–24 rich	0.84	0.86	0.95
New France settlers	1.20	0.53	0.58
Washington	0.91	0.94	0.84
Average, all groups	0.94	0.84	0.83

Although the sampling for attorneys contains more possibilities for error, the attorney evidence is largely consistent with that from physicians and suggests even lower rates of social mobility. It confirms that the social mobility rates found for physicians indicate a generally slow rate of social mobility and are not just an artifact of the physician population.

Some surname groups are significantly over- or underrepresented among both physicians and attorneys. Although that representation is gradually converging toward the average for all these groups, the rate of convergence is surprisingly low, given conventional mobility estimates. Social mobility is no higher for highly visible minorities, such as the Jewish and black population, than it is for less visible minorities: the descendants of the French settlers of Acadia and Quebec, the descendants of the rich of 1923–24, and the descendants of Ivy League graduates of 1850.

New France Surnames

The low representation of the surnames of New France settlers among physicians and attorneys is a surprise, as this group has not typically been identified as an underprivileged minority in the United States.

By design, the surnames selected in this group were those for which less than 5 percent of holders in the census declared themselves black. Thus they largely exclude the common surnames of the Cajun population of Louisiana, such as *Landry*, for which 12 percent of holders were black. New France surnames instead tend to be concentrated in New England, as a result either of the takeover of parts of Acadia in the eighteenth century by the American colonies or of immigration between 1865 and 1920 of French Canadians from Quebec and New Brunswick. So low representation of these names in the physician and

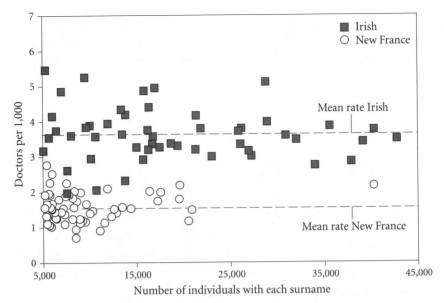

FIGURE 3.11. Physicians per thousand surname holders, most common Irish and New France surnames.

attorney elites cannot be attributed to their being geographically concentrated in poor areas of the United States. Moreover, because this group is not a highly visible minority, its low representation among the current medical and legal elites is unlikely to stem from acts of discrimination. No one bears a grudge against the *Gagnons* or holds prejudicial views of their abilities.

What, then, explains the low social status associated with these surnames? One possible explanation that George Borjas has emphasized in his work is the "cultural capital" of those of New French descent.[15] Could this community have inherited a cultural legacy that impedes upward social mobility? There are claims that Franco-Americans were more committed to maintaining their language and religious practices than the assimilationist Irish and Italians. Certainly in 1970 a surprising number of Franco-Americans with parents born in the United States still retained French as their mother tongue.[16]

Supporting this view is the remarkable pervasiveness of New France disadvantage. Figure 3.11 shows the rate of occurrence of the most common New France surnames among physicians, compared to the most common Irish sur-

[15] Borjas 1995.
[16] MacKinnon and Parent 2005, table 1.

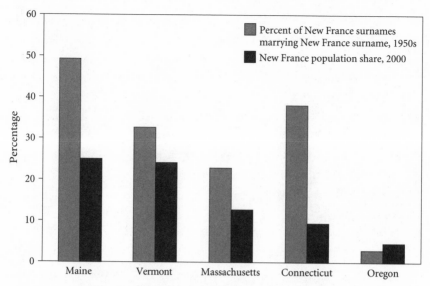

FIGURE 3.12. Marital endogamy among New France descendants, 1950s.

names.[17] The New France surnames look as though they are drawn from a completely different distribution than the Irish surnames. There is something pervasively different about these two groups.

Interestingly, even going back to the 1950s and considering data from states with many people of New French descent, rates of intermarriage between those with New France surnames and those of surnames of other heritages have been substantial. This is not an isolated social group.

Figure 3.12 shows the percentage of individuals of Franco-American heritage in four New England states and in Oregon, according to the 2000 census. Also shown is the percentage of those in the 1950s with common New France surnames who married a partner with any New France surname. By the 1950s, a large majority of New France descendants were marrying outside that community, even in Maine and Vermont, where they still constitute a quarter of the population. This has been a largely open community for generations. Interestingly, despite the evidence of persistently lower status, many of these exogamous marriages were with individuals bearing Irish and Italian surnames, who

---

[17] New France surnames were included only if fewer than 5 percent of the holders were black. The figure excludes the three most common Irish surnames, *O'Brien*, *Gallagher,* and *Brennan,* which each had more than forty-five thousand holders.

were coreligionists, and there is a substantial overlap between the New France and Irish populations in New England.

The low average occupational status of New France surnames cannot be the result of recent assimilation into U.S. society. Some of the New France population was incorporated into the United States in the colonial era. The rest arrived as immigrants from Quebec and New Brunswick, mostly between 1870 and 1930.[18] So the vast majority of those in the current stock of physicians and attorneys are from families who have been in the United States for three or more generations.

An alternative explanation of the low socioeconomic status of this group is that it was drawn, for reason of accidents and history, from the lower end of the French status distribution. U.S. citizens of French colonial origin typically experienced selection through two migration experiences. First, the modern population of seven million people of New French descent derives from a small stock of migrants to France's North American colonies in the seventeenth and early eighteenth centuries. It is estimated, for example, that the French population of Canada in the late nineteenth century derived from fewer than nine thousand original French settlers.[19] Within this settler population, some people were much more reproductively successful than average, and they are the progenitors of a disproportionate share of the modern population. The high incidence of Mendelian (single-gene) disorders in the Province of Quebec, for example, has been argued to stem from a disproportionate contribution of a small share of the founder population to the modern genetic stock in French-speaking Canada: according to one researcher, "as few as 15% of the founders could account for 90% of the total genetic contribution from the founders."[20]

The surname *Gagnon*, as noted, is rare in France, with only about nine hundred holders now, and presumably less than three hundred possessing the surname in France in 1700. Yet there are 54,000 *Gagnons* now in North America, most of whom must have derived from a tiny group of *Gagnon* migrants to New France.

Another distinctive feature of the demographics of Quebec in the seventeenth to nineteenth centuries was that the most reproductively successful

[18] MacKinnon and Parent 2005, appendix, table 1.

[19] Scriver 2001, 76.

[20] Scriver 2001, 78. This is not to imply that the source of Franco-American disadvantage in the modern United States is genetic in nature. The possible mechanisms of status transmission are discussed in chapter 7.

group in the population was of lower socioeconomic status.[21] So the founder population of the French population of North America could well have been a draw from the lower end of the French occupational distribution.

In addition, there is evidence that French Canadian immigrants to the United States between 1860 and 1920 were negatively selected from the Francophone population of Canada. Byron Lew and Bruce Cater show that from 1900 to 1920, illiterate French Canadians were significantly more likely to emigrate to the United States than their literate counterparts.[22]

It is possible, then, that the low status of modern Franco-Americans stems from the persistence of an ethnic culture maladapted to economic success. But it seems more plausible that their low status in the United States stems from the fact that they are a twice-selected low-status subgroup of the parent French population. Their continued low occupational status is witness to the slow processes of social mobility revealed once we turn to surnames as a measure.

Japanese Surnames

Today, people bearing Japanese surnames are an elite group in the United States with respect to occupational status. Unusually, Japanese Americans until recently showed no tendency to regress toward the mean. Instead, from 1940 to 2000, they became more distinctive as a population subgroup (see figure 3.13). Only since 2000 has there been regression to the mean among Japanese Americans of the kind seen among the descendants of Jewish immigrants from the 1980s onward.[23] The Japanese experience also contrasts strongly with that of New France descendants, although these groups arrived in the United States at roughly the same time. Their experience in the medical profession reflects a general tendency for Japanese Americans to become a highly educated, high-income subgroup in America.

We can attribute the delayed rise of Jewish Americans among physicians at least in part to the quota systems that operated increasingly in East Coast universities from the 1930s until the 1950s. The delayed rise of Japanese Americans as an elite group is less plausibly explained by such barriers. On the West Coast

[21] Clark and Hamilton 2006.

[22] Lew and Cater 2012, table 2. In contrast, literate English Canadians were more likely than illiterate English Canadians to emigrate to the United States.

[23] The decline in representation among physicians from 2000 to 2012 is statistically significant, indicating that regression has begun.

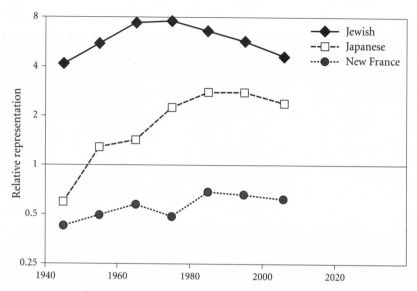

FIGURE 3.13. Relative representation of Jewish, Japanese, and New France surnames among physicians, United States.

and in Hawaii there do not seem to have been such barriers. Unlike Jewish Americans, Japanese Americans were not graduating from colleges at a much higher rate than the rest of the local population, which was what led to quotas being placed on Jewish admissions in the East. Also, they represented a smaller share of the population in states like California than Jews did in New York.[24]

Masao Suzuki argues that one factor that explains the high status of the Japanese is that emigrants from Japan were always a relatively elite group and became more so as barriers to Japanese immigration were set in place. Table 3.4 shows the occupational distribution of Japanese immigrants entering the United States from 1899 to 1931, compared to the occupational distribution in Japan as a whole in 1920. Even in the period before the Gentleman's Agreement of 1907 (a tacit agreement between the governments of the United States and Japan that placed informal limits on Japanese immigration), the immigrants of 1899–1907 would have likely been more skilled than the Japanese home population in those years. Because the Japanese economy was rapidly modernizing,

[24] The internments of 1942–45 applied to only a minority of the total Japanese population, and this seems too brief an episode to explain the long-delayed rise in their representation among physicians.

TABLE 3.4. Occupational distribution of Japanese immigrants to the United States and Japanese domestic population, 1899–1931

	Immigrants			Domestic population, 1920
	1899–1907	1908–24	1925–31	
Professionals, businessmen, and skilled workers	20	39	61	17
Farmers and other occupations	21	31	17	26
Farm laborers, laborers, and domestic servants	59	30	21	57

the occupational distribution in 1920 would have been more skilled than twenty years earlier. After the Gentleman's Agreement, Japanese immigrants to the United States became distinctly more skilled.

The rise in status of the Japanese American community until the 1980s was substantially driven by the high skills that Japanese immigrants brought with them in the years 1908–70, when Japan was a substantially poorer economy than the United States. According to the 1960 census, of Japanese Americans born in the 1920s, 16 percent were born in Japan, and for those born in the 1930s the figure is 27 percent. The high skill level of Japanese immigrants in the early to mid-twentieth century is evident from the AMA register of physicians. Of those physicians with Japanese surnames completing medical school in the 1940s, 69 percent were trained in Japan. In the 1950s, 52 percent were still Japanese trained, and in the 1960s 44 percent.

Conclusions

This chapter establishes through analysis of surname distributions that the underlying social mobility rates in the United States since 1920 are much lower than conventional estimates would suggest. Although surname groups tend to regress to the mean in occupational status, they do so far more slowly than conventional estimates imply.

Looking at ethnic groups such as Jews, blacks, Japanese Americans, and Franco-Americans, it might seem that this slow social mobility is connected to some shared social capital, or lack thereof. But we see the same slow rates of mobility within groups of surnames that are not ethnically or culturally homogeneous, such as the bearers of the rare surnames of the rich of 1923–24. Chapter 6 offers explanations of why these surname estimates of social mobility rates reveal the true underlying rates of social mobility in a society such as the United States.

We do not, however, find any evidence for the dystopia that Charles Murray fears in his recent book, *Coming Apart: The State of White America, 1960–2000*. Murray argues that there is an increasing disparity between the values of the white upper class and the white lower class, and increasing geographic, educational, and social isolation of that lower class. The data presented and discussed in this chapter give no indication that social mobility rates have declined in the past few decades in the United States. They are slow, but not any slower than in the previous forty or fifty years.

FOUR

Medieval England

Mobility in the Feudal Age

MEASURED USING SURNAMES, social mobility is surprisingly low in modern Sweden and in the United States. How do mobility rates compare for the preindustrial era, before the whole panoply of public education and fair-employment laws of the modern state? Using surname evidence, we can estimate social mobility rates in England back to 1300 and the feudal world of lord and bishop, serf and slave.

What most people would expect from this study is obvious: the illustration of a class-ridden past, with the majority of the population trapped under the feudal yoke, condemned to a brutish existence cultivating the heavy sod of the medieval fields. This unfortunate majority would have been supporting an entrenched and tyrannical elite who sustained their position through control of land, politics, and violence. We would then expect to see the liberation of the Industrial Revolution, which eventually freed the population from the constraints of the past, followed by a series of political reforms that enfranchised ever-larger shares of the population. After World War II we would note the introduction of redistributive taxation, mass higher education, and a modern world of social mobility. The stately ossification of the world of *Downton Abbey* would be replaced by the hectic social turbulence of the rude boys of the City and finance.

We have seen that modernity did not bring rapid social mobility in Sweden and the United States. But was there gain at least relative to the bad old days of the Middle Ages? Do the modern English at least live in a society of greater social mobility than in medieval times?

The Rise of the Artisans

In using surnames to measure mobility in medieval England, the first set of surnames employed are those of medieval artisans: workers with some skills, located at the middle or lower middle of the social scale. More than one in ten of all modern surnames in England derive from the occupation of some medieval ancestor. *Smith, Baker, Clark, Cook, Carter, Wright, Shepherd, Stewart, Chamberlain,* and *Butler* are all easily identified occupational surnames, but there are plenty of others whose etymological origin is more obscure, such as *Webb* or *Webber* (weaver), *Coward* (cowherd), *Walker* (fuller), *Coulthard* (colt herd), *Baxter* (baker), and *Dexter* (dyer).

In addition to *Smith* (the most common surname in England, Australia, and the United States), the whole range of the building trades is represented in surnames: *Carpenter* or *Wright, Mason, Thatcher, Plumber, Glazier, Painter, Sawyer, Slater,* and *Tyler.* The one trade that is not well represented is bricklaying. Surnames were well established in England by the fourteenth century, and brick became an important building material in England only after 1500, too late to leave a mark on surnames.

Farming contributes such occupational surnames as *Carter, Shepherd, Coward, Plowman,* and *Thresher.* Textile and clothing production, important occupations in medieval England, generate *Taylor, Webb, Webber, Webster* and *Weaver, Walker* and *Fuller, Barker* and *Tanner, Lister, Dyer* and *Dexter, Skinner,* and *Glover.* The female versions of occupational surnames in medieval England were derived from the male forms by changing the ending to *-ster* or *-xter.* There are however, few *Spinners,* despite the importance of this occupation, because spinning was exclusively female work and would not become the stuff of an inherited surname.[1] Food production gave us *Baker* and *Baxter, Butcher, Coke* and *Cook, Brewer* and *Brewster, Salter, Miller* and *Milner,* and *Spicer.* All these artisan occupational surnames connote the medieval origin of a family not at the bottom of society, among the laborers in town and field, but in the middle, below the landowners, the manorial officials, the clerics, the merchant class, and the attorneys.

When were these surnames first affixed as heritable surnames? The exact period is unknown, but by 1381 these surnames were largely transmitted through inheritance. We know this from the surviving returns of the 1381 poll tax. Some

---

[1] But from *spinner* we get *spinster,* which came to refer to any unmarried woman.

of these returns show not just the surnames of taxpayers but also their current occupations. An occupational surname that differs from its holder's occupation must be an inherited surname. By 1381, only 38 percent of people with artisan surnames were doing the job their name described, so a minimum of 62 percent of people with artisan surnames had inherited them.[2] But given that many sons would follow their father's or grandfather's profession, by 1381 most surnames must have been inherited. The fact, however, that 38 percent of artisan surnames still described the occupation of the bearer suggests that these surnames could not have existed as hereditary surnames for more than three or four generations. Thus it seems likely that artisan surnames became hereditary around 1250–1300.

There are four major sources that identify the elite in medieval England. The first is people associated with the ancient universities of Oxford and Cambridge, whose membership records start around 1170. The second is those whose wills were proved in the highest will court in the land, the Prerogative Court of the Archbishop of Canterbury (PCC), whose records span the period 1384–1858. Because of its location in London, this was the court for the elites of English society until 1858. The third is those whose wills were proved in the PCC who are referred to as *Sir* or *Gentleman,* suggesting even higher status. The fourth is members of Parliament, the House of Commons, from 1295 onward. What do these sources suggest about the social mobility rates implied by the distribution of artisan surnames over time?

Figure 4.1 shows the percentage of Oxford and Cambridge members entering the universities between 1170 and 2012 who had artisan surnames. These surnames are very rare at the universities before 1350, but their frequency increases substantially in the late Middle Ages to achieve its modern level by 1500. Also shown is the percentage of probates in the PCC associated with artisan surnames, shifted back thirty years for comparability with university entrants.[3] Finally, the figure shows "elite" PCC probates, cases in which the deceased person was referred to by a title indicating high status, such as *Gentleman.*

At this scale, medieval England looks like a world of astonishing mobility. Artisans in 1300 were mostly illiterate workers scattered across English villages,

---

[2] This analysis is based on 129 occupational surnames for which the holder's current occupation was also revealed.

[3] People entered Oxford and Cambridge at age 16–18 and typically died at age 50 or later. So to compare people of the same birth cohort, we need to shift the probate data backward by thirty years or more.

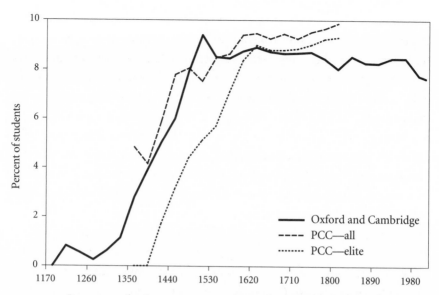

FIGURE 4.1. Percentage of artisan surnames among English elites, 1170–2012.

yet by 1500 their descendants were fully incorporated into the English universities. And by 1620 they were fully represented even among the gentry whose wills were proved in the PCC. Even before the Enlightenment proclaimed the idea of the fundamental equality of humanity in the abstract, the social and economic system of medieval England was delivering equality of opportunity in the concrete.

The intergenerational correlation implied by this pattern depends on two things, however. First, how elite was the population at Oxford and Cambridge in this period? One way to calculate its exclusivity would be to look at the share of males in each generation who attended the universities, which in the fifteenth century was 0.3–0.7 percent. This would make the universities potentially as exclusive as the top 0.5 percent of the medieval status distribution.

However, while the universities attracted those seeking a career in the church or administration, there were other career paths for medieval elites. Those seeking a legal career would enroll at one of the Inns of Court in London. Young men aspiring to a career in commerce might apprentice with a merchant or banker. Youths pursuing a military career would train at the tournament and the campaign. As a result, university attendees would have represented a larger share of the population, as much as the upper 2 percent.

The second factor that affects the calculation of mobility rates is the place of artisans in the status distribution of society in 1300. They ranked above unskilled laborers, who constituted a quarter or a third of the society, and above the semiskilled husbandmen of the farm sector. But they ranked below the many landowners, manorial officials, farmers, clerics, merchants, civil servants, and attorneys.

Here persistence rates are calculated assuming that artisans started between the fortieth and sixtieth percentile from the bottom of the socioeconomic distribution. The higher the starting position of artisans on the social ladder, the lower the estimated mobility rates. Assuming Oxford and Cambridge students represented the top 0.5–2 percent, and that artisans were at the median or the upper fortieth percentile of the status distribution, the persistence rate implied by figure 4.1 lies between 0.77 and 0.85. Figure 4.2 shows the best fit of 0.8 for the preferred assumption: Oxford and Cambridge represented an elite of 0.7 percent of the general population, and artisans started in the middle of the status distribution. The figure also shows that there was no possibility that the intergenerational correlation was as low as 0.7 or as high as 0.9.

This finding means that medieval England had mobility rates similar to, though perhaps modestly higher than, those of the modern United States and

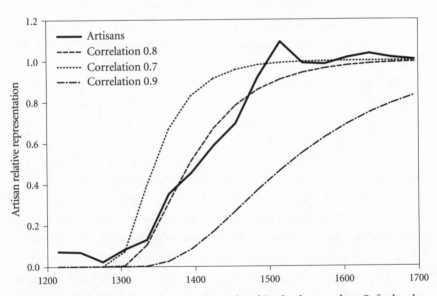

FIGURE 4.2. Alternative persistence rates for medieval England versus data, Oxford and Cambridge students.

Sweden. In terms of social mobility, then, what did the Scientific Revolution, the Enlightenment, and the Industrial Revolution achieve? Very little. Social mobility existed long before people even thought of it as a feature of the good society. It was never fast, but over generations, all ranks of society could enter equally into its upper echelons. By implication, the early elites eventually saw substantial downward mobility.

A good example of the operation of social mobility in these years is Geoffrey Chaucer (1343–1400), the celebrated author of *The Canterbury Tales*, itself a satirical commentary on the various strata of English social life (figure 4.3). The surname *Chaucer* is believed to derive from the French word for a shoemaker, *chausseur*. But the Chaucers had left shoemaking generations before Geoffrey. Both his father and grandfather were prosperous vintners, a higher-status occupation. Though he was of completely common background, Chaucer became, by dint of his abilities, a courtier, diplomat, and civil servant in the court of Richard II.[4] By 1386 he was member of Parliament for Kent, and by 1389 clerk of the king's works, an important administrative position. His son Thomas was later speaker of the House of Commons. Thomas's daughter Alice married William de la Pole, Duke of Suffolk. Geoffrey's great-great-grandson, John de la Pole, Earl of Lincoln, was named heir to the English throne by Richard III in 1485 (but executed after Richard's overthrow). Thus during the medieval period, the Chaucer family went from shoemakers to claimants to the English throne, albeit under a different surname.[5] Chaucer's family history conveys the fluidity and flexibility of medieval English society, as opposed to the common stereotype many have of a rigid and static preindustrial social world.

Since in the medieval period artisan surnames would have connoted low status, there is some chance that as people rose in social position, they adopted higher-status surnames. A man could do this by taking his wife's surname at marriage or adopting the surname of a patron. English citizens may have lost the right of their American cousins to wield death-spitting weaponry, but they have long held the right to change their surnames to whatever they wish by personal fiat, as long as there is no intention to deceive. If this practice was common, the rate of mobility measured through surnames would be lower than the actual mobility rate, since there would be spurious continuation of the status of

---

[4] By marriage, Chaucer also became the brother-in-law of the immensely powerful John of Gaunt.

[5] Like many other rare names, the surname *Chaucer* itself is now lost to history.

FIGURE 4.3. Portrait of Geoffrey Chaucer ca. 1415–20 by his friend, the poet Thomas Hoccleve.

surnames. So for artisans, we can be confident that the mobility rate for the Middle Ages measured by surnames is the lower bound of actual mobility rates.

The Decline of Elites: Locative Surnames

If medieval artisans enjoyed upward mobility, what signs are there of the concomitant downward mobility of thirteenth-century elites? A large elite group of surnames in medieval England are those surnames that came from town and village names: locative surnames.

In preindustrial England, where most people lived in one place all their lives, identifying the average person by the name of their town or village would make no sense. However, among the elite, who left their places of origin to go to court, to the universities, to the religious centers, and to the towns and cities to work as merchants, lawyers, and bankers, the most typical surname was one that identified their ancestral home or place of origin.

This locative naming practice started with the Norman conquerors of England. This new elite took surnames that linked them to their home villages in Normandy, such as *Mandeville, Montgomery, Baskerville, Percy, Neville,* and *Beaumont.*[6] But as the Norman elite was gradually displaced by an indigenous English propertied class, new locative names associated with high status appeared: *Berkeley, Hilton, Pakenham,* and so on.

---

[6] The original surnames would have included the particle *de,* but this was eventually dropped in most cases, except in such names as *de Vere* or *D'Arcy.*

These surnames are prominent in the early records of Oxford and Cambridge: they account for nearly half of the names associated with the universities in the thirteenth century. But these surnames were a much smaller share of the overall population stock of surnames. The frequency of high-status surnames tended to increase in preindustrial England until 1800. Thus while the locative surnames used here account for 7.1 percent of all surnames among marriages from 1800 to 1829, they account for only 6.7 percent in 1650–79 and 6.1 percent in the period 1538–59. Projecting backward from the growth rate by generation between 1538 and 1800 gives an estimated share of 5 percent in 1250.

The advantage of using these locative surnames as a measure of mobility is that they represent a large share of the stock of all surnames, and most of them are not associated with any notable status or distinction. The most common locative surnames, for example, are *Barton, Bradley, Greenwood, Newton, Holland,* and *Walton.* Such names would not themselves influence the status of the holders.

Figure 4.4 shows the relative representation of a sample of locative surnames at Oxford and Cambridge from 1200 to 2012, calculated, as before, as the ratio of their share in the universities to their share in the general population. Until 1350, the relative representation of these surnames remains close to four. The reason for the absence of any downward mobility for these surnames in

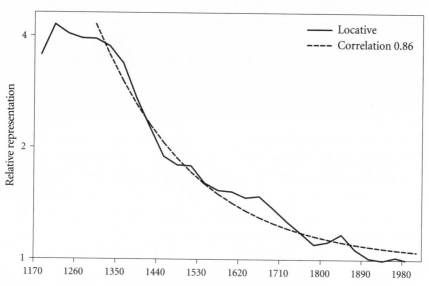

FIGURE 4.4. Locative surnames at Oxford and Cambridge, 1170–2012.

these years is likely that locative surnames were still being adopted by people of higher status. So the initial period for measuring rates of social mobility is taken here as 1320–49. We see above that artisan surnames did not begin to displace other surnames at the universities on a significant scale until after 1350.

From 1350 all the way until the present, locative surnames decline steadily in relative representation at the universities. One persistence rate, 0.86, turns out to fit the data well for the period 1320–2012, a span of almost seven hundred years. But this is a high persistence rate. It implies that nearly three-quarters of the variation in general social status across families derives from inheritance in any generation. Thus mobility was consistent even in the Middle Ages, but very slow.

The estimated intergenerational correlation for the downward mobility of the locative surnames is quite consistent with the 0.75–0.85 range suggested for persistence in the upward mobility of the artisan surnames.

Thirteenth-Century Property Owners

An even more elite group of thirteenth-century surnames is the rarer surnames belonging to landowners appearing in the *Inquisitions Post Mortem* (IPM) for the years 1236–99. These were inquiries held at the death of tenants of the English crown to establish what lands they had held and who should succeed to those lands. The holders of these properties were typically members of the medieval upper classes. The surnames chosen for this sample were those of decedents who transmitted the largest average amounts of property to their heirs. They were also surnames for which the modern English form of the surname is known or easily inferred.

Table 4.1 lists some sample surnames as they appear in the IPM and in their modern forms. Many of these surnames, being derived from the names of French villages, lost their meaning to the later English-speaking bearers of the names and thus mutated into names with a similar sound that had a meaning in English. *Taillebois,* for example, is now sometimes *Tallboys.*

It is necessary to follow all possible derived variants of the initial surname, because the less well-connected variants are likely to be associated with lower-status descendants of the original surname holders. *Baskerville,* for example, began as the Norman surname *de Basqueville,* from a village in Normandy. By the thirteenth century it had become *de Baskerville.* In a further mutation, it

TABLE 4.1. Some medieval surnames from the IPM and their modern English equivalents

IPM	Modern
De Bello Campo, De Beauchamp	*Beauchamp, Beaucamp, Beacham*
De Berkele, De Berkelegh, De Berkeley	*Berkeley, Barclay*
De Kaygnes, De Kaynes, De Caynes, De Keynnes, De Kahanes, De Keines	*Keynes, Kaynes*
De Menwarin, De Meynwaring, De Meynwaryn	*Mainwaring, Manwaring*
De Mortuo Mari, De Mortymer, De Mortimer	*Mortimer, Mortimor*
Taillebois, Tayleboys, Talebot, Talbot	*Talboys, Talbot, Talbott, Tallboy*

became *Baskervilde* and then *Baskerfield*. The *-field* variant is lower in status on average then the *-ville* variant: this difference is predictable because the mutation to *-field* was much more likely to occur among lower-status and illiterate holders of the surname.

Many of the surnames of the English elite in the thirteenth century originated as surnames of the Norman conquerors of 1066. But in the two intervening centuries, a new class of English property owners had also emerged, such as the rich and influential Berkeley family.[7]

Figure 4.5 shows the status over time of this group of surnames as represented by their incidence among students at Oxford and Cambridge. As expected, this is an even more elite group of surnames than those shown in figure 4.4, which are simply associated with places. The IPM surnames peaked in status in 1230–59, when they were thirty times more common at the universities than in the general population. After that, they immediately began regressing to the mean. They show a persistence rate very similar to that of the locative surnames until about 1500.

Had that rate of regression to the mean been maintained, then by 2012 these surnames would have been only 14 percent more frequent in the top 1 percent of the status distribution than an average surname. But after 1500 the rate of regression to the mean slowed down further, and from 1500 to 2012 the per-

---

[7] The Berkeley family took their name from their home castle in Berkeley in Gloucester. There are actually two branches of the Berkeley family. One is of Norman descent, and the other, more prominent one is allegedly descended from a high official of the Saxon king Edward the Confessor (r. 1042–66). Edward II was murdered while imprisoned by Lord Berkeley at Berkeley Castle in 1327.

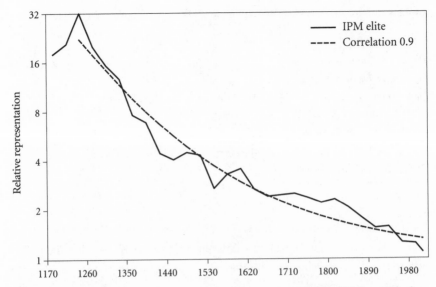

FIGURE 4.5. Incidence of surnames from the *Inquisitions Post Mortem* (IPM) at Oxford and Cambridge, 1170–2012.

sistence rate that fits the data throughout these years is 0.93, an extraordinarily high number. This implies that modern England actually has lower rates of social mobility than medieval England did. Surnames loosely associated with the rich of the thirteenth century still appear among Oxford and Cambridge students at a rate 25 percent more than expected 1980–2009. Since these results differ from those for the locative surnames, we have to consider other possible explanations of this outcome.

One important possibility is that elites deliberately adopted these high-status names in recent centuries. When a high-status man with a common surname such as *Smith* married a woman with a high-status surname such as *Darcy*, he might choose to adopt her surname after the marriage rather than follow the convention of the woman adopting the husband's surname.

Consider, for example, the *Stanley* family, the earls of Derby and descendants of an original medieval *Stanley*. In the eighteenth century, seeking cash through a matrimonial alliance with a rich heiress, Lucy Smith, *Stanley* became *Smith-Stanley*. In the later nineteenth century, the déclassé *Smith* was again dropped from the family name. Such selective name changing could give an artificially low impression of downward mobility by holders of high-status medieval surnames.

The Norman Conquerors

We can follow one group of surnames even further back than the propertied elite of the thirteenth century. These are the names of the Norman conquerors of England in 1066 who are recorded as property holders in the Domesday Book of 1086. What happened to this medieval super-elite?

Once he had vanquished Harold and his followers in battle, Duke William of Normandy's first order of business was to secure his hold on the English throne by granting lands and positions to the adventurers from Normandy, Brittany, and Flanders who had won it for him. There was thus a wholesale replacement of the former Saxon upper class with a new Continental elite.

The Domesday Book, the record of property holders in England under William, records for the first time the names of the Norman adventurers. Detailed work in the arcane historical field of prosopography by the splendidly named Katharine Stephanie Benedicta Keats-Rohan has established the origins of many landholders in the Domesday Book.[8]

It is not clear how heritable surnames were in the eleventh century. However, of the nearly five hundred surnames identified in the Domesday Book, many seem likely to be unique to the Norman, Breton, and Flemish upper classes that dominated England after the conquest. Many of these surnames, which were associated with the holders' villages of origin, have disappeared, but some have survived into modern England. Table 4.2 shows a sample of these names in the form that appears in the Domesday Book and in their modern form.

The table shows that one of these surnames, *Sinclair,* had more than seventeen thousand bearers in England and Wales in 2002. Could all of these people have descended from one family, or a small group of families? Once again we witness the amazing power of exponentiation. Thirty-one generations elapsed between 1086 and 2002. A population of seventeen thousand people with a given surname in 2002 implies 8,500 males. For one forefather to produce 8,500 descendants in the course of thirty-one generations would require that each generation produce an average of only 1.34 surviving sons per family. There is evidence that the upper classes of preindustrial England easily achieved such fertility levels.[9] So even these outlier surnames with large numbers of holders

[8] Keats-Rohan 1999.
[9] Clark 2007, 112–121.

TABLE 4.2. Some Norman surnames, 1086 and 2002

Original	Modern	Number in 2002
Baignard	*Baynard*	54
De Belcamp	*Beauchamp, Beacham*	3,252
De Berneres	*Berners*	49
Burdet	*Burdett*	3,973
De Busli	*Busly*	52
De Cailly	*Cailey*	32
De Caron	*Carron*	613
De Colavilla	*Colville, Colvill*	1,271
Corbet	*Corbett*	12,096
De Corbun	*Corbon*	—
De Albamarla	*Damarel*	122
De Arcis	*D'Arcy, Darcey, Darcy*	4,039
De Curcy	*De Courcy, Courcy*	219
De Ver	*De Vere, Vere*	556
Giffard	*Gifford, Giffard*	2,382
De Glanville	*Glanville*	2,826
De Lacy	*Lacey, Lacy*	14,782
Malet	*Mallett*	4,948
De Magnavilla	*Mandeville, Manderville, Manderfield*	514
De Maci	*Massey, Massie, Macy*	15,056
De Montague	*Montague*	3,282
De Montfort	*Montford, Monford*	298
De Mon Gomerie	*Montgomery, Mongomery*	7,524
De Mortemer	*Mortimer*	12,008
De Molbrai	*Mowbray*	2,059
De Nevilla	*Neville*	7,998
De Percy	*Percy, Percey*	3,284
De Pomerai	*Pomeroy, Pomery, Pomroy*	2,312
De Sackville	*Sackville*	64
De Sai	*Say, Saye*	1,230
De Sancto Claro	*St Clair, Sinclair*	17,143
Taillebois	*Tallboy(s), Talbot*	16,857
De Tournai	*Tournay, Tourney*	61
De Venables	*Venables*	3,857
De Villare	*Villars, Villers, Villiers*	1,054

could have descended from one family, if it was consistently reproductively successful over the generations.

There is evidence that the population share of Norman surnames continued to increase from 1560 to 1881. For the sample used here, the share of Norman-derived surnames in the population as a whole was 0.32 percent in the years 1538–99, 0.46 percent in 1680–1709, 0.47 percent in 1770–99, and 0.50 percent by 1881. The Norman surname share in the population for the period 1200–1538 is thus calculated assuming the same growth rate in the generations before 1538 as for 1538–1709.

Figure 4.6 shows the relative representation of Norman surnames at Oxford and Cambridge from 1170 to 2012. Again there is steady regression to the mean, so that today Norman surnames are only about 25 percent overrepresented at the universities compared to other indigenous English surnames. The distribution of these surnames across social positions in England is now close to the average.

Again, however, the rate of regression to the mean is startlingly low. It has been 947 years since the Norman conquest of 1066. The fact that Norman surnames had not become completely average in their social distribution by 1300, by 1600, or even by 1900 implies astonishingly slow rates of social mobility

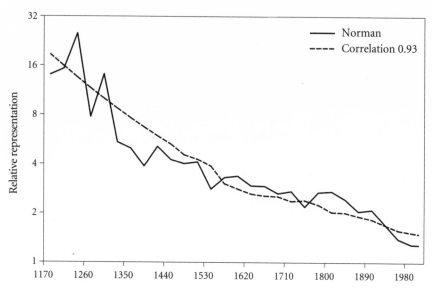

FIGURE 4.6. Relative representation of Norman surnames at Oxford and Cambridge, 1170–2012.

FIGURE 4.7. Gary Neville, football's representative of the Norman elite.

during every epoch of English history. The estimated intergenerational correlation for the period 1170–1589 is 0.90. For the years 1590–1800, the rate of regression to the mean is even slower, as with the propertied elite surnames of the thirteenth century, but this period of slow regression was followed by a period of somewhat faster social mobility from 1800 to 2012. As a result, the persistence rate of 0.90 correctly predicts the Norman surname share at Oxford and Cambridge now (figure 4.7).

A persistence parameter of 0.90 over twenty-eight generations implies two things. The first is that there is a consistent and stable regression of status toward the mean: in the long run, we are all equal in expectation. The second is that if this parameter is valid for medieval and modern England as a whole, then more than four-fifths of social and economic outcomes are determined at birth. Again we have to ask whether selective name changing has artificially boosted the status of some of these Norman surnames in more recent years. Chapter 14 discusses some other surprising persistence associated with Norman surnames in England.

Wealth

The records of the Prerogative Court of Canterbury (PCC), the probate court of the upper class of England from 1380 to 1858, show a broadly similar pattern for wealth mobility as for educational status. The index of the PCC contains nearly a million estates probated before 1858, so this is a rich source of data on social

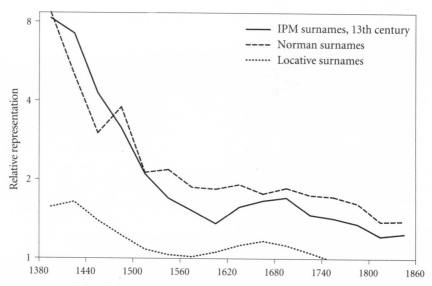

FIGURE 4.8. Medieval elites in PCC probates, 1380–1858.

status before 1858. As figure 4.1 shows, artisan surnames have a normal overall representation in this court by 1550 and proportional representation among higher-status groups (such as "gentlemen") by 1620. This is a modestly slower rate than that of their diffusion into the universities. The implied persistence rate for the artisan surnames is thus slightly higher than from the Oxford and Cambridge data, on the order of 0.80–0.85.

Figure 4.8 shows the relative representation of the three medieval elite surname groups among all PCC probates: locative surnames, the IPM surnames of the thirteenth century, and the Norman surnames of the Domesday Book. Counting these probates as the top 5 percent of the wealth distribution, which they represented from 1680 onward, gives the best-fitting estimates of persistence shown in table 4.3 for four surname groups (the three elite groups and artisans). These estimates fall in the range 0.74–0.85. The rate of upward mobility for the artisan surnames is just as slow as the rate of downward mobility for the medieval elite surnames.

There is a yet more elite group revealed in the probate records: those whose wills were proved in the PCC and who were also described by an honorific such as *Sir, Gentleman, Earl, Duke, Lord, Lady, Countess, Count, Baron, Bishop,* or *Reverend.* These persons account for only one in ten probates in the Canterbury court, a group that is taken to represent the top 0.5 percent of wealth. Figure 4.9

TABLE 4.3. Persistence estimates for different surname types among elite groups, 1380–1858

	All PCC probates, 1380–1858	High-status PCC probates, 1440–1858	Oxford and Cambridge students, 1170–1590
Artisan surnames	0.85	0.85	0.80
Locative surnames	0.74	0.84	0.86
Surnames from IPM	0.79	0.84	0.86
Norman surnames	0.85	0.88	0.90
Average	0.81	0.85	0.85

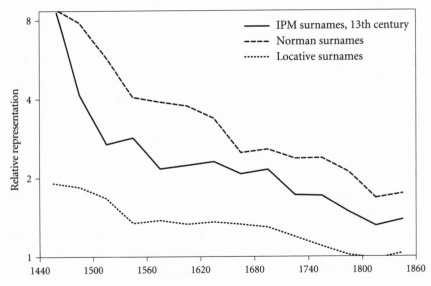

FIGURE 4.9. Medieval elites in high-status PCC probates, 1440–1858.

shows the relative representation of the three elite surname groups among the high-status PCC probates. These are shown for the period from 1440 onward because their numbers are too small in earlier generations to calculate meaningful persistence rates. Table 4.3 shows the best-fitting persistence rate for this more exclusive stratum. Persistence here is somewhat stronger than among the less exclusive PCC probates, but the estimates are very consistent across the groups, at 0.85–0.88.

Table 4.3 also shows, for comparison purposes, the persistence estimates for those attending the universities up to 1590. These numbers are consistent in the picture they paint of early English society. There was very slow but consistent social mobility generation after generation, which brought the descendants of the artisans and the propertied elites of the thirteenth century to nearly equivalent social status by the eve of the Industrial Revolution. By 1770, the high-status locative surnames of the Middle Ages had dropped to average social status, measured in terms of their representation at the universities and in PCC probates. At the same time, the artisan surnames had risen to average status. However, social mobility occurred at such a stately pace that those bearing the surnames of the propertied elite of the thirteenth century identified from the *Inquisitions Post Mortem* of 1236–99 and those bearing surnames derived from the Norman conquerors were still modestly overrepresented among the wealthy and educated in 1770. For example, in 1770 Norman surnames occurred 2.5 times as frequently as expected among Oxford and Cambridge students, 2.1 times as frequently among high-status PCC probates, and 1.6 times as frequently among all PCC probates. But since those bearing such surnames made up less than 1 percent of the English population, the obverse side of this finding is that more than 97 percent of those attending Oxford or Cambridge, or whose wills were proved in the PCC, had non-Norman surnames.

Conclusions

We see in medieval England slow but persistent rates of social mobility similar to those in modern Sweden and the United States. The surname data we examine show absolutely no sign that any of the intellectual, social, and economic advances between 1300 and 2000 in England produced much increase in social mobility. Neither the Reformation in the sixteenth century, nor the Enlightenment of the early eighteenth century, nor the Industrial Revolution of the late eighteenth century, nor the political reforms of the nineteenth century, nor the rise of the welfare state in the twentieth century, seems to have had much effect on intergenerational mobility.

The next chapter looks more specifically at mobility rates across many dimensions in modern England, before chapter 6 theorizes about what all this means about the process of social mobility.

FIVE

Modern England

The Deep Roots of the Present

THIS CHAPTER ESTIMATES SOCIAL MOBILITY RATES in England for the
period 1830–2012. It does so using rare surnames, as most common surnames in England now differ little in social status: regression to the mean
may be slow, but over the seven hundred years since surnames were formed
in England, it has done its work in this respect. The use of rare surnames
offers a means of addressing one objection to the conclusions in chapters 2–4:
that if people know that certain surnames convey high or low status, then
this awareness itself may affect social mobility rates. If the name *Darcy* is
perceived as being of high status, then perhaps *Darcys* are more readily admitted to the right schools and recruited for prestigious jobs. If *Bottom* is perceived as connoting low status, then perhaps *Bottoms* never get a chance to
show their worth. If *von Essen* is perceived by Swedes to be a surname of
noble lineage, then perhaps the *von Essens* receive unmerited promotions
and privileges. So it may be that, by measuring social mobility rates using surnames, we are incorporating effects that reduce mobility for those with distinctive surnames.

Consider, for example, the following list of names drawn from the list of
barristers in England in 2011: *Franklin St Clair Melville Evans, Durand David
Grenville Malet, Michael John Davy Vere-Hodge, Michael David Melville-
Shreeve, Matthew Sean de la Hay Browne Brotherton, Jeremy Gaywood Grout-
Smith, Alexandra Marika Niki Smith-Hughes, Mungo William Wenban-Smith,
Alexander George Lavander Hill-Smith.* These are not people you expect to
meet at your local chip shop or job center. These names reek of class, privilege,
and distinguished lineage.

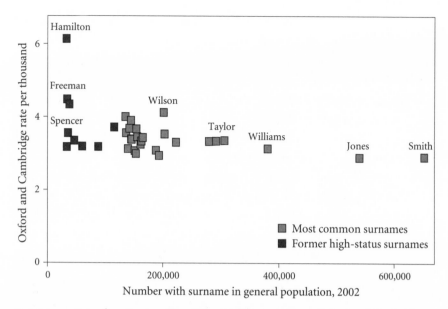

FIGURE 5.1. Rate of occurrence of common English surnames at Oxford and Cambridge per thousand of these names in the population in 2002.

These names stand out in part because they are uncommon. As the previous chapter shows, common surnames tend to have close to average social status in modern England. One measure of the average status of a surname is the rate at which it shows up at Oxford and Cambridge compared to its incidence in the general population. Figure 5.1 shows the incidence of the twenty-five most common indigenous English surnames among students at Oxford and Cambridge from 1980 to 2012. These surnames tend to show up at very similar rates among this social elite. *Smith* and *Jones,* the two most common surnames, have slightly lower incidences than the average surname, a result found for these names among other elites. This is probably because some high-status people with the mundane surname *Smith* abandon it in favor of a more distinguished one. But even here, the effect is small.[1]

Even common surnames that originated in the Middle Ages from the occupations of people of higher social status have reverted to average status. These include my own name, *Clark(e),* from *cleric,* which referred to both members of the church and attorneys. Other names derive from the titles of high manorial

[1] *Smith* is also a very common surname among the Traveller population, which sends few students to Oxford or Cambridge.

officials, such as *Chamberlain, Butler, Bailey, Reeve,* and *Spencer* (from *dispenser*). And there were high-status trades such as *draper.* Figure 5.1 shows the most common of these higher-status occupational surnames: they have no higher status now than the average common surname does.

Rare surnames, by contrast, can vary significantly in social status, just from the forces of chance that affect the circumstances of the average holder of such a name. Fortunately for our purposes, some societies, including England, have always had many rare surnames. The occurrence of very rare names (held by only 1–4 people) in such records as censuses is probably artificially increased by errors of spelling and transcription in recording common names. But most names held by 5–50 people are genuine rare surnames. Thus in England in 1881, 5 percent of the population (1.4 million people) held 112,000 such rare surnames. In 2002, the same percentage (now 2.8 million people) held 215,000 such rare surnames.

Rare surnames originated in various ways. The arrival of the Huguenots from France after 1685 brought names such as *Abauzit, Bazalgette,* and *Bulteel* to England. Spelling mutations from more common surnames created names like *Bisshopp.* And some names were always held by very few people, such as *Pepys, Binford,* and *Blacksmith.*

Francis Galton, the Victorian polymath, cowrote a paper in 1874 that predicted the extinction of most rare surnames over time.[2] There was concern at this time that the distinguished surnames of the aristocracy were dying out. However, in England, the stock of rare surnames has been replenished by immigrants bringing in new surnames and by the widespread adoption of hyphenated surnames by the English upper classes from the nineteenth century onward. There is no lack of rare surnames.

As noted, the advantage of measuring social mobility with rare surnames is that most carry no status association. Table 5.1, for example, lists the first fifteen names from the samples of rare English surnames from the mid-nineteenth century used in this chapter from three different social groups: rich, prosperous, and poor. These surnames were held by 0–40 people in the 1881 census. They are labeled just as sample A, sample B, and sample C. Can you discern which is which? (The source note to the table reveals the answer.)

In the analysis of social mobility using rare surnames, the first set of names examined are those of people dying between 1858 and 1887 (one generation),

[2] Watson and Galton 1875.

TABLE 5.1. Rare English surname samples, 1858–87

Sample A	Sample B	Sample C
Ahmuty	Aller	Agace
Allecock	Almand	Agar-Ellis
Angerstein	Angler	Aglen
Appold	Anglim	Aloof
Auriol	Annings	Alsager
Bailward	Austell	Bagnold
Basevi	Backlake	Benthall
Bazalgette	Bagwill	Berthon
Beague	Balsden	Brandram
Berens	Bantham	Brettingham
Beridge	Bawson	Brideoake
Berners	Beetchenow	Broadmead
Bigge	Bemmer	Broderip
Blegborough	Bevill	Brouncker
Blicke	Bierley	Brune

with names held by forty or fewer people in the 1881 census. This starting date was chosen because it was in 1858 that the modern comprehensive probate register was adopted (superseding an obscure complex of overlapping ecclesiastical-court records). From the comprehensive probate register, which gives an assessed value for all probated estates, the average wealth at death can be estimated for all surnames in England and Wales from 1858 to the present.

The first such surname sample is 105 rare surnames from the top 5 percent of the wealth distribution in 1858. These are a mixture of rare indigenous names and foreign imports. Some of the surnames are well known: *Brudenell-Bruce, Cornwallis, Courtauld, Leveson-Gower,* and *Sotheby.* Charles Cornwallis, the first Marquess Cornwallis, was one of the leading British generals in the American War of Independence. The *Courtaulds* were of Huguenot heritage and founders of a famous textile firm. The *Leveson-Gowers* were among the richest aristocrats in England. The *Sotheby* family founded the famous auction house. The *Brudenell-Bruces* are an aristocratic family, marquesses of Ailesbury and earls of Cardigan, who now serve as an illustration of the power of social mobility. Their name appears frequently in the social pages of the English press. But their ancestral seat, Tottenham House, is in sad decay, as figure 5.2 illustrates.

FIGURE 5.2. Decay at the family seat: regression to the mean among the *Brudenell-Bruces.*

And the current Earl of Cardigan, David Brudenell-Bruce, has fallen on such reduced circumstances that he at times subsists on a jobseeker's allowance of £71 a week.[3]

Most of these surnames, however, are too obscure to signal any particular social status: *Bigge, Buttanshaw, Hilhouse, Skipwith, Taddy,* and *Willyams,* for example. A typical foreign name from this sample is *Bazalgette,* discussed in chapter 1. All of the fifty-seven *Bazalgettes* in England in 2002 seem to be descended from one man, Jean-Louis Bazalgette, a Huguenot immigrant from southern France, who became tailor to the prince regent, later George IV. The prince must have had quite extravagant tastes in clothes, because Jean-Louis left the enormous fortune of £250,000 at his death in 1830. Jean-Louis had two wives and many children. Within a generation, his family had become thoroughly English, with at least seven of his grandchildren serving in the British armed forces. His grandson Joseph William was well known in his own right as the designer of the London sewer system (see figure 5.3). But for all that, the name *Bazalgette* is unfamiliar to most people.

[3] "I'm So Broke" 2013.

FIGURE 5.3. London monument to Sir Joseph Bazalgette.

The second sample of surnames from the probate register is drawn from families in the top 5 to 15 percent of the wealth distribution. This comprises seventy-six similarly diverse and mostly obscure surnames. The notable ones are *De Grey, Pepys, Pigou,* and *Rothschild.* But, as before, most of these names are largely unknown: *Brandram, Brettingham, Brideoake, Broadmead, Broderip,* and so on.

The third sample is 237 rare surnames held by poor people. The first source of such names is a list published by the government in 1861 of habitual paupers, people who had been on poor relief (public assistance) continuously over the last five years. The surnames used here are a subset of that list. No one with these surnames dying between 1858 and 1887 evidenced any wealth at all. The names themselves signal nothing of their low status, and indeed some are surprising. The list includes *Defoe,* the surname of the famous writer Daniel Defoe (1660–1731). Though *Defoe* is a French-sounding surname, it is very rare in modern France, and Defoe himself was born Daniel Foe, adding the *De-* as a pseudo-aristocratic affectation.[4] Because Daniel Defoe had surviving sons, and there is

[4] As noted, it has ever been the right of the English to call themselves whatever they want, as long as there is no intention to deceive. This ability to change surnames is something we

no record of any *Defoe* in English births or marriages before his birth, the modern English *Defoe*s likely mostly descend from Daniel. The poverty of the *Defoe*s who died between 1858 and 1887 reflects downward mobility.

The Inheritance of Wealth in Modern England

The people identified in these initial rare-surname groups were born, on average, around 1813. How did their descendants fare in the four to six generations up to the present?

As noted, the probate records give an indicator of wealth at death for every adult dying in England and Wales from 1858 onward. A variable fraction of adults was probated at death in each year: only 15 percent in 1858 but 42 percent by 2011. Of the estates probated, all have an assessed value. For wills not probated, we have no measure of the value of the estate. But since most of those avoided probate because their assets were of insufficient value, we can assume for this group an average estate value of half the minimum value of those requiring probate. In this way we can assign an average probate value to all rare surnames by generation of death, starting in the period 1858–87.

Figure 5.4 shows the result. Wealth for each surname group in each period is measured relative to the wealth of the average adult at death. The initial wealth of the rich surname group is 187 times that of the average, and for the prosperous group, it is 21 times the average. Both rich and prosperous surname groups regress toward the mean with each generation, but by 1999–2012, four generations later, they are both still much wealthier than the average person at death: the rich are four times as wealthy, the prosperous three times as wealthy. The initial wealth of the poor group is half the average. By 1999–2012 this figure was an estimated 90 percent of the average. Figure 5.4 demonstrates that even among the great-great-grandchildren of the Victorian generation, wealth disparities between surname groups persist.

Table 5.2 shows the implied intergenerational correlation for wealth in each generation for each group of surnames.[5] Because many of these surnames are

---

have to guard against in the examples below. But surprisingly few English people have made use of this right, even when their birth name has unfortunate connotations. Shakespeare, for example, when he wants a comic surname for one of his "rude mechanicals" in *A Midsummer Night's Dream* (1594), chooses *Bottom*. But there were still 549 *Bottoms* in England in 1881, as many proportionately as in the marriage records of 1594.

[5] In each case, wealth was measured as a logarithm to limit the effects of outliers of extreme wealth on the results. See Clark and Cummins 2013 for details.

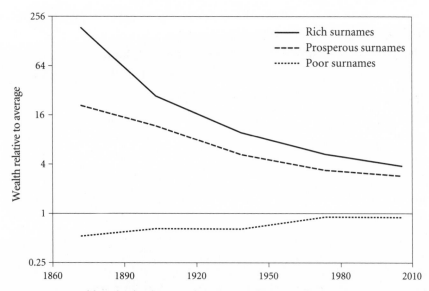

FIGURE 5.4. Wealth at death relative to the average, by surname type.

TABLE 5.2. Intergenerational correlations for wealth at death

Generation	Conventional estimate	Rich	Prosperous	Poor
1888–1917	0.48	0.63	0.81	0.67
1918–59	0.41	0.69	0.67	1.02
1960–87	0.41	0.73	0.73	0.23
1999–2012	0.46	0.80	0.87	1.10
Average, all generations	0.44	0.71	0.77	0.64

so rare, we can identify individual fathers and sons for more than four thousand cases. Thus the first column of the table shows the estimated intergenerational correlation for individual families using conventional measures to estimate the persistence rate. This persistence rate, ranging from 0.41 to 0.48, is in line with the other, limited evidence on wealth inheritance within English families. Notice also that there is no sign of any increase in wealth mobility between the generation dying in the years 1888–1917 and that dying in the years 1999–2012, despite the many institutional changes in the intervening years.

The other columns show the intergenerational correlations for average wealth across rich, prosperous, and poor surname groups. For all three groups, the correlation averaged over the entire period is much higher than that revealed by conventional measures: for the rich it is 0.71, for the prosperous 0.77, and for the poor 0.64. The estimate for the poor, however, is one potentially contaminated with random error, as can be seen by the large fluctuations in estimates for different generations. So the estimates for the rich and prosperous are the focus here. For these groups, again, we see no sign of any increase in wealth mobility between 1888 and 2012. Yet the earlier generation held wealth in an era when taxation and redistribution of income and wealth were very modest compared to more recent periods.

The maximum inheritance tax rate in England for those dying between 1858 and 1887 was 4 percent. Thus this generation could pass on wealth almost intact to their heirs. In contrast, for those dying between 1960 and 1993, the maximum inheritance tax averaged 69 percent (see figure 5.5). The wealth inherited by the generation dying between 1999 and 2012 thus would have been heavily taxed, and this taxation should have pushed their wealth much more quickly toward the mean than was the case for previous generations. Yet no such trend is apparent in the data. The persistence of wealth remained just as high for the last two, heavily taxed, generations as for the previous two, which escaped significant inheritance taxation.

Under the various inheritance-tax laws in effect in England and Wales from 1858 to 2012, considerable wealth could be exempted from tax. Since allowances sometimes varied for unmarried and married testators, it is not possible to estimate the exact tax burden in each period. But for members of the rich surname group dying between 1960 and 1993, of all wealth bequeathed, roughly 57 percent was absorbed in taxes. It is thus surprising that the persistence of wealth in the fifth generation, the beneficiaries of these bequests, is just as strong as in previous generations.

Other evidence of the strong persistence of wealth differences by surname comes from probate rates in each surname group. Since typically only the wills of people with wealth at death were probated, and a large fraction of the population has no wealth at death, these rates are another good indicator of surname-group wealth.

Figure 5.6 shows the probate rates for the three surname groups at death over five generations. Wills for those in the rich and the prosperous surname groups are currently probated at a rate of 60 percent, compared to 45 percent for the general population. Probate rates for the poor are converging toward

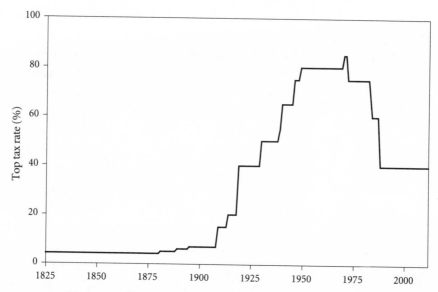

FIGURE 5.5. Maximum inheritance tax rates, United Kingdom, 1825–2012.

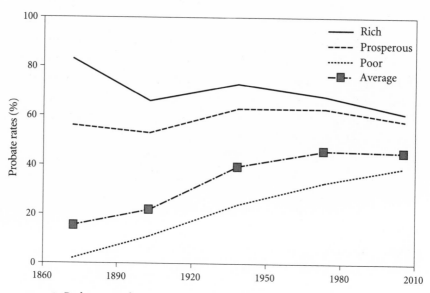

FIGURE 5.6. Probate rates for surname groups, by generation.

that of the average surname, but only in the fifth generation, and even that convergence is not yet complete.

From these probate rates, we can infer the intergenerational persistence of wealth in England, using the method given in appendix 2. Table 5.3 shows the estimated correlations for the rich, prosperous, and poor groups by generation and averaged over generations. These confirm the estimates above based on actual wealth estimates.

These wealth measures have drawbacks as a general index of social mobility. First, it may be objected that of various components of social status—education, occupation, earnings, health, and wealth—the most persistent is wealth, since it can be directly inherited. Second, the measures of wealth discussed above may not fully reflect the social changes that took place in Britain in the twentieth century. For the last generation we observe, those dying in the years 1999–2012, the average date of birth was 1924. These people would, on average, have completed their schooling by 1946, before many of the social changes of the postwar era. This raises the question of whether social mobility might be much greater for people in England born more recently.

Greater longevity is making the circulation of wealth in modern economies increasingly socially dysfunctional. In 1858–69, when our data on deaths begins, the average age for those whose wills were proved was 62. Given an average gap of thirty years between generations, wealth was inherited by children on average at age 32, just as they were rearing their own children and buying housing. But now people are, on average, fifty years old when they inherit any wealth from their parents. By then they typically own their own house and cars, and their own children have completed much of their education. If longevity continues to increase, then, despite increases in the average age at which women produce children, wealth will increasingly pass from the ancient to the aged.

TABLE 5.3. Wealth correlations from probate rates

Period	Rich	Prosperous	Poor
1888–1917	0.60	0.73	0.43
1918–1959	0.74	0.70	0.98
1960–1993	0.66	0.74	0.74
1994–2011	0.73	0.81	0.22
Average	0.68	0.77	0.64

Inheritance of Educational Status

As a way of measuring social mobility in current generations, we can turn to education. Specifically, we look at the fraction of people admitted to Oxford and Cambridge as an index of educational status. This measure can be applied to people born as late as 1994.

From 1830 to 2012 these universities typically enrolled only 0.5 to 1.3 percent of each cohort of the eligible domestic population. The data used here provide a complete record of Oxford and Cambridge attendees from 1800 to 1893, and thereafter four-fifths or more of attendees through 2012—a total of six hundred thousand students. The last birth cohort observed is those born in 1993–94.[6]

For this purpose, because the surname sample is small and admission to the universities is a low-frequency event, the rare surnames of the rich and the prosperous dying between 1858 and 1887 are combined into one group. Figure 5.7 shows the relative representation of these surnames at Oxford and Cambridge by thirty-year generations starting in 1830, ending with a current cohort of entrants, 2010–12. The figure shows how overrepresented these surnames are at Oxford and Cambridge relative to their incidence in the general population.

The rare wealthy surnames show up at very high rates in the initial generation of university entrants, 1830–59. Someone with one of these surnames was fifty times more likely to enroll at Oxford or Cambridge than someone from the general population. Over the next six generations, the last observed being university entrants from 2010 to 2012, there is a substantial decline in the relative representation of these surnames. By the last generation, a member of this surname group was only six times as likely to enter Oxford or Cambridge as someone in the general population. This finding implies that simply by knowing that people with a given surname born circa 1813 on average died wealthy, it is predicted that people born circa 1990 with the same surname are six times more likely than the average person to attend Oxford or Cambridge. This is a remarkable persistence of status over six generations.

There are thirteen observations of the wealthy rare surnames at Oxford and Cambridge for the period 2010–12, compared to an expected two. This high number could be in part just the result of luck. Admission to Oxford and Cambridge depends on exam results, secondary school location, and sympathetic

---

[6] This database was assembled from a variety of sources, such as exam results published for Oxford from 1976 to 2009 and the e-mail directories of Oxford and Cambridge for 2010–12.

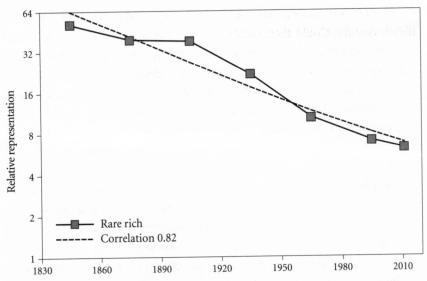

FIGURE 5.7. Relative representation of rare wealthy surnames at Oxford and Cambridge, 1830–2011.

interviewers, among other factors. However, the probability that this high representation between 2010 and 2012 is all due to random chance can be shown to be one in a thousand. Rare surnames that were elite in the early nineteenth century remain elite today.

Even so, the admissions data show a decline in relative representation for this surname group. What does this trend imply about the intergenerational correlation of educational status in England? The figure also shows the pattern of decline that would be predicted if the correlation of educational status across generations were always 0.82. The fit is generally good, despite the small numbers of observations in later generations.

Educational status persists for this group even more strongly than wealth. Moreover, as with wealth mobility, there is no sign that educational mobility has increased in the past few generations. An intergenerational correlation of 0.82 fits the pattern reasonably well across all generations. The implied rate of mobility is so low that the rich elite surnames will not approach an average representation at Oxford and Cambridge for another seventeen generations (510 years).[7]

[7] This is calculated defining average representation of a surname as a representation at Oxford and Cambridge no more than 10 percent above its share in the general population.

The rare surnames in this sample are all associated with wealth in the nineteenth century. Could their persistence as an educational elite be due to the association of these surnames with wealth? Have other families in the educational elite of 1830–59 regressed to the mean much more quickly?

To test this hypothesis, we draw from the university records another, larger rare-surname group that consists of any surnames with five hundred or fewer holders in the 1881 census that appear on the lists of entrants to Oxford and Cambridge between 1800 and 1829. Thus all we know about these surnames, apart from their rarity, is that they show up on the university rolls sometime in this period. In 1830, this group of surnames represented just over 1 percent of the population of England but nearly 12 percent of all Oxford and Cambridge students. Figure 5.8 shows the relative representation of this much larger surname group in subsequent generations at Oxford and Cambridge.

Again the high educational status associated with these surnames erodes very slowly. They are still overrepresented in the current student population, although that overrepresentation is now modest. Such surnames are only 65 percent more frequent in the universities as in the population of all eighteen-year-olds. But again, this finding implies a strong intergenerational correlation of status over six generations. The persistence rate that best fits this pattern is 0.73.

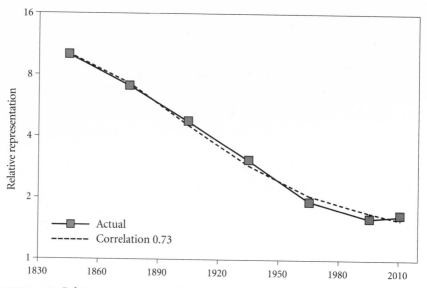

FIGURE 5.8. Relative representation of Oxford and Cambridge rare surnames from 1800–1829 among Oxford and Cambridge students, 1830–2012.

The pattern of declining relative representation predicted by such a level of persistence in educational status is shown in the figure: it fits the observed pattern of decline very well across almost all the generations. The implied intergenerational correlation of status seems constant between 1830 and 2012. Later generations show no increase in social mobility. The only deviation is that in the years 2010–12, an unexpectedly high number of the elite surnames from the period 1800–1829 are observed. But this anomaly may be due to the fact that our data for current students comes from a different source (the university e-mail directories).

Thus intergenerational persistence is just as high for education as for wealth. And in this case, the persistence extends to the generation born 1992–1994. Both the wealthy and the educationally privileged of 1800–1829 are losing their elite status only slowly. Yet since that time the nature of universities and the way in which they recruit students have changed dramatically.

The finding about the persistence of rarer surnames at Oxford and Cambridge is remarkable. Suppose you are now eighteen and have a surname that was held by five hundred or fewer people in 1881. Even if all we know about you is that someone with your surname was enrolled at Oxford or Cambridge in the years 1800–1829, then we can predict that you have a 65 percent better chance of being admitted to one of those universities now. If you have a surname that was even rarer in 1881, held by forty or fewer people, we can improve on that prediction: if a person with your surname attended Oxford or Cambridge between 1800 and 1829, then your chances of admission are 3.5 times better than those of the average eighteen-year-old in England.

These findings hold despite significant changes in admissions policies and financial support for students in the intervening years. In the early nineteenth century, Oxford and Cambridge were largely closed to those outside the established Church of England. Not until 1871 were all religious tests for graduation finally removed. As late as 1859, one member of our wealthy surname group, Alfred de Rothschild, who was Jewish, had to petition to be excused from Anglican services at Trinity College, Cambridge. This exemption was granted as a special indulgence.[8]

Before 1902 there was little or no public support for university education. Oxford and Cambridge offered scholarships, but most of them went to students from elite endowed schools, who were coached to excel at the scholarship

[8] Winstanley 1940, 83.

exams. In the years 1900–1913, nine schools, identified as the elite of English secondary education in the Clarendon report of 1864 (including Eton, Harrow, and Rugby), supplied 28 percent of male entrants to Oxford.[9] In addition, entrance requirements favored students from more exclusive educational backgrounds: before 1940, entrants to Oxford, regardless of their intended field of study, were required to complete a Latin entrance exam.

From 1920 to 1939, local authorities provided financial support that enabled less affluent students to attend university. After World War II, there was a major increase in government financial support for secondary and university education. Oxford and Cambridge eventually devised entry procedures that should have reduced the admissions advantages for students from the traditional, endowed feeder schools. These measures would seem to imply a much faster regression to the mean for elite surname frequencies at Oxford and Cambridge after 1950. Yet there is no evidence of such a trend in figures 5.7 and 5.8.

Political Status

An even more elite group than the wealth holders or Oxford and Cambridge students is members of Parliament. There were about five hundred MPs on average from England and Wales in the nineteenth century, rising to around 550 in the twentieth century.

Records of members of Parliament extend back to 1295 and thus allow us to observe the mobility implied by movements in and out of the English political elite since the high Middle Ages. Here we take the list of rare surnames found at Oxford and Cambridge for the years 1800–1829. As a social elite, this group of surnames is also overrepresented in Parliament. Figure 5.9 shows the relative representation of these rare surnames in Parliament in the years 1830–2012. The Parliament measure starts in 1830 so that the sample corresponds to the birth cohort associated with entry to university between 1800 and 1829.

The relative representation of these rare surnames in Parliament follows the same pattern as their association with wealth and Oxford and Cambridge attendance. It again shows a relatively steady decline over generations, though the process becomes noisier at the end because of the small numbers of MPs and the many chance factors that determine whether any particular person becomes an MP. But five generations later, in the 1980–2009 cohort, these rare

[9] Greenstein 1994, 47.

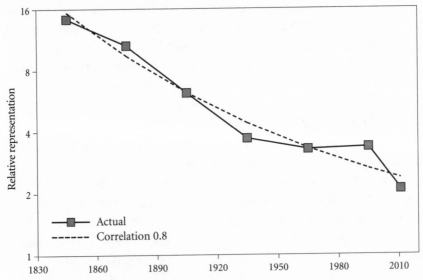

FIGURE 5.9. Relative representation of Oxford and Cambridge rare surnames from 1800–1829 among members of Parliament, 1830–2012.

surnames are still more than three times as frequent in Parliament than in the general population. The implied intergenerational correlation of status is high, at 0.8.[10]

The remarkable thing about this finding is that over this period, significant changes in political institutions brought new parties and new groups into the House of Commons. Why did these changes not have a greater effect on the representation of surnames among MPs? The allocation of seats in Parliament for counties and boroughs was largely unchanged from the medieval pattern as late as the election of 1831; it failed to reflect the growth and redistribution of the population. Medieval boroughs, such as Dunwich in Suffolk, were entitled to elect two MPs. Over time, with changes in trade and industry, many of these once-thriving boroughs became depopulated villages or hamlets with tiny electorates. Most of Dunwich, in fact, fell into the sea.

These fossilized borough constituencies became known as rotten boroughs. The landowners of these boroughs effectively controlled the election of MPs. Voting was public in these years, and the small number of electors could be

[10] We assume in this calculation that MPs represent the top 0.1 percent of the status distribution.

bribed or intimidated to vote as directed. The most notorious example was Old Sarum, which in 1831 had a population of seven and an electorate of four. In the 1831 election, just before reform, 152 out of 406 MPs, more than a third, were elected by fewer than one hundred voters. Thus a large part of the House of Commons was in the control of the traditional landed classes.

The Reform Act of 1832 disenfranchised 56 such boroughs in England and Wales and reduced the representation of another 31 to only one MP. It also created 67 new constituencies and extended and regularized the franchise. In 1867, a second Reform Act disenfranchised a further two rotten boroughs and reduced a further 35 boroughs to one MP. Ancillary legislation in 1867–68 eliminated another 9 rotten boroughs. The 1867 act also resulted in another major extension of the franchise (though it was still restricted to men). Yet these reforms had no perceptible effects on the rate of intergenerational mobility among the political class.

Along with these reforms, over time the electoral franchise was extended to men (and then women) lower on the social scale. The franchise extended to only 13 percent of men in 1830 but to 100 percent by 1918. The extension of the franchise was associated with the rise of the Labour Party as the voice of the urban working class. By 1923 the party had 191 MPs, including members from Scotland. From then on large numbers of Labour MPs were returned at every election.

But, as figure 5.9 shows, the rise of a working-class party in the early twentieth century was not associated with a rapid replacement of traditional elite surnames in Parliament. Whatever the political arrangements, this surname group maintained its overrepresentation in Parliament and in the halls of Westminster. Lineage dominated ideology and party.

Conclusions

The tracking of rare surnames shows that social mobility rates for wealth, education, and political power are low in modern England. The intergenerational correlation of status in these various dimensions is on the order of 0.73–0.80 and has not decreased since the nineteenth century, despite the advent of modern economic growth, mass public education, the extension of the political franchise, and the welfare state. Modern rates of social mobility also represent only very slight increases on mobility rates in the medieval period, when for artisan surnames the estimated persistence rates for education and wealth were on the order of 0.80–0.85. These rates are similar to those found in Sweden for recent occupational and status mobility and in the United States for recent occupational mobility.

The intergenerational correlation of wealth in England is estimated at 0.73 from an analysis of surname groups. Yet conventional estimates of intergenerational wealth persistence, which look at individual families, are always in the range 0.41–0.48. How do we reconcile these different estimates of social mobility rates? Which of these estimates is correct? In the next chapter we offer a theory as to why surname estimates consistently reveal much lower social mobility rates than the conventional estimates do, and why surname estimates are the better guide to overall rates of social mobility and to the underlying structure of status inheritance in societies.

SIX

A Law of Social Mobility

Even a fool learns something once it hits him.
  Homer, *The Iliad*

THIS BOOK ESTIMATES SOCIAL MOBILITY RATES by measuring the rate at which surnames that originally had high or low social status lose that status connotation. If a surname such as *Pepys* or *Brudenell-Bruce* had a high status in 1800, how rapidly does that surname regress to average status? If *Baskerville* was an elite name in the Domesday Book of 1086 in England, is there any echo of that distinction in 1300, 1500, or now? The book examines how surnames reflect the rate of social entropy, the rate at which original status information leaves the social system.

The four previous chapters reveal not one but many surprising results from using surnames as measures of mobility. The first is that in all the cases examined, social mobility measured from surnames is much lower than from conventional measures. The conventional measure, as discussed in appendix 1, just looks at the correlation between parent and child for any aspect of status. Surname status shows regression to the mean in all cases, but the process is slow. Elite surnames can take ten or fifteen generations (300–450 years) to become average in status.

The second surprising result is that social mobility seems to occur at a similar rate for different measures of status: wealth, education, occupational status, and membership in political elites. Wealth would seem to be much more heritable than education or occupational status. You can leave your indolent or idiot son or daughter a pile of money, but that money won't get them into medical school without superior MCAT scores. Why, then, does wealth show the same rate of persistence as these other aspects of status?

The third surprise is that the rate of persistence is close to constant across wildly different social systems. It is little higher for the feudal England of the

Middle Ages than for the progressive, equality-loving, social-democratic Sweden of today.

If individual family estimates of social mobility suggest intergenerational correlations of 0.15–0.60 for these measures of social status, why do surname studies suggest correlations of 0.75–0.80? Why are the results so different when we examine surname groups rather than individual families?

A Simple Theory of Social Mobility

The theory proposed here to explain the above findings is simple, but it has significant implications for estimates of the rate and nature of social mobility. The proposal is that we must distinguish between a family's surface or apparent social status and their deeper social competence, which is never observed directly.[1] What is observed for families is their attainment on various partial indicators of social status: earnings, wealth, occupation, education, residence, health, and longevity. Each of these derives from underlying status, but with a random component.

Thus if y_t, for example, measures the earnings of a family in generation t, this assumption just formally translates into the statement

$$y_t = x_t + u_t$$

where x_t is the family's underlying social competence, and u_t is the random component.

The random component of aspects of social status exists for two reasons. First, there is an element of luck in the status attained by individuals. With respect to earnings, high-earning people happen to choose a successful field to work in or a successful firm to work for. They go to work for Facebook rather than Myspace. They just succeed in being admitted to Harvard, as opposed to just failing. They marry a supportive spouse instead of ending up shackled to a needy partner. Second, people trade income and wealth for other aspects of status. Someone might choose a career as a philosophy professor as opposed to a lower-status but more lucrative career selling plumbing hardware.

The second assumption in this simple theory of all social mobility is that underlying social status in families regresses only slowly toward the mean, with

---

[1] In psychometric terms, underlying status is a latent variable.

a persistence rate, b, of 0.75. And this high rate of persistence is constant across all societies. Formally,

$$x_{t+1} = bx_t + e_t,$$

where e_t is a second random component.[2] This is the social law of motion that is tested in the rest of this book. The claim of this book is that these two assumptions are sufficient to describe social mobility in all societies. This insight leads to powerful predictions about social mobility and its sources, predictions that are successfully tested below.

The above implies, for example, that the conventional studies of social mobility, based on estimating the intergenerational correlation β in the relationship

$$y_{t+1} = \beta y_t + v_t$$

for various partial measures of status—earnings, wealth, education, occupation, and so on—underestimate the true intergenerational correlation b that links underlying social status across generations. In particular, the expected value of conventional estimates, β, is not the underlying b but instead θb, where θ is less than one. Further, the greater the random components of any measured aspect of status, the smaller will θ be.[3]

Figure 6.1 shows the structure being proposed. The determining variable here is underlying social competence. Because the correlation of earnings with this variable is less than one, the correlation of earnings over one generation is $b\rho^2$, where ρ is the correlation of earnings with underlying social competence.

Since we have these two measures—b for underlying social mobility and β for partial measures of status—why is it that the underlying b is the true rate of social mobility? The reason is that if we were to measure families' status by an average of the various observed aspects of status, $\bar{y}_t$, then

$$\bar{y}_t = x_t + \bar{u}_t$$

where $^-$ indicates an average of the various random components. But as we average status across many aspects—earnings, wealth, residence, education, occupa-

---

[2] To keep the mathematics simple, x_t and x_{t+1} are assumed to have a mean of zero and a constant variance.

[3] This is shown in appendix 2.

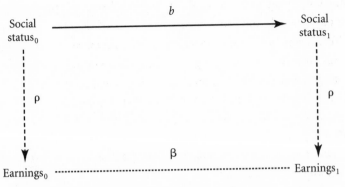

FIGURE 6.1. The intergenerational transmission of status.

tion, health, longevity—the average error component shrinks toward zero. Thus the intergenerational persistence of average social status approximates to b as opposed to β.[4] The underlying b gives us a better measure of the persistence of status on average for families, as opposed to the persistence of any particular aspects of status. Thus b best measures the true rate of social mobility.

Conventional estimates of social mobility, based as they are on estimating the correlation of parents and children on partial measures of social status, systematically overestimate the underlying mobility rate. It is the underlying mobility rate that determines overall social mobility rates for families and social mobility over multiple generations.

What causes the conventional measures to overestimate underlying social mobility rates is the presence of the error term linking partial measures of status with underlying competence. By looking at groups of people (as long as they are grouped by identifiers that do not correlate with this error term, such as race, religion, national origin, or even common surnames), we can reduce this error term by averaging across the group. While

$$y_i = x_i + u_i$$

at the individual level, at the group level,

$$\bar{y} = \bar{x}.$$

Now the $\bar{y}$ accurately tracks $\bar{x}$ without the intrusion of the errors, and we can correctly estimate social mobility. When we look at such groups of individ-

[4] A good example of the lower heritability of one aspect of a more general trait is IQ. Overall IQ is much more highly correlated between generations than any specific subcomponent.

uals, the underlying, slow rate of social mobility becomes apparent even when we can observe only the usual partial indicators of underlying social competence. This is why the surname groups provide a measure of underlying rates of social mobility. But any grouping that is independent of the current random elements determining a partial measure of status will do the same. That is why it will always seem that racial, ethnic, and other minorities within societies experience slower than expected social mobility.

For this argument to hold, it must be the case that the various manifestations of social status are all only loosely correlated with underlying social competence. This loose correlation can be shown both by illustrations and systematically. As an illustration, the State of California conveniently makes available to the public the salaries of all faculty in the University of California system. This information reveals that professors who would be regarded as equivalent by such criteria as level of education and occupational status in fact earn vastly different amounts. Figure 6.2 shows median salaries in 2012 for some disciplines. Professors of English and music earn about one-third the salaries of professors of management. If we were to infer status based only on earnings, we would conclude that there was a vast social gap between these species of academic.

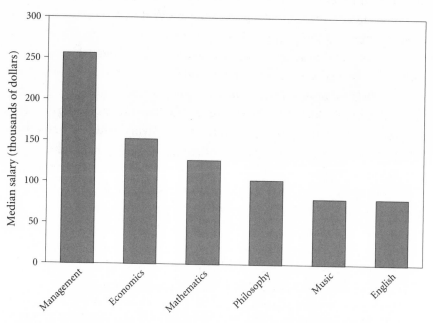

FIGURE 6.2. Median professors' salaries by subject, University of California, Davis, 2012.

TABLE 6.1. Correlations between different aspects of status

Status element	Cognitive ability (IQ, etc.)	Education	Occupational status	Earnings	Wealth
Cognitive ability	—	0.53	0.23	0.26	0.16
Education		—	0.63	0.33	0.30
Occupational status			—	0.52	0.23
Earnings				—	0.60

Table 6.1 confirms that any partial measure of social status, such as earnings, wealth, education, or occupation is only a very indirect measure of the underlying social competence of individuals. The table shows the average reported correlation for the same individual for several aspects of status: cognitive ability (typically represented by IQ), occupational status, education, earnings, and wealth. The correlations for any two attributes average 0.43. That means, for example, that if we know the cognitive ability (the IQ) of a child, we can typically predict less than one-fifth of the variation in the child's possible educational achievement, occupational status, earnings, and wealth.[5] This loose association of the various aspects of status for any person means that each aspect of status must also be only weakly correlated across generations.

This simple switch in thinking about the mechanism of social mobility can explain many of the puzzles noted in the existing literature on social mobility. It also enables us to make quite strong predictions about the nature of social mobility. Here are the predictions of this model.

The observed rates of regression to the mean for individual aspects of status are determined by how well they are predicted by the underlying status of families. The lower their correlation with this underlying status, the lower their intergenerational correlation. Thus mobility rates appear to differ for different aspects of status, depending on how closely each is linked to underlying status. And measured mobility rates vary across societies, again depending on how closely such as earnings correlate with underlying social status.

In the long run, all aspects of status regress to the mean at the same rate. Underlying mobility, as measured through earnings, wealth, education, or occupational status, will be the same.

[5] Bowles and Gintis (2002) point out that this loose association between IQ and other social outcomes creates puzzles about how these other attributes are inherited as strongly as they are. IQ inheritance cannot be the primary pathway.

The underlying process of social mobility is Markov: it proceeds at the same rate across all generations.[6] In particular, once we know the underlying status of your parents, no further information about your prospects in life can be derived from your earlier lineage. But using conventional family estimates, it appears that the status of grandparents and great-grandparents influences the current status of individuals.

Some social groups, such as Jews, blacks, Latinos, and Native Americans in the United States, appear to have lower rates of social mobility than the general population on conventional measures, but in fact they exhibit the same rate of regression to the mean as the society as a whole. Slow mobility rates for blacks and Latinos do not reflect an enduring racism in American society; they just reflect the fact that the rate of regression to the mean for underlying social status is inherently low.

Variation in Measured Social Mobility Rates

As shown in chapter 1, measured mobility rates for earnings in Sweden are much greater than in the United Kingdom or the United States. Yet when we measure mobility in these three societies using surnames, we find no difference. The explanation of these findings is that the greater the random components in measures of status such as income, relative to the systematic elements stemming from underlying status, the greater the mismatch between measured earnings mobility and the underlying rate of social mobility.

The United States, for example, has much greater inequality in earnings than does Sweden. Figure 6.3 shows the salaries in 2010 for some comparable high- and low-status occupations in Sweden and the United States. A U.S. doctor earns six times the wage of a bus driver, while in Sweden the ratio of their earnings is only 2.3. A U.S. university professor earns 60 percent more than a bus driver; a Swedish professor earns only 40 percent more.

As noted above, the larger the share of variation in any particular status outcome (such as earnings) that is driven by random forces, as opposed to underlying differences in social competence, the greater the attenuating factor, θ, driving down the standard estimate of β below the underlying correlation of social status across generations. The compression of earnings in Sweden compared to the United States will lead to a lower value of θ for Sweden and thus

---

[6] For the statistical purists, it is first-order Markov.

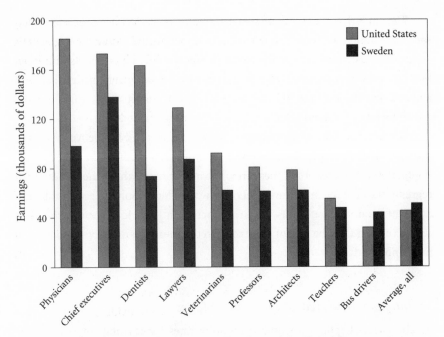

FIGURE 6.3. Average earnings by occupation, Sweden and the United States, 2008.

the appearance of more social mobility in general. Earnings in the United States are a better indicator of the underlying social status of families, and so income is more persistent across generations than it is in Sweden. This explanation also counters the popular belief that as earnings inequality has increased in the past forty years in the United States, social mobility rates have declined.[7] All that has happened is that the standard measures of mobility now more accurately reflect the low underlying mobility rates that always existed.

The mismatch between measured social mobility rates from partial aspects of mobility and underlying social mobility are dramatically illustrated in the inheritance of longevity. Across groups of people, longevity is highly correlated with social status. Longevity in England, as in other societies, has been dependent on socioeconomic status, at least since the nineteenth century. For professionals in England and Wales, recent life expectancy averaged eighty-two years. For unskilled manual workers, it averaged only seventy-five years.[8]

[7] Though this notion has gained currency (see, for example, Foroohar 2011), there seem to be no academic studies supporting it.
[8] U.K., Office of National Statistics 2007.

Many people assume that there is a high correlation between their likely longevity and that of their parents. After all, we would expect strong genetic inheritance of characteristics that lead to a longer life. Thus people with long-lived parents save more for retirement, assuming that they will need to support themselves over a longer period.

But in fact the correlation of longevity between individual parents and children is very low. For the people dying in England in the period 1858–2012 with the rare surnames used in chapter 4, we can measure the correlation of longevity between fathers and sons for more than four thousand sons surviving to at least age 21. That correlation is only 0.13. If we take the average of both parents' ages at death, that correlation increases to 0.26. But it is still low.[9] In reality, your age at death is not strongly predictable from your parents' age at death. All those saving more for retirement simply because both their parents are fit, healthy, and in their nineties should stop immediately. Your expected additional longevity relative to the average is only three years.

However, at the level of social groups rather than individuals, we see a very strong correlation of longevity across generations. Table 6.2 shows the average longevity of the rich, prosperous, and poor rare surname groups in England, classified into generations according to date of death. In the generation 1866–1887, the average age of death differs dramatically among surname groups: it is 51 for the rich, 32 for the poor. Average longevity converges steadily over time, but even for the fifth generation, those dying 1994–2011, the average longevity for two richer surname groups was 80, compared to 77 for the poor surname group.[10] The descendants of the original rich surname groups are still living longer.

The reason for the extreme difference in measured average longevity in the first generation is actually a combination of lower death rates for the rich at each age and greater fertility among the poor, which exposed the poor population in the early years to high child-mortality risks. If we look instead just at longevity for those surviving to age 21 and above, the difference is more modest.

Figure 6.4 shows average adult longevity for each surname group by generation. Even though at the individual level there is little correlation across generations in longevity, the figure reveals that at the group level, there is extraordinary persistence of longevity differences between the descendants of

[9] This finding is consistent with the intergenerational correlation in other family studies. See Beeton and Pearson 1899; Cohen 1964.
[10] Since the estimated standard error of the difference of mean ages at death is 0.68, this difference is highly significant statistically.

TABLE 6.2. Longevity by rare-surname wealth groups, England

Generation	Average age at death		
	Rich	Prosperous	Poor
1866–87	51	46	32
1888–1917	58	55	35
1918–59	67	67	56
1960–93	75	75	71
1994–2011	80	80	77

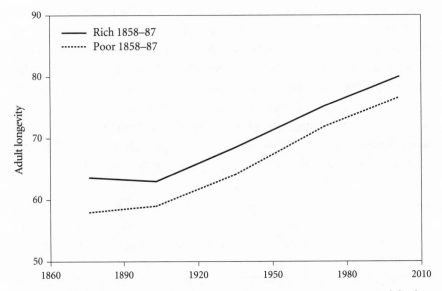

FIGURE 6.4. Average longevity for adults (age 21 and over), by surname group and death generation.

the rich and the poor of the nineteenth century. The underlying persistence of attributes such as longevity across generations is disguised by the large random component determining individual longevity.

Mobility Measured by Various Characteristics

Another feature of conventional estimates of social mobility is large differences in suggested rates of mobility for different characteristics. Cognitive abilities in Sweden, for example, are found to be strongly correlated across generations, with an intergenerational correlation of 0.77. But, at least in Nordic countries, other characteristics, such as income, education, and wealth, have a much lower heritability, with correlations often less than 0.3.

The simple theory here makes a startling and powerful prediction, which is that underlying mobility rates for all aspects of social status, such as earnings, wealth, occupational status, education, health, and longevity, are the same. The apparent variations in these rates of social mobility come only from the effect of random elements. The data for England for the period 1800–2012 support this prediction. Evidence from the period 1830–2012 for those with rare surnames at Oxford and Cambridge suggests an underlying persistence rate of 0.73 for educational status. We can estimate the persistence rate for wealth in this surname group by measuring the probate rate of the surnames between 1830 and 1966 (with higher relative representation among probates signifying higher wealth). Figure 6.5 shows this probate rate, as well as the best-fitting estimate of the persistence rate for these years. A constant persistence rate of 0.78 fits the data very well.

This intergenerational correlation is slightly higher than the educational persistence rate of 0.73. But the two numbers 0.73 and 0.78 are remarkably close, given the completely different aspects of social status that they represent.

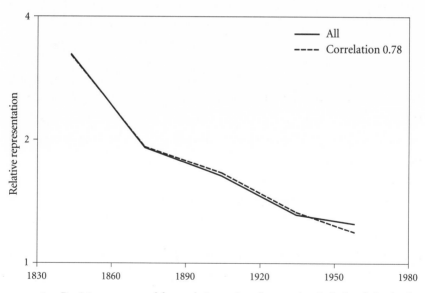

FIGURE 6.5. Persistence measured from relative probate frequencies, Oxford and Cambridge rare-surname elite, 1800–1829.

Suppose social mobility rates for different aspects of status really were very different. Suppose, for example, that wealth mobility was much slower than educational mobility. In that case, over the course of centuries, we would end up with a society where there was very little correlation between the various aspects of status. We would find a lot of wealthy, uneducated people and a lot of educated people with no assets to their names. Overall, the wealthy would be average in terms of their educational attainment: there would be little or no correlation between these two attributes. This is not the world we observe. Instead, there tends to be a consistent correlation between the various aspects of status. Maintaining such a correlation demands that the persistence of these attributes across generations be very similar.

The Influence of Grandparents

This simple model also explains another puzzle of conventional mobility estimates, which has emerged as researchers have begun to establish connections between the status of grandparents and grandchildren and even between great-grandparents and great-grandchildren. These estimates consistently show stronger correlations between the status of grandparents and grandchildren than would be expected from the correlations between parents and children. They also show that even if we control for the status of parents, the status of grandparents is predictive of the outcome for their grandchildren.[11] Current social status seems to be the result of a complex web of linkages, as pictured in figure 6.6.

Whatever the status of your parents, high-status grandparents predict a better outcome for you. Low-status grandparents predict a poorer outlook. This finding has been interpreted as showing that grandparents play a causal role in the outcomes for their grandchildren through such means as giving them money, helping them make social connections, and providing care that enhances their life chances.

Such a web of ancestral linkages, if they are causal, would also establish that the persistence of status has important social and institutional elements. The discussion below of what might underlie the patterns of status persistence shows that if persistence is mainly driven by genetic inheritance of abilities,

[11] See, for example, Long and Ferrie 2013; Lindahl et al. 2012; Boserup et al. 2013.

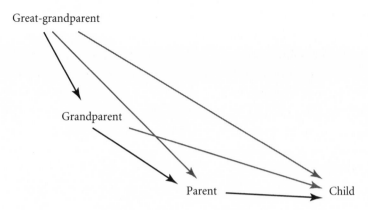

FIGURE 6.6. Apparent linkages between generations.

then grandparents and other, more distant relatives can have no direct influence on the current generation's life chances. The status of grandparents and great-grandparents predicts outcomes for descendants only because it provides more information about the true underlying social status of the parents. All the salient information is contained in the genetic code of the parents.

The simple model outlined above, however, predicts all these observed lineage effects, and even their magnitude, without ascribing to more-distant relatives a direct causal role in outcomes. It predicts these outcomes even though it assumes that grandparents, great-grandparents, and others farther back in a person's lineage in fact play no direct role in social outcomes.

Consider first the strength of correlations between grandparents and great-grandparents and the current generation. If the correlation between parents and children is 0.4, then we would intuitively expect the correlation with grandparents to be 0.16, the square of the one-generation correlation, and with great-grandparents a mere 0.06. However, our model of a much more persistent underlying social status predicts that a person's link to more distant ancestors will be stronger than expected from this simple reasoning.

The reason for this in technical terms is that the link between children and parents, the intergenerational correlation β normally estimated, relates to the underlying persistence of status such that the expected value of β is θb, where θ, as above, is the attenuation factor caused by the random components linking observed status on any one dimension with underlying status. When we look, however, at the correlation between grandparents and grandchildren, and esti-

TABLE 6.3. Intergenerational correlations of wealth in England, 1858–2012

Earlier generation	Number of observations	Observed correlations	Predicted correlations from conventional estimates	Implied underlying correlation
Fathers	4,312	0.43	—	—
Grandfathers	1,709	0.29	0.19	0.67
Great-grandfathers	487	0.25	0.08	0.87

mate $\hat{\beta}_2$, the correlation across two generations, we find that it is not $\hat{\beta}^2 = \theta^2 b^2$, as would be expected from simple models of social mobility, but instead θb^2. For family members n generations apart, the expected correlation is

$$\theta b^n.$$

The downward bias in the estimate of the intergenerational correlation of status caused by the error component in any measure of status is the same across all generations.

The information discussed in chapter 5 on the wealth of a large sample of people in England with rare surnames allows us to test the predictive power of the simple model of intergenerational links. Table 6.3 shows the results. Although the correlation between the wealth of parents and children averages 0.43, that between great-grandparents and their great-grandchildren is still 0.26. The intergenerational connections fade away much more slowly than would be expected. The rate of decline is consistent, with an underlying persistence rate of 0.67–0.87, just what the surname evidence implies in this case.[12]

When multigenerational studies predict grandchild outcomes from grandparent outcomes, controlling for the characteristics of parents, they typically find that grandparents' status is still predictive of child outcomes. However, the simple model of persistent underlying social status implies exactly these effects and their magnitude.[13] Using the wealth data from England for the period 1858–2012, we can check whether the magnitudes of the effects match the pre-

[12] The other studies of intergenerational correlations between grandparents and grandchildren all find a stronger than expected correlation, consistent with an underlying intergenerational correlation in the range 0.5–0.7.

[13] This prediction is detailed in appendix 2.

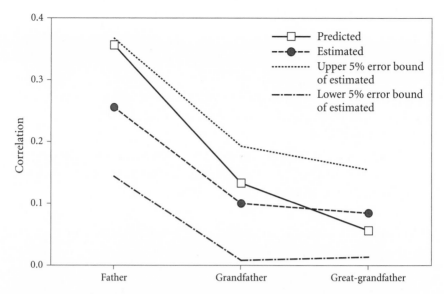

FIGURE 6.7. Predicted versus estimated intergenerational correlations for wealth for four generations, England, with error bounds, 1858–2012.

dictions. Figure 6.7 shows the actual correlations across four generations, controlling for the influence of other ancestors as well as the ones whose influence is predicted if the underlying persistence is 0.72. Because of the small numbers of observations—only 454 cases in which we can observe the wealth at death of all four generations—the correlations here are estimated with some potential error, shown by the dotted lines, for the 95 percent confidence intervals. But in each case the predicted correlation falls within the observed error bounds of the estimate. The pattern of wealth correlations across generations is consistent with the simple model outlined above.

Controlling for fathers and grandfathers, there still appears to be a significant correlation in wealth between great-grandfathers and great-grandchildren. In this simple model of underlying social competence, however, grandfathers and great-grandfathers have no independent influence. They merely supply more information on the true underlying social status of the fathers.

In the model above, all the information useful to predict the outcomes for children is conveyed by the status of their parents. If we know the true underlying status of the parents, then the status of their ancestors is unimportant and uninformative. Children have the same prospects whether they come from a distinguished lineage of elites or a background of poverty and neglect.

Knowing whether a person's prospects in life indeed depend solely on the status of their parents is of crucial importance in understanding the nature of social mobility. Can we test this implication of the simple model? The problem with existing data on families across multiple generations is that we do not know the true underlying status of the parents. Thus earlier ancestors, who supply more information on this, always show up as significant predictors of the status of the next generation.

However, it is possible to set up such a test using the data for attendance at Oxford and Cambridge. The crucial question is, when we have two groups of known status in a given generation, does the one with the more distinguished lineage maintain higher status in subsequent generations? If the status of grandfathers and great-grandfathers directly affects outcomes, as pictured in figure 6.6, then the children with the more distinguished grandparents and great-grandparents will do better, relative to their parents, than the others.

As before, we look at people with rare surnames, those with fewer than five hundred holders in 1881, who attended Oxford and Cambridge between 1800 and 1829. But here we divide these surnames into two groups. The first group includes people with surnames also found among those attending the universities in the previous generation, 1770–99. This is the group with the more distinguished lineage. The second group includes people with surnames that are not found among the previous generation of students at Oxford or Cambridge between 1770 and 1799. They have a less distinguished lineage. For the period 1740–69, the surnames of the elite lineage are more than four times as overrepresented at Oxford and Cambridge than are the surnames of the inferior lineage.

Figure 6.8 shows the correlation of status for generations after 1830 for these two groups of different backgrounds. The elite lineage regresses to the mean at exactly the same rate as the less distinguished lineage. The implied intergenerational correlation for the elite lineage for the period 1830–2012 is 0.738. The correlation for the inferior lineage is 0.734. The different histories of these two groups of surnames have no effect on their subsequent rates of social mobility. The tendency to regress to the mean is just as strong for the group with the richer and more distinguished set of ancestors. The history of families does not matter in predicting the status of future generations: all that matters is the status of the parent generation. Again the surprisingly simple model of mobility outlined at the beginning of this chapter seems to be all that is needed to explain the world of social mobility.

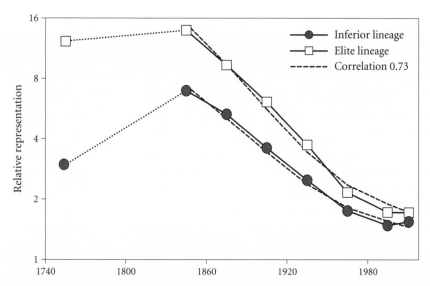

FIGURE 6.8. The effects of lineage on rates of social mobility, Oxford and Cambridge, 1740–2012.

The Mobility of Social Groups

One of the most powerful implications of the simple model of mobility outlined here is that it explains the often-observed slow rates of social mobility for specific social, ethnic, racial, and religious groups without having to posit discrimination, ethnic capital, or ethnic social connections as contributing factors. It has long been noted that social groups seem to experience a much slower rate of social mobility than can be observed for individual families. In the United States, the Jewish and Japanese populations are not regressing downward to the mean at the expected rate. Conversely, black and Latino populations are not tending upward toward the mean as fast as would be predicted by studies of the rates of social mobility achieved by the white population.

Thus in the United States, Tom Hertz shows that just knowing that a family is Jewish predicts a 33 percent higher than average income for children relative to their parents. Knowing just that a family is black or Latino similarly implies that children's incomes will be 30 percent lower than would be expected from the general correlation of incomes across generations.[14] A recent study by the Pew Charitable Trust found that among families with middle-class incomes,

[14] Hertz 2005.

black and Latino children were more likely to fall into the bottom 30 percent of the income distribution than white children. For whites the chance was 25 percent, for blacks 37 percent, and for Hispanics 29 percent.[15]

What is happening here? One interpretation is that there are still racial barriers in the modern United States that constrain opportunities for blacks and Latinos, for example through their concentration in low-income neighborhoods and underperforming schools.[16] But the lack of upward social mobility is observed not just among low-income groups but also among middle-class blacks and Latinos—those who attend racially mixed schools and have benefited from affirmative action programs in universities and employment. And the failure of Jewish or Japanese children to regress to the mean as rapidly as expected is not due to any advantage they gain in U.S. society, where both these groups form small minorities of the population.

George Borjas earlier found a similar result from looking at immigrant groups in general in the postwar United States, many of whom, such as the Irish, would not be classed as particularly identifiable minorities.[17] For fathers with a given level of income or education, the greater the average income or education of men from the same immigrant group, the better were the predicted outcomes for their sons.

Borjas attributes this effect to the idea that different groups of immigrants to the United States have different levels of *ethnic capital*. Sons from ethnic groups with high average education levels, for example, do better than would be predicted from the education of the father alone because of spillover effects from the education of others in the community. More highly educated uncles, cousins, and neighbors improve the outcomes for children from these communities through information, help, and example. Such an interpretation could also be applied to the results Hertz finds for Jewish, black, and Latino families. However, there is little or no evidence for these hypothesized community benefits to individuals. The descendants of Japanese immigrants to the United States, as noted, are a group with high average status. Yet this is a small, dispersed community that has integrated strongly into white American society through intermarriage.

With the simple model of a slowly changing underlying social competence of families, we can explain all the above results without having to invoke racial barriers, ethnic capital, or the importance of social connections.

[15] Arcs 2011, 14.
[16] This is the explanation favored by Hertz himself.
[17] Borjas 1995.

Consider, for example, two families with annual incomes of $90,000, one Jewish and the other black. Since median household income in the United States is $52,000, we expect that the children of such families will have incomes lower than their parents' and closer to the median. However, this income level is close to the median for the Jewish community.[18] Thus the random component in this family's household income, the part that deviates from what we would expect from their underlying social capabilities and is not heritable, will be on average zero. So their children will regress only modestly toward the social mean. In contrast, a black family with a median income of $90,000 has nearly three times the median income of the black community, which is only $35,000. Families who have incomes well above the average of their community typically have benefited from a positive random shock to their income that has placed them above their underlying social status. On average, the random component affecting their family income is substantial and positive. Their true underlying social status is typically lower than their income indicates, and it is this underlying social status that predicts the income of the children in the next generation. So the black children will show, on average, a greater drop in income relative to the parents than the Jewish children.

With this model, there is no need to invoke racial discrimination, social networks, or ethnic capital to explain such effects. However, this model does leave open the question of why the underlying social competence of the Jewish and Asian communities is higher than that of the black and Latino populations.

In Summary: The Power of a Single Equation

Surname evidence shows that all social mobility can essentially be reduced to one simple law,

$$x_{t+1} = bx_t + e_t,$$

where x is the underlying social competence of families. The persistence rate, b, is always high relative to conventional estimates, generally 0.7–0.8. It seems to be little affected by social institutions.

There thus seems to be a simple law of social mobility, which we explore and test in the subsequent chapters.

[18] US Census Bureau 2010; Pew Forum on Religion and Public Life 2008, appendix 1, 78.

SEVEN

Nature versus Nurture

THE PRECEDING CHAPTERS EXPLAIN why social mobility is lower than traditionally measured. But why are mobility rates seemingly constant across very different social regimes? Here I conjecture that this is because status inheritance is indistinguishable in form from the inheritance of genetically controlled attributes. This is not to say that social status is determined genetically. But whatever drives it is, on the tests performed here, indistinguishable from genetic inheritance. Status may or may not be genetically inherited, but for all practical purposes, nature dominates nurture.

Discussion about the mechanisms that drive the inheritance of social status has been limited. The standard approach in economics assumes that social status is transmitted through three channels: genetic transmission of underlying abilities from parents; transmission of cultural traits within families; and transmission of abilities through parental investment of time and resources in child rearing (in economic parlance, investment in "human capital").

Economists assume that because higher-ability parents have higher incomes, they can create more human capital in their children through education, ensuring a greater persistence of status than stems from the biological and cultural connections alone. Nature and nurture both matter. The paths of transmission envisioned by economists are shown in figure 7.1.[1] There is an independent causal effect of family income in the parent generation on income in the next. This model of inheritance implies that the observed correlations across generations for earnings, wealth, and education are greater than predicted by

[1] This approach was first formalized in Becker and Tomes 1979, 1986. Goldberger (1989) argued that the Becker-Tomes economic model did not imply anything distinct from the simple regression to the mean in all human characteristics posited by Galton (1889). Mulligan (1999) tried to find features of inheritance that would disprove the Galton hypothesis, but with little success.

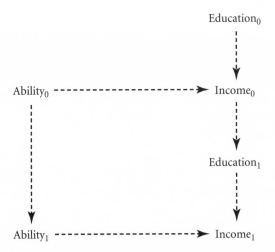

FIGURE 7.1. Economists' conception of intergenerational earnings links, where 0 indicates the parent generation.

the correlation of underlying abilities. This is because education and nurture investments are correlated with underlying abilities.[2]

The economists' conception seems intuitive and is shared by many people. Differences in innate talent are magnified by differences in individual families' income and resources.

This picture of mobility mechanisms also implies that the intergenerational correlation of outcomes in the free-market economy is higher than is socially desirable. Children with the same innate abilities do not get equal chances in life. Those from higher-income families do better. Children of parents of modestly lower innate abilities become adults with substantially poorer outcomes because they receive fewer resources from their parents. Assuming that education and nurture investments by higher-income families are productive, the state should intervene to subsidize such investments in poorer families and promote equality of opportunity.

[2] Gary Solon recently formulated a simple model of the contribution of each of these paths of inheritance that concludes that the intergenerational correlation of earnings, assuming a constant variance of earnings, will be $b_y = \dfrac{(\gamma + \tau)}{(1 + \gamma\tau)}$, where τ is the parent-child correlation of abilities independent of investments in children, and γ is the elasticity of earnings with respect to human capital investment. If such investments have no effect on income, then $\gamma = 0$, parents do not invest, and $b_y = \tau$, from the biological and cultural correlation. But if $\gamma > 0$, $b_y > \tau$ so that investment increases child income (Solon 2013).

The further implication of this proposed mechanism is that windfall gains to a family will raise the next generation's social status. Conversely, unexpected losses will depress it. Also, the more extensive the government's provision of educational investments, the higher social mobility rates will be.

However, suppose that even half of the variation in this generation's income is caused directly by the variations in income in the parent generation and the effects of those family-income variations on investments in training and education. That is, assume that parent income matters as much as children's abilities in determining outcomes. Those conditions preclude the pattern of correlations of measures of status across multiple generations that researchers are now finding. The correlations in measures like income should decline quickly over multiple generations.[3] To get slow long-run mobility at the same time as fast short-run mobility, the great majority of outcomes must be attributed to underlying abilities. Income can play only a very modest direct role in producing outcomes if the process is to describe the low long-run mobility we observe.

If family characteristics are to account for observed dynastic connections in status across as many as ten generations, they must be much more persistent between generations. The persistent element cannot be earnings, income, or wealth, because these have been demonstrated to be fluid across generations within individual families. This is not to imply that resource investments in children have no effect on the outcomes of the next generation, but that effect must be modest.

There are multiple ways to test the claim that resource transfers between parents and children are only modest determinants of status inheritance. The first is to examine the variation across societies in the effect of parental investments on children's outcomes. Where the state provides extensive educational support for all children, parental investments will matter less, and the rate of social mobility should be higher.

Another implication of this theory is that, other things being equal, elite families with larger numbers of children should see faster regression to the mean. With a finite stock of family resources, the greater the number of children parents must provide for, the less each child gets. By the same reasoning, lower-status families with fewer children should regress upward to the mean more rapidly.

---

[3] Using the Solon 2013 model, for example, if correlation of incomes over one generation is 0.47, over two generations it will be 0.16, and over three 0.06. Table 6.3 shows that the correlation of wealth in England is in fact 0.43 across one generation and 0.26 over three generations.

This chapter considers two tests of the idea that parental resources explain a small minority of the inheritance of status. Other tests are discussed in chapter 15. These include the relative roles of biology and rearing in determining outcomes for adopted children, and the effects of windfall gains—chance additions to wealth—on outcomes for future generations.

Public Support for Education

The amount of human capital that parents can develop in their children should vary across societies. In some societies, richer parents can do much more to improve their children's relative education, income, and social status than in other societies. Where the return to such investments is high, rich parents invest more resources in children, and the persistence of status is greater. Where the social landscape reduces the benefits from such familial investments, this connection between parents and children should be weaker, with status transmitted only through biological and cultural channels. Thus in the preindustrial world, largely without public education, we would expect the gains from parental investment to be large and persistence correspondingly great.

In modern societies such as Sweden and the United Kingdom, a lot of human-capital investment is publicly financed. Elementary, secondary, and even university education is provided free of charge. Often even the living costs of university students are covered.

Sweden, in particular, offers extensive state support for education. From age 6 through tertiary education, tuition is free, and for younger children, schooling includes free meals. All students in postsecondary education are eligible to receive student aid, in the form of grants and loans, to finance up to five years of study. The statement of the Swedish National Agency for Higher Education is that "the Swedish system of student finance is designed so that higher education is accessible to all those who can benefit from it regardless of socioeconomic background. . . . As tuition at higher education institutions in Sweden is free-of-charge . . . student finance is intended to cover living expenses and the cost of study material. Everyone below the age of fifty-four has the right to apply for student finance for a maximum of 240 weeks." Student finance consists of grants and loans.

Those age 16–20 attending higher secondary schools are eligible for student aid for living expenses. For the youngest children, municipal governments are responsible for providing preschool places at a modest price, with meals always included. In 2009 the tuition cost for preschool in Sweden was a maximum of $200 per month, a modest amount for most parents.

In a society like this, what contribution can parental spending make to the human capital of children? Some parents choose private schooling for their children at institutions that yield strong academic results, such as the Internationella Engelska Skolan (IES). But the overwhelming majority of these private schools emerged after 1992, when the government began paying an equivalent to the state-school tuition cost to private schools. In return, these schools have to admit students tuition-free and on a first-come, first-served basis. They are thus popularly referred to as "free schools" and now enroll one in ten students.

So what can a highly resourced Swedish family do to increase the human capital of their offspring that a poorer family cannot? Some families might hire private tutors to supplement public-school instruction, but if children are attending well-organized schools, the gain from each kroner spent in this way will be minimal. That is why, if human-capital investments by parents are an important contributor to status persistence, Sweden should be the society with the lowest persistence, or the highest social mobility rates.

England has less extensive public support for education than Sweden and thus a potentially higher return to private investments to increase children's human capital. Education is tuition-free in state schools from age 3 to age 18. From 1962 to 1998, tertiary education was also free, and maintenance grants were available to lower-income students to offset living costs.[4] Since 1998, students have paid tuition fees for higher education (recently raised by many universities to £9,000, or about $14,000 annually), but they can borrow to finance these fees. Students can also get grants and loans to cover their living costs.

Private schooling paid for by parents is much more extensive in England than in Sweden: 7 percent of all elementary and secondary students attend such schools, with the figure rising to 18 percent for students age sixteen and above. Fees for such schools range from $4,000 to $48,000 annually, the highest fees being for boarding schools.

Such private schools on average have much better academic results than state-supported schools. Their graduates are three times as likely as state-school graduates to be admitted to Oxford or Cambridge. So it is more advantageous

---

[4] My parents, for example, paid nothing for my thirteen years of elementary and secondary education in state schools. Nor did they pay fees or maintenance for the four years I spent at Cambridge University, in those days a deluxe education that included a servant to make your bed and clean your room.

for parents to transform their resources into enhanced human capital for their children in England than in Sweden.[5] But even many of the private schools provide extensive scholarship aid for poorer students who pass their qualifying exams, so the gains from such investment are again modest.

Certainly contemporary England should, on the basis of returns to human capital investment, display much less status persistence than England before 1870. Schooling in the earlier period was entirely a private matter, with parents paying for schooling or relying on charity schools.

In comparison to Sweden and England, the United States has many more children attending privately financed primary, secondary, and tertiary institutions. From kindergarten through twelfth grade, 15 percent of children are privately educated at fee-charging schools. In areas like the Northeast, these schools can be very expensive, charging as much as $45,000 annually for day students.[6] Thus it is easily possible to spend as much as $600,000 on a child's elementary and secondary education.

At the tertiary level, the United States again has a much larger private sector, with 27 percent of students attending private institutions. Most state institutions also charge tuition fees. Net of discounts and grants, nineteen million tertiary students paid $53 billion in tuition in 2009.[7] In addition, they had to cover their living costs while attending college. The ability to attend a selective college depends much more on the financial resources of parents in the United States than in Sweden or the United Kingdom. Consequently, the United States is the society where parental resources should be able to do the most work and should thus be the society with the greatest persistence of status.

The evidence of similarly slow rates of social mobility in modern Sweden, preindustrial Sweden, medieval England, modern England, and the United States is thus at variance with the human-capital account of intergenerational mobility. Instead it seems that social status is transmitted within families independently of the resources available to parents. This raises the possibility that it

---

[5] Recent evidence suggests that attending private school improves the A-level results for a student of a given ability over those of an equivalent student at a state school. This conclusion is derived, however, from the fact that students from state schools perform better than those from private schools with the same A-level scores once admitted to university. Thus private students gain some advantage in admissions, but it is eroded in terms of degree results.

[6] In 2013–14 the most expensive school in the United States was the Lawrenceville School in New Jersey, with fees of $44,885 for day students ("The 50 Most Expensive Private High Schools" 2013).

[7] Geiger and Heller 2011, 3, 9.

is nature, much more than nurture, that propagates social status so persistently across the generations. Bryan Caplan is potentially correct when he concludes, "While healthy, smart, happy, successful, virtuous parents tend to have matching offspring, the reason is largely nature, not nurture."[8]

Demography and Social Mobility

One clear prediction of the human-capital theory is that, other things being equal, the more children parents have, the poorer the children's outcomes. The more children there are, the fewer family resources can be devoted to bolstering the human capital of each. Over time, however, there have been remarkable differences in the correlation of fertility and social status. Sometimes it has been strongly positive, at other times strongly negative.

Currently, in high-income societies such as the United Kingdom, Sweden, and the United States, the correlation is relatively weak, with high-status parents having as many children as lower-status parents, or modestly fewer. But in other historical periods there was a strong negative association between social status and fertility, as in England for parents who married between 1890 and 1960. High-status families had much lower fertility than those of low status. In contrast, in the preindustrial world, fertility was typically strongly positively associated with status. In England before 1780, this effect was so strong that the wealthiest parents had twice as many children as the average family. Between these two periods, for parents who married between 1780 and 1880, there is no association between fertility and social status.[9]

Figure 7.2 illustrates the number of surviving children for men who first married between 1500 and 1780 and those who married between 1780 and 1879, classified by their wealth at death. Marriages of high-status people before 1780 in England led to six births on average, with four children surviving to adulthood. At death, the richest men in the earlier period left more than four children; the poorest of the testators (in the middle of the overall status distribution since only richer men were probated) left only half as many. But for men marrying in the later period, there is no correlation of fertility with wealth.

The lineage of Charles Darwin is a nice illustration of how large the families of the middle and upper classes could be in preindustrial England. He descended

---

[8] Caplan 2011, 34.
[9] Cummins and Clark 2013.

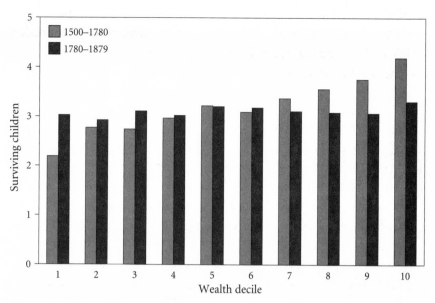

FIGURE 7.2. Surviving children per father by wealth at death.

from a line of successful and prosperous forebears. His great-grandfather Robert Darwin (1682–1754) produced seven children, all of whom survived to adulthood. His grandfather Erasmus (1731–1802) produced fifteen children (born to two wives and two mistresses), twelve of whom survived to adulthood. His father, Robert Waring (1766–1848), produced six children, all of whom survived to adulthood.[10]

In a social environment where all these children had to be privately educated, dowries needed to be provided for daughters, and estates were divided among children at death, human-capital theory would predict that the heedless fecundity of the English social elites of these years would lead to rapid downward social mobility. The lower classes of preindustrial society, producing only modestly more than two surviving children per family on average, would be able to concentrate resources on the care and education of their offspring and see them rise rapidly on the social ladder.

In contrast, by 1880 in England, upper-class men seem to have produced far fewer children than those of the middle or lower classes. Indeed, from 1880 to 1940, the richest English families seem to have been dying out. Based on the

[10] Jenkins (2013) supplies the genealogical information on the Darwin family.

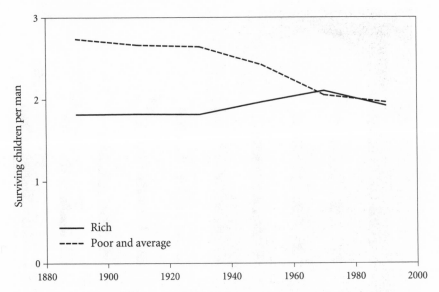

FIGURE 7.3. Surviving children per adult male by twenty-year period, rich and poor.

rare-surname samples of chapter 5, the upper-class males produced, on average, fewer than two children who survived to adulthood. At the middle and bottom of society, however, men were producing an average of 2.5–3 children who survived to adulthood, in reversal of the pattern observed before 1780. Figure 7.3 shows, by twenty-year periods, the estimated total number of children surviving to adulthood per adult male for two wealth cohorts: initial rich and initial poor or average-wealth rare surnames. Fertility for the richer lineage is consistently less than that of the poorer in the years 1800–1959.

This major change in the relationship between fertility and status can be illustrated again by the Darwin family. Charles Darwin (figure 7.4), marrying in 1839, had ten children, though only seven survived childhood. These seven children produced only nine grandchildren, an average of only 1.3 per child. (This figure is unusually low for this era, but there was great randomness in individual fertility.) The nine grandchildren produced in turn only twenty great-grandchildren, 2.2 per grandchild. This figure was less than the population average for this period. The great-grandchildren, born on average in 1918, produced 28 great-great-grandchildren, 1.4 each.[11] Thus by the time of the last generation, born around 1918, average family size for this still rather elite group had

[11] Jenkins 2013.

fallen to substantially less than replacement fertility. The Darwin lineage failed to maintain itself in genetic terms.

Interestingly, with respect to social mobility rates, the twenty-seven adult great-great grandchildren of Charles Darwin, born on average nearly 150 years after Darwin, are still a surprisingly distinguished cohort. Eleven are notable enough to have Wikipedia pages, or the like, such as *Times* obituaries, devoted to them. They include six university professors, four authors, a painter, three medical doctors, a well-known conservationist, and a film director (now also an organic farmer).[12]

But we see no signs that social mobility rates in England slowed as the upper-class groups produced fewer children. Instead, as chapter 5 shows, the intergenerational correlation of status remained constant for education and wealth. By implication, human-capital effects on social mobility must be modest. Status is strongly inherited within families mainly through genetic or cultural transmission, or both.

[12] It is also interesting that Darwin's fourth-generation descendants included Adrian Maynard Keynes and William Huxley Darwin, showing the intermarriages between the lineages of John Maynard Keynes, Aldous Huxley, and the Darwins. This illustrates the intermarriage of the English intellectual elite in these years.

Biology versus Culture

If nature dominates nurture in the transmission of status, to what extent is the transmission genetic as opposed to cultural? The evidence presented here cannot answer this question. The best we can do is suggest some tests that would rule out genetic transmission as a significant cause of the high intergenerational correlation of status. There is an extensive list of these tests, which are discussed here and in subsequent chapters.

First, we can ask whether social mobility mimics processes that we know to be largely genetically driven, such as the intergenerational transmission of height in affluent societies. That is, does social status show a constant rate of regression to the mean regardless of a family's position in the status distribution? Or is social mobility higher at one or the other end of the status distribution?

To illustrate the nature of biological transmission of traits such as height, which are the product of many different genes acting in combination, we can consider the data from Francis Galton's famous study of the connection between the heights of parents and children. Presented to the Royal Society in 1885, this study introduced the concept of regression to the mean. Figure 7.5 shows Galton's 928 observations, grouped into seven clusters of average parent heights (at one-inch intervals for the five central groups).[13] Also shown is the best linear fit of the 928 observations, where the implied persistence rate is 0.64. All across the parent height distribution, the observations lie close to the fitted straight line. One persistence rate predicts intergenerational height mobility for those close to the mean as well as for the extremes of short and tall.

In comparison, consider the transmission of wealth across generations. Simon Boserup, Wojceich Kopczuk, and Claus Kreiner have assembled a wonderful data set from Danish tax records that allows them to compare the wealth of 1,155,564 children with that of their parents.[14] The Danish state apparently keeps its Big Brother eye on the economic fortunes of its citizens. The only limitation of this data is that because the wealth of parents comes from the years 1997–99 and that of the children from 2009–11, the children's wealth is observed much earlier in the life cycle than that of parents. But the authors control for the age profile of wealth in making the comparison.

---

[13] Hanley 2004.
[14] Boserup, Kopczuk, and Kreiner 2013.

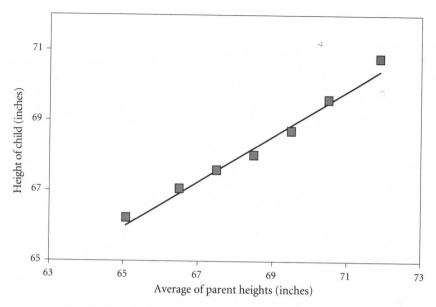

FIGURE 7.5. Francis Galton's observations of biological inheritance of height.

The huge size of the Danish wealth data set means that the authors can divide the parents into percentiles and look at the average wealth of children for one hundred sets of parents, measured again as a percentile of the child wealth distribution. Other than the top and bottom 3 or 4 percent of parental wealth, the picture has the same linear character as that for height inheritance. One persistence rate, 0.20, describes inheritance across the middle 90 percent of the distribution (figure 7.6).

The greatest deviation appears in the bottom 4 percent of parental wealth, where the children are much richer than we would expect. But the parents at the bottom of the distribution in Denmark have negative wealth—that is, debt. This suggests not chronic, grinding poverty (no one, after all, lends much to the truly poor), but more likely indebtedness to finance a business venture or training. The fact that this is not truly the bottom of the wealth distribution explains the breakdown of the stable relationship.

Children in the top 3 percent of the parental-wealth distribution also show slightly greater wealth inheritance. Although this effect is statistically significant, it represents only modest deviations from the single persistence rate in real terms: the persistence rate implied for the top percentile is 0.24, as opposed to 0.20 for the rest of the distribution. For the second percentile, it is 0.23, and for the third 0.22.

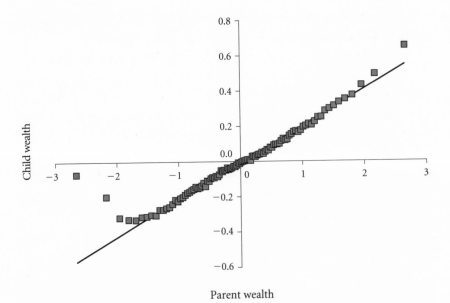

FIGURE 7.6. Social inheritance of wealth, Denmark, 1997–2012.

This result, showing the same intergenerational correlation all across the status distribution, is found also in England. For the period 1858–2012, we can measure social mobility by looking at the representation of surnames among Oxford and Cambridge students, which typically describes the upper 1 percent of the educational distribution. We can also measure social mobility by looking at probate rates: the probated elite was typically 15–45 percent of the population, much closer to median status. The estimated mobility rates are the same from these two sources.

There is at least one exception to this rule of uniform persistence rates across the status distribution. A study by Anders Björklund and others found that in Sweden, although the overall correlation of income across one generation was 0.26, for the top 0.1 percent of the income distribution, it was much higher, at 0.9.[15] However, their study found that this effect was caused largely by the exceptionally high levels of wealth among the sons of the very high-income fathers. There was no unusually strong transmission among the top 0.1 percent of educational attainment, high cognitive abilities, or high noncognitive abilities. Thus while there may be exceptions to the rule of a constant persistence

[15] Björklund, Roine, and Waldenström 2012.

rate across the status distribution, it may only be found for the very wealthy, and only for wealth transmission (not for other status indicators).

One argument for a potentially important role for genetic transmission in the inheritance of underlying social status is the tendency of status indicators to regress to the mean. Genetic processes, unlike other inheritance processes, have built into them an inherent tendency for characteristics to so regress. Why would the transmission of cultural traits also show such a consistent tendency to regress toward the mean? Even if family culture were transmitted with some error between generations, as long as positive errors were as likely as negative errors, the result would be increased dispersion of outcomes for an elite group, not consistent regression to the social mean.[16]

If there were an important genetic influence on intergenerational correlations, furthermore, groups that marry endogamously (within the group) would not regress to the mean in social status. Suppose, for example, we were to take everyone over six feet tall in the United States and decree that from then on they could only mate with other people in this group and their descendants. The first generation of descendants would regress toward mean height, because the six-foot-and-above club includes many people whose genotypic height is below their phenotypic height. But after this first generation, there would be no further regression of the height of the descendants toward the mean. For a genetic trait like this, endogamy would ensure persistence. If genetics is important in transmitting social status, the degree of endogamy is an important controller of the rate of social mobility.

For even if marriage is perfectly assortative, those in an elite group who choose marriage partners from the general population experience more downward mobility than those who marry within the elite. This is because the partners from the general population, even if they have observed characteristics identical to those of alternative partners from within the elite, have a greater random component to their status on average, since they are drawn from a population with a lower mean underlying status.

If, to the contrary, we think that the advantage of elite families is a cultural trait, then endogamous marriage would not lead to any more faithful a transmission of that trait than exogamous marriage to someone with the same observed characteristics as the elite group. We show below that endogamy is

---

[16] The one way that such an error could produce reversion to the mean is if there were an upper bound on family competence, so that errors at the extreme effectively had to lead toward the mean.

associated with a complete absence or a slowing of the process of regression to the mean for elite groups.

In different social systems where marriage is exogamous, are rates of social mobility the same? Again, if genetic transmission of innate abilities is the key driver of status, then we would expect it to be constant.

Is social mobility Markov in character?[17] That is, is all the information useful for predicting the status of the next generation contained in the parent generation, or does the more extended lineage matter in determining outcomes for children? If genetics is the most important element, the process has to be Markov.

Chapter 6 presents important evidence from the Oxford and Cambridge cohorts showing that the history of an elite group does not seem to affect its subsequent social mobility. It also shows that the extended lineage can appear to matter even within a framework where the true process is Markov. Such a process, as specified by the law of mobility proposed here, further implies that mobility rates for any group must be constant over time. If the longer history is not significant, every period will look the same as any other. Thus persistence rates must be constant across generations. All of these characteristics are observed in the mobility data over longer periods for Sweden and England.

Finally, if genetics is an important vehicle of social and economic success, then elite and underclass groups should always be formed as a selection from the upper or lower tails of a larger population. No entire population will become elite or underclass through ideological or cultural transformation. If genes are important carriers of social competence, elite groups will be formed only as a selection from a larger population.

Under these conditions, individual families will become elite as a result of a series of random accidents. Below we test whether that prediction is borne out by the trajectories of several generations of such families. But if the world is characterized by persistent regression to the mean, balanced only by random shocks to maintain status dispersion, how do large social groups end up systematically above or below the mean in the first place? If the differences between groups are genetic as opposed to cultural, one process that could produce such differences would be selective affiliation to a social group by people at the top or the bottom of the status distribution. Again we examine below whether there is any historical evidence of such processes at work.

[17] Technically it is first-order Markov.

PART TWO

TESTING THE LAWS
OF MOBILITY

EIGHT

India

Caste, Endogamy, and Mobility

INDIA IS AN INTERESTING SOCIETY in which to test two aspects of the theory of social mobility outlined in chapters 6 and 7: that social institutions can do little to change the rate of social mobility and that a key controller of mobility rates is the degree of marital endogamy among elite and underclass groups. This chapter calculates social mobility rates for colonial and modern India for Hindu groups of different original status and for Muslims. These social mobility rates are low—much lower than the rates calculated for India by conventional methods. By some measures, social mobility is nonexistent.

As the simple theory of mobility predicts, religious and caste endogamy are associated with low rates of social mobility. Thus as long as religion and caste continue to play a strong role in marital sorting in India, social mobility rates will remain unusually low.

One factor that might be predicted to increase social mobility in India is a form of affirmative action known as the reservation system, whereby up to half of public-sector jobs and places in educational institutions are reserved for disadvantaged social groups. This chapter also calculates the effect of the reservation system on social mobility rates since 1947. It concludes that its dramatic interventions have had modest effects on overall social mobility rates. This is because although it has modestly increased downward mobility among Hindu and Christian elites, its main effect has been to create a new elite composed of groups that were never significantly disadvantaged. In practice, the system has largely hurt the prospects of the truly disadvantaged.

Background

India entered the modern era at Independence in 1947 with the legacy of the Hindu caste system, which was echoed in the Muslim community also. Intermarriage and even social intercourse between different castes were limited. This system of exclusion was so powerful that different castes and subcastes, even within small geographic areas, can now have distinct genetic profiles.[1]

The Hindu community was traditionally divided into four castes. In descending order of status, these were Brahmins, priests; Kshatriya, rulers, administrators, and soldiers; Vaishya, farmers, bankers, and traders; and Shudra, laborers and servants. Each caste had hierarchically ranked subcastes. Under British rule, the lowest social groups were referred to as the depressed classes. These groups included the untouchables, who were believed to confer defilement on higher-caste groups through mere contact, as well as indigenous tribal communities not incorporated into Hindu or Muslim society.

After Independence, for purposes of social action, these various castes and other social groups were classified under Indian law as "forward castes," "scheduled castes" (the former untouchables), "scheduled tribes," and "other backward castes." The classification was based on the British census of 1931. While that classification broadly correlated with social status, as figure 8.1 shows, many groups that were not particularly disadvantaged ended up classified as scheduled castes or other backward castes.[2] Membership in the legally defined scheduled caste group now derives strictly from inheritance and is independent of social status. But for the other backward caste group, those of higher social status, described under Indian law as the "creamy layer," are excluded from benefits. Thus those in this group need to obtain a certificate of "non-creamy-layer" status to get the benefits of membership.

Figure 8.1 shows the share of twenty-three-year-olds who graduated from universities in India in 2000 by caste and religion under these classifications.

---

[1] There is contention about this claim, but a paper in *Nature* concludes that "allele frequency differences between groups in India are larger than in Europe, reflecting strong founder effects whose signatures have been maintained for thousands of years owing to endogamy" (Reich et al. 2009). Chapter 13, by contrast, shows that subcastes in England and Ireland, such as the Traveller population, are not genetically distinct from the general population.

[2] The list of scheduled castes was initially promulgated by the colonial government in 1936. The British classification was largely adopted by the government of India in 1953 in establishing the current system of reservations (Jadhav 2008).

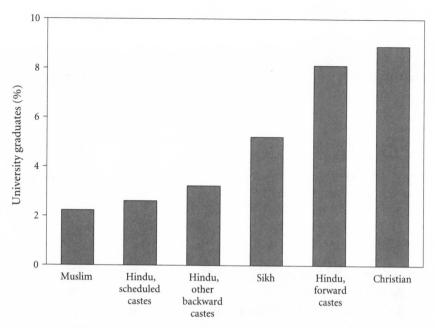

FIGURE 8.1. University graduation rates by social group, India, 2000.

Caste affiliations determined centuries ago still strongly predict current educational outcomes.

One factor that might be expected to promote mobility, however, is the reservation system. Since Independence, the number of places reserved and the number of groups eligible for reserved places has increased. Up to half of available educational places and government jobs are now reserved.[3] If the caste system trapped many potentially talented people at lower levels of society in the premodern era, then modern reservation policy could be expected to rapidly increase social mobility. Thus, while figure 8.1 implies continuing dramatic social inequalities, it is not clear whether we should expect high or low rates of social mobility today, given Indian social policy.

Table 8.1 shows numbers of candidates in various admissions categories admitted to the All India Institute of Medical Sciences for the Bachelor of Med-

[3] The Indian Supreme Court has ruled that no more than half of available positions can be reserved for disadvantaged groups, but some states have higher quotas. Tamil Nadu, for example, has reservations for 69 percent of positions. The legality of these quotas is still being litigated.

TABLE 8.1. Admissions to the All India Institute of Medical Sciences, Delhi, by reservation-system category, 2012

Category	Number	Numerical rank on admission test
Unreserved	36	1–36
Scheduled caste	11	288–1,164
Scheduled tribe	5	177–2,007
Orthopedic physically handicapped	1	1,201
Other backward classes (non-creamy layer)	19	41–116
All	72	1–2,007

icine degree in 2012, as well as their rank on the entrance exam. Of the seventy-two candidates admitted, only half were admitted solely on the basis of their admissions exam score. The lowest ranking for any student in the open category on this exam was 36, compared to 2,007 for the reserved category.

There are surprisingly few formal studies of social mobility in India.[4] Thus the two recent international surveys of social mobility discussed in the introduction, one for earnings and the other for education, do not include India.[5] However, a recent study estimated the Indian intergeneration income correlation to be 0.58, making social mobility rates in India among the world's lowest.[6]

The estimated persistence rate for income in India of 0.58, however, is not much higher than those for the United Kingdom (0.5) or the United States (0.47). The share of income variance in the next generation attributable to inheritance from parents in India is still only $(0.58)^2$, or 0.34. This suggests that even in India, an individual's position in the income ranks is not primarily derived from inheritance. Thus, by conventional estimates, modern India has become a society of rapid social mobility, where three to four generations might see the elimination of all traces of millennia-old patterns of inequality.

---

[4] The large agricultural population makes it difficult to classify occupational status. Mobility studies based on occupation are thus difficult to interpret and to compare with those from more developed economies. See, for example, Nijhawan 1969; Kumar, Heath, and Heath 2004; Hnatkovska, Lahiri, and Paul 2013.

[5] Corak 2013; Hertz et al. 2007.

[6] Hnatkovska, Lahiri, and Paul 2013. The researchers actually estimate the income elasticity, which equals the correlation only if the variance of log incomes is constant.

Social Mobility in Bengal, 1860–2011

This chapter examines social mobility in Bengal from 1860 to the present. At the partition of India in 1947, this region was divided into the Pakistani province of East Bengal (now the nation of Bangladesh) and the Indian state of West Bengal. With a population of ninety-one million today, West Bengal is one of the larger Indian states. Its income per capita is only about three-quarters that of India as a whole, so it is also one of the poorer areas of the country. It was chosen because of the availability of the electoral register for Kolkata (Calcutta), the largest city in West Bengal, which allows estimates of the relative population shares of each surname. But it has a mix of castes and religions that it is representative of India in general, so it can be expected to be representative of other conditions as well.

For the upper classes in Bengal, family surnames date from the arrival of the British in the eighteenth century or earlier. Petitioners to the East India Company courts in Bengal in the late eighteenth century typically have surnames, and these names are still common in Bengal: *Banarji, Basu, Chattarji, Datta, Ghosh, Haldar, Khan, Mandal, Mitra, Sen*.[7]

If there had been substantial social mobility in Bengal, even with a persistence rate as high as 0.6, then over the last two hundred years (seven generations), even the high-status surnames of the eighteenth century should have regressed to an average representation in the top and the bottom strata of society. However, common surnames vary enormously in their relative representation among elites in modern Bengal. Figure 8.2 shows the relative representation of six groups of surnames among physicians and judges in West Bengal. These surname groups are presented below. Since they differ significantly in their social status, we can use them, as in other cases, to estimate social mobility rates.

Among Bengali Brahmins, the highest subcaste is the Kulin, who supposedly migrated to Bengal from north India in the tenth or eleventh century CE. Seven surnames are associated with this group: *Bandopadhyaya/Banerjee, Bhattacharya/Bhattacharjee, Chakraborty/Chakravarty, Chattopadhyaya/Chatterjee, Gangopadhyaya/Ganguly, Goswami/Gosain*, and *Mukhopadhyaya/Mukherjee*.[8] These surnames form the Kulin Brahmin group shown in figure 8.2.

[7] Government of Bengal, Political Department 1930.

[8] The association of these surnames with the Kulin Brahmin subcaste can be confirmed by examining the surnames of those listing themselves as Kulin Brahmin on matrimonial websites. All these surnames are also found, however, among other subcastes of Brahmins.

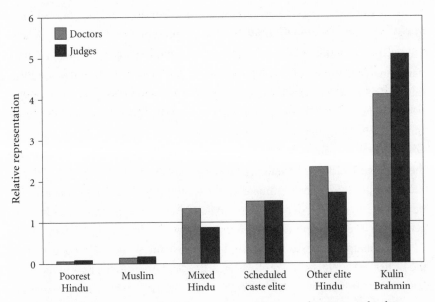

FIGURE 8.2. Relative representation of surname groups among physicians and judges.

The surnames of Kulin Brahmins are the most overrepresented of all surname types among modern Bengali elites. They are more than four times as frequent among physicians registered in recent decades as in the general population. These names are likely to be familiar to anyone who has met Indian physicians, professors, or engineers in the United States.

Other surnames associated with the high-status Brahmin and Kayastha castes in Bengal are also overrepresented, though not to the same degree as Kulin Brahmin surnames. These include the surnames *Basu/Bose, Datta/Dutta, Ghosh, Kundu, Mitra,* and *Sen* or *Sengupta,* which were all high status in the nineteenth century. These surnames form the "other elite Hindu" group in figure 8.2. *Basu, Ghosh,* and *Mitra,* for example, are associated with the Kulin Kayastha (scribe) subcastes, which were regarded as next in status after Brahmins in premodern Bengal. As with Brahmins, *Kulin* denotes a superior subcaste.

In contrast, the surnames of the Muslim population are dramatically underrepresented among both physicians and judges. Muslims formed a large proportion of the population in Bengal before Independence and continue to do so in the contemporary state of West Bengal. Because Muslim and Hindu first names are also distinctive, the fraction of Muslim physicians in Bengal in the years 1860–2011 is easily estimated.

Also still very underrepresented are some Hindu surnames that are included here because they had little or no representation among physicians before Independence. The main one is *Shaw/Show*, held by 3.7 percent of men on the Kolkata voting rolls. Others are *Rauth/Routh, Paswan, Dhanuk, Balmiki,* and *Mahata/Mahato*. Together these surnames are held by 7 percent of the population of West Bengal. These constitute the "poor Hindu" surname group in figure 8.2.

Two additional surname groups of intermediate social status are tracked. The first is surnames associated with scheduled castes (those eligible for reserved positions), identified from lists of those admitted to universities in West Bengal and successful candidates for police jobs in Kolkata. These names are *Barman/Burman, Biswas, Haldar/Halder, Mandal/Mondal,* and *Naskar*. They account for 3.8 percent of the population age 20–29 in Kolkata. Because they are overrepresented among physicians and attorneys in Bengal, they are labeled in figure 8.2 as "scheduled caste elites."

The second intermediate group is "mixed Hindu" surnames. These are mixed in the sense that they are found mainly in the general admission lists for universities and the police but also in significant numbers in the scheduled caste lists. These surnames are *Das/Dasgupta, Majumdar, Ray/Roy, Saha,* and *Sarkar.*

Figure 8.3 summarizes the relative representation of these surnames among five generations of physicians. The information on physicians for the years 1910–2011 comes from the Indian Medical Registry, which includes physicians registered in Bengal from 1915 onward. For the period before 1910, surname frequencies among physicians were estimated from a list of registered physicians in the province of Bengal in 1903 and from lists of physicians registered in Bihar and Orissa, and in Burma, in 1930 who were trained in Bengal. This list includes people first registering in the years 1904–09.

For the Muslim population, relative representation is shown relative to the entire population and is always very low. Muslims have always been a tiny share of doctors compared to their population share. The partition of Bengal in 1947 into largely Hindu West Bengal and mainly Muslim East Bengal significantly reduced the Muslim population share in West Bengal. The removal of a large fraction of the population that contained very few doctors had the effect of decreasing the relative representation of all the Hindu surname groups among physicians after 1947. Their share of physicians increased little as their population share increased. Since this politically created decline gives a spurious impres-

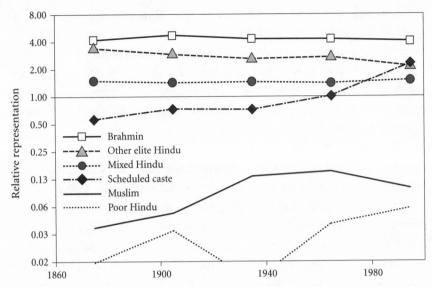

FIGURE 8.3. A summary of social mobility by surname type, 1860–2011.

sion of social mobility, for these other groups relative representation is shown always with respect to the non-Muslim population only.

Measured by this standard, there has been very little social mobility among Hindu surname groups in Bengal since 1860. The Brahmin group of surnames is almost as heavily overrepresented among the non-Muslim population in the period 1980–2011 as it was in 1860–89. Other elite Hindu surnames show a slow rate of decline in status. But the relative representation of mixed Hindu surnames, which are modestly elite, does not change. And the relative representation of poor Hindu surnames of the nineteenth century, those with the highest potential for regression to the mean, also changes little. The only group showing a marked change in status is the group of surnames associated with scheduled caste lists for positions in universities and the police. This group went from being modestly disadvantaged among non-Muslim groups in 1860 to being one of the most elite surname groups, as measured by their relative representation among physicians now.

Table 8.2 summarizes the persistence rates associated with these surname groups. These rates show how quickly the status of these groups is moving toward the population mean. With a stable variance of status across generations, they are also the intergenerational correlation of status. In that case they will be between zero and one. However, these persistence parameters are often

TABLE 8.2. Intergenerational persistence rates (b) for various groups and periods

Surname group	Percentage of population (age 20–29), 2010	Persistence rate			
		1860–1947, all	1950–2009, all	1860–1947, non-Muslim	1950–2009, non-Muslim
Muslim	31.1	0.91	1.20	—	—
Kulin Brahmin	3.4	1.05	1.05	1.03	0.97
Other elite Hindu	5.0	0.87	0.85	0.86	0.85
Poorest Hindu, pre-1947	7.0	1.01	0.85	1.02	0.83
Scheduled castes	3.8	—	—	0.84	—
Mixed Hindu	11.8	1.10	1.70	—	—
Average, all		0.99	1.13	0.91	0.88

greater than one, meaning that some of these groups are diverging from the mean rather than trending toward it. The persistence rate for the scheduled caste surname group cannot even be calculated for the period 1950–2011, since it crosses the mean, moving from below-average status to above-average status.

THE MUSLIM POPULATION

Census reports exist giving the Muslim share of the population in Bengal and West Bengal for each decade from 1871 on. Thus there are good measures of the relative representation among physicians in Bengal from 1860 on. The striking feature is the very low representation of Muslims among physicians in all periods. Under British rule, Muslims experienced limited upward mobility. The implied persistence of status was high, with a calculated intergenerational correlation of 0.91.

However, from the 1970s until very recently, the Muslim community in West Bengal saw a further decline in representation among physicians, with no implied regression to the mean. Indeed, starting with the generation entering practice since Independence in 1947, the implied persistence coefficient is 1.2, indicating that the Muslim community has been diverging further from the mean.

Bengal's system of reserving educational places and employment opportunities for disadvantaged castes and tribes explicitly excludes Muslims and Christians: only Hindus, Sikhs, and Buddhists are eligible. West Bengal, unlike some other Indian states, has not yet introduced reserved educational places for "other backward classes," which would include Muslims. Such a system will not take effect until 2014.[9]

Thus Muslims have been disadvantaged in admission to medical practice in West Bengal, compared to the Hindu, Sikh, and Buddhist populations, since Independence. They could compete on equal terms for the unreserved positions in medical schools, but the advantages offered by the reservation system to other disadvantaged groups effectively penalized Muslims. This situation helps explain the surprising negative social mobility implied for the Muslim community in recent generations. It emerges below, however, that even if the pernicious effects of the reservation system were removed, upward mobility rates for this group would be low.

It is possible that because there are so few Muslim physicians, this profession does not provide a useful measure of social mobility rates in the Muslim community in general. However, Muslims are similarly underrepresented in other, somewhat less elite occupations. Figure 8.4, for example, shows the relative representation of Muslims among new sergeants and subinspectors in the Kolkata police force in 2009, compared to their relative representation among physicians for the period 2000–2011. These lower-level police posts are coveted positions for which only a high school diploma is required. Muslims are similarly underrepresented in higher ranks in the police force, such as inspector. The medical profession is representative of a more general pattern.

THE BRAHMIN POPULATION

The seven Kulin Brahmin surnames have always been well represented among physicians in Bengal. Since Independence, they have accounted, on average, for more than 16 percent of physicians. The Brahmin-surname population share from 1860 to 2011 is estimated as described in the notes to figure 8.3. Figure 8.5 shows the implied relative representation of Kulin Brahmin surnames among physicians in Bengal under British rule and in West Bengal after Independence.

Relative representation declines from 5.8 times the average in 1860–89 to 4.2 in 1980–2011. This result implies very low social mobility rates. The recent overrepresentation of the Kulin Brahmins among physicians is, however, lower than the overrepresentation of Ashkenazi Jews among U.S. physicians, who have a relative representation of 5.6. So while Kulin Brahmin descendants are

---

[9] In 2013 a law was passed reserving 17 percent of places in state-run universities for other backward classes.

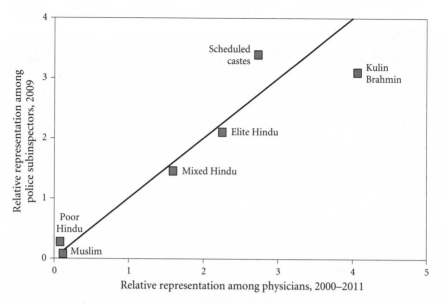

FIGURE 8.4. Relative representation of surnames among physicians and police sergeants.

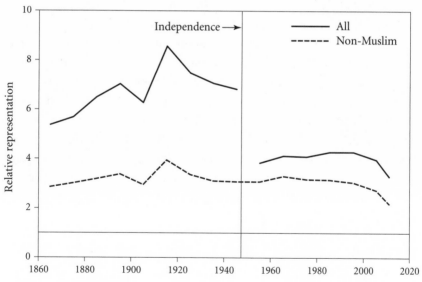

FIGURE 8.5. Kulin Brahmin relative representation among Bengali physicians and non-Muslim Bengali physicians, 1860–2011.

an elite, they are less distinctive in Bengal than Ashkenazi Jews are in America. There are plenty of poorer Brahmins.[10]

However, as the figure shows, the apparent decline in the relative status of Kulin Brahmins is mostly due to the partition of Bengal at Independence in 1947 and the loss of a large portion of the low-status Muslim population. After Independence, these surnames show little sign of regressing toward average representation among physicians. Only since 2000 has Brahmin overrepresentation declined, and this may just be a blip. During the colonial period, Kulin Brahmin relative representation was rising, though this was mainly because of the relative growth of the poor Muslim population.

Looking at the representation of Brahmin physicians among only the non-Muslim population (as represented by the dotted line in the figure), the relative representation of Brahmins shows very little sign of regression to the mean in either epoch. Even in the period since Independence, the persistence coefficient is 0.97. Surprisingly, the reservation system in Bengal, which sets aside 28 percent of medical-school places for scheduled castes and tribes, has produced little downward mobility among the Kulin Brahmin surname group since the colonial era.

As shown below, the reservation system did sharply increase the representation of a group of surnames associated with scheduled castes. What would the rate of downward mobility of the Brahmin surnames have been had the system not been implemented? Assuming that the system caused the Brahmin community to lose access to 28 percent of medical-school places and adjusting the data accordingly, the relative representation in the final period 1980–2011 would rise to 4.1 among the non-Muslim population, which is higher than the rate before Independence.[11] The implication is that absent reservation, there would have been no downward mobility among the Brahmin community in Bengal from the mid-nineteenth century to the present. India would be an example of a society with no mobility for some social groups.

OTHER ELITE HINDU SURNAMES

Our group of other surnames associated with high status shows a nearly fivefold overrepresentation among physicians in Bengal in the years 1860–89. The

[10] The press now publishes articles on the plight of lower-class Brahmins, who are disadvantaged in competition for university places and government positions.
[11] Candidates from scheduled castes and tribes who score high enough on the entrance requirements are allotted unreserved places. So the reservation system reduces the number of places available to members of the higher castes by the share of reserved places.

implied intergenerational correlation of status for the colonial period differs modestly depending on whether it is calculated for the population as a whole or only for the non-Muslim population. But, as table 8.2 shows, across both the colonial and Independence eras, it is around 0.86, also a high rate (though lower than for the Brahmin surname group). Somewhat lower on the social scale than the Kulin Brahmins, this group seemingly faced more competition for unreserved places at universities. But again, the implied rates of downward social mobility for this group of surnames remain low, even despite the expected effects of the reservation system in reducing their share of physicians. As with the Kulin Brahmin surnames, without the reservation system, the relative representation of these surnames among the non-Muslim population in the period 1980–2011 would be 2.2, very modestly less than the rate of 2.4 in the period 1860–89 under British rule. The underlying rate of social mobility for this group between 1860 and 2011 is consistent with an intergenerational correlation of 0.95 or higher. Thus inherent mobility rates are again very low.

THE POOREST HINDU GROUPS

Despite the establishment of the reservation system, surnames associated with the poorest Hindu groups of the colonial era are extremely rare among physicians even now. Among the non-Muslim population, they appear among physicians at 4 percent of the expected rate. They are also greatly underrepresented among lower-status occupations such as police sergeants and subinspectors in Kolkata (see figure 8.4).

As table 8.2 shows, the implied persistence rate for this group is 1.01 under British rule, implying no upward mobility. Since Independence, the calculated persistence rate has fallen to 0.83–0.85, depending on the reference group. But representation of this surname group among physicians is so low that this change in measured mobility rates may be the result of random chance.

Despite ample room for improvement of status, these surname groups have benefited little from the reservation system. Some of these surnames, such as *Dhanuk,* belong to groups which, although poor, did not qualify as scheduled castes because the British did not list them as such in 1931. While at least some *Shaw/Shows* were among the scheduled castes, many clearly were not. Thus in the list of nearly five hundred recruits to the Kolkata police with the rank of sergeant or subinspector, the four *Shaws* were all found in the "general," or unreserved, category. In a sample of medical-school admissions for 2010–11, three of the four *Shaws* were in the general category.

The peculiarity of the scheduled caste surnames identified above is that al-though all of them figure prominently in the scheduled caste list, they also fig-ure significantly in the list of Bengal physicians from before Independence. Indeed, as figure 8.6 shows, these surnames were already fully represented among physicians relative to their share in the population in the last generation before Independence. Looking just at the share of these surnames among the non-Muslim population, they were at less than half their expected representa-tion in the period 1860–89 but were converging toward proportional represen-tation, with a persistence rate of 0.84.

The success of this surname group under the reservation system has led to these surnames becoming as overrepresented as many higher-caste Hindu sur-names among both physicians and police recruits (see figure 8.2). Because they start just below the mean representation in the first generation after Indepen-dence, there is no implied regression to the mean for this group. They are defy-ing the law of social mobility presented in chapter 6, which predicts that all groups regress to the mean.

This recent overrepresentation of these surnames among physicians, even with respect to the non-Muslim population only, seems to be driven by the reservation system. In a list of recent admissions to medical schools in West

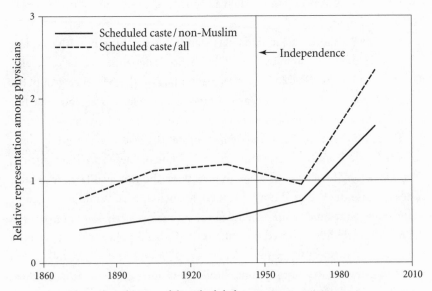

FIGURE 8.6. The curious history of the scheduled caste surname group.

Bengal that identifies some students by their reservation-system category, this surname group, accounting for 141 admissions, was at double the average representation for the non-Muslim community. Only 30 percent of this group were admitted to unreserved places; the rest were assigned places reserved for scheduled castes.[12] In the absence of reserved places, only fifty-eight surnames from this group would have appeared, and the group would have had a relative representation of only 0.84 instead of 2.04.[13]

These results seem to be driven by the arbitrariness of the original scheduled caste and scheduled tribe lists drawn up by the British, which ended up classifying even moderately prosperous groups as "untouchables" and reserving places for them. These misclassified groups thus gained a disproportionate advantage from the reservation system.[14]

THE MIXED HINDU SURNAMES GROUP

The group of mixed Hindu surnames includes surnames that were elite during the colonial era and showed no tendency then to regress to the mean. Since Independence, these names have tended to diverge from the mean, becoming more elite relative to the general population. But with respect to the non-Muslim population, these surnames show close to average representation among physicians both during the colonial period and since Independence. It is thus not possible to estimate a rate of regression to the mean for them because they already are at the mean.

This surname group both benefits and suffers from the reservation system. Those not designated as members of scheduled castes have a lower chance of admission to university, but those who are members of scheduled castes have a comparable advantage. Looking at lists of admissions from the two medical schools that made public their admissions in the reservation-system categories, 58 percent of this surname group were admitted to unreserved places. In the absence of reserved places for this group, the relative representation of this group of surnames, compared to other non-Muslim surnames, would have dropped from slightly above 1 to 0.8.

[12] Bankura Medical College, entry year 2012, and Kar Medical College, entry years 2010 and 2011, had admissions lists showing candidates' reservation-system status. These give the status of 395 admitted students in total.
[13] This assumes that absent the reservation system, admissions rates for this surname group in the unreserved category would remain as they are currently.
[14] Susan Bayly notes that the British caste designations of 1931 were often so broad as to include many groups not suffering any social disabilities (Bayly 1999, 277).

Social Mobility Rates Without the Reservation System

The strange pattern of convergence and divergence seen in figure 8.3 and table 8.2 seems to be an artifact of the reservation system for university admissions. Table 8.3 shows the relative representation of each of the six surname groups among physicians first registering in Bengal between 2000 and 2011. Using the cases noted above from universities that reported the reservation-system status of their admitted students, it is possible to estimate the share of reserved-place admissions to medical school for each surname group. Because this sample is small, for one group, the poorest Hindu surnames, there are only four people observed.

With this information, we can estimate the representation of the various surname groups for the years 2000–2011 had all admission been by open competition. Column 4 of the table shows the implied relative representation in this case. Figure 8.7 shows the estimated relative representation for each group for 1920–2011 without the reservation system.[15]

From this counterfactual estimate of relative representation, the implied persistence coefficient between the generation of physicians in the periods 1920–47 and 2000–2011 (seventy years or 2.33 generations later) is estimated. These estimates are shown in the rightmost column of the table.

These calculations imply that without the reservation system, for Kulin Brahmins, other high-status Hindus, and Muslims, there would have been little or no regression to the mean. The mixed and poorest Hindu surname groups regress toward the mean at a slow rate. For the poorest Hindu surname group, however, the numbers of physicians observed is so low that this result may be spurious.

The scheduled caste surname group still shows the odd transition from an underrepresented to an overrepresented group among physicians. But the attempt here to control for the effects of the reservation system is only partial: it does not control for the effect of the reservation system on the previous generation, which might have created more middle-class families whose children were better able to compete for unreserved places.

The effects of the reservation system between 1950 and 1999 cannot be fully inferred. On balance, it may have reduced the persistence rate for the initially

[15] The relative representation of the surnames in the period 1920–47 was calculated assuming (counterfactually) that the Muslim population share was the same as in 1980–2011. This was done to exclude from this exercise the effects of a shifting Muslim population share on measured social mobility rates.

TABLE 8.3. Implied persistence of status with and without the reservation system, medical-school admissions, Bengal, 2000–2011

Surname group	Relative representation, 2000–2011	Percent admitted through reservation system, 2010–12	Relative representation 2000–2011, no reservation system	Implied intergenerational correlation, 1935–2005, no reservation system
Kulin Brahmin	3.96	0	5.49	1.08
Other elite Hindu	2.25	3	3.02	1.07
Mixed Hindu	1.70	45	1.30	0.87
Scheduled caste	2.90	70	1.20	—
Poorest Hindu	0.10	25	0.10	0.77
Muslim	0.12	0	0.17	0.96

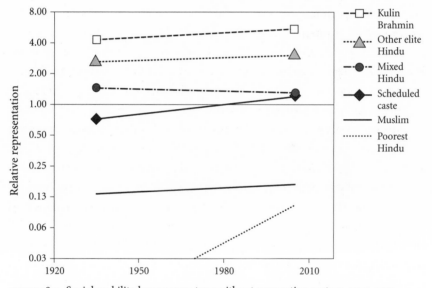

FIGURE 8.7. Social mobility by surname type without reservation system, 1920–2011.

high-status groups. But it has also served to increase persistence for a large and growing underclass of Muslims and poor Hindus who are ineligible for scheduled caste status.

It is also not clear whether the system is doing much to increase these overall slow rates of social mobility. As evidenced by surname distributions, the two-thirds of the population outside the reserved categories in Bengal has seen little change in relative social position over the past two generations. Among the groups included in the reserved categories, a few seem to have reaped disproportional gains, while others seem to have experienced few benefits. Thus despite the intergenerational mobility injected by the reservation system in the short run, the impression from the surname-group analysis is of an overall rate of social mobility close to zero. India seems to be a uniquely immobile society.

Does Marital Endogamy Explain Low Mobility?

The social mobility rates for Bengal estimated above are among the lowest observed, lower than those of preindustrial England, Sweden, or China. They are lower than those in highly unequal contemporary societies such as Chile, and are certainly lower than those of the modern United States, England, Sweden, China, Taiwan, Japan, and Korea. What makes India different from these other societies? Does this finding suggest that there is no universal constant of social mobility?

The hypothesis preferred, in line with the argument of chapter 7, is that Bengal's low social mobility rates are due to uniquely low rates of intermarriage between members of traditional elites and underclasses in Bengal. Chapter 7 argues that an important source of social mobility is marital sorting driven by the current social and economic status of families. With such sorting, those of high underlying social status tend to marry those of lower underlying status, and their children consequently regress to the mean. If, however, groups of high average status marry only within that group, then, although there is social mobility within the group, the group's average status will not revert to the mean. So if Indians conform to this pattern of associative marriage and also operate with rigid barriers to marriage across religious and caste lines, then religious and caste groups will not revert to the mean.

If marriage is endogamous, then there is no mechanism to eliminate underlying differences in the average levels of ability or competence of different castes or religious groups, and they will exhibit little or no social mobility.

Despite the importance of religion and caste in Indian history and politics, there has been surprisingly little study of intermarriage between different social groups in India in general or in Bengal specifically. As late as the 1960s, caste endogamy still seemed to be the rule for most marriages in Bengal, as seen in a

TABLE 8.4. Most common female first names among religious groups, Kolkata, 2009

Kulin Brahmin	Other high-caste Hindu	Muslim	Christian/Jewish
Krishna	*Geeta/Gita*	*Salma*	*Mary*
Soma	*Krishna*	*Yasmin*	*Elizabeth*
Geeta/Gita	*Soma*	*Shabana*	*Maria*
Arati	*Arati*	*Asma*	*Margaret*
Swapna	*Meera/Mira*	*Sultana*	*Helen(a)*
Meera/Mira	*Namita*	*Anwari*	*Agnes*
Kalpana	*Kalpana*	*Shabnam*	*Veronica*
Ratna	*Anjali*	*Afsana*	*Rosemary*
Sumita	*Swapna*	*Shahnaz*	*Dorothy*
Anjali	*Pratima*	*Farzana*	*Teresa*

detailed study of a modest-sized town in Bengal in the late 1960s.[16] Another study, looking at marriages in rural villages in Karnataka and Uttar Pradesh for the years 1982–95, found that of 905 marriages in the study, none involved couples who differed in their caste status.[17] In Hyderabad, among Kayasthas, only 5 percent of marriages were outside the caste even in the period 1951–75.[18] Information on the degree of endogamy for marriages in Bengal in the 1970s and 1980s, which produced the most recent crop of physicians, is not readily available.

One source of information on the likely endogamy rate is the 2010 Kolkata voter roll, which gives surnames, first names, and ages of all voters. Many first names are highly specific to the Hindu, Muslim, and Christian/Jewish communities. Table 8.4 shows the most common ten first names for women in each religious group. Women who marry into one of these groups from another group will almost always have different first names from women born in within the group. Also, if families with surnames associated with one group are assimilated into another group, then, as a result of intermarriage and adoption of at least some elements of the culture of the wives, the children again would typically have different first names.

[16] Corwin 1977.
[17] Dalmia and Lawrence 2001.
[18] Leonard and Weller 1980, tables 1–3.

As table 8.5 shows, the percentage of women in the Kulin Brahmin surname group with non-Hindu first names is extremely small. Because Muslims constitute nearly a quarter of the Kolkata population, this implies that intermarriage rates between Kulin Brahmin men and women of Muslim origin are extremely low, on the order of 0.1 percent. A similar result holds for other high-caste Hindu surnames.

More women with Muslim surnames have Hindu first names: 0.9 percent. But given the near-total absence of any sign of Muslim women's marriage into high-caste Hindu groups, if these findings are indicative of marriage alliances, they are likely with lower-caste Hindus.

Intermarriage between Christians and high-caste Hindus appears to be substantially more common. Christian surnames account for a very small share of the surname stock in Kolkata, about 0.3 percent, and are mainly Portuguese in origin. Given this small Christian population, the small share of women with high-caste Hindu surnames who have Christian first names is nevertheless suggestive of significant intermarriage.

An alternative explanation for these female Christian first names may be that high-caste Hindu girls are given Christian first names at birth. The possibility of significant intermarriage between Christians and Hindus is, however, supported by the fact that just over 30 percent of women with Christian surnames have first names that are Hindu. Also, almost 12 percent of women with Christian surnames have a combination of Christian and Hindu first names.

The first-name and surname evidence suggests almost no intermarriage between the largely poor Muslim community and either Hindus or Christians.

TABLE 8.5. Female first-name origins by surname group

| | Incidence in surname group (%) | | | |
First-name type	Kulin Brahmin	Other high-caste Hindu	Muslim	Christian
Hindu	99.6	99.3	0.9	30.2
Muslim	0.1	0.1	98.9	0.4
Christian	0.3	0.6	0.2	57.4
Hindu and Christian	0.0	0.0	0.0	11.9

Within the Hindu community, first-name evidence does not allow us to determine the degree of marital endogamy within castes because many female first names are common to high- and low-caste groups.

One of the few exceptions is the name *Munni,* found at the rate of 0.007 percent among high-caste surname women and 0.20 percent among other Hindu surname groups. If *Munni* were distributed representatively in the rest of the Hindu population, maintaining this incidence disparity would require that less than 4 percent of men with elite surnames married women from the general Hindu population. This would indicate a high degree of marital endogamy among elite populations.

However, the incidence of the name *Munni* is inversely proportional to the wealth of the group. Among the poorest Hindu surname group, it is found at a rate of 0.9 percent. Thus the absence of the name *Munni* among women with elite surnames may not reflect general marital endogamy among these caste groups but only a lack of intermarriage between men with high-caste surnames and low-status women. This type of marital sorting would be the same as that observed in societies such as the United States, England, and Sweden and thus would not suffice to explain the lack of social mobility in India.

Another source of evidence of the persistence of marital endogamy is websites advertising for potential wedding partners in Bengal. We recorded the characteristics of two hundred women identified as Kulin Brahmin on one of these sites. 83 percent specified that they were seeking a Brahmin husband, 2 percent specified Brahmin or other high-caste, and only 15 percent stated that caste status was no barrier to a potential union.[19] However, that 15 percent includes 8 percent who listed their preference in a form such as "Brahmin-Kulin, caste no bar." Thus a full 93 percent of respondents indicated a preference for a Brahmin spouse. And listings on websites presumably are biased toward the least traditional families of the Brahmin community.

If the marital endogamy of castes and religions in India explains low average social mobility for surname groups, we should find higher rates of social mobility for individual families within these groups. Families sharing the surname *Banerjee,* for example, will have the same rates of mobility as in any other society. It is just that the average status of the *Banerjees* will not converge toward

[19] Bengali Matrimony, n.d.

that of the *Shaws*. We should also find that over time, all the major Kulin Brahmin surnames have the same average social status. This hypothesis is borne out by the incidence of these surnames among physicians.

This consideration implies that in India, the estimates of social mobility for surname groups correctly estimate persistence at the group level but overestimate persistence at the family level. While the Brahmins may have stayed at the top of the social scale for thousands of years, individual family lineages within the Brahmin caste should show the normal slow turnover of elite and underclass families every three to five hundred years.

The Beneficiaries of the Reservation System

We show above that the reservation system has been of enormous benefit to some families in admission to university and government positions. Some surnames that are associated with scheduled castes, such as *Mandal/Mondal*, now appear, according to many measures, to belong to the social elite of Bengal. If the reservation system were to end now, what would be the long-run status of these surnames? Would they decline toward their 1947 social status? If not, could we conclude that affirmative-action policies can permanently change the outcomes for social groups? And if affirmative-action policies bring about such effects, does this prove that biology is not the major factor determining the social status of the next generation?

The information does not exist to answer these questions. There is, however, one piece of information that suggests that the reservation system in India may have less effect on the overall social status of its beneficiaries than the data on physicians and university admissions in Bengal would suggest. The horizontal axis of figure 8.8 shows the percentage of physicians in Bengal registered between 1950 and 2011 from each of the six surname groups discussed above, plus those with Christian surnames. Large numbers of physicians who complete medical school in Bengal end up working in the United States. The American Medical Association directory for 2012 shows 1,168. The vertical axis of the figure shows what percentage of these Bengali physicians in the United States come from each surname group.

For some surname groups, such as the Kulin Brahmins, the percentages of physicians employed in Bengal and the United States are the same. Other groups, such as Christians, have a much greater presence in the United States. Notably, the group for which it was estimated that as many as 70 percent were admitted

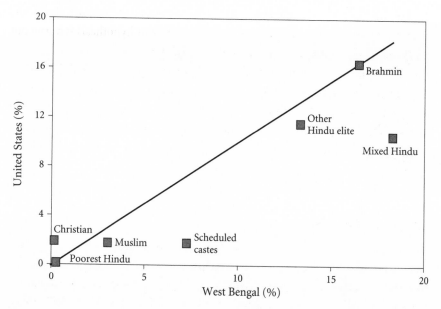

FIGURE 8.8. Surname group shares among Bengali physicians in West Bengal versus in the United States.

to reserved places in medical schools is heavily underrepresented among Bengali physicians working in the United States. Their representation in the United States is only a quarter of that in Bengal. The mixed Hindu surname group, of whom an estimated 45 percent were admitted to reserved places, show up in the United States at about 40 percent less than the rate expected from their representation in Bengal.

There could be many explanations of these findings. But one possibility is that physicians admitted to Indian medical schools through the reservation system find it harder to meet the onerous requirements to practice medicine in the United States: passing the U.S. Medical Licensing Examination and completing the required residencies. Though the reservation changes the measured social status of these individuals, it does much less to change the underlying social competence of these families. If the reservation system were ended, the measured social status of these groups would soon also decline substantially. Another possibility, however, is that groups that benefit from the reservation system have fewer of the family resources needed to relocate to the United States and practice medicine there. But the observed patterns contain nothing that clearly contradicts the biological explanation.

Conclusions

Long-run social mobility rates in India, as measured by the frequency of sur-name types in high-status occupations such as physicians or judges, are even lower than in England, the United States, and Sweden. The reservation system may actually be restricting mobility because it helps only a small portion of the lower classes, and even there it tends to benefit families who were not of partic-ularly low social status in the first place. But without the reservations system, the estimated status persistence rate would be, on average, a very high 0.91.

This unusually low rate of social mobility is consistent with the argument in chapter 7 that group marital endogamy leads to persistent classes of the ad-vantaged and disadvantaged. In Kolkata, for example, there is little or no inter-marriage between the very low-status Muslim community and the prosperous communities of high-caste Indians and Christians. Matrimonial listings on the Internet still show strong preferences, even within the Hindu community, for partners of the same caste.

NINE

China and Taiwan

Mobility after Mao

IN ALL THE SOCIETIES WE HAVE LOOKED AT so far, mobility rates have been slow—or, in the case of India, almost nonexistent—at the group level. But these are all societies whose institutions and social structures have been stable and continuous over many centuries.

England famously had only one lasting Political Revolution, the Glorious Revolution of 1688–89.[1] And even that revolution was made by the upper classes of English society for their own benefit and did not involve fighting on English soil. A new king and queen were invited in, and the tiresome old one, bereft of support, conveniently fled the scene. There were precious few imprisonments, dispossessions, or exiles as a result. The United States was born in a long and bloody revolution, but it was a revolution of the colonial upper classes against an external tyrant.

In Sweden, there is debate about whether there ever was any political revolution. Thus, according to one author, "Conventional wisdom holds that Sweden's transition to democracy was exceptionally gradual, stepwise and non-revolutionary."[2] In India, the British were expelled, and a new country was born in the violence of Partition and its mass population movements in 1947. Even so, in most parts of India the transition was smooth. The new rulers of India in the Congress Party were the same Brahmin elite who had governed as part of the Indian Civil Service under the British. In fifty of the sixty-six years of Indian independence, the prime minister has been a Brahmin.

---

[1] The Civil War of 1642–49 saw only a temporary overthrow of the traditional elite, and they returned in full force with the Restoration of 1660.

[2] Schaffer 2012, 2.

China, by contrast, experienced in the twentieth century a revolution unparalleled in its ferocity, bloodlust, class hatred, and mass dispossession. The sclerotic Qing imperial regime collapsed by 1912. Although the Nationalist Party won the election of 1912, warlords remained in control of the central government in Beijing. The Nationalists by 1925 established a rival capital in the south. It took more than a decade of fighting for Chiang Kai-shek, leader of the Nationalists, to defeat his northern rivals and reunify China under Nationalist rule in 1928. But this unity was fragile, beset by continuing armed conflict with remnant warlords, the Communist Party, and in 1937 open conflict with the Japanese, who had previously seized Manchuria. The Communists came to power in 1949 after decades of social turmoil.

The final Communist victory produced a generation of unprecedented social dislocation. Perhaps a million mainland Chinese fled to Taiwan with the Nationalists, including many Nationalist functionaries and sympathizers from the middle and upper classes. Many Shanghai businesses transferred their operations to Hong Kong, which also received hundreds of thousands of refugees.

Under the agrarian reform of 1946–53, as much as 43 percent of the farmland of China was seized from the landlord class and redistributed.[3] In the process, some 800,000 landlords were executed.[4] This was because land reform was mainly a political movement to eliminate opponents and potential opponents of the revolution. These executions represented only perhaps one in a thousand of the rural population, but this figure represented a significant fraction of the old elite.[5]

The Cultural Revolution of 1966–76 saw another round of mistreatment and purges of "class enemies"—relatives of former landlords, businessmen, and anyone suspected of having a bourgeois background. Teachers and intellectuals, particularly those in positions of authority, were frequent targets. Thousands died at the hands of the Red Guards, the militant youth wing of the Communist Party. As many as half a million in the cities were shipped to the countryside for reeducation through labor. The institutions of society—universities, hospitals, government ministries—were paralyzed, placed under the control of erratic teenage revolutionary committees. But by 1967 the Cultural Revolution had dissolved into a bloody mess, into which the army entered both on the side of the

[3] Stavis 1978, 67.
[4] Moïse 1983, 142; Stavis 1978, 75.
[5] Stavis 1978, 75.

FIGURE 9.1. Administrator of the *Heilongjiang Daily* denounced by the newspaper staff for following the capitalist line, 1966.

Red Guards and in defiance of them. All across the countryside, alleged class enemies were being confronted, abused, and killed (figure 9.1). The total death toll from the chaos of the Cultural Revolution is unknown but has been estimated to be as high as ten million.

Institutions of higher education effectively closed between 1966 and the early 1970s. Even after this, large numbers of urban students were sent out to labor in the countryside, denied the opportunity for higher education. It is estimated that as many as eighteen million people were forced to relocate to the countryside in these years. Admission to universities in the years 1970–76 was largely determined by political qualification and connections: only students without the taint of bourgeois background were admitted. In 1977 the National

College Entrance Examination was restored, allowing "bourgeois" students to compete for university places. But not until 1980 were all those exiled to the countryside during the Cultural Revolution allowed to return to the cities. Thus the universities were effectively closed to those with bourgeois family backgrounds for more than ten years.

Mao Zedong may not have had the lasting impact on Chinese society that he sought through such movements as the Cultural Revolution. But did he create a period of unusually rapid social mobility though the elimination, repression, and dispossession of the upper and middle classes?[6]

Some recent studies suggest that postreform China has achieved high rates of social mobility. The urban intergenerational correlation of income in this period, for example, is only 0.3–0.6.[7] But these estimates are based on one dimension of status and on only two generations, and we see above from examination of such examples as Sweden that such estimates can be completely misleading about underlying social mobility rates. This chapter again applies surname-group analysis to attempt to arrive at a more realistic estimate of social mobility.

Chinese Surnames

The problem with measuring social mobility in China using surname distributions is that the Chinese have few surnames, and these surnames have been employed for millennia. There are estimated to be only about four thousand surnames in use among Han Chinese. The hundred most common Chinese surnames are held by nearly 85 percent of the population, with the three most common Chinese surnames, *Wang* (王), *Li* (李), and *Zhang* (張), held by more than 270 million people (21 percent of the population).[8] These "big three" surnames are used below as a benchmark for the average representation of surnames among elite groups. In England and Wales, by contrast, in 2002 there were 270,000 surnames shared by five or more people. Because almost all Chinese surnames are so common, they typically carry little information on the social status of their holders.

---

[6] The irony is that Mao himself was the son of a rich farmer and so himself a "class enemy."

[7] Guo and Min, 2008; Gong, Leigh, and Meng 2010. Wu and Treiman (2007), however, argue that taking into account urban-rural inequality, the intergenerational correlation of incomes would be significantly higher.

[8] Supposedly these surnames appeared at a similar frequency even during the Song dynasty, 960–1279 CE (Liu et al. 2012, 342).

FIGURE 9.2. Imperial examination hall with 7,500 cells, Guangdong, 1873.

However, it is possible to identify thirteen relatively rare surnames that appear with unusually high frequency among those who attained the highest qualification under the Qing exam system, that of *jinshi* (进士). A complete list has been published of all the Qing *jinshi*. Indeed, in the front courtyard of the Confucius Temple in Beijing are hundreds of large stone tablets bearing the names of the more than fifty thousand *jinshi* of the Yuan, Ming, and Qing dynasties. These thirteen elite surnames were identified as those that showed a relative representation among Qing *jinshi* between 1820 and the end of the imperial exam era in 1905 that was at least four times that of the big three surnames.[9] Though relatively rare by Chinese standards, the thirteen elite Qing surnames are held by nearly eight hundred thousand people today.[10] So there is plenty of evidence by which to judge the current status of these surnames.

The imperial examinations were the meritocratic path to high-level positions in the bureaucracy. The gains from various levels of achievement on these exams were so great that to limit cheating and nepotism, they were held under strict supervision, with the candidates isolated in individual cells for the two to three days of the exam (see figure 9.2). Individual examinations were numbered, and candidates' answers were copied out by clerks so that the graders could not recognize candidates by their calligraphy. Candidates spent years studying to attempt the various levels of the exams. The gains were not just the emoluments

[9] It is assumed that the relative frequency of surnames was the same in the period 1645–1905 as in 2010.

[10] These surnames represent, however, only 0.055 percent of the modern population.

of imperial service but also the protection and business advantages the degrees afforded to the families of successful candidates. Extended families thus had interests in furthering the success of the most academically able of their relatives.

Geography still matters to social status in China, a fact that slows mobility at the national level. The populations bearing the thirteen Qing elite surnames are all concentrated in the lower Yangzi River valley. These surnames are overrepresented among both exam passers in the imperial era and in modern Chinese elites. Here, to exclude geographic causes of persistence in status, social mobility rates are measured relative to the common surnames of the lower Yangzi. The mobility rates estimated for modern China would be even lower were the geographical elements in immobility not excluded.

The relative representation of these thirteen Qing elite surnames among modern elites was calculated by comparing them to three equally regionally favored surnames, Gu (顾), Shen (沈), and Qian (钱), the "regional three," that have only average status in the lower Yangzi. These three surnames, held by more than ten million people now, offer a large and stable comparison group.

Figure 9.3 shows the relative frequency of the Qing elite surnames in various modern Chinese elites with respect to the "big three" and "regional three" surnames. The modern elites employed are high officials in the Nationalist government in China from 1912 to 1949; professors at the ten most prestigious Chinese universities in 2012; chairs of the boards of companies listed in 2006 as having assets of US$1.5 million and above; and members of the central government administration in 2010. Compared to the big three surnames, the thirteen elite Qing surnames are nearly as prominent among Chinese elites in recent years as are Brahmin surnames among elites in India. But, as noted above, geography is responsible for much of this effect.

Relative to the regional three surnames (Gu, Shen, and Qian), the thirteen Qing elite surnames are less overrepresented but still distinctive in the Qing and modern eras. Their relative representation was 2.28 among high Nationalist officials, 1.88 among professors at elite universities in 2006, 1.62 among chairs of company boards, and 1.46 among central government officials. Had these surnames declined to average status by now, all the measures of relative representation would be one.

The stock of professors, company board chairs, and government officials in 2006–12 consists almost entirely of people born after 1940 and therefore educated under communism. (Only those age 60 or older would have completed their education before the Cultural Revolution and the disruption of higher-

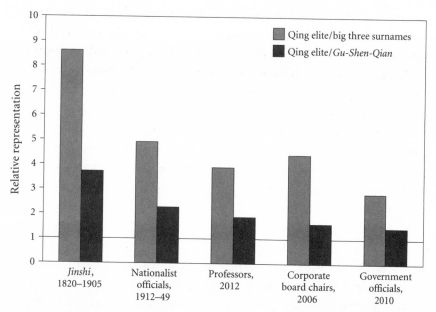

FIGURE 9.3. Relative representation of Qing elite surnames among modern Chinese elites.

education institutions between 1966 and 76.) These three groups are observed roughly seventy-five years, or 2.5 generations, after the high Nationalist officials of 1912–49. Assuming that the Nationalist officials were a similarly exclusive elite, the intergenerational correlation of status for these surname groups between the Republican era and 2006 is 0.9 for professors, 0.8 for company board chairs, and 0.74 for central government officials.

Assuming that the *jinshi* elite of 1820–1905 and the Nationalist officials of 1912–49 were also comparably elite groups, it is also possible to calculate the mobility rate between these two eras.[11] The decline of the relative representation of the thirteen Qing elite surnames among the Nationalist officials implies an intergenerational correlation of status of 0.8.

These results are supported by data on student admissions to Tsinghua University from 2003 to 2011. As one of the top ten universities in China, Tsinghua again represents an elite at the pinnacle of the education distribution. The relative representation of the thirteen Qing elite surnames, even relative to the three regional surnames, was still 1.62. Since these students, entering university

[11] Based on the numbers listed per year, there were more *jinshi* than high Nationalist officials.

at age 18, are a full three generations removed from the Nationalist officials of 1912–49, this figure again implies an intergenerational correlation of 0.83. Despite the disruptions of civil war, land reform, and the Cultural Revolution, the data show a very slow decline in status of the Qing elite within Communist China.

These results are all subject to random errors, because the sample sizes of some of the elites are modest. The samples include 9,363 Qing *jinshi*, 26,738 Nationalist officials, and 26,429 elite university professors. Of these samples, only 39, 62, and 51, respectively, hold one of the thirteen Qing elite surnames. Just by chance, the number of Qing elite surnames could deviate significantly from the underlying trend in any of these samples. So none of the individual estimates of intergenerational correlations from these samples can be relied on. The true value of each could deviate substantially from the estimate.

Nevertheless, it is clear from these samples that these thirteen Qing surnames remain elite. And there is another sample so large as to give absolute confirmation of their continuing enhanced status: the household registration details of all 1.3 billion Chinese in 2008. This database records whether individuals have completed a university degree. There are 29,604 people with one of the Qing elite surnames who have a university degree. Now the sampling error is minuscule.

The household registrations reveal that in 2012, 2.6 percent of all Chinese held university degrees; for holders of the regional three surnames, the figure was 3.5 percent. Degree attainment is 58 percent higher for the Qing elite surnames than for the big three surnames and 30 percent higher than for the regional surnames. The relative representation of the Qing surnames is lower among university graduates than among professors, but this is exactly what we would expect given that university graduates in general are a much less elite population.

Degree attainment has expanded rapidly in the last ten years, and therefore the average date for the awarding of these degrees is 1998. Thus this population is three generations separated from the Nationalist elite of 1912–49. Allowing for this, and for the lower exclusivity of the pool of modern university graduates, the implied intergenerational correlation over these three generations is 0.78, very similar to what was implied by the smaller more elite samples.

There is still random error associated with the smaller sample of Nationalist officials. This could lead to under- or overestimation of the rate of social mobility between 1912–49 and 2008. Taking this into account, we can be 95 percent confident that the true intergenerational correlation of status for Communist

China lies in the range 0.71–0.92. Even at the lower bound of this range of estimates, this is a remarkable degree of status persistence by the elite in a society that experienced the degree of turbulence and anti-elitist actions in the early years of Communist rule.

Surname–Place of Origin Identifiers

Other evidence for rates of social mobility in Communist China is supplied by identifiers that combine surnames and places of origin. Given how common most surnames are in China, families and lineages distinguished themselves in the imperial and Republican eras by associating the name with the family's place of origin. Such combinations include the Fan family of Ningbo (宁波范氏), the Zha family of Haining (海宁查氏), and the Weng family of Changshu (常熟翁氏). The surnames themselves—*Fan, Zha,* and *Weng*—are average in social status at the national level. But these particular combinations of surnames with places of origin represent an imperial elite whose later regression to the mean can be measured.

To measure social mobility in this way, the focus here is on two regions in the lower Yangzi, South Jiangsu and North Zhejiang, which lie, respectively, north and south of Shanghai (see figure 9.4). This has long been one of the most economically advanced areas of China. Required for this local mobility estimate are the frequency in these regions of each surname–place of origin combination and the frequency of these combinations among various local elite groups over time.

For want of a better source, surname–place of origin population shares are estimated from the records of twenty thousand soldiers from the lower Yangzi who died in the civil wars of 1933–36 and 1945–49 and the external wars of 1937–45 and 1950–53.[12] (Modern population censuses might seem better sources from which to estimate these population frequencies, but no modern population count gives name frequencies by surname and place of origin.) It is assumed that the share of surnames among soldiers who died between 1933 and 1953 represent the population shares in these areas as a whole and that the population share of surnames has been constant over time.[13]

[12] Of these soldiers, 12,737 were from South Jiangsu and 8,907 from North Zhejiang.

[13] This assumption seems reasonable because there is evidence that common surnames in the lower Yangzi did not change in frequency between 1645 and 2010. And the common surnames are found at the same frequency among dead soldiers as in other local sources.

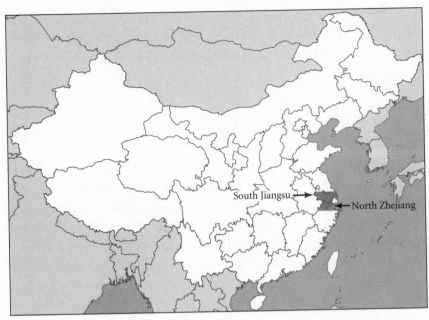

FIGURE 9.4. The areas of the lower Yangzi used in the surname–place of origin mobility estimates.

Again, unusual Qing-era success on the imperial exams is used to identify the early elite surname–place of origin combinations in these two regions. The records used in this case are the far more numerous ones of the *juren,* those who succeeded at the provincial level of the imperial examinations. Surname-location combinations that occurred at five times or more of the expected frequency among *juren* in each location from 1871 to 1905 were classified as constituting local surname elites.

To trace the status of these groups into the present, we need to know the family place of origin for members of various later elites. This information is available for the Republican era because it was included in university rosters and alumni records, which provide data for eleven thousand students.

Under communism, such forms of identification became less common. The Communists, after all, wanted to remake society, not perpetuate the ancient lineage of successful families. But fortunately, two sources from the Communist era still reported family places of origin at the county level. For modern Zhejiang, the Zhejiang Provincial Archive lists notable Zhejiang people born between 1930 and 1990 and includes the family place of origin. This list covers a spectrum of occupations, such as entrepreneurs, artists, professors, and officials; of these, only those with a university degree were counted as elite. The notable people list also includes, conveniently, people who migrated from the region.

Data on later elites is obtained for South Jiangsu from the Nanjing University archive, which records students by name, place of origin, and year of graduation for the years 1952–2010. This institution ranks third among Chinese universities, and two-fifths of its students are from Jiangsu. To enroll, students must rank among the top 3 to 5 percent of those taking the National College Entrance Examination (*gaokao* [高考]). Since less than half of each cohort typically took this exam in the Communist era, Nanjing students represent the top 0.6 to 2.5 percent of the South Jiangsu distribution of scholastic achievement.

Comparing the relative representation of the 1871–1905 exam elite in two subsequent Republican elites—students and officials—in the years 1912–49 gives an estimate of persistence rates for the Republican era of 0.78–0.81, consistent with estimates in many other societies (see table 9.1).

The implied social mobility in North Zhejiang for the Communist era is not significantly higher: the persistence rate is still 0.74. This mobility estimate is partly based, however, on the achievements of people born in Zhejiang who emigrated to Taiwan, Hong Kong, or the United States but were still included on the list of notable people.

In South Jiangsu, based on the Nanjing student records for 1952–2010, social mobility rates for the Communist era were higher than before. But there was still a strong connection between surname–place of origin combinations overrepresented in 1952 and those overrepresented in 2010. (Again, given the modest sample sizes, there may be considerable sampling error underlying these estimates.)

Overall, although these local estimates do suggest faster social mobility in the Communist era, they also imply a remarkable persistence of status in a soci-

TABLE 9.1. Persistence rates for the lower Yangzi, 1871–2010

Period	Surname groups	North Zhejiang	South Jiangsu
1871–1949	*Juren,* University students	0.78	0.81
1930–90	Notable people	0.74	—
1952–2010	Nanjing University students	—	0.66

ety convulsed at times by revolutionary fervor and a determination to root out "class enemies."

Mobility among the Nationalists: Taiwan, 1949–2012

More than a million supporters of the defeated Republican government of China retreated to the island of Taiwan in 1949. These people, most of whom had been part of the mainland elite, immediately formed a new political and social elite on an island populated by only six million people before their arrival. With the arrival of this immigrant elite, what were social mobility rates in Taiwan after 1949?

As a matter of policy, the Taiwanese government does not collect or publish information about the relative status of the descendants of natives and mainlanders in modern Taiwan. But as Yu Hao shows in his recently completed PhD dissertation, it is possible to identify groups from each community using surnames.[14] Using information from 1956, when the population census reported surname totals by ethnic status, Hao identifies three hundred surnames whose holders were at least 95 percent mainlanders, and thirty surnames whose holders were at least 98 percent native Taiwanese. These surnames had average status in their respective communities.

Using records of university students, doctors, and business leaders, Hao then estimates social mobility in Taiwan for the period 1949–2012. The isolation of Taiwan from the mainland before 1990, and the ban even today on students from mainland China pursuing graduate degrees in Taiwan, means that we can be relatively certain that the holders of the three hundred mainland surnames in Taiwan now are the descendants of those who held the name in the previous generation.

Table 9.2 summarizes Hao's persistence rate estimates across the last two generations for three different elite groups: National Taiwanese University students, medical doctors, and business leaders. As a background to these estimates, note that individual-level estimates show high rates of intergenerational income mobility in Taiwan. The intergenerational correlation is estimated to be on the order of 0.17–0.24, as low as in Nordic countries.[15]

As always, the estimates in table 9.2 show much greater persistence than those for individual families. However, these estimates, in the range 0.55–0.64,

[14] Hao 2013.
[15] Hao 2013, chapter 2.

TABLE 9.2. Persistence rates for Taiwan, 1949–2012

Group	Persistence rate	
	Unadjusted	Adjusted for emigration of mainlander elite
National Taiwan University students	0.55–0.66	0.61–0.72
Medical doctors	0.53–0.65	0.59–0.71
Business leaders	0.58–0.62	0.64–0.68

are low compared to those seen in the other surname studies. They certainly suggest, ironically, that social mobility after 1949 was faster in class-ridden Taiwan than in the class-free society Mao built.

However, after the 1950s there was significant migration from Taiwan to the United States and Canada, mainly by the more-educated mainlander population. In the United States, these immigrants and their descendants have among the highest university graduation rates of any community. Such migrants in the United States and Canada now number 0.7 million, equivalent to 3 percent of the population of Taiwan. The subtraction of this mainlander elite from the population of Taiwan by emigration increased estimated social mobility rates within Taiwan. There are consequently fewer mainlanders at National Taiwan University or working as medical doctors and business leaders. There are correspondingly more native Taiwanese in these positions who are descended from families that were lower class in 1949.

The information does not exist to allow Hao to estimate what the true persistence rates would have been absent this migration. He cannot observe exactly how selective the migration was or how concentrated among mainlanders. We can be confident, however, that the mobility rates reported in table 9.2 overstate true rates of social mobility.

Yu Hao estimates counterfactually that this effect could have reduced measured persistence rates for educational status by as much as 0.06.[16] Table 9.2 shows the estimated persistence rates with this upward adjustment. The average measured persistence rate is 0.66, which is now not far below the estimates found for other countries. And, as noted, the effects of emigration are hard to estimate.

[16] Hao 2013, chapter 3.

Conclusion

The startling observation in this data is that social mobility rates in China under communism, even with the execution and exile of significant numbers of the middle and upper classes, have been just as low as in countries that have not experienced such social turmoil. The Qing elite are still overrepresented at the top of Chinese society. In particular, despite Mao's best efforts, even in the machinery of central government, the thirteen Qing elite surnames are more prevalent than expected. Despite Mao's best efforts, "class enemies" are strongly entrenched within the current Communist government of China.

These results are in line with some more-conventional studies of social mobility in modern China. Studies that examine social mobility by classifying people into groups according to the social background of their families should, according to the interpretation of social mobility in chapter 6, show much less mobility than would be expected from conventional estimates of mobility rates in recent years. One such study is that of Robert Walder and Songhua Hu, who classify people as descendants of the old elites (地富反坏右), landlords and businessmen before 1949, or descendants of the old poor (贫下中农), those whose forebears were tenants and workers before 1949. The descendants of the old elites had to pursue professional careers instead of politics after 1949 because they were discriminated against in the Communist Party. Nonetheless, they maintained advantages in educational attainment. Once discrimination inside the party was officially ended after 1976, they performed much better in all occupations relative to the descendants of the old poor.[17]

This slow rate of mobility in the modern era echoes similarly slow social mobility rates in the imperial era (see chapter 12). Despite the classic study of Ping-ti Ho, suggesting rapid social mobility and an open meritocracy in China in the exam era, surname distributions imply strong persistence of elite surnames among exam-degree attainers.[18]

Some scholars, such as Cameron Campbell and James Lee, have interpreted this slow mobility and long persistence of elites in China as revealing the importance of kin networks and extended-family strategies.[19] In the imperial era, given

---

[17] Walder and Hu 2009.

[18] Ho 1964.

[19] Campbell and Lee 2010, 2011. In a recent paper, Avner Greif, Murat Iyigun, and Diego Sasson argue that these kin networks were important enough in preindustrial China to explain

the low pass rates on the provincial and national exams (the pass rate for the provincial exams was typically less than 1 in 200), it was unlikely that a nuclear family could produce *juren* or *jinshi* over consecutive generations. For any individual child, luck was as important as talent in determining success in the exams.[20] The best strategy, then, was for the heads of kin groups to pool resources and try to secure an exam pass for the best candidates from each generation. The successful candidates then had to reciprocate by providing aid to the kin group that had secured their appointment.

This kinship strategy was pursued in various ways. Kin groups allotted a portion of land as "land for education" (学田), with the rent being used to pay for education and exam preparation. These funds supported lineage-based schools (族学) in which the most academically talented children within the kin group were coached for the exams by the best available teachers. To diversify risk, other children were assigned to alternative occupations.

Success in the exams not only brought glory to the common ancestor of the chosen candidates but also secured protection for the property rights of the entire kin group. As it obtained more land and wealth, the group had more resources to invest in education. Thus the pooling of resources made the status of kin groups more stable over generations than that of individual families.[21] On this interpretation, it is the kin network that explains the strong persistence of some family surnames among the Qing elite as well as elites in Republican and Communist China.

However, the status persistence observed in China is no greater, either now or in the past, than in highly individualistic societies such as Sweden, England, or the United States. In these Western societies, aid from kin networks is limited and rare. Thus kinship networks are not an essential factor in accounting for slow social mobility. The law of mobility presented in chapter 6 assumes nuclear families with no collateral transfers. It is more parsimonious, then, to assume that China has simply experienced the same strong underlying transmission of social competence within families that we see in the rest of the world, and that kinship associations did little to further reduce rates of social mobility.

---

why Chinese technological development was much slower than European (Greif, Iyigun, and Sasson 2012).

[20] Elman 1992.
[21] Hymes 1986.

TEN

Japan and Korea

Social Homogeneity and Mobility

CONVENTIONAL STUDIES SUGGEST that modern Japan is a socially mobile and meritocratic society. In this view, although Japan before the Meiji restoration of 1868 was a society of rigid class divisions, the reforms of 1868 and 1947 transformed it into an egalitarian, homogeneous, and classless society. Does a society such as Japan, with a high degree of cultural homogeneity, have faster social mobility than societies such as the United States, which are fractured by religious, racial, and ethnic differences? Korea is a society of similar cultural homogeneity, profoundly remade after World War II as a supposedly modern and meritocratic society, so the same questions arise there also.

Japan

The largest traditional elite in Japan was the samurai, the former warrior class (figure 10.1). By 1868 they had evolved mostly into bureaucrats and administrators. Because by then they constituted 5 percent of the population, their economic circumstances were diverse, but on average they remained an elite. With the Meiji restoration, the samurai lost the legal privileges they had enjoyed under the shogunate. The new government did, however, compensate them for their hereditary land revenues with government bonds. In 1871 the government ordered all samurai to surrender their swords, made commoners free to intermarry with samurai, and abolished restrictions on the occupations samurai were allowed to pursue. A new education system was launched in 1872, premised

FIGURE 10.1. Samurai of the Satsuma clan during the Boshin War period (1868–69).

on selection for higher-level institutions through competitive examination. The samurai thus soon lost all class privileges in the rapidly modernizing Japanese economy.

As part of its modernization program, the Meiji government sought to enforce a shared cultural identity and set of cultural practices. The reformed educational system promoted a standard form of spoken Japanese nationwide. The government was aided in this effort by the relative homogeneity of language, culture, and even physiognomy among most Japanese.

After the Meiji restoration, the new leadership, as part of its Westernization program, merged the *kuge,* the ancient court nobility of Kyoto, with the *daimyo,* the feudal lords, into an expanded aristocratic class. The resulting *kazoku* peerage initially consisted of just 427 families. However, the Meiji government expanded the hereditary peerage by adding to its ranks persons who had made distinguished contributions to the nation. As table 10.1 shows, the total membership grew most rapidly between 1884 and 1907. Thus the *kazoku* families represented an elite of wealth and position in Japan that dates mainly from before 1907, though new families were being added even after 1928.

The *kazoku* had a number of privileges in addition to any private wealth that they retained from pre-Meiji times. Some received hereditary pensions from the state. The titles and pensions passed by inheritance to the eldest son. Only the holder of a title was considered part of the *kazoku:* other children had no special status. The *kazoku* elected representatives from their ranks to serve in the House of Peers.

TABLE 10.1. Number and rank of *kazoku* families, 1884–1946

Year	Prince/marquess/count	Viscount	Baron	Total
1884	111	324	74	509
1887	117	355	93	565
1899	144	363	221	718
1907	151	376	376	903
1916	155	380	398	933
1928	166	379	409	954
1946	—	—	—	1,011

The new constitution of 1947 eliminated the imperial elite: the *kazoku* was abolished, and these families were all rendered ordinary citizens. Thus for the last two generations Japan has been a society of exceptional social homogeneity. Visible racial and ethnic minorities are few: they include the Ainu, some islanders, and the descendants of Korean immigrants from the colonial era. Social policy has even managed to render invisible the *burakumin,* the descendants of the outcast communities of the feudal era whose occupations rendered them defiled and impure. Religious minorities, such as Christians, have remained a small share of the population. And in general the Japanese now register in the World Values Survey as the most secular population in the world.[1]

Sociological studies support the idea that Japan is an intergenerationally mobile society. One study, for example, looked at the occupations of three cross sections of fathers and sons in 1965, 1975, and 1985.[2] If we assign an income level to each of these occupations, we can translate these results into the intergenerational earnings correlation. Using average earnings by occupation gives an implied persistence rate of 0.3 in all these cohorts.[3] A more recent study of intergenerational income mobility found implied intergenerational correlations of 0.3–0.46.[4] Thus, on conventional measures, Japan has plenty of intergenerational mobility.

[1] Inglehart and Welzel 2010, 554.
[2] Jones, Kojima, and Marks 1994.
[3] Clark and Ishii 2013.
[4] Ueda 2009.

TABLE 10.2. Class status of university graduates, 1890–1900 (%)

	1890		1900	
	Samurai	Commoners	Samurai	Commoners
Imperial universities	63	37	51	49
Other universities	62	38	48	42

SOCIAL MOBILITY AMONG THE SAMURAI IN THE EARLY MEIJI ERA

As the class of bureaucrats and officials, the former samurai began the Meiji era with considerable advantages. These were reflected in admissions to the newly formed universities and technical colleges, in which the descendants of the samurai class were heavily overrepresented. Table 10.2 shows the percentages of samurai and commoners in the major higher-education institutions in 1890 and 1900. Since the descendants of the samurai constituted 5.3 percent of the population, in 1890 the samurai were graduating at twelve times the expected rate from imperial universities, and commoners at less than half the expected rate.[5]

The proportion of commoners in the universities rose quickly, however. By 1900, samurai were graduating at only nine times the expected rate. However, because the samurai were so heavily overrepresented initially, the rate of decline in their advantage is still slow once we calculate the implied persistence rate.

Table 10.3 shows the implied relative representation of the samurai in the universities and the implied intergenerational correlation of educational status. This analysis assumes that university students represented the top 1 percent of the status distribution and that by 1890 the samurai had the same variance of underlying social status as the general population. The implied intergenerational correlation is high, 0.66–0.72. A wider estimate, based on a more comprehensive set of higher-education programs, suggests an average persistence rate of 0.73 for this period.[6] Thus even though the raw data of table 10.2 might appear to suggest high rates of social mobility, it actually implies slow mobility rates during the Meiji era.

This intergenerational correlation in status is calculated assuming that the samurai share of the university-aged population remained constant between 1890 and 1900. There is reason to believe that, if anything, their population share was declining. For example, the source that gives samurai and commoner pop-

[5] Amano 1990, 192.
[6] Clark and Ishii 2013.

TABLE 10.3. Implied persistence rates for the samurai, 1890–1900

	Relative representation			Implied persistence rate
	1890	1895	1900	
Imperial universities	11.9	11.1	9.6	0.72
Higher schools	11.6	11.2	9.0	0.66

TABLE 10.4. Percentage of samurai government officials and persistence rates, 1872–82

Year	Central government	Local government
1872	78	70
1876	78	—
1882	61	58
Implied persistence rate	0.71	0.72

ulations in 1881 estimates an average family size for samurai of 4.54, compared to 4.78 for commoners.[7] Any decline in the share of samurai in the young population between 1890 and 1900 would imply a smaller decline in relative representation of samurai at universities and professional schools and hence an even higher persistence rate.

Harry Harootunian gives the share of central and local government employees in 1872 to 1882 who were of samurai origin.[8] These findings are summarized in table 10.4. The share of samurai among government officials also greatly exceeded their share in the general population in 1872. But as with graduates of the universities, this share began immediately to decline. Again, however, the rate of decline was consistent, with a high rate of persistence of 0.72. (This persistence rate again is calculated assuming that the samurai population share was constant over time.) So despite the many social and economic changes occurring in Japan in the Meiji period, the rate of downward mobility of the former samurai is once again the standard rate. This was another social revolution that had surprisingly little bite on the social elite.

[7] Sonoda 1990, 103.
[8] Harootunian 1959.

After 1947, Japanese sources no longer categorize people by samurai or *kazoku* ancestry. These earlier distinctions of caste and privilege have been washed away in the world of the salaryman. But again it is possible to measure the fates of these earlier elites, and their rate of social mobility, by turning to the rare surnames that were associated with samurai or *kazoku* ancestry.

A candidate list of samurai surnames was formed from a genealogy of samurai families assembled by the government in 1812.[9] Similarly, a genealogy compiled by descendants of the *kazoku* allows construction of a complete list of surnames once held by *kazoku*.

By 1898 surnames in Japan had become strictly hereditary, with little possibility that the rare surnames of the elite were being adopted by less distinguished families. The 1898 Family Registration Law dictated that each household have a surname inherited by children, with a married woman adopting her husband's surname.[10] Adopted children took the surname of the head of the family.[11] The Family Registration Act of 1947 established that only the head of a family could apply for a surname change; if granted, it applied to the entire family. Surname changes were to be granted only in cases of "unavoidable reasons." We thus assume little surname changing after 1947.

Measuring inheritance of position by surname for Japanese elites is potentially complicated by the prevalence of adoption among upper-class groups. In Japan, where there is no male heir, it has always been quite common for high-status families to adopt a son-in-law to carry on the family name and lineage. Indeed, figures on adult adoptions in Japan in recent decades suggest, remarkably, that as much as 10 percent of each male cohort has been adopted by another family, and that this pattern has prevailed since at least 1955.[12] Samurai and *kazoku* families without sons traditionally engaged in this practice on a large scale.[13] A study of the samurai in the Tokugawa era, for example, suggests substantial rates of adult male adoption.[14]

---

[9] Takayanagi, Okayama, and Saiki 1964.

[10] Ando 1999, 259.

[11] Kitaoji 1971, 1046.

[12] Mehrotra et al., 2011, table 1. The number of adult adoptions in 1955 suggests that about 7 percent of each male cohort were adopted as adults.

[13] Lebra 1989, 106–32.

[14] Moore 1970.

Since men will only be adopted as sons if they are at least moderately successful socially, adoptions potentially bias estimated persistence rates upward. However, the bias is likely modest. Suppose, for example, that a quarter of the inheritors of high-status surnames are adopted sons. Suppose also that in these cases, the sons match the status of the adoptive fathers exactly. If the true intergenerational correlation of status is 0.75, as we observe for other societies above, then in Japan the upward bias in the measured intergenerational correlation would be 0.06. Thus even large-scale selective adult adoptions have only a modest and predictable effect on measured persistence rates.

The original surname lists include many widely held surnames. To narrow the list to surnames that were more closely associated with *kazoku* and samurai families, only rarer surnames from the list were employed in measuring mobility. Rarer surnames were defined as those now held by fewer than ten people per million (1,270 or fewer people). Unlike China, Japan has considerable surname variety: there are an estimated 110,000 Japanese surnames. So there are reasonable numbers of rare surnames associated with these earlier elites.

One complication of this approach involves the romanization of Japanese names. Both the sources of the candidate elite surnames give surnames in kanji, the Japanese character system. The source for the modern frequency of these surnames is Public Profiler's World Family Names, an Internet surname database. Its data for Japan are derived from the surnames associated with forty-five million of the estimated total of fifty-two million households in Japan in 2007. But these names are romanized on the basis of pronunciation, a method that creates difficulties in matching the modern names with the original kanji versions.[15] Table 10.5 shows the numerical composition of our two rare surname samples.

The relative representation of the rare elite surnames was calculated for a variety of high-status occupations in modern Japan: medical researchers, 1989–90;[16] attorneys, 1987; corporate managers, 1993; university professors, 2005; and scholarly authors, 1990–2012. In all cases these surnames are overrepresented with respect to their incidence in the general population, as shown in figure 10.2. The average rate of representation is three times the expected rate for the *kozaku* and 4.3 times the expected rate for the samurai surnames.

Thus these rare surnames are on average overrepresented in modern Japanese groups of high social status across a broad range of occupations. Interest-

---

[15] See Clark and Ishii 2013.
[16] No sources were available listing only regular physicians.

TABLE 10.5. The rare surname samples

Estimated number of surname holders	Kazoku		Samurai	
	Number of surnames	Implied number of people with names	Number of surnames	Implied number of people with names
0–99	59	1,658	68	1,638
100–199	15	1,890	18	2,450
200–399	19	5,940	19	5,714
400–999	33	24,098	69	48,480
1,000–1,240	7	7,757	15	16,514
All	132	41,343	189	74,797

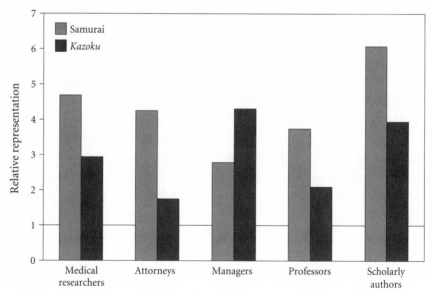

FIGURE 10.2. Relative representation of rare surnames among high-status groups, Japan, 1989–2012.

ingly, the samurai surnames, despite their being selected from a genealogy of 1812, are still much more heavily overrepresented in four of the five high-status groups in the modern era than are the *kazoku* surnames.

The expectation is that the rarer these surnames are today, the more likely that the holders are actually samurai or *kazoku* descendants. Thus the rarer the

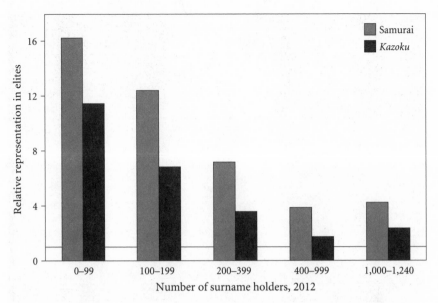

FIGURE 10.3. Relative representation of samurai and *kazoku* surnames by estimated frequency of surname in Japanese population, ca. 2007.

surnames, the greater their predicted overrepresentation among elites. Figure 10.3 shows relative representation controlling for the frequency of the surnames. Several things stand out. First, the rarer the surname, the higher indeed its relative representation. The rarest surnames are 12–16 times overrepresented, whereas the most common are only 2–4 times overrepresented. Some of this effect may, however, be a statistical artifact. Since these surname frequencies are based on only a sample (though a very large one) of family surnames in Japan, they give an imperfect measure of the stock of each surname in the population at large. Thus the surnames assigned to the rarest groups tend to be those whose true frequency in the population is greater. Experience elsewhere suggests that the true frequency of these rarest surnames is at least a quarter greater than reported.

But the overrepresentation of the rarest surnames is so great that even if their true frequencies were double the reported figure, they would still be greatly overrepresented. This supports the idea that the rarer the *kazoku* or samurai surnames now, the more likely it is that modern bearers of the name are descendants of *kazoku* or samurai forebears.

Second, as before, samurai surnames, even controlling for frequency, are now more overrepresented among elites than *kazoku* surnames. If samurai descendants never intermarried with descendants of commoners, then, assuming

FIGURE 10.4. From samurai to salarymen.

the same fertility, their descendants would now constitute 5 percent of the population. But figure 10.3 suggests that samurai descendants may be as much as ten times overrepresented among modern Japanese elites. That rate implies that half the modern elites are descended from the samurai. Intermarriage would greatly expand the share of the modern population of samurai descent. But if the samurai are really ten times overrepresented in modern elites, intermarriage must have been limited, so that their descendants constitute no more than 10 percent of the modern population.

Tracking the most common surnames provides confirmation that the samurai and *kazoku* descendants are still heavily overrepresented among modern Japanese elites (figure 10.4). Most commoners acquired surnames only after 1868, when the government required all families to adopt surnames to aid military conscription, taxation, and postal delivery. Many previously high-status surnames were adopted by commoners. Thus the name Fujiwara, originally the name of a powerful and distinguished medieval family, is now held by more than three hundred thousand Japanese. It is clear that any very common surname in Japan must have been held disproportionately by commoners in the Meiji era. Thus, if we look at the status of the most common surnames, we can determine the relative status of the descendants of the commoners of 1868 in modern Japan.

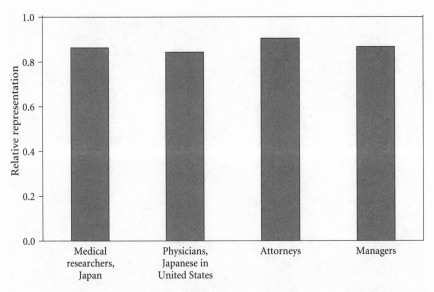

FIGURE 10.5. Relative representation of common surnames among elites, Japan, 1980–2012.

Taking the fifty most common surnames in Japan, which together account for a quarter of the population, we find that their relative representation among elites in Japan is always less than one. Typically these surnames occur at only 85 percent of the rate expected from their population shares (see figure 10.5). Interestingly, they are equally underrepresented among physicians in Japan and among physicians trained in Japan who are now practicing in the United States.

SOCIAL MOBILITY RATES, 1900–2012

To calculate the relative representation of *kazoku* and samurai surnames among elites as far back as 1900 requires knowing the share of these surnames in the general population in earlier generations. There is some evidence of lower fertility among elites, which would imply smaller elite-surname population shares earlier. In the years 1940–67, for example, marriages involving highly educated husbands or wives produced one-fifth fewer births than those of couples with lower educational attainment.[17] But the prevalence of adult male adoption among the elite would create a countervailing tendency for elite-surname population shares to increase, if some of the adoptees originally had average-status sur-

[17] Hashimoto 1974, S184.

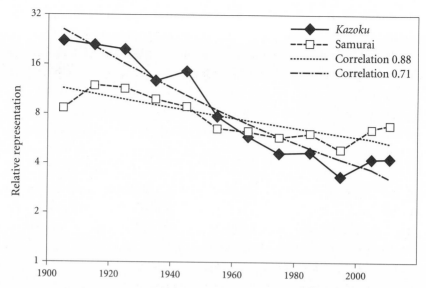

FIGURE 10.6. Relative representation of *kazoku* and samurai surnames among authors of scholarly publications, 1900–2012.

names. Absent better data, it is assumed that the population share of these surnames was the same in 1900 as in 2007.

Google Scholar gives measures of the number of publications associated with samurai, *kazoku*, and common surnames for the period 1900–2012.[18] To calculate the relative representation of these surnames among publications by Japanese authors requires, however, that the total stock of such publications be estimated for every decade. This is done by measuring publications by authors holding the ten most common Japanese names in each decade.[19]

Figure 10.6 plots the relative representation of samurai and *kazoku* rare surnames among authors of scholarly publications by decade from 1900. Both the samurai and *kazoku* surnames are heavily overrepresented in the initial decades, with publication rates of eleven and twenty-one times those of the average person in Japan, respectively. That relative representation declines over time, but is still more than four for both groups from 1990 to 2012. Indeed, for

[18] Clark and Ishii (2013) detail some complications that arise in performing this exercise.

[19] This stock of all publications is adjusted upward by 13 percent to allow for the expected underrepresentation of common surnames among elite groups such as authors, as seen in figure 10.5.

both groups, there is an increase in relative representation in the years 2000 and later.

The implied intergenerational correlation of publication rates, assuming a standard thirty-year generation, is 0.71 for the *kazoku* and 0.88 for the samurai. There is no sign of any increase in mobility rates after the reforms of 1947. Again, adult male adoption may bias these estimates up by as much as .06. But even allowing for this, social mobility rates are clearly just as low in Japan as in the other countries studied, and they are just as low after 1900 as they were in the early Meiji period.

The magnitude and pattern of these results for authors is confirmed by the representation of these surnames among medical researchers. Listings are available of medical researchers in Japan for 1965–66 and 1989–90, a twenty-five-year interval. Table 10.6 shows the relative representation of the *kazoku* and samurai rare surnames among medical researchers in each year. The names are again distinctly overrepresented. In the bottom row of the table are the implied persistence rates, adjusted to a thirty-year generation. The values are slightly lower than for the publications, at 0.63 for *kazoku* and 0.82 for samurai surnames. But this difference could be due to chance. Because of the small populations bearing these rare surnames (41,000 and 75,000 respectively circa 1990), the number of observed medical researchers in each period is small.

Another estimate of social mobility in Japan comes from the 2012 American Medical Association directory. This lists more than a thousand Japanese-trained physicians practicing in the United States, a fifth of whom hold one of the fifty most common Japanese surnames. The AMA data also give the date of graduation of each registrant. The Japanese physicians can thus be divided into two generations, those graduating between 1950 and 1979 and those graduating

TABLE 10.6. Relative representation of samurai and *kazoku* among medical researchers, 1965–89

Year	Samurai	*Kazoku*
Observed 1965–66	30	13
Observed 1989–90	70	23
1965–66	5.99	4.95
1989–90	4.69	2.94
Implied persistence rate	0.84	0.64

between 1980 and 2012. The relative representation of physicians with these common surnames among this group is 0.77 for the period 1950–79 and 0.85 for 1980–2012. Thus, again, we see signs of regression toward the mean. But, assuming that doctors represent the top 0.5 percent of the society, the persistence rate implied by this rate of convergence is 0.65. This estimate has a very high potential measurement error, but it is another sign that the rate of social mobility in Japan is much lower in the modern era than conventionally estimated.

SAMURAI VERSUS *KAZOKU* MOBILITY RATES

The persistence rates estimated for the *kazoku* for 1900 and later are in the range 0.64–0.71, and for common surnames the rate is 0.65. This is similar to but perhaps a bit lower than in other countries. However, the persistence rates for the surnames associated with the samurai are 0.84–0.88, higher than elsewhere. There is also evidence that the samurai surnames are now more elite than the *kazoku* surnames, even though circa 1900 the *kazoku* were the most elite group in Japanese society. Why has regression to the mean across all these measures been faster for the *kazoku* than for the samurai descendants?

One interesting difference between the two groups is that all the samurai surnames were identified as belonging to at least one samurai family in 1812, whereas the *kazoku* surnames were identified as belonging to families added to the *kazoku* between 1869 and 1946. Only 42 percent of the *kazoku* derived from the hereditary nobility; the other 58 percent were people awarded titles in recognition of distinction in the military, administration, commerce, and other professions between 1869 and 1946.

According to the theory posited in chapter 6, observed status on any dimension is related only with some degree of error to an underlying social status, which regresses slowly to the mean. When we observe samurai publication rates for 1900 onward, using Google Scholar, to get a measure of observed status, the selection of surnames is based on samurai names from 1812. Thus the expected value of the underlying status equals that of observed status for 1900 and later. Publication rates are an accurate indicator of samurai status overall. We thus observe in the publication rates the rate of regression of underlying status, even though publications are just a partial indicator.

However, in the case of the *kazoku*, many of whom achieved prominence only after 1880 and constituted the initial cohort of this elite, those showing up as authors between 1900 and 1949, and even in the 1950s and 1960s, include many individuals newly appointed to the *kazoku* because of their distinction in scholarly or technical fields. Thus for this group, the expected error relating observed status (measured by number of publications) to underlying status is positive on average. The observed regression to the mean for observed status is thus greater than that for underlying status, because in the succeeding generations the average error linking publication rates to underlying status is once again zero.

Despite this observed faster regression to the mean of the *kazoku*, then, there may well be no inherent difference in the social mobility rates of the *kazoku* and the samurai descendants after 1947. If that is the case, however, we would expect that by the 1970s, when most of the first-generation *kazoku* were dead, then the rate of regression to the mean of both groups should be the same. The expected error term relating their observed status on any measure to underlying status is now zero for both groups. However, even in this later period, the samurai descendants regress more slowly to the mean than the *kazoku* descendants. The reason for this difference remains a puzzle.

Korea

In South Korea, as in Japan, since 1948 there has been a profound remaking of the political and social order that has displaced previous elites from any privileged social position. The period of Japanese colonial rule, 1910–45, and the disruptions created by the regime in North Korea after 1945 could be expected to have led to a profound dislocation by 1948 of the traditional elites of the long-lasting Joseon dynasty. This was followed by a period of sustained and rapid industrialization, with substantial migrations of people to urban areas. Korea is also, like Japan, a society of great ethnic and cultural homogeneity, a fact that, again, would lead us to expect a great deal of social mobility in South Korea in the period 1948–2013. Korea also appears by conventional measures to be a society of high social mobility: a recent study of income mobility across generations reports a persistence rate of 0.35.[20]

Korea does not initially seem like a promising society in which to study social mobility using surnames. The three most common surnames in Korea—*Kim, Lee,* and *Park*—are held by two-fifths of the population. However, as in China, the lack of variety in surnames led to the convention of identifying people both by surname and by family place of origin. Thus, for the surname *Kim,*

[20] Ueda 2013.

which is held by a quarter of all Koreans, in 2000 the census in Korea recorded 348 different clans, or *bon-guan*. Membership in these clans is patrilineal. Clan membership was important in Korea for delineating possible marriage partners: traditionally, marriage had to be to someone outside the *bon-guan*. Indeed, until 1997, it was not legal for Koreans to marry within their *bon-guan*.

In total, these surname–place of origin combinations provide 3,783 distinctive family names by 2000. There have been claims that although clan membership is supposed to descend strictly through the male line, in the nineteenth century many arrivistes from lower-status groups affiliated themselves fraudulently with clans of distinguished lineage. Even if that is correct, by 1898, under the Japanese Family Registration Law all family names became fixed in Korea, so the modern surname-*bon-guan* combinations indicate with high fidelity relationships to people born more than a hundred years ago.

In a recent paper, Christopher Paik applies the methods of this book to estimate educational mobility rates in South Korea for the years 1955–2000, using these surname–place of origin designations.[21] Korea, like China, had a national examination system in the Joseon imperial era (1368–1894). Extensive records exist of the names of successful candidates in these exams. From these records, Paik assigns to each surname and *bon-guan* combination (taken from the 1985 census) a weighted average exam-success rate, the weights being based on the prestige of the exam. These rates vary from 0 to as high as thirty-six per thousand for the Suh of Daegu, a clan that constituted 0.34 percent of the 1985 Korean population. The largest surname–place of origin group in Korea today is the oldest branch of the Kim of Gimahae, to which nearly 1 percent of Koreans belong. But their exam-success rate was only 0.05 per thousand.

For both 1985 and 2000, the Korean census records surname-*bon-guan* frequencies for all of the country's 192 districts. Paik can thus calculate the average exam status of surnames within each district. The censuses of 1955, 1970, 1985, and 2000 also give the average years of education attained per district for those age 25–39. Paik can thus also assign to each district in each of these years a standardized educational achievement score.

If the past history of families before 1898 has no effect on current outcomes, then there should be no correlation between the average exam status score by district and current educational achievement. But for all four years

---

[21] Paik 2013.

examined, Paik finds a significant association.[22] The higher the exam lineage status for the average surname in the district, the higher was the educational attainment of the 25–39 age group in each census year.

But Paik also observes that the relationship between exam status and district education levels for the 25–39 cohort is strongest for 1955 and weakest for 2000. This weakening is due to social mobility. From the rate of decline in correlation, it is possible to infer the underlying persistence parameter for modern Korea. The implied intergenerational persistence rate is 0.86 from 1985 to 2000, 0.86 from 1970 to 1985, and 0.74 from 1955 to 1970. On average, the implied persistence rate for educational status in Korea from 1955 to 2000 is thus 0.82.

Thus despite the homogeneity of Korean society and the remaking of social institutions on a large scale several times in the past century, social mobility in Korea is no faster than in other countries and potentially slower. Like Sweden and Japan, Korea illustrates how widely conventional estimates of social mobility can vary from underlying rates of social mobility.

Conclusion

The samurai and *kazoku* show surprising persistence as elites in modern Japanese society, despite the samurai having lost any legal privileges by 1871 and the *kazoku* having lost theirs by 1947. In particular, if the descendants of the samurai constitute 5 percent of the modern Japanese population, then they could still constitute anywhere between 20 and 50 percent of modern Japanese elites. The homogeneity of Japanese society does not lead to a higher rate of social mobility than we observe in more ethnically, racially, and religiously diverse societies, such as the United States. Reinforcing this finding, Korea, another highly homogeneous society, again shows rates of social mobility that are no faster than in socially and ethnically fractured societies such as the United States.

[22] For 1970 and 1955, exam status in each district is assumed to be the same as in 1985.

ELEVEN

Chile

Mobility among the Oligarchs

C HILE IS NOW ONE OF SOUTH AMERICA'S more prosperous economies. Its income per capita equals that of Argentina, although it is still only about one-third that of the United States. But like its neighbors, Chile is characterized by inequalities in income and wealth that are among the highest in the world. The Gini coefficient measuring income inequality is 0.55 for Chile, compared to 0.26 for Sweden (see figure 1.3). Despite Chile's relatively high average income, poverty is highly visible, as illustrated by the shanty town in the port city of Valparaiso shown in figure 11.1.

A trope of modern discussions of mobility has been that inequality breeds immobility. Empirical studies of the connection between inequality and mobility rates across countries appear to confirm this assertion. In these studies, South American countries register high degrees of inequality and low levels of social mobility.[1]

However, the mechanisms that might explain this empirical association between inequality and immobility are unclear. One explanation is an analogy: the greater the distances between the rungs of the economic ladder, the harder it is for people at the bottom to climb up the ladder. But this analogy is entirely spurious as an argument for lower social mobility. In a society such as the United States or Chile, where the rungs in the income ladder are further apart, the same rate of occupational mobility as in Sweden produces much greater changes in income. So the ordinary processes of occupational mobility ensure

[1] There is debate about how social mobility in Chile compares with that of other South American countries, but no question that it is lower than in the Nordic countries.

FIGURE 11.1. Shantytown, Valparaiso, Chile.

the same proportional movements in income toward the mean as are seen in Sweden, where the rungs of the income ladder are closer together. If the rungs on the income ladder are farther apart in the United States or Chile, the upward steps that are possible through occupational mobility are correspondingly greater. So the distance between the analogical ladder rungs explain nothing about rates of social mobility.

In chapter 6 it was argued that the inequality-immobility association is an illusion created by the fact that common measures of social status, such as income, indicate only with some degree of error the true underlying status of families. In societies like Sweden, where ranges of income and wealth are compressed, these measures are particularly poor indicators of underlying social status. Consequently, these societies seem to have rapid rates of social mobility.

In contrast, in a society of great income and wealth inequality such as Chile, these factors are much better indicators of the true social status of families: income mobility comes closer to measuring the true underlying rate of social mobility. This chapter investigates whether social mobility rates in an inegalitarian society such as Chile truly are lower than in egalitarian Sweden.

The 2004 Chilean Electoral Register

Chile provides a nice instrument which can be used to estimate social mobility over the past sixty years: the 2004 electoral register. This data set provides the full name, date of birth, profession, and place of residence of all voters—more than eight million people. Using this register, the population can be divided into two birth generations, 1920–49 and 1950–79, and average social status measured across these generations. The youngest persons under this division were age 25 at the time of the census and so already had an occupation. Alternatively, people can be divided into six birth decades, starting in 1920–29 and ending with those born 1970–79.

The electoral register does not provide data on income or wealth, but knowing individuals' occupations, their income can be estimated from the average income for those occupations (this information is available for more than three hundred occupations).[2] Knowing average earnings by location, it is also possible to calculate for each person earnings based on their location. These "locational earnings" provide a nice check on occupational earnings, since for some occupational categories (e.g., "employee," "merchant," or "farmer") the occupational-income measure involves much error. Estimating earnings in multiple ways with different sources of error makes the results more robust.

Evidence that these occupational and locational earnings estimates are informative about social status is shown in figure 11.2. Each *comuna* (municipality) in Chile has an estimated average measure on the Human Development Index (HDI) calculated for 1990–98 by the United Nations Development Program in its study of the Chilean economy.[3] The figure groups the *comunas* in Chile into five categories with ranks 0.5–0.59 through 0.9–1.0 on this index. The average occupational earnings for each of these *comuna* groupings is calculated using the 2004 electoral register. These are shown on the vertical axis. Because average earnings by location are also known, average earnings for each of the *comuna* are also calculable. The figure shows that the two inferred earnings measures are highly correlated and, further, that both these earnings measures are highly correlated with the broader measure of HDI by *comuna*. Thus

[2] Students, retirees, and housewives are excluded. Chile, Ministerio del Trabajo y Prevision Social 2008.

[3] Chile, Ministry of Planning and Cooperation 2006. HDI is a measure that includes life expectancy, education, and income.

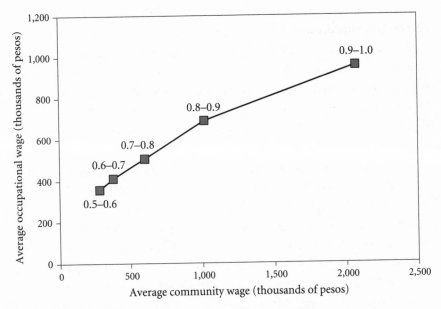

FIGURE 11.2. Salaries by community, Human Development Index grouping.

there is good information from the electoral census not just on implied earnings, but also on more general implied living conditions.

Underclass and Elite Surname Groups

As in earlier chapters, social mobility in Chile is estimated by identifying surnames that had high or low status before 1920 and then measuring how quickly the average status of these surnames regresses to the mean using the information from the electoral register.

One general feature of Chile's population is an inverse correlation between social class and degree of indigenous ancestry. Studies suggest that for the upper class, 73–91 percent of their genetics is Caucasian, for the middle class 68–70 percent, and for the lower class 41–48 percent.[4] So the Mapuche, the major indigenous population of Chile, would be expected to be at the lowest rung of the social ladder.

[4] Cruz-Coke and Moreno 1994, table 2.

When the Spaniards first arrived in Chile, the Mapuche had been fending off the Incas for decades. They occupied a vast amount of land in southern Chile, from Talca to Valdivia. The rich natural terrain had allowed them to maintain a population estimated in the hundreds of thousands while remaining hunter-gatherers. The Spaniards eventually recognized the Bío-Bío River as the border between the areas of Spanish control and independent Mapuche terrain. Under Spanish influence, the Mapuche economy shifted to subsistence agriculture and cattle herding.

From 1861 to 1883, the Chilean government progressively conquered Mapuche territory and incorporated it, and the Mapuche people, into Chile. By 1900 the Mapuche held titles to only one-tenth of their original land. They lacked the technology and know-how to compete in the new economic environment they had been compelled to enter. They became indebted and a source of low-skill labor for the main landowners.

Four percent of the contemporary Chilean population is of Mapuche origin. The Mapuche have distinctive surnames, over four hundred of which can be identified.[5] This cohort of surnames thus represents the lowest-skilled and most disadvantaged community in Chile. Although they used to be a rural population, confined to southern Chile, today nearly half the Mapuche reside in the largest city, Santiago.

At the other end of the social scale in colonial times were the *encomenderos*. These were Europeans supposedly appointed as protectors of the indigenous population, but in reality grandees living off the labor of their charges. The tributes and benefits obtained by the *encomenderos* varied over time, but they undoubtedly represented the dominant socioeconomic elite of a polarized society.[6] The list of *encomendero* surnames used here consists of rare surnames such as *Oyarzun, Ureta,* and *Iparaguirre,* all of which had at least one *encomendero* holder but fewer than fifty holders in 1853 and 2004.[7] These were the original oligarchs of the colonial era.

Another influential and prosperous colonial elite was the Basque community. A significant proportion of governors under the Spanish had Basque last names. By 1800, a quarter of the Chilean population was of Basque origin. The Basques specialized in trade and commerce, employing important connections

[5] Galdames (2008) uses phonetic transcription to generate a compilation of Mapuche surnames that is used here.

[6] González Pomes 1966.

[7] The *encomendero* surnames were derived from Amunátegui Solar 1932 and Góngora 1970.

with their relatives in Europe. They eventually married into the landed colonial elite and formed the Castilian-Basque aristocracy that played a substantial role in Chilean history. To track their social status, a randomly chosen group of Basque last names appearing in the 1853 census is employed. Most of them are rare surnames.[8]

Another means of identifying elites is by landholdings. An agricultural yield report was compiled in 1853 to determine land taxes.[9] This report includes the records of a large sample of landowners, who together possessed nearly fifteen thousand parcels of land. Owners with rare surnames (those appearing only three to thirty times in the 1853 census) were selected and divided into four wealth groups. These were based on the average annual value in pesos of the land owned: 350 or less (small); 350–1499 (medium); 1500–4999 (large); and 5,000 or more (very large). The last group represents the landowning elite in Chile in 1853.

In the 1920s, Juvenal Valenzuela created a detailed list of the major agricultural estates in Chile.[10] He visited them and estimated the land quality and area irrigated to estimate the value of each estate. He found that in 1920, 10 percent of the landowners held 90 percent of the land, and he created a list of the top one thousand owners. From this list have been selected the surnames that had a frequency of three to thirty in the earliest-born cohorts in the 2004 electoral register. These are the large landowners of 1920.

One additional wealth-based elite is a set of the rare surnames of the rich of the nineteenth century. After independence, between 1830 and 1930, Chile experienced a period of territorial expansion and economic growth (along with social unrest and recurrent civil war), due in part to the exploitation of mineral resources. The population quadrupled as the economy grew. The benefits of the expansion were perceived as being primarily enjoyed by the elite. From the work of Sergio Villalobos and Ricardo Nazer Ahumada, among other sources, it is possible to create a list of the rare surnames of the nineteenth-century commercial and mining elite.[11]

Another elite group of the nineteenth century was Italian immigrants. Half of the Italian immigrants who entered Chile in 1853 were involved in commerce or were skilled professionals. More than 80 percent of Italian immigrants could

[8] Basque surnames were identified from Irigoyen 1881 and Narbarte 1992.
[9] Chile, Estado que manifiesta la renta agrícola 1855.
[10] Valenzuela O. 1923.
[11] Villalobos 1990; Nazer Ahumada 1993, 2000.

read and write in 1865, compared to 35 percent of the host Chilean population.[12] The Chilean electoral register of 2004 lists over six hundred thousand Chileans of Italian descent. A sample of surnames of the more successful Italian families was obtained from the *Commercial and Industrial Census of the Italian Colony in Chile for 1926–27,* from which were selected surnames held by dentists, doctors, jewelers, factory owners, and the like.[13] Most of the surnames are rare.

The Germans were arguably the most notable of all the more recent immigrant groups in Chile, due to both their numbers relative to other groups and their strong presence in economic, military, and social elites. The most important of the early waves of German immigration came after the enactment of the 1845 Law of Selective Immigration, which gave special incentives to more skilled and wealthier Germans and Austrians. This law aimed to promote economic growth by populating the south-central part of the country. The idea was to create a backbone of Western work ethics and culture and to dilute native influences. Favored immigrants were given five-year loans, livestock, land, and free transportation to Chile for the entire family. Thus 54 percent of all Germans who entered Chile in 1865 were skilled workers, craftsmen, or involved in commerce. More than 82 percent of them could read and write.

Lists of successful Germans circa 1920 are drawn from the *Gazette of the Austral Region of Chile* of 1920, which lists commercial and industrial firms and their owners, as well as professionals dedicated to the service industry, passenger listings, and a genealogical dictionary of surname origins.[14] Most of the German surnames are rare in Chile, although, again, the surnames were not selected on that basis.

French immigration to Chile was concentrated in the late nineteenth century. By 1930, well over twenty thousand French immigrants had been recorded. Like their Italian and German counterparts, they were merchants, artisans, and professionals, with above-average literacy rates. The list of French surnames used here is derived from a list of over five hundred significant French businessmen and entrepreneurs recorded in Chile between 1907 and 1920 in consular reports. Since most of these surnames are rare in Chile, this constitutes a list of surnames of prosperous French immigrants circa 1920.[15]

[12] Chile, Oficina del Censo 1866.
[13] Pellegrino 1927.
[14] Valenzuela O. 1920.
[15] Sloan, n.d.

Table 11.1 summarizes the numbers of people from each of these surname groups in the 2004 census who were born in the periods 1920–49 and 1950–79. The ratio of the numbers born in the later period and the earlier reveals the relative social status of these groups. For the country as a whole, the ratio is 2.3. For the Mapuche, the lowest-status group, this ratio is higher, at 2.47. The difference reflects a combination of likely higher fertility among poorer groups and lower longevity in the older age cohort.

Confirmation that the ratio is closely linked to status comes from the surnames of the 1853 landowners. Ranking these by in increasing order by value of their land, the ratios are 2.26, 2.10, 1.91, and 1.89. Thus 150 years later, in 2004, the status of landowners in 1853 continues to influence outcomes, suggesting that there is considerable intergenerational persistence in Chile.

Table 11.2 shows average occupational income by surname group relative to the average for all persons for those born in the periods 1920–49 and 1950–79. Also shown is the implied intergenerational correlation of average income. The individual estimates vary from 0.70 to 0.95, with an average of 0.84. Estimated

TABLE 11.1. Surname samples in 2004 Chilean electoral register

Group	Notes	Number in birth cohort		Ratio (1950–79/ 1920–49)
		1920–49	1950–79	
Encomenderos	Early elite	839	1,557	1.86
Mapuche	Indigenous	7,036	17,389	2.47
Basque	Early elite	8,755	17,841	2.04
French	1920 elite	1,402	2,494	1.78
German	1920 elite	2,452	4,337	1.77
Italians	1920 elite	1,132	1,981	1.75
Landowners				
1853, small		15,988	36,070	2.26
1853, medium		824	1,731	2.10
1853, large		1,874	3,580	1.91
1853, very large		857	1,621	1.89
1920, large		1,680	3,069	1.83
Rich, nineteenth century		1,058	2,012	1.90

TABLE 11.2. Intergenerational correlation of occupational and locational income by surname group from 2004 electoral register

Group	Occupational income relative to birth-cohort average		Implied correlation, occupational income	Implied correlation, locational income
	1920–49	1950–79		
Encomenderos	1.54	1.45	0.76	0.83
Mapuche	0.68	0.75	0.79	0.63
Basque	1.35	1.27	0.75	0.79
French	1.57	1.51	0.88	1.01
German	1.63	1.56	0.93	0.86
Italians	1.67	1.53	0.85	0.89
Landowners				
1853, small	1.01	1.01	—	—
1853, medium	1.41	1.27	0.70	0.85
1853, large	1.59	1.53	0.92	0.82
1853, extra large	1.74	1.71	0.95	0.81
1920, large	1.79	1.73	0.92	0.81
Rich, nineteenth century	1.61	1.54	0.90	0.86
Average	—	—	0.84	0.83

correlations using locational estimates of average income are shown in the last column. The individual estimates of persistence vary here, but the average is very close to that for occupational income, at 0.83.

As in the other countries, the social mobility rates estimated here are much slower than those estimated by conventional methods. Núñez and Miranda, for example, derive estimates of only 0.52–0.67 for income and educational persistence using conventional methods.[16]

The estimates of the intergenerational correlation for the Mapuche, the one poor group in the table, are lower in each case than the average: 0.79 for occupational income and 0.63 for locational income. These results may reflect higher

---

[16] Núñez and Miranda 2007. These are high for conventional estimates compared to those for Nordic countries, or even Canada, the United Kingdom, and the United States.

social mobility by the Mapuche than in the rest of the society: as noted, the Mapuche have relocated in large numbers from rural areas to Santiago. But these figures may also reflect the difficulty in estimating occupational and locational earnings for this still heavily rural group.

There is a distinct possibility that these correlation estimates are systematically biased upward. Earnings vary substantially within each occupation. An elite group, such as the descendants of the landholders of 1920, is likely to produce attorneys who earn more than the typical attorney and doctors who earn more than the average doctor. As this elite group regresses toward the mean, so will the salaries of group members in high-income occupations. Thus there is a second type of earnings regression for elite and underclass groups that is not reflected in the average figure for occupational earnings. The intergenerational correlations reported represent upper bounds for the intergenerational correlation of earnings and of underlying status.

The analysis so far shows that the underlying rate of social mobility in modern Chile is indeed low. Surnames that were high status in the colonial era, such as those of the *encomenderos* and the Basques, have remained high status in the generation born in the years 1950–79. The way that elite surname groups were identified does not affect the measured rates of social mobility. If they are defined as ethnic groups—Italians, French, Germans, Mapuche—then they show the average rates of social mobility. If the elite surnames are defined purely based on their earlier wealth, such as landholdings in 1853 or 1920, or wealth in the nineteenth century, then mobility rates are very similar.

Thus the low mobility rates observed using surnames in Chile are not the result of ethnic groups walling themselves off and marrying only endogamously. In the surname groups defined by wealth, only rare surnames were used, so the mobility being measured here is for individual families of landowners or industrialists, which do not experience much faster rates of social mobility. It is not that there is plenty of individual family mobility within ethnic groups such as the German community, but a tendency within that group for everyone to regress to a higher German mean occupational status. Mobility is generally low.

However, there is no evidence that Chile's social mobility rates are any different from those of the United States, the United Kingdom, Sweden, or even Communist China. Chile serves instead to confirm the hypothesis that social mobility rates are mainly determined within families and are mostly independent of social institutions.

Mobility by Decade

Above, mobility is measured by generation. But it is also interesting to consider mobility by decade, even though with this approach random fluctuations appear because of the smaller amounts of data. This approach is of interest for Chile because of its relatively short-term but dramatic social disruptions in the later twentieth century. The years 1964–73, under the presidencies of Eduardo Frei and Salvador Allende, saw significant attempts to improve the educational outcomes for the poorer sections of Chilean society. That social experiment came to a calamitous end with Augusto Pinochet's coup d'état of 1973 (figure 11.3) and the ensuing years of repression under military rule. During Pinochet's dictatorship (1973–1990), there was reduced expenditure on public education and programs targeted at the poor and an expansion of the private sector in higher education. If public support had any effects on social mobility, then we would expect that the people born in the decade 1950–59, many of whom enjoyed the benefits of the Frei and Allende social programs as they attended secondary school and college, would experience enhanced mobility. In contrast, the people born in the decade 1970–79, most of whom were educated in the Pinochet years, should experience more restricted mobility.

FIGURE 11.3. The assault on the presidential palace during the 1973 Chilean coup d'état.

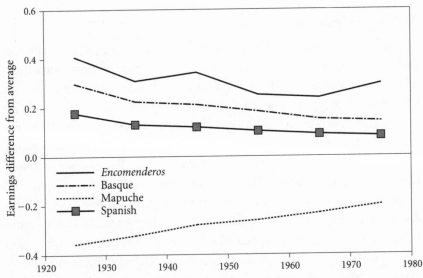

FIGURE 11.4. Earnings variation by birth decade by surname type, colonial elites and underclasses, 1920–79.

Figure 11.4 shows occupational incomes by decade for a set of surname groups from the colonial era, including the *encomenderos* and the Mapuche. The incomes are shown essentially as their variation above and below the mean occupational income for people of that decade.[17] The scaling of the figure means that social mobility rates are portrayed by the slope of the line. It is evident that the political regimes of 1964–73 and 1973–90 had little perceptible impact on social mobility rates. The 1950–59 birth cohort did not see any systematic increase of mobility rates, despite the enhancement of educational opportunities for the poor under Frei and Allende. The 1970–79 cohort did not see any systematic decline in social mobility. There was indeed an apparent increase in occupational status for the *encomendero* surnames. But that is based on small numbers and may be subject to sampling error.

Figure 11.5 shows the variation in occupational incomes by decade for other elite-surname groups: French, German, Italian, and the rare surnames of medium and large landowners in 1853. Again there is no sign of any systematic enhanced mobility for the 1950–59 birth cohort. There is a modest sign, however, of a decline in downward occupational mobility for those educated in the Pinochet years.

[17] Technically the figure shows average log income for each surname group minus the Chilean average log income.

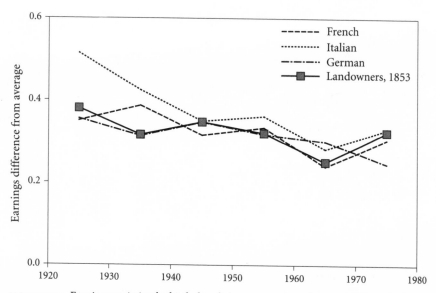

FIGURE 11.5. Earnings variation by birth decade by surname type, later social elites, 1920–79.

Thus the case of Chile seems to underscore a theme of earlier chapters: social and political movements have a surprisingly modest effect on the rate of social mobility. Events that at the time seem crucial, powerful, and critical determinants of the fate of societies leave astonishingly little imprint in the objective records of social mobility rates. Allende tried to remake Chilean society and died bravely when the military intervened to destroy his dream. Thousands were imprisoned, tortured, and murdered under Pinochet's brutal military regime. But if social mobility rates were the only record of the history of Chile in the past hundred years, we would detect no trace of these events. Despite the cries, the suffering, the outrage, and the struggle, social mobility continued its slow shuffle toward the mean, indifferent to the events that so profoundly affected the lives of individual Chileans.

TWELVE

The Law of Social Mobility and Family Dynamics

CHAPTER 6 CONJECTURES that all social mobility is governed by a simple underlying law, independent of social structure and government policy:

$$x_{t+1} = bx_t + e_t$$

where x_t is the underlying social status of a family in generation t, e_t is a random component, and b is in the region 0.7–0.8.[1] This simple law of mobility makes surprising predictions about the earlier history of social elites and underclasses observed at any point in time.

The social status of any individual family can follow any possible path over many generations. But when we observe that a family has high or low status in some earlier period, such as 1800–1829, this law of mobility implies that on average, the status of the descendants will move toward the mean for the society generation by generation. When the persistence rate, b, is as high as 0.8, this is a slow process, taking many hundreds of years for families who are initially far above or below the mean. Once we look at large groups of families of high or low status, the movement on average to the mean becomes deterministic and predictable.

This law of motion has, however, a counterintuitive implication about the history of current elites and underclasses. For it predicts that on average, a family's path as it diverges from and regresses toward the mean will be symmetrical. The law of motion implies that we can infer the average history of the rich and poor families of any generation as reliably as we can predict their future.

---

[1] Remember that social status here is measured such that the average is zero.

We have a fascination with rags-to-riches stories. Biographies of Charles Dickens, for example, rarely neglect to mention that he came from a childhood where he was removed from school at age 9 and set to work in a blacking factory before he rose to become the richest and most celebrated writer of nineteenth-century England.[2] Similarly, biographers of Andrew Carnegie tend to dwell on his birth in a one-room cottage in Dunfermline, Scotland, as the son of an impoverished handloom weaver.[3]

But the law of mobility tells us that the rags-to-riches path is the anomaly and the exception. The elite of any generation typically come from families only modestly less elite. On average, the fabulously rich and the extravagantly talented are the offspring of the moderately rich and moderately talented. The truly poor and completely talentless are the children of the modestly poor and somewhat untalented.

This law can be demonstrated empirically. Figure 12.1 shows the average path of a random group of families toward and away from the upper and lower tails of social status, using the above equation and assuming b is 0.8.[4] This figure shows simulations for five hundred families over fifty generations. For any family that achieves either high or low status in any generation, the figure shows its average status for the ten generations preceding and following. Even with random errors included, there is an elegant symmetry in the rise and decline of social status. The persistence rate estimated for the high-status group in the ten generations preceding is 0.81, and for subsequent generations it is 0.85. For the low-status group, the respective persistence rates are 0.81 and 0.77.

The paths for individual families vary widely. Figure 12.2 shows the paths of six randomly chosen individual families underlying the averages for the elite group in figure 12.1. Even with extensive individual variation, the figure shows that for the preceding and following four generations, these families consistently have above-average status.

---

[2] Dickens's father, however, was at least lower middle class. He was a clerk in the Royal Navy unable to manage his finances: as a result, he was consigned to debtors' prison and young Charles to the blacking factory.

[3] Handloom weaving was far from the bottom of the occupational hierarchy in preindustrial Britain. Weavers were skilled craftsmen who often owned their looms and cottages. But by the time of Carnegie's birth in 1835, handloom weaving had gone into rapid decline, devastated by competition from factory weaving. Carnegie's father reacted entrepreneurially, pursuing better economic prospects by moving the family to the United States.

[4] For this purpose we define the top and bottom of the status distribution as at least three standard deviations from the mean status, roughly the top and bottom 0.1 percent.

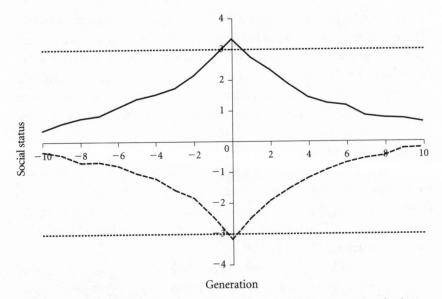

FIGURE 12.1. The implied path through twenty-one generations for elite and underclass families of the base generation.

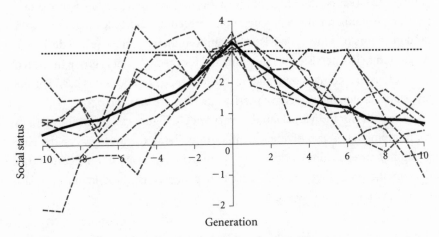

FIGURE 12.2. Paths of six elite families compared to the average.

The empirical result shown in figure 12.1 can be shown mathematically in a few lines.[5] The law of motion implies that for any social group, where the ‾ indicates average status, on average

$$\bar{x}_{t+1} = b\bar{x}_t.$$

But it also implies, paradoxically, that on average

$$\bar{x}_{t-1} = b\bar{x}_t.$$

That is, if we observe any group of families that now deviate from average social status, then they will have deviated on average by a lesser amount, determined by b, in the previous generation. For these groups, expected future and past trajectories are precisely symmetrical.

This symmetry implies that if a group deviates in the current generation from the mean social status, set at zero, then on average it will have deviated by a smaller amount, determined by b, in the previous generation. A group of families now of high social status will have arrived at this status over many generations by a series of upward steps from the mean. And the length and speed of that ascent, paradoxically, are determined by the rate of persistence, b. The greater this persistence rate, the longer the implied path to the elite, or indeed to the lower class.

Social mobility rates can be measured equivalently by how long it takes an existing elite to regress to the mean and by how long it took them to depart from the mean and attain their current position.

To grasp intuitively why the dynamics of social position must ever be thus, note that the fundamental equation of social mobility posits a deterministic component, bx_t, and a random component, e_t, to any family's underlying social position. The bigger is b, the smaller is the typical random component. When b is large, to move from a social position at or below the mean to the top in one generation would require an enormous positive random shock. It would require winning an El Gordo of a lottery in the random components of status.

Thus if the intergenerational correlation is 0.75, the equation predicts that the chance of a family going from the mean of the status distribution to the top 0.5 percent in one generation is roughly one in five hundred million. It is quite likely that it has never happened in England. The chance of going from the bot-

[5] See appendix 2.

tom 0.5 percent to the top 0.5 percent in one generation is essentially zero. It has never happened in the history of any society.

In contrast, although high-status families are being constantly pulled back to the middle by the forces of regression to the mean, they are also subject to the same random shocks, and for them even a relatively modest shock can overcome the force of regression to the mean and move them higher in the social ranks. Thus the typical family found in an elite in any generation was recruited from a cadet elite of somewhat lower status in the previous generation. Since this is true across all generations, the typical path of a family to its current elite status involves a series of modest positive shocks over many generations.

This implies that if the rate of persistence is indeed 0.75 or higher, families observed at any time in the elite spend twenty or more generations (six hundred years) at above-average status. The same holds for families observed at low status: they typically linger at below-average status for twenty generations or more. A high persistence rate implies very slow regression back to the mean; it also implies the persistence of some families above or below the social mean for astonishingly long periods.

It may appear that some strange causal mechanism is consistently propelling some families toward the upper reaches of social status. It may also seem that as soon as we observe an elite, we ensure its destruction, its decline toward the mean. As in quantum mechanics, we somehow influence the outcome just by making an observation. But both of these impressions are incorrect. We are simply observing the patterns predicted by the random processes of the fundamental equation. Although we may be able to infer that the elite families of 1850 have been on an upward social path since 1550, we cannot predict which of the average families of 1550 will join the 1850 elite.

The empirical strength of this result can be demonstrated for England using two rich sets of surname observations introduced in chapter 4 above. The first is the set of people whose wills were proved in the probate courts of England from 1384 to 2012, indicating greater wealth. The second is the set of people attending Oxford and Cambridge from 1500 to 2012, indicating greater educational attainment.

One elite group we can observe all the way from 1384 to 1858, for example, is the people whose wills were proved in the highest probate court in the land, the Prerogatory Court of the Archbishop of Canterbury (PCC). The share of men dying in England with wills proved in the PCC was fairly stable over the years 1680–1858, averaging 5 percent of all adult male deaths. Thus we can take

TABLE 12.1. Representation of rare surnames in PCC probates

Generation	All probates	Rich rare surnames, 1858–87	Poor rare surnames, 1858–87	Relative representation, rich, 1858–87	Relative representation, poor, 1858–87
1680–1709	56,672	129	26	2.6	0.81
1710–39	69,899	187	26	3.7	0.58
1740–69	90,493	223	32	3.9	0.60
1770–99	108,573	257	25	4.6	0.50
1800–29	154,137	404	27	5.6	0.40
1830–58	197,218	602	16	7.2	0.20

the testators proved in this court after 1680 as representing the wealthiest 5 percent in English society. Not all were men: by 1680 a quarter of the wills probated in this court were from women, typically widows or spinsters. Thus this measure of status indicates the general inheritance of wealth within families, not only through the male line.

Table 12.1 shows the numbers of estates probated in the PCC by generation of death, 1680–1858, and the sizes of the rich and poor rare-surname groups of 1858–87 discussed in chapter 5. By dividing the share of probates from the rich-surname group by the share of population represented by that group in each generation, we obtain the relative representation of these surnames among the probates.[6]

The rich surnames of 1858–87 are always overrepresented in the earlier probates. But as we go back in time, that relative representation declines from 7.2 to 2.6. Conversely, the poor surnames are always underrepresented, but as we go back in time, their relative representation rises from 0.2 to 0.8.

Figure 12.3 shows the pattern of relative representation for these groups. Also shown is the relative representation predicted by the persistence rate that best fits the pattern. For the rich rare surnames, that rate is 0.85. Again wealth is predicted to regress very slowly to the mean in the years 1680–1858, this time measured by the rate of increase in wealth for later elite families. For these same surname groups in the period 1858–2012, the best-fitting intergenerational correlation is 0.82. These numbers are not identical, as the theory would predict, but they are close.

[6] The incidence of the surnames in the population as a whole is estimated from their frequency in marriage registers.

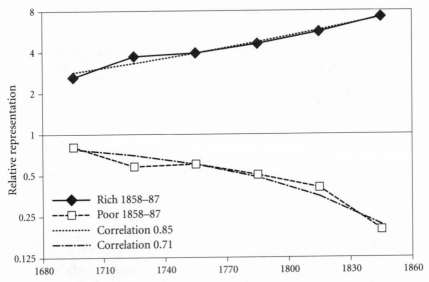

FIGURE 12.3. Relative representation in PCC probates for rich and poor surname groups of 1858–87.

For the poor rare surnames, the best-fitting implied persistence is 0.71. The estimate of persistence rates for the poor for the period 1858–2012 is 0.64, but this later estimate has a great deal of imprecision. Thus downward mobility is close to symmetrical with upward mobility. Families who end up at the bottom of the status distribution follow a trajectory that looks very similar in shape to that followed by families who end up at the top.

Using the PCC records, we can also systematically measure upward and downward mobility at the time of the Industrial Revolution, 1680–1860. Were they equal, as the law of mobility predicts? For each thirty-year period, starting in 1680–1709 and ending in 1830–58, a set of rare surnames was identified that were associated with estates probated in the PCC. The bearers of these surnames were typically four to six times as likely to be probated in the PCC than the average surname, represented here by *Clark(e)*, in periods immediately before and after they were identified.[7]

Figure 12.4 shows the regression of these surname groupings toward average representation in the PCC in later generations. As before, these patterns

---

[7] Their relative representation is even higher in the period in which they are identified, but in this period their relative representation is higher than implied by their true underlying social status because of the prevalence of positive errors (see appendix 2).

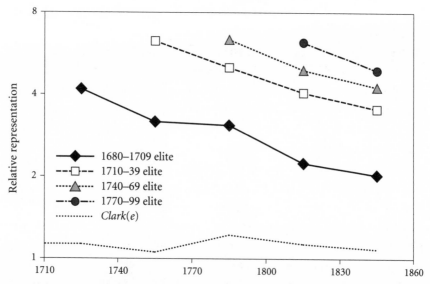

FIGURE 12.4. Relative representation in PCC probates for elite-surname cohorts, 1710–1858.

can be used to estimate social mobility rates in each of these generations, and these estimates are shown in table 12.2. They confirm what is by now a familiar story. The average persistence rate for downward mobility during the entire Industrial Revolution period is 0.82, despite the huge structural transformation of the economy in this period. The rise of new industries, and new wealth, from 1760 onward makes no impression on these measured mobility rates. The decline of the old landed aristocracy has no effect either. Intergenerational wealth mobility was extremely slow in Industrial Revolution England (1710–1858), just as it was in modern England (1858–2012). Consequently the high-

TABLE 12.2. Implied persistence rate for downward mobility for PCC elite, 1710–1858

Generation	1680–1709 elite	1710–39 elite	1740–69 elite	1770–99 elite	Average
1740–69	0.77	—	—	—	0.77
1770–99	0.97	0.84	—	—	0.90
1800–29	0.68	0.83	0.81	—	0.78
1830–58	0.86	0.88	0.88	0.83	0.86
Average	0.82	0.85	0.85	0.83	0.82

status surnames of preindustrial England (1710–39) retain relatively high status in the period 1830–58, four generations later, and well after the Industrial Revolution effected major changes in economy and society. You can transform a society, but you do not change the slow march of social mobility.

We can use the same PCC data to measure rates of upward mobility for the years 1680–1829 by looking at the rate of rise in relative representation of the surnames that formed elites in later periods. Figure 12.5 shows these patterns. If upward social mobility rates are the same as downward, then the slopes of the upward and downward curves showing relative representation for the same surnames across multiple generations should be the same. The symmetry between figure 12.5 and figure 12.4 is very clear. Upward and downward mobility are symmetrical processes. Table 12.3 summarizes the implied persistence rates from the rate of rise of later elites. The overall average estimate of persistence for upward mobility is 0.77, close to the 0.82 calculated for downward mobility. Allowing for the random fluctuations inherent in any measure that involves sampling, rates of upward and downward mobility are indeed similar. The laws of social mobility show remarkably stable and predictable patterns over very different epochs and social regimes in England.

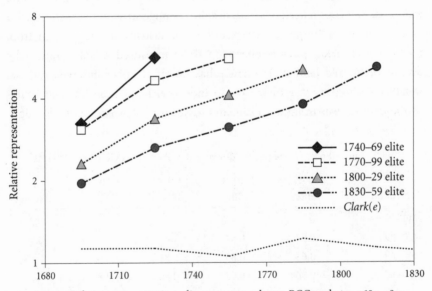

FIGURE 12.5. Relative representation, elite-surname cohorts, PCC probates, 1680–1829.

TABLE 12.3. Implied persistence rate of upward wealth mobility for PCC elite, 1710–1858

Generation	1740–69 elite	1770–99 elite	1800–1829 elite	1830–58 elite	Average
1710–39	0.61	0.68	0.65	0.67	0.65
1740–69	—	0.86	0.83	0.83	0.84
1770–99	—	—	0.84	0.83	0.83
1800–29	—	—	—	0.77	0.77
Average	0.61	0.77	0.77	0.77	0.77

Educational Mobility

We can show the same symmetrical rise and fall of families in educational mobility over the period 1530–2012 (seventeen generations). The source is the rare surnames of students at Oxford and Cambridge.

The first elite set of rare surnames is those of the rich who died in the years 1858–87. Figure 5.8 shows the slow downward mobility of these surname groups as measured by their relative representation at the universities from 1830 to 2012, with an intergenerational correlation of 0.82. Figure 12.6 shows their relative representation at Oxford and Cambridge from 1530 to 2012. The start date of 1530 was chosen because measures of the relative population shares of surnames are possible only from 1538 on, with the beginning of parish registers of baptisms, marriages, and burials. This surname group shows the expected symmetrical rise from 1530 to 1799, with a persistence rate of 0.83.

The second set of elite rare surnames consists of those that just happen to appear at Oxford and Cambridge in the years 1800–1829.[8] Figure 12.6 shows the relative representation of these surnames. Again the pattern is as predicted. The persistence parameter implied by the relative representations for 1830–2012 is 0.77, exactly the same as that estimated for 1530–1799.[9] Thus, again, the law of mobility for status holds good over a period of five hundred years during which England underwent profound social changes: the reformation of the Church of England, the Scientific Revolution, the Civil War, the Glorious Revolution, the

[8] As before, we define a rare surname as one held by forty or fewer people in the 1881 census.

[9] The period 1800–1829 is not included in either the forward or backward estimation because the social mobility observed between that period and the adjacent generations is the ordinary type, as opposed to the underlying persistence rate we seek here.

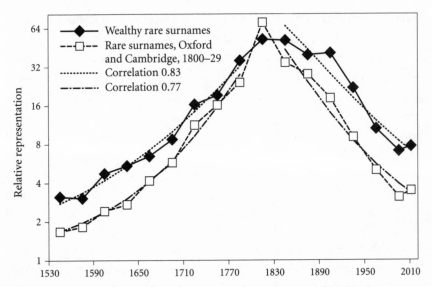

FIGURE 12.6. Relative representation and implied persistence of wealthy and rare surnames at Oxford and Cambridge, 1530–2012.

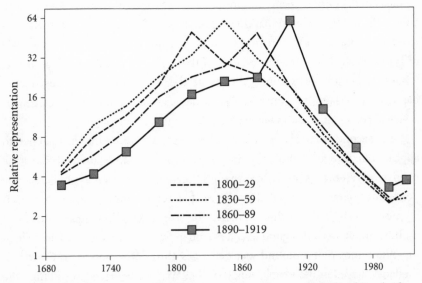

FIGURE 12.7. Relative representation for rare-surname cohorts at Oxford and Cambridge, 1680–2012.

Industrial Revolution, the move to universal male suffrage and mass public education, and the rise of the welfare state.

For both these groups, the persistence rates are the same for education as for wealth. For 1680–1858, the persistence rate for wealth was estimated above as being in the range 0.71–0.85. The persistence rate for education is in the range 0.77–0.82.

What is true for the 1800–1829 rare surnames that show up at Oxford and Cambridge is true for every such cohort of rare surnames. Figure 12.7 shows the path of educational status for cohorts of rare surnames found at the universities in the thirty-year periods starting in 1800, 1830, 1860, and 1890. All of them show the symmetrical inverted-V shape predicted by the simple law of mobility.

These findings show two things. The first is the apparent stability of status persistence rates across a whole variety of social regimes in England between 1680 and 2012. The second is the very deep roots of elites at any given time. The rare surnames overrepresented in 1890–1919, for example, are already three times overrepresented at Oxford and Cambridge in 1680–1719. The modern elite has a long history of overrepresentation at the universities.

A Tale of Two Pepyses

Can all social mobility in England from 1500 to the present be explained by our simple law of mobility? Some examples of persistence seem remarkable even in a world where the overall persistence is in the range 0.75–0.8. Consider, for example, the *Pepys* family, mentioned in the introduction. This is one of the prosperous rare surnames we identify among the cohort dying in the years 1858–87. Evidence from parish records of marriages and baptisms suggests that from the sixteenth to the eighteenth century, no more than forty *Pepyses* were ever alive at one time. Such rare surnames always flirt on the edge of extinction, as the famous Watson-Galton result predicts. *Pepys,* with only eighteen holders in 2002, seems to be edging closer to annihilation.

Pepys seems to be a surname of modest origins. There is no record of any *Pepys* in the medieval records of substantial property owners such as the *Inquisitions Post Mortem* (see chapter 4) or among members of Parliament. The name does not appear in the probate records of the PCC before 1620. The marriage and baptism records suggest only that it originated in rural areas of Cambridge and Norfolk. The *Pepyses* are sons of the soil.

Yet since at least 1496, *Pepys* has consistently been a high-status surname. In the years 1496–1699, there could have been no more than fifty-six *Pepys* males who reached age 21. Yet twenty-eight of them attended Oxford or Cambridge, at a time when fewer than 2 percent of all men attended these universities. The family's university attendance rate declined somewhat in the eighteenth and nineteenth centuries but was still twenty-two out of an estimated seventy adult male *Pepyses,* thirty times the rate for the general population. In the twentieth century, that attendance rate has declined further, but it is still more than twenty times that of the general population.

Can this five-hundred-year record of educational attainment be due solely to random forces, or is it due to a special *Pepys* legacy or advantage, such as the fame of the surname, that transcends the ordinary pull of mediocrity? The answer suggested here is that exceptional as the *Pepys* family record is, its centuries-long pattern of overrepresentation at Oxford and Cambridge, with a persistence rate of 0.8, is also precisely what we would expect. Figure 12.8 shows the expected arc of rise and fall of the status of the surname over many generations. There was nothing special about the *Pepyses* except for the fact that between 1450 and 1650 they had a lot of random good luck.

This random luck lay in good fortune in the shuffling of the genes on reproduction and good luck in the underlying characteristics of the women that

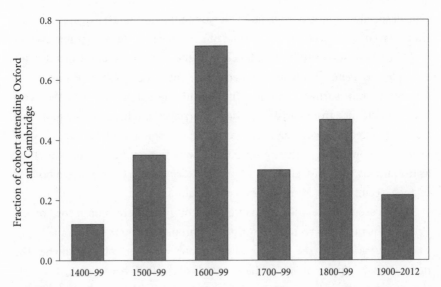

FIGURE 12.8. Occurrence of surname *Pepys* among Oxford and Cambridge students, by century.

Pepys men married. The rise of the *Pepyses* was not due to anything other than their skill and abilities. They were not the bastard offspring of kings, the recipients of patronage, or the inheritors of caste privilege. They prospered under medieval Catholicism, through the Reformation, and then under Puritanism, through the Restoration, the Glorious Revolution, and into the Victorian era. They prosper now. The General Medical Register in the United Kingdom shows four *Pepyses*.

In contrast to the long arc of success for the *Pepys* family, there is another family that is likely related, with the similarly rare surname of *Peeps*, which is completely unremarkable. As with the *Pepyses*, the earliest parish records of births and marriages of the *Peeps* family appear in Cambridge. It is likely, given the vagaries of early spelling, that the *Peeps* and *Pepys* lineages had the same ancestors. Two *Peepses* are recorded at Cambridge in the 1530s, but none since. This is not in itself remarkable, as in 1881 there were only forty-six *Peepses*, and by 2002 that number had shrunk to twelve. While the PCC court records forty-nine probates of *Pepyses* between 1620 and 1858, not a single *Peeps* will was probated in this court.

But the divergent fates of these two surname lineages through the generations have no greater meaning than as examples of the way that random shocks affect the underlying social competence of families. This is not the story of Cain and Abel, of those blessed and cursed in the eyes of God. There is nothing special about these families: their trajectories simply demonstrate that the law of social mobility tends to produce a long arc of privilege or want for those who end up at the extremes of the status distribution.

This is all just the operation of chance. The *Peepses*, should the name survive, will sometime in future eons have their time in the *Sun*. The *Pepyses* are almost certainly destined for mediocrity. But the persistent effects of accidents of chance alarm many people. The idea that the abilities and status of our ancestors twelve generations in the past can predict our chances of entering university, being a doctor, or becoming wealthy somehow violates the sense that a fair society should offer equality of opportunity for all in the current generation. This issue is considered below.

Qing China

Another case that demonstrates the counterintuitive effect of the law of mobility on the rise of families is Qing China (1645–1905). Using surname–place of origin combinations, such as the Fan family of Ningbo, it is possible to track social mobility in the Republican era (1912–49) and the present (see chapter 9). From the records of *juren*, successful candidates on the provincial exam in the imperial era, in South Jiangsu and North Zhejiang, the status of these surnames can also be traced all the way back to 1645 and the beginning of the Qing era.

What is the earlier history (1645–1870) of the surname–place of origin combinations identified as elite, based on their numbers of *juren* in the period 1871–1905? Figure 12.9 shows the relative representation of these surnames by generation from 1661 to 2010 for both Jiangsu and Zhejiang. It illustrates exactly the pattern in the earlier years (1721–1870) that the law of mobility would predict. For both sets of surnames, there is a near-symmetrical rise of the names in status over the previous seven generations. For Zhejiang, this increase implies an underlying persistence of 0.81, very close to the persistence parameter of 0.78 estimated for the decline of status in the Republican era.

However, the pattern is not as predicted for the years 1661–1720. The relative representation of these surname–place of origin combinations is as high or higher in 1661–90 as in 1721–50. One possible explanation is that rare surnames declined in frequency with time. Absent better information, it is assumed here that these surname–place of origin combinations were the same share of the

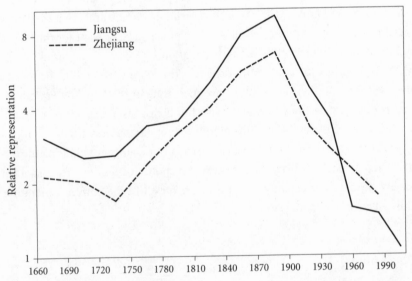

FIGURE 12.9. Relative representation among *juren* of 1871–1905 surname–place of origin elites, Jiangsu and Zhejiang, 1661–1990.

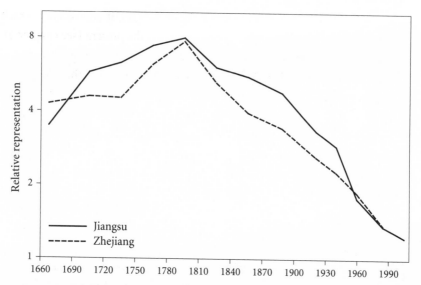

FIGURE 12.10. Relative representation among *juren* of 1781–1810 surname–place of origin elites, Jiangsu and Zhejiang, 1661–1990.

population in 1661–90 as in 1912–49. Experience in England, for which we can track surname frequencies all the way from 1538 to 2010, shows that a rarer surname in the period 1912–49 tends to account for a larger share of surnames in 1661–90. Surnames that were even more infrequent in 1661–1690 typically disappear by 1912. If these Chinese surname–place of origin combinations were, on average, twice as frequent in the population in 1661–90, then the puzzle would disappear.

Figure 12.10 shows the same pattern for surname–place of origin combinations identified as elite in 1781–1810 from their appearance in the *juren* lists of this period. We see the predicted symmetry, but in a much looser-fitting way than in England. Again, difficulties in fixing the population share of these surname–place of origin combinations over time could explain the roughness of the fit.

Thus the Qing *juren* data offer qualified support for the idea that status dynamics for elite families always follow the pattern found in England and shown in figures 12.6 and 12.7. Overall, this simple and counterintuitive prediction of the social law of motion holds up well.

THIRTEEN

Protestants, Jews, Gypsies, Muslims, and Copts

Exceptions to the Law of Mobility?

THE CASES EXAMINED ABOVE INDICATE THAT across a broad range of societies and epochs, there appears to be a general rule of social mobility. All groups feel the pull of regression to the mean. Variations in social position are maintained by random shocks to families' underlying social competence.

It is assumed, however, that each population has a given, similar, distribution of talent, and that elites and underclasses are simply draws from this pool of God-given talent. Within societies, social mobility acts as though it were a biological phenomenon, as if the factors affecting mobility were genetically inherited.

Some features of social mobility, however, seem to defy such simple quasi-biological laws. The law of mobility explains why individual families become elite or underclass, and the surprising dynamics of that process are laid out in the previous chapter. But it cannot explain how large social, religious, and ethnic groups in some societies attain and maintain high social status or are condemned to persistent low status. Such an outcome is not contemplated in the law of mobility.

How did Jews emerge as a social elite in Eastern Europe and the Middle East in the Middle Ages or earlier? How did the Gypsy or Traveller population of England end up at the bottom of the social ladder in the sixteenth and seventeenth centuries? Why are Christian minorities typically economic elites in the Muslim world?

The emergence of elite social groups has often been linked to their embrace of religious ideologies that privilege and foster the aptitudes and aspirations favorable to social success. Thus Maristella Botticini and Zvi Eckstein argue that the rise of the Jews as an educated elite in the Middle East between 70 and 700 CE was driven by the emergence within Judaism of a religious ideology that emphasized that each male should learn to read the Torah, the book of laws.[1] Adherence to this emerging religious precept molded the history of the Jewish people in the preindustrial world. It gave them an advantage in the world of commerce, finance, and scholarship and transformed them from farmers into traders, scholars, and financiers.

Protestantism in early modern Europe similarly emphasized that people should be able to read the Bible for themselves, rather than have their religious knowledge mediated by a priestly caste. The effect of this tradition on literacy rates has been invoked to explain why Protestants enjoyed higher economic status than Catholics in preindustrial Europe. If this explanation is correct, and religious or ethnic affiliation indeed plays an independent causal role in the social competence of families, then the law of mobility will fail to predict many outcomes.

The law of mobility also fails to explain the persistence of status over centuries of some groups, with no regression to the mean. Why are Jews still a social elite in most societies more than two thousand years after their emergence as a distinct group? Why are Brahmins still an elite and Muslims still lower class in Bengal? How did Copts and other Christians in the Middle East and North Africa maintain above-average social status for more than a millennium after the Muslim conquests?

Here it is shown that these outcomes are, in fact, compatible with the law of mobility detailed in the chapters above. Incompatibility would arise if religious ideology itself could change the social competence of families. An alternative explanation for the emergence of elites and underclasses is that religions tend to recruit selectively (either positively or negatively) from the existing pool of talent in a society. And the duties that different religions impose on their followers may dictate from where in that talent pool their adherents are drawn.

Why Are Jews Unusually Successful?

Botticini and Eckstein highlight that by 1490 CE, the Jewish population was a modest subgroup of descendants of a much larger parent population. They date the emergence of an emphasis on literacy for all Jewish males to the period

[1] Botticini and Eckstein 2012, 71.

TABLE 13.1. Jewish population as a percentage of parent groups, Europe, North Africa, Asia Minor, Arabia, and western Asia, 65–1492 CE

Year (CE)	Total population	Jewish population	Percent Jewish
65	55	5.5	10
650	51	1.2	2.4
1170	70	1.5	2.1
1490	88	1	1.1

around 70 CE. Assuming that Jews in the period 65–1490 CE had the same net fertility as the surrounding populations, by 1490 only about 10 percent of the descendants of the parent Jewish population of 70 CE was still Jewish (see table 13.1). The rest of the Jewish population had converted to other religions, probably mainly Christianity. These conversions occurred in environments where forced conversion was rare.

Botticini and Eckstein explicitly present the decision to stay with Judaism or convert to one of the many competing sects as an economic one.[2] What drove the decision was, first, the occupation of the family, because literacy is assumed to have had an economic value only to traders and craftsmen. There must also have been some selection based on talent, though this is not explicitly modeled, and the authors are ambiguous on the importance of this feature in determining conversion.[3]

Botticini and Eckstein's main idea is thus that a religion that emphasized a duty of literacy attracted adherents among those who engaged in the urban occupations of trade and manufacture. But if the adoption of such urban occupations was driven by the underlying talents of different families, as seems likely, then Judaism would also have been retained by the most talented among the earlier Jewish population. Much of their evidence is consistent with the possibility that conversion from Judaism was mainly driven by the social competence of families. They observe that "passages by early Christian writers and

[2] Botticini and Eckstein 2012, 80–94.
[3] "Families with low-ability sons or with sons who do not like studying . . . will be less likely to invest in children's literacy" (Botticini and Eckstein 2012, 93).

Church Fathers indicate that most Jewish converts to Christianity were illiterate and poor."[4]

One possible test of whether selection based on ability has shaped the fortunes of the Jewish population is the economic status of Jews in the modern world. Suppose the current Jewish population is just a random subset of descendants of an original Jewish population of 65 CE. Now that literacy is universal, and inculcated by the state, Judaism should offer no economic and social advantage. But even a hundred years after the arrival of universal literacy, Jewish populations are still heavily concentrated in the upper parts of the status distribution in every society they reside in. What could be the source of this abiding economic advantage in the modern world, if not that Judaism selectively retained the talented from its parent populations?

Selective Conversion

Nice evidence of the tendency of religions to selectively attract adherents is provided by the experience of Ireland before Partition. Irish society is notable for the long-standing differences in status between the Catholic and Protestant populations. From the seventeenth to the twentieth century, the Protestants, a settler population largely established in the seventeenth century, remained the elite. There was a sharp and continuing social division between Catholic and Protestant, particularly the Presbyterian Protestants of Scottish origin, and seemingly impermeable barriers to social intercourse. From the arrival of the largely Scottish Protestant settlers in Ireland in the seventeenth century until the present, these two communities apparently developed in splendid isolation from one another. Thus we would expect the Protestant population now to be exclusively the descendants of Protestant settlers, and the Catholic population exclusively the descendants of the native Irish.

Surname evidence, however, suggests that there have been considerable exchanges of population between the two religious groups.[5] If we take a sample

---

[4] Botticini and Eckstein 2012, 120. However, a model of selective survival of Judaism among elite Jewish families would show a relatively uniform decline of the Jewish population across different geographic areas. Botticini and Eckstein also emphasize that Jewish populations disappeared from much of the Middle East and North Africa by 650 CE, the surviving populations being concentrated in Mesopotamia and Persia.

[5] See Kennedy, Gurrin, and Miller 2012. The discussion here just amplifies their observations.

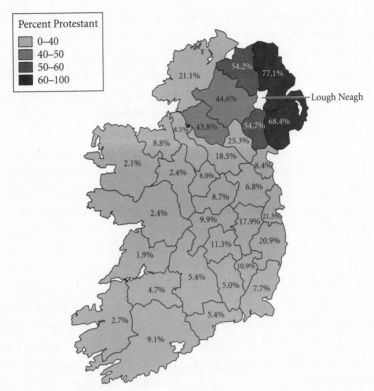

FIGURE 13.1. Distribution of Protestants in Ireland, by county, 1911.

of surnames of exclusively Scottish origin and look at the religious affiliation of their holders in the 1911 Irish census, we find that a full 14 percent of them were Catholic.[6] And similarly, if we take a sample of native Irish surnames, once exclusively Catholic, 12 percent of the holders in 1911 were Protestants.[7] There was thus a significant two-way movement of population across an apparently impenetrable religious divide.

To understand what drove these exchanges, it is useful to divide Ireland into the six counties with the greatest share of Protestants—Armagh, Antrim, Down, Fermanagh, Londonderry, and Tyrone, which together became Northern Ireland—and the rest. Figure 13.1 shows the Protestant share of the popula-

---

[6] The following surnames were chosen as exclusively Scottish in origin: *Bothwell, Buchanan, Cathcart, Fullerton, Girvan, Hamilton, Laird, McGregor, Orr,* and *Sproule.*

[7] These Irish surnames are: *Boyle/O'Boyle, Doherty/O'Doherty, Grady/O'Grady, Han(n)away,* and *McBride. Hanaway* was included because it is the surname of my maternal grandfather, who himself appears in the census.

tion of Ireland by county. Figure 13.2 shows the share of the population of each surname type by religious affiliation and age group (ages 0–29 and 30 and over) in each region in 1911.

Figure 13.2 reveals that surnames were changing to those of the predominant religion of each region. In the south, the overwhelming majority of the Irish surnames were still Catholic, whereas in the six northern counties, only two-thirds of Irish surnames remained Catholic. In counterbalance, in the northern counties, 93 percent of Scottish surnames remained non-Catholic, while in the south one-third of the Scottish surnames were held by Catholics.

Figure 13.2 also suggests that this process had been under way for generations. When we divide people in the census into two age groups, those age 30 and older, and those younger, we see that the transition of Irish surnames toward Protestantism, and of Scottish surnames toward Catholicism, is only modestly greater for the younger cohort.

The two groups, Catholics and Protestants, were socially differentiated. As figure 13.3 illustrates, throughout the country, Catholics were less literate than Protestants. And as figure 13.4 shows, Protestants were more likely to be found in skilled occupations all over Ireland. However, as these figures also show, the transitions from one religion to another helped perpetuate differences in social

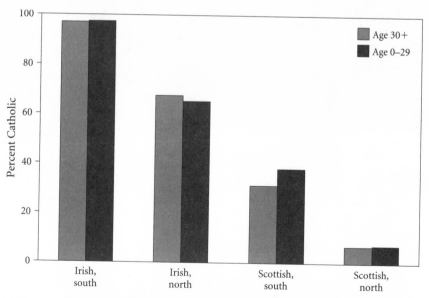

FIGURE 13.2. Percentages of Irish and Scottish surnames held by Catholics, 1911.

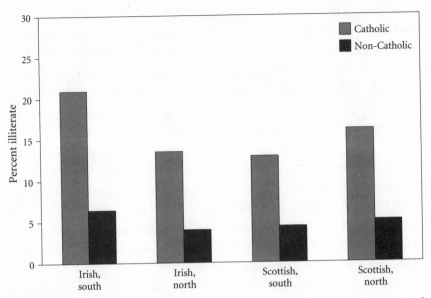

FIGURE 13.3. Percentages of Irish and Scottish surnames held by illiterate males age 16 and over, 1911.

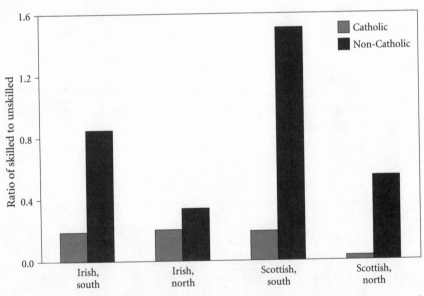

FIGURE 13.4. Ratio of skilled to unskilled males age 18 and over, 1911, by surname type and religion.

status between the two religions. Catholics with Scottish surnames had much lower social status than Protestants with the same surnames, even controlling for regional differences: they were more likely to be illiterate and to hold less-skilled occupations. Similarly, Protestants with Irish surnames had much higher status than Catholics with the same surnames: they were more likely to be literate and to hold more skilled occupations.

Thus Irish history shows how even communities as mutually antagonistic as Irish Catholics and Protestants can undergo not only a significant movement of people from one group to the other but also a movement that solidifies the positions of the respective elites and underclasses within of the two groups. Those at the bottom of the social scale in the Protestant surname group were much more likely to have transferred their religious affiliation to Catholicism sometime in the previous three hundred years. Those at the top of the social scale in the Irish surname group were much more likely to identify as Protestant by 1911.[8]

The Origins of the Modern Jewish Population

Suppose Jewish populations interacted with the surrounding populations in Europe, North Africa, and the Middle East in the same way as the Protestant minority in Ireland did with the majority Catholic population. Then Jewish economic advantage later might be explained by selective flows between the local and Jewish populations.

There are, however, some puzzles about the origin of the modern Ashkenazi Jewish population, descended from communities concentrated in Slavic Eastern Europe in the early nineteenth century. In 1170 the Sephardic and Mizrahi Jews of the Middle East, North Africa, and southern Europe represented the great majority of the known Jewish population. By the early twentieth century, the Sephardic and Mizrahi population had grown little and was still only about one million. There is clear information on their origins and lineage: Sephardic and Mizrahi Jews are plausibly all the descendants of the Jewish population of 1490 CE, with some local admixtures and losses from conversions to

---

[8] Though, as Kennedy, Gurrin, and Miller (2012) note, there is a question of causation here: "Whether lower socio-economic status preceded or coincided with absorption into the Catholic community, or gave rise to this outcome in the form of downward social mobility, opens a further intriguing set of possibilities" (p. 21).

other religions (as in Spain after 1492). In contrast, the Ashkenazi population, which was estimated in medieval times to account for 4 percent or less of all Jews, had come to constitute the overwhelming majority of Jews by the early twentieth century, numbering as many as eight million.[9] Despite the Holocaust, it is estimated that the Ashkenazi now constitute more than 80 percent of the world Jewish population.

How the Ashkenazi emerged by the nineteenth century as the bulk of the world Jewish population is an intriguing historical mystery. It is ironic that a community renowned for its early embrace of literacy has no written records to show its own origin or migration to Eastern Europe. As one scholar of the origins of Yiddish, Robert King, notes: "The legacy of early Jewish life in the Slavic East was very largely the bones of its dead."[10]

It used to be accepted without controversy that the Ashkenazi were an offshoot of the Sephardic community that migrated from Italy to western Germany in the Middle Ages. Later, this group was supposedly driven east under the pressure of persecution in Germany following the onset of the Black Death in 1347. This is the so-called Rhineland hypothesis. However, it would require extraordinary rates of population growth in Eastern Europe between the Middle Ages and the nineteenth century to produce the eight million Ashkenazim observed in 1900: consistently more than 1.5 percent per year, or 50 percent per generation—much faster than the general growth of population in Eastern Europe. This rate is not implausible: in societies such as preindustrial England, elite groups did have much faster population growth rates than the general population. In England, for example, the richest lineages had increases in family sizes of 50–100 percent per generation.[11] A common origin of Ashkenazi and Sephardic Jews from a subgroup of no more than 10 percent of a larger parent population in the Roman Empire would fit with the hypothesis on the biological transmission of status advanced here.

Some scholars have questioned, however, whether the Ashkenazi population growth rate required by the Rhineland hypothesis is consistent with other evidence on the demography of preindustrial Jewish communities.[12] An alternative proposal is that the Ashkenazim were descended from a mass conver-

---

[9] Botticini and Eckstein 2012, 40.
[10] "Scholars Debate the Roots of Yiddish, Migration of Jews" 1996.
[11] Clark 2007, 116–121.
[12] Van Straten and Snel 2006; Van Straten 2007, 43.

sion of the Khazars, originally from the Caucasus, to Judaism in the ninth century. After the collapse of the Khazarian Empire in the 960s CE, the remnants of the Khazars supposedly migrated to Eastern Europe, bringing Judaism with them. This would contradict the hypothesis offered here on the source and nature of elite populations. A whole population converted to Judaism should not become elite, since religious precepts in themselves are irrelevant to social competence except insofar as they lead to selective recruitment to a religious affiliation.

However, the genetic evidence seems to support the Rhineland hypothesis on the origins of the Ashkenazi.[13] A recent survey of the genetic evidence on Jewish populations, including evidence from the whole genome, the Y chromosome, and mitochondrial DNA, concludes that Ashkenazi are indeed closely related to other Jewish populations. Further, they are most closely related genetically to the Italian, Greek, and Turkish Jewish populations, a finding that fits with the conventional story of the migration of the Ashkenazi to northern Europe.

The genetic evidence also suggests that the Ashkenazi population had a very small number of both male and female founders and so must have undergone a rapid expansion to reach its present size. Four women, for example, account for 40 percent of the mitochondrial DNA of the Ashkenazi, with a modest number of others contributing the rest. The evidence from the Y chromosome also suggests that only 5 to 8 percent of the Ashkenazi genetic material comes from admixture of European males.[14] Thus the Ashkenazi may represent an elite within an elite, a finding that would be entirely consistent with the hypothesis on social mobility advanced here. And the limited admixture of European DNA from the Ashkenazis' long sojourn in Eastern Europe is consistent with the proposition that a group retains its elite status over the long run either by practicing endogamy or by selectively losing its lower-status members.[15]

---

[13] There is dissent on this point. Elhaik (2013) reports genetic evidence favoring the Khazarian hypothesis.

[14] Ostrer and Skorecki 2013, 123.

[15] Gregory Cochran, Jason Hardy, and Henry Harpending (2006) have argued that the elite status of the modern Ashkenazim stemmed from the greater reproductive success of more-intelligent members of the community in Eastern Europe because of their occupational concentration in finance and trade. This is another potential mechanism consistent with the law of mobility. However, greater reproductive success in the preindustrial era by the elites in society is not a pattern unique to Ashkenazi Jews: in preindustrial England, for example, economic success was associated with reproductive success (Clark 2007).

Minorities in Muslim Societies

Evidence for the role of selective affinity with minority populations can also potentially explain the emergence of Christians, Jews, and Parsis as elites in predominantly Muslim societies. This mechanism is laid out for Egypt in an interesting study of Coptic Christians by Mohamed Saleh.[16] Muslim societies had two characteristics. First, subject populations were not forced to convert to Islam: Muslim societies were, at their inception, tolerant of religious minorities.[17] But under Islamic law, non-Muslim males were subject to a head tax called the *jizya(h)*. This was a fee for permission to practice another religion, designed as an inducement to convert.

The head tax was sometimes levied at variable rates. Thus Abu Yusuf, the chief justice of Baghdad in the eighth century, in his treatise on taxation and public finance (*Kitab al-kharaj*), stipulated that the *jizya* should be forty-eight dirhams for the richest men, twenty-four for those of moderate wealth, and twelve for craftsmen and laborers. But such rates would still have made the tax much more burdensome on the poorest laborers than on wealthier members of religious minorities.[18]

Saleh shows that in Egypt, Coptic Christians, who formed the vast majority of Egyptian society on the eve of the Arab Muslim conquest, selectively converted to Islam in the centuries following the Arab conquest of 641 CE. He finds evidence that under the pressure of the *jizya,* the poorest Copts converted to Islam: the conversion rate was greater in areas where heavier taxes were imposed. Moreover, in areas where the conversion rate was highest, the remaining Coptic population was more elite by the nineteenth century. In the Byzantine Empire, Copts had the lowest status in society, below the Jews and upper-class Greek Orthodox Christians; in Muslim Egypt, the remaining Copts became, like these two other minorities, an elite. In the nineteenth century, in both urban and rural areas, Copts had higher occupational status than Muslims despite being a political minority.

The situation in Egypt is echoed in other Muslim societies. In Iran, for example, an analysis of the 1966 census found that the high-income capital, Tehran,

---

[16] Saleh 2013.

[17] Once someone converted to Islam, or a child was born Muslim, however, conversion to another religion was punishable by death.

[18] Muslims had their own taxes to pay under Islamic law, though these were generally, by design, less burdensome than the *jizya.*

with about 10 percent of the country's population, contained two-thirds of Armenian Christians and Jews, and half of Zoroastrians and Assyrian Christians. The explanation was that after modernization began in 1921, many of the early physicians, engineers, mechanics and teachers of foreign languages with Western training came from minority groups. Tehran was in the vanguard of modernization and presented a high demand for such professionals. Thus minorities were attracted to the city.[19]

However, minorities in Iran even in 1966 constituted only 1.2 percent of the population, large numbers of Jews, Zoroastrians, and Christians having previously emigrated because of Shia Islam's intolerance toward minorities. In Lebanon, Syria, Jordan, and Iraq, Christian minorities all constituted elites after the Muslim conquests, presumably because of a similar pattern of conversion to Islam under the *jizya* system.

Once created, minorities in Islamic societies seem to have maintained their high status over more than a millennium through high rates of marital endogamy. A study of the ABO blood groups of Iran concludes that the Jewish, Armenian, Assyrian, and Zoroastrian minorities were genetically isolated from the rest of the Iranian population for long periods.[20] These groups account for such a small share of the population, however, that although it can be concluded that they gained few members from Muslim population groups, the possibility cannot be ruled out that they lost members to assimilation with Muslim groups.

All these experiences of the creation of elite subgroups and the persistence of elites are consistent with the simple model of social mobility outlined in chapter 6. Elites and underclasses are formed by the selective affiliation to a religious identity of some upper or lower share of the distribution of abilities within the population. In Islamic societies, the practice of imposing taxes on religious minorities tended to recruit to Islam the lowest socioeconomic strata of conquered societies.[21] Elites and underclasses have maintained themselves over periods as long as 1,300 years because of very high rates of endogamy, which preserves the initial advantage of elites from regression to the mean by preventing intermarriage with less advantaged populations.

[19] Firoozi 1974, 65.

[20] Walter, Danker-Hopfe, and Amirshahi 1991.

[21] It is not clear whether this same mechanism accounts for the low socioeconomic status of Muslims in India by the time of the British Raj. See Eaton 1993.

Gypsies and Travellers in England

Do such explanations also hold for the major English underclass for the last four hundred years, the Gypsy or Traveller community? This community has long been at the bottom of the socioeconomic ladder in England. The U.K. Equality and Human Rights Commission notes that they are "one of the most deprived groups in Britain. Life expectancy for Gypsy and Traveller men and women is 10 years lower than the national average. Gypsy and Traveller mothers are 20 times more likely than the rest of the population to have experienced the death of a child. In 2003, less than a quarter of Gypsy and Traveller children obtained five GCSEs and A*–C grades, compared to more than half of students nationwide."[22]

Table 13.2 reports the result of a survey of nearly three hundred adult British and Irish Gypsies/Travellers in 2006. About half the people surveyed no longer traveled, and about a quarter traveled only in the summer. Even so, only two-thirds of the Travellers had ever attended school, and their average age on leaving school was thirteen. Nearly three-fifths of them smoked. Half reported a chronic cough, and more than a quarter reported suffering from anxiety or depression. Women on average had given birth to 4.3 children, and some were still of childbearing age.

A comparison group was composed, somewhat mysteriously, of poor English whites, Pakistanis, and blacks of Caribbean origin. The outcomes for the comparison group were, systematically, significantly better than for the Traveller population. The comparison group had more schooling and better health. They also, notably, had much lower fertility.

The mythology of the Gypsy/Traveller community is that they are the descendants of the Roma (Romany), with origins in India. However, there is plenty of evidence to suggest that the community is almost entirely of native British origin. Consider, for example, figure 13.5, which shows two Traveller children at the 2011 eviction of Travellers from an illegally occupied site at Dale Farm, Essex. These do not look like people of Indian origin.

Evidence from the surnames of Gypsies and Travellers in England suggests that they are indeed of domestic origin. Other immigrant groups in England, such as the Jewish population that emigrated to England in the seventeenth century and later, exhibit an unusual distribution of surnames by frequency.

---

[22] U.K., Equality and Human Rights Commission 2009, 5.

TABLE 13.2. Characteristics of Travellers and comparison disadvantaged group, England

Status	Travellers	Comparison group
Average age	38.1	38.4
Ever attended school (%)	66	88
Average age on leaving school	12.6	16.4
Current smoker (%)	58	22
Average number of children born (for women)	4.3	1.8
Reports anxiety/depression (%)	28	16
Chronic cough (%)	49	17

Figure 13.6 compares surname frequency in the general population to that among people with characteristically Jewish first names, such as Solomon and Golda, who were born in England between 1910 and 1914. The most common surnames in the native population in 1881 were very infrequent among Jews. Half the Jewish population had surnames held by fewer than two hundred people in 1881.

Gypsy or Traveller families tend not to have similarly distinctive surnames (figure 13.7). These families can be identified in the 1891 census as those whose housing is described in such terms as "in canvas tent," "in caravan," and "on the

FIGURE 13.5. Young Travellers look on as bailiffs evict Travellers from a settlement without planning permission at Dale Farm, Essex, 2011.

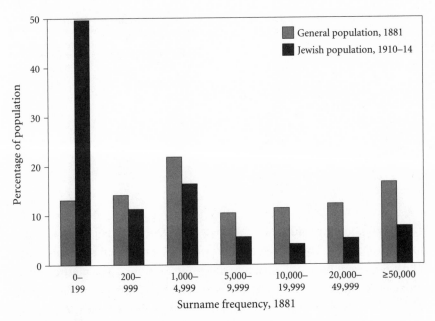

FIGURE 13.6. Surname frequencies among general population, 1881, and Jewish population 1910–14, England.

common" and their occupations as "travelling hawker" or "showman." Apart from one peculiarity, surname frequency in this group echoes that of the general population. That peculiarity is the unusually high frequency of the surname *Smith*. This is the most common surname in England: in 1891 it appeared at a frequency of 1.4 percent among the general population. Among Travellers, its frequency was 7.7 percent. Travellers do not seem to have had unusual surnames of non-English origin: their surnames are a representative sample of rare, intermediate, and common English surnames.

These findings suggest that the Gypsy and Traveller population of England is not descended from some exotic band of imported Roma, an underclass many generations old, but is almost entirely indigenous and more recent in origin.[23] It is likely that among the indigenous English population, by random chance, some families ended up at the margins of society as traveling harvest workers, hawkers, basket makers, and showmen. But this marginal group, perhaps even drawing inspiration from the few genuine Roma they encountered,

[23] Since I am Scottish and Irish in origin, I know at first hand how one's supposed cultural heritage can turn out to be largely a modern invention.

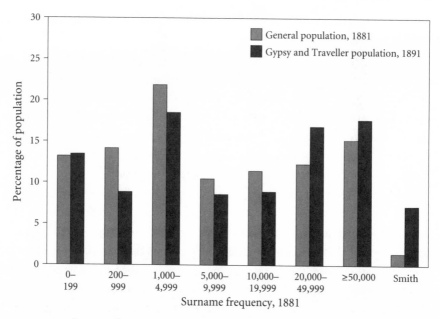

FIGURE 13.7. Surname frequencies among general population, 1881, and Gypsy and Traveller population 1891, England.

adopted a romanticized version of the Gypsy lifestyle and a creation myth of their own.[24]

By the nineteenth century, the first names of Gypsy and Traveller children were sometimes colorful. For boys, favored names allegedly included Goliath, Belcher, Dangerfield, Gilderoy, Nelson, Neptune, and Vandlo. Favored girls' names included Britannia, Cinderella, Dotia, Gentilia, Fairnette, Freedom, Mizelli, Ocean, Reservoir, Sinfai, and Vancy.[25] Are these timeless Gypsy names, passed down by Roma forefathers? Not likely. If we look at the extensive records of baptisms in England 1538–1837, we find that almost all these supposed Gypsy and Traveller surnames first appear only in the late eighteenth and nineteenth centuries. Thus the first recorded Cinderella baptism was in 1798, the first Goli-

[24] In line with this hypothesis, genetic testing suggests that the Irish Traveller community is entirely of Irish origin (North, Martin, and Crawford 2000). This article concludes that "these data support that the origin of the Travellers was not a sudden event; rather a gradual formation of populations" (p. 463). There are no equivalent genetic studies of the origins of English Gypsies and Travellers.

[25] These first names are from the Romany and Traveller Family History Society, n.d. In later periods, these names are associated with surnames held by many Traveller families.

ath 1817, the first Ocean 1797, the first Freedom 1803, and the first Gilderoy 1785.[26] (The late appearance of *Cinderella* is not surprising, since the Cinderella story, based on a French tale, was first published in English in 1729.)

The name evidence thus suggests that many of the modern-day Gypsies and Travellers of England are not descended from those of the seventeenth century. The normal process of social mobility should have brought those descendants closer to the social mean. Instead there is a steady flow of people into and out of Gypsy and Traveller communities. The more economically successful members of these communities acquire permanent homes and occupations more typically associated with the majority population. Because they are in no way racially distinct from the rest of the indigenous English population, and because their surnames do not reveal much about their background, they can at any time blend into the larger society. But at the same time that people leave the group, others from the margins of society flow in. These entrants adopt the lifestyle and mores of the Gypsies and Travellers. For example, the recent addition to the traveling community, the New Age Travellers who took to the road in the past generation, will likely merge into future generations of Gypsies and Travellers.

This hypothesis of an open Gypsy and Traveller community predicts that surnames concentrated in the Traveller community in 1891 or earlier, such as *Boswell, Penfold, Loveridge, Brazil,* and *Beeney* should trend upward toward the mean in social status.[27] Each generation, some of the Travellers with these surnames will move up and be incorporated into the settled society, so that the average surname status will rise. But only those who do not experience this upward mobility will continue to identify as Travellers. Thus self-identified Travellers would seem to be a minority not subject to social mobility.

However, testing this hypothesis by looking at the social status of a Traveller surname, such as *Loveridge,* from 1858 to the present does not yield the expected result. Figure 13.8 shows a measure of the social status of the surname *Loveridge* from 1858 to 2012, by decade. The status is measured by comparing the fraction of people called *Loveridge* whose estates were probated to the fraction of the general population whose estates were probated. For a surname of

---

[26] FamilySearch, n.d.

[27] Modern surnames associated with the Traveller community in England can be identified by their unusually fast population growth and their high rate of intermarriage with *Smiths,* since *Smith* is unusually prevalent among Travellers.

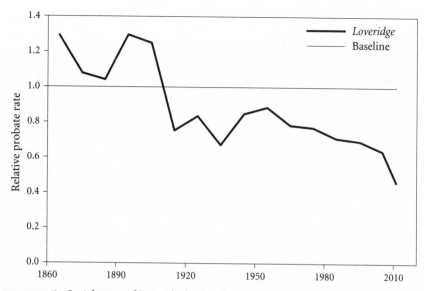

FIGURE 13.8. Social status of *Loveridge* by decade, 1858–2012.

average status, this fraction is one. For names of above-average status, the figure is greater than one, and for names of below-average status, it is less than one. Interestingly, until 1910, *Loveridge* was a relatively high-status surname. But since then its average status has declined steadily, so that by 2000 the probate rate of *Loveridges* was only about 60 percent of the average.[28]

What is happening here? Although rare surnames can move away from the social mean of status as a result of random forces, *Loveridge* is so common as to make such a random movement wildly improbable. By 2002 there were more than five thousand *Loveridges* in England and Wales. Does the decline of this name suggest that the law of mobility sometimes does not predict social outcomes? Can social groups systematically move downward in status?

The likely solution to this puzzle, which does not violate the law of mobility, is the following. *Loveridge* had exceptional growth in frequency for a common surname in England in the years 1881–2002. In that interval, the stock of the average indigenous surname did not quite double. Yet in the same interval, *Loveridges* increased nearly fourfold. This disproportionate increase may be

[28] There are other signs of the low social status of the *Loveridges* in recent years. A search on the Internet for recent arrests and convictions in England and Wales showed eight times as many *Loveridges* as *Barclays*, even though the name *Barclay* has about 20 percent more holders than *Loveridge*.

attributed to the very high fertility rates among Gypsy and Traveller families in modern times, illustrated in table 13.2 above. Such fertility rates would double the population of Travellers in each generation and could explain why, even though a substantial fraction of *Loveridges* are not Travellers, the overall stock of the name could increase so much over time. If fertility is much higher for low-status families with a given surname, then even if every family conforms to the law of mobility, the average social status of the surname can move downward from the mean over time.

The implication here is that the children of the low-status *Loveridges* are indeed regressing to the mean over generations, and they have so many more children than the high-status families that the surname group is diverging toward the bottom end of the status distribution. Figure 13.9 simulates this effect for a population that starts in the first generation with average social status, and in which status regresses to the mean with a persistence rate of 0.7. Fertility, however, is at twice the average rate at the bottom of the distribution and half the average rate at the top. In this case, mean status moves downward from the mean, despite every family's regressing to the mean.

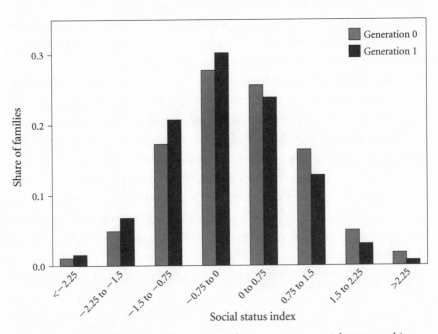

FIGURE 13.9. Simulated downward movement of surname-group social status resulting from fertility effects.

The downward mobility in this example above will continue until the average status reaches an equilibrium at which the mean for the group is sufficiently low that regression to the mean can balance the excess fertility at the bottom end of the status distribution. Thus another explanation for long-lasting underclasses in a society, even with intermarriage between the underclass and the rest of the population, is that the underclass has much higher fertility rates than the society as a whole. The effects of marital exogamy in pulling the group toward the mean are offset by the higher fertility of poorer members of the group. However, in preindustrial society, poor groups typically had lower fertility rates than richer groups, so this effect could operate only in the modern world (in this case, since 1880).

The example of the *Loveridges* does suggest, however, that under current conditions, no matter how many campsites and social services are provided by local authorities in Britain, a distinct and poor Gypsy and Traveller population is likely to persist in England and Ireland for the foreseeable future, beyond the reach of the normal processes of social mobility.

Elites and Underclasses in the Modern United States

The proposition that elites and underclasses are not created by religion, culture, or race is supported by evidence from the United States on current elite and underclass populations. A quick confirmation of this proposition can be obtained by looking at surnames identified with particular ethnic or national groups and counting the numbers of registered physicians per thousand of each surname type in 2000. We can divide this number by the average number of physicians registered per person in the United States in 2000. For the population as a whole, this number will be one.

Figure 13.10 shows the implied elite populations in descending order. Topping this list, surprisingly, are names of Egyptian Coptic origin. For such surnames, there are a remarkable forty-eight physicians per thousand holders of the surname in 2000. This rate of representation among physicians is thirteen times that of the average surname in the United States. Next come Hindu surnames, then Indian Christian surnames, then Iranian Muslim surnames, then Maronite Christian surnames, originally from Lebanon. All these groups are represented among physicians at a frequency six or more times that of the general population. All are relatively more frequent among physicians than even Ashkenazi and Sephardic Jewish surnames. These new elites in the United States

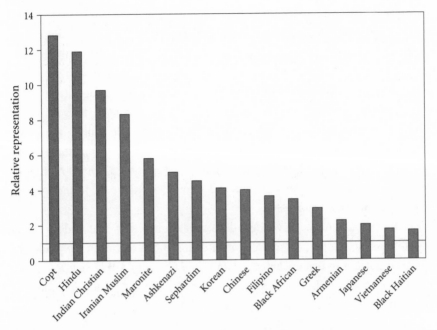

FIGURE 13.10. Elites in the modern United States, measured by relative representation among physicians.

span three major religious traditions: Christian, Muslim, and Hindu. But the Christian groups here represent mostly a very traditional, unreformed Christianity. The Coptic Church, for example, has a liturgy in Coptic, a language no longer spoken by church members. Part of the Maronite liturgy is in Aramaic, again not spoken by the congregants. Many Indian Christians are of Portuguese descent or from families converted by the Portuguese, or are from the even older Syriac tradition. U.S. elites exhibit an astonishing diversity now of backgrounds and cultural heritage.[29]

The remaining elite groups are Koreans and Chinese, followed by Filipinos, black Africans, and Greek surnames, and finally Armenians, Japanese, Vietnamese, and black Haitians. Almost every major race and religious tradition is represented—except for European Protestants.

[29] The measure here of the social status of groups correlates well with other measures, such as average household income by country of origin, where these surname groups can be identified with nationalities. See U.S. Census Bureau 2010.

Many of these modern elites are creations of U.S. immigration policy, which for countries far from the United States is biased strongly in favor of skilled immigrants. The elite status of Hindu, Indian Christian, and black African surnames can be attributed almost entirely to this factor. But other elite groups are the product of events in other countries that led to selective migration by groups within these countries. During the rule of the Shah of Iran, many Iranian students attended U.S. universities. With the revolution of 1979, many of these students chose to stay in the United States, and many other highly educated Iranians fled the new Islamic republic to take up residence in the United States. Similarly, before the fall of South Vietnam to the Communists in 1975, Vietnamese immigration to the United States was negligible. But in the initial years of the new regime, many Vietnamese associated with the previous regime fled, including many skilled and educated families. Other groups, such as the Copts, the Maronites, and Jews, already constituted elites in their home societies. But for the Copts, immigration to the United States has because of immigration policy attracted higher-status Copts, which has made this group even more elite in the United States.

In a recent study, Cynthia Feliciano examines the educational attainment of migrants to the United States relative to the average for their home country. She creates an index of selectivity in migration for each sending country, which is based on the relative education level of migrants to the United States compared to nonmigrants. The correlation of physician frequency in the United States with this measure of migration selectivity is 0.75 for the eleven countries where there is national-level information, as shown in figures 13.10 and 13.11. The countries with the greatest educational disparities for migrants to the United States include Iran and India, which also have among the greatest disproportions in physician frequencies.[30]

Figure 13.11 shows, in contrast, surname groups underrepresented among physicians in the United States. An interesting variation among the long-established, largely white population is the underrepresentation of Cajun and New France surnames relative to Dutch and English surnames.[31] This finding,

---

[30] Feliciano 2005, 140.

[31] The Cajun community of Louisiana originated in groups expelled in 1763 from Acadia by the British. Many of their surnames overlap with those of other New France groups, but some are distinct. Here they are identified as names ending in *-eaux*, an ending common in Louisiana but generally uncommon elsewhere in North America, of which less than 10 percent

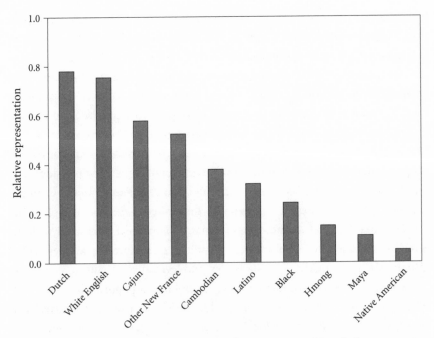

FIGURE 13.11. Underclasses in the modern United States, measured by relative representation among physicians.

as discussed in chapter 3, seems to relate to the history of French settlement in North America and negative selection in migration of French Canadians to the United States.

The other surnames heavily underrepresented are Cambodian, Latino, black American, Hmong, Mayan, and Native American. The Hmong engaged mainly in subsistence farming in the hills of Laos before coming to the United States. The U.S. Hmong community seems to represent a broad cross section of the Hmong population of Laos, entire communities having moved to refugee camps in Thailand out of fear of the Communist Laotian government and then been admitted en masse to the United States. Thus an entire disadvantaged refugee community in Laos has been transplanted to the United States. As a conse-

---

of holders in 2000 were black. The most prominent such name is *Boudreaux,* which is twenty times more common in Louisiana than in any other U.S. state or Canadian province, and sixty times more common in the United States than in France.

quence of these processes, there are eighty times as many physicians per capita with Hindu Indian surnames such as *Banerjee* or *Ganguly* than there are with Hmong surnames such as *Her, Lor,* or *Vang.*[32]

For Latino surname groups, selective immigration again seems to be a powerful force shaping social status in the United States. Much of this population originates from Mexico and Central America, and a considerable proportion of the original migrants entered or remained in the United States illegally. Illegal migration should not be an attractive option for educated populations, given the manifest disadvantages that illegal status imposes in the United States. There has been considerable debate about whether Mexican migrants to the United States are negatively selected. Recent research suggests convincingly that Mexican migrants to the United States in recent years have substantially less schooling than nonmigrants and earned considerably less in Mexico before migrating than did nonmigrants.[33]

We saw above in figure 3.3 that long-established populations descended from European origins, aside from the French, tend to have social status close to the average. These populations mainly arrived in the era of open immigration before 1914. A recent study of Norwegian migration in this period finds that, consistent with this, the forces of selection for emigrants were not strong. There was definite negative selection for migrants from urban areas in Norway. But for the more numerically important rural areas the evidence was ambiguous as to whether selection was positive or negative.[34]

Thus the accidents of geography, immigration policy, and social and political events in countries around the world are even now creating new upper and lower social classes in the United States. These classes will be a feature of U.S. society for many generations to come, until the processes of intermarriage eventually eliminate these distinctions.

---

[32] These were identified as surnames whose greatest concentration was in the six main centers of Hmong settlement: Fresno, Merced, and Sacramento, California; Saint Paul and Minneapolis, Minnesota; and Milwaukee, Wisconsin.

[33] Moraga 2011. The average male migrant in the period 2000–2004 had 7.2 years of schooling, compared to 8.5 for the average nonmigrant, and on average earned only 71 percent of nonmigrants' earnings. Women migrants had 8.4 years of schooling compared to 7.9 for nonmigrants but earned only 77 percent of average nonmigrants' earnings. Since four-fifths of migrants were male, the net effect is one of strong negative selection (p. 76).

[34] Abramitzky, Boustan, and Eriksson 2012.

Conclusion

The persistence of high and low status for some groups in various societies would seem to contradict the simple law of mobility for social status. However, in each of the anomalous cases discussed above, there are factors at play that can make even extreme persistence consistent with the same universal tendency for families to regress toward the mean over time. Elites and underclasses seem to be created by mechanisms that select them from the top or bottom of the established status distribution. They can also be created, as in the case of the Gypsy/Traveller community in England, by differential fertility between higher- and lower-status members of a group.

Once established, these differences in social status can be maintained by marital endogamy, as seems to have happened with Christian and Jewish minorities in the Muslim world, or they can be maintained by selective movement between social groups, as in the case of Catholics and Protestants in Ireland.

FOURTEEN

Mobility Anomalies

The same Norman nobility which surrounded the throne of the Conqueror, continues, in its remote posterity, to occupy the same place in the reign of the Conqueror's latest descendant, our present sovereign—continues to occupy its baronial place in Parliament—continues to preside on the judicial bench— continues to lead our armies and navies in battle, and continues generally to control and direct the affairs of the English empire.

The Norman People and Their Existing Descendants in the British Dominions and the United States of America, 1874

THE PREVIOUS CHAPTER LISTED SOME seeming deviations from the social law of motion that can be explained by processes of selection, selective affiliation to groups, or differential fertility within groups. There are some other anomalies that are not so easy to explain and that violate the idea that there is one underlying rate of persistence for all social groups.

One of these anomalies concerns the composition of the English and Welsh Members of the Westminster Parliament. We have records of the composition of Parliament since 1295. It is a small group: until the seventeenth century, MPs numbered between two and three hundred, expanding to 513 by 1678. The England and Wales membership of the U.K. Parliament has remained in the range 485–573 down to the present. MPs represent a tiny fraction of the population, and their social status is somewhat unclear.

Parliaments began to assemble regularly in the reign of Edward I (r. 1272–1307), who engaged in significant numbers of expansionary military campaigns against the Welsh and Scots and needed parliamentary approval to raise the taxes required to fund them. Before the 1832 Reform Act, the Parliament contained two sorts of representatives. First, there were two knights from each county, 74 MPs in all. Second, there were variable numbers of representatives of boroughs, the burgesses, with 170 towns in England at various times having the right to send representatives to Parliament.

The county knights seem to have had higher status: in the fourteenth century they were paid forty-eight pence per day for attending Parliament and burgesses only twenty-four pence. However, given that the day wage of a laborer was no more than threepence per day, these were clearly all high-status individuals. The representatives came from the most influential commoners in each town and county. Absent better evidence, it is assumed that Parliament represented the top 0.5 percent of society throughout these years.

Based on the evidence of social mobility in education and for wealth, as illustrated by surname groups (see chapters 4 and 5), artisan surnames would be expected to have had a proportional representation among MPs in England. But that is not the case. Figure 14.1 shows the share of artisan surnames in Parliament compared to their share among Oxford and Cambridge students. There is a lot of variation, because of the small size and infrequent meetings of early Parliaments, but artisan surnames are systematically underrepresented until the late nineteenth century.

The absence of a representative share of people with artisan surnames before 1900 is reflected in a surprising abundance of the surnames of medieval elites. Figure 14.2, for example, shows the relative representation of locative surnames and Norman surnames in Parliament.

The Norman surnames are the most striking anomaly. Until 1800, Norman surnames were eight times more likely than the typical surname to appear

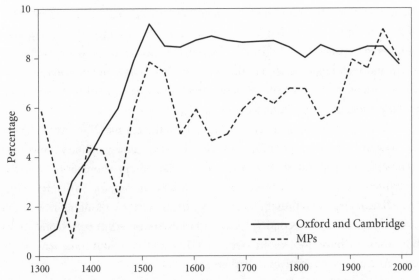

FIGURE 14.1. Percentages of artisan surnames among MPs and among Oxford and Cambridge students, 1300–2012.

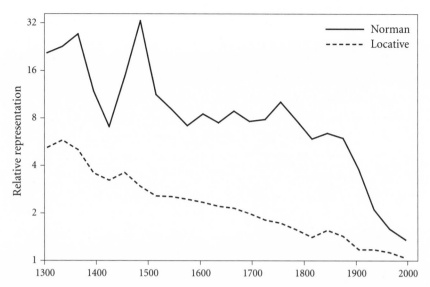

FIGURE 14.2. Relative representation of Norman and locative surnames among MPs, 1300–2012.

among MPs. This implies an astonishing persistence of political status for the descendants of the determined band of adventurers who triumphed on the bloody battlefield of Hastings on October 14, 1066. More than seven hundred years later, their descendants were still heavily overrepresented in Parliament.

High-status locative surnames from the medieval period also show unusual persistence in Parliament. By 1700 their relative representation was still about twice the expected rate. By the eighteenth century, the persistence rate for both the locative and the Norman surnames had declined to the levels we find for surname groups in general. Thus, as figure 14.3 shows, the intergenerational correlation for locative surnames between 1700 and 2012 is 0.84. By the twentieth century, the overrepresentation of locative surnames among MPs had declined to a mere 10 percent. But even in the twentieth century, Norman surnames remained overrepresented among English and Welsh MPs in Parliament.

The persistence among MPs of the surnames of the medieval elite remains something of a mystery. Moreover, it seems to have been unaffected by changes to the composition of Parliament in the nineteenth and early twentieth centuries. As can be seen in figure 14.3, the parliamentary and voting reforms of 1832, 1867, and 1918 are not associated with any sudden changes in the surname composition of MPs.

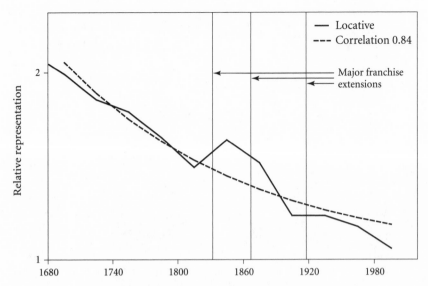

FIGURE 14.3. Social mobility rate of locative surnames among MPs, 1680–2012.

Norman surnames are also significantly overrepresented in English armies in the years 1369–1453, more than three hundred years (ten generations) after the Norman Conquest. This was the period of the Hundred Years' War, the long struggle between the French and English crowns for control of the English-held territories in France. The evidence on the composition of armies comes from surviving muster rolls, which list soldiers engaged in English armies in France, Scotland, Wales, and elsewhere.[1]

Table 14.1 shows the numbers of those serving at various ranks in the English armed forces and also the percentage of their surnames that come from the Norman-derived surname sample discussed in chapter 4. Norman surnames clearly still represented an elite. The higher the social status of the person in the army, the greater the share of Norman surnames. At the top level—earls, barons, and bishops—approximately a fifth of those recorded have Norman surnames, as opposed to less than 0.3 percent of the general population in England who bore such surnames.

What is surprising, however, is the heavy concentration of Norman-derived surnames at all ranks of the armed forces. Even among the lowest ranks of the

[1] The database is available online at www.medievalsoldier.org/index.php. The details of its construction are given in Bell et al. 2013.

TABLE 14.1. Norman surnames in English muster rolls and universities, 1369–1453

Rank	Number	Percentage with Norman surname
Earl	56	39.3
Baron, bishop	153	13.1
Knight	1,729	10.6
Gentleman	47	0.0
Esquire	8,463	3.0
Man-at-arms	17,742	2.5
Archer, crossbowman, hobelar	58,220	1.0
Oxford and Cambridge students	12,640	1.0

army, the archers, Norman surnames still show up at three or four times the frequency predicted by their population share. Archers were skilled workers, with wages comparable to artisans, but did not rank particularly high on the social scale. The preponderance of Norman surnames among them thus does not stem from the relatively high social status of these names: to the contrary, this should have led to Norman surnames' being underrepresented in these ranks. Instead it seems to suggest that even ten generations after the conquest, the descendants of the Norman conquerors still had a taste and facility for organized violence. This hypothesis is supported by the share of knights and esquires in these armies with Norman surnames. This was 3–11 percent, much greater than the share of Norman surnames found in the more pacific realm of Oxford and Cambridge at the same time.

This particular concentration of Norman surnames in the realm of violence is not contemplated in the general theory of social mobility advanced here and thus represents an unexplained anomaly.

PART THREE

THE GOOD SOCIETY

FIFTEEN

Is Mobility Too Low?

Mobility versus Inequality

R EPORTS IN EARLIER WORKING PAPERS that the true persistence rate of social status is on the order of 0.75, even in the United States and Sweden, were greeted by many commentators with dismay.[1] And indeed, even with the earlier reports of persistence rates of 0.5, many people already regarded U.S. society as mired in unfairness. Thus James Heckman, the eminent economist, states in a recent essay titled "Promoting Social Mobility": "While we celebrate equality of opportunity, we live in a society in which birth is becoming fate. . . . This powerful impact of birth on life chances is bad for individuals born into disadvantage. And it is bad for American society. We are losing out on the potential contributions of large numbers of our citizens. It does not have to be this way. With smart social policy, we can arrest the polarization between skilled and unskilled."[2]

This general dismay has multiple sources. First, the American Dream, embodied in the phrase "all men are created equal" in the Declaration of Independence, has been believed to hold only if social mobility rates are high. America may be a violent society and one with scant safety nets for those on its bottom margins. But to many, rapid social mobility is the proof that Americans live in a country of equal opportunity, no matter the circumstances of their birth. It is the proof that however great the disadvantages of birth—and however indifferent the polity to the plight of the poor—talent, hard work, and enterprise will be rewarded. It is the evidence that the talentless or idle children of the upper

[1] See, for example, "Nomencracy" 2013.
[2] Heckman 2012.

261

classes cannot secure their status in life merely through inherited wealth and social connections.

The conditions for those at the bottom of U.S. society, in terms of material wealth, health, and personal safety, may be grim. But with rapid mobility, no one with desire and determination is condemned to live forever in that squalid netherworld. However, the surname-mobility estimates seem to imply that the founding document of the United States should instead read: "All men are created equal, but some are more equal than others."

The second source of unease is the ability to predict so much about the general social prospects of any individual at birth. This capacity appears to deny the importance of human agency and free will. That so much is knowable at birth seemingly implies that there are people whom we can instruct at age 5, "Don't bother with education, for we can be confident that you will spend your life at the lower margins of society."

A third source of discomfort is the perceived waste of potential. It is assumed that if social mobility rates are low, there are people who, if born into other families, would have had very different life outcomes. This is Heckman's major point in the passage quoted above. Even in the modern United States or Sweden, people with potentially great contributions to make to society are trapped in unskilled jobs well below their capabilities.

A fourth source of disquiet comes from the fact that a century of redistribution, public education, and social policy seems to have done nothing to improve the social mobility rates. Social mobility is no higher in modern Sweden than in the United States or even preindustrial England.

The response to the first concern is that it is true that the absence of rapid social mobility means that we lack proof that America is a meritocracy. But slow mobility does not itself prove the opposite—that America is rife with nepotism and privilege. As is discussed below, a completely meritocratic society would most likely also be one with limited social mobility. Slow mobility does not, in itself, imply a rigidly hierarchical society.

The second concern, the worry about the elimination of human agency, is misdirected. Even with an intergenerational correlation of 0.75, more than two-fifths of variation in outcomes in generalized social status is still unpredictable. True, for those at the bottom, the chance of making it to the top in one generation is dauntingly small. But there is still plenty of room for people to improve their social position compared to their parents'. And indeed, the prediction for those people at the bottom is that their prospects, while limited, are generally better than those of their parents.

The second reason that this concern with agency is misdirected is that although we may be able to predict to a high degree your success in life, whatever success you do attain will still be achieved only through struggle, effort, and initiative. We can predict only that you are likely to be the type of person who can make the effort and endure defeats along the way in order to succeed socially and economically in the end. Predicting social success, even if that success comes from genetics, is not like predicting height. In high-income societies there is very little that individuals can do to change their preordained, genetically determined final height. But social and economic outcomes are determined by the agency of the person.

The response to the third concern, waste of potential, is more complex. The simple law of social mobility detailed in chapters 6 and 7 assumes that mobility is driven by the strong inheritance of underlying abilities. If existing rates of social mobility imply a loss of potential for society, then it must be possible to improve underlying abilities through transfers to families of money or other resources. Conversely, if it is impossible to significantly improve the next generations' outcomes through any intervention, then there is no waste of potential, and social mobility rates are optimal. All is for the best in this best of all possible worlds.

In his recent book *Coming Apart: The State of White America, 1960–2010,* Charles Murray documents the many ways in which the white underclass differs in behavior from the white upper class.[3] Satisfaction with marriage is lower, divorce is more common, and children live more frequently with just one parent and much less frequently with both biological parents. Both men and women work less. Criminal behavior—both violence and theft—is more common. Church attendance is lower. Voting is less common. Trust in the fairness and integrity of others is lower. Murray's message is simple: as long as the behaviors and values of the white underclass differ from those of the white upper class, the outcomes will differ substantially.

Another important part of Murray's message is that in the years 1960–2010, the behaviors of the white upper class and underclass steadily diverged, increasing the inequality in outcomes in modern America and entrenching the positions

---

[3] Murray 2012.

of the privileged and deprived groups. But the examination of social mobility in the United States above finds no sign that social mobility rates have in fact declined in recent decades (see chapter 3).

But is there evidence to support the views of such thinkers as Heckman and Murray that smart social policy, or a reeducation in the Protestant ethic of the Founding Fathers, would greatly improve the outcomes for low-status families and hence rates of social mobility? One way to test such claims is to look at the outcomes for adoptees. If status outcomes are heavily socially determined, then adoptees will resemble their parents as much as biological children do, and they will also significantly resemble their genetically unrelated siblings.

The research on adoption outcomes, however, implies strongly that most of the variation in outcomes for adopted children stems from their biological parents or from chance, not from their adoptive parents. Biology may not be everything, but it is the substantial majority of everything. However, the adoption studies do leave open the possibility that social interventions could change outcomes for children from the most disadvantaged backgrounds.

Studies of the inheritance of intelligence, for example, find that adoptive parents matter a lot for outcomes among younger children, but that as children approach adulthood, their intelligence more closely matches that of their biological parents. Thus one long-running study in Colorado, which compares adopted children with a control group of children from nonadoptive families, finds that at age sixteen the correlation of the IQ of adopted children with that of their adoptive parents is effectively zero, whereas it averages 0.3 for the matched control families. Figure 15.1 shows how the pattern varies with age.[4]

One limitation of adoption studies, however, is that the range in variation among adoptive parents does not include "the environmental extremes of disadvantage, neglect, and abuse."[5] Adoptive parents are subject to screening by adoption agencies that biological parents do not face. Thus when we compare the effects of nature and nurture in these studies, we exclude some of the variation in nurture that occurs in practice. But the authors of a series of papers on the Colorado Adoption Project note that adoptive families "are reasonably representative of the middle 90% of the population."[6]

---

[4] Plomin et al. 1997, table 1. The correlation of intelligence with fathers is as high as with mothers, even though for the children studied, born in the years 1975–82, mothers would have interacted with children more than fathers.

[5] Plomin et al. 1997, 446.

[6] Plomin et al. 1997, 446. Two other adoption studies, in Minnesota and Texas, found more

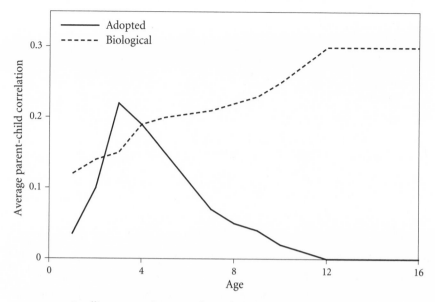

FIGURE 15.1. Intelligence correlations with age for adoptees.

Studies looking at the outcomes in the adult lives of adopted children are rarer. They support the idea that biology dominates nurture but suggest that nurture has some effect. One elegant study is that of Bruce Sacerdote, who looked at various outcomes for Korean adoptees in the United States.[7] These children were randomly assigned to approved families with varying degrees of education and economic resources. The adoptive families did not include those at the lower end of the income distribution: U.S. law required the adoptive families to have incomes of at least 125 percent of the poverty level. But in other respects the adoptive families spanned a wide range of income and education.

Table 15.1 shows the share of variation in each outcome for the Korean adoptees and their nonadopted siblings that is explained by nurture as opposed to nature. The proportion of outcomes explained by nurture is just the correlation between these outcomes for nonrelated adopted siblings, assuming that the family assignments were indeed random. The proportion explained by nature is derived from how much closer the correlations of biological siblings were for

---

correlation between adoptive parents and children at age 18 than did the Colorado study. But these correlations averaged just 0.12 and 0.06, still very low. The overall average across the three studies is thus 0.07 (Richardson and Norgate 2006, 320).

[7] Sacerdote 2007.

TABLE 15.1. Proportion of outcomes explained by nature and nurture for Korean adoptees

Outcome	Proportion explained by nurture	Proportion explained by nature
Height	0.01	0.86
Family income	0.11	0.33
Four years of college	0.14	0.41
Smokes	0.15	0.27
Drinks alcohol	0.34	0.06
Selectivity of college	0.34	0.24

these same families.[8] We can see that height is indeed largely biologically determined, whereas alcohol consumption is almost entirely socially determined.

For characteristics other than height, adopted siblings were always significantly correlated, despite their absence of genetic connection. Their shared family environment had an influence. But family environment appears to have only a very modest influence on the later earnings of children. Genetic inheritance explains three times as much of children's income variation as does family environment. Figure 15.2 shows an adopted child's adult income relative to the adoptive parents' income at the time of adoption. There is no connection. So the correlation of incomes for adopted siblings is due to aspects of their shared family environment other than parental resources. There is no sign here that giving extra income to families would result in higher incomes for the next generation.

For educational attainment, the correlation between children and their adoptive parents was higher than for income. But again, nature explains three times as much of the variation as does nurture. As figure 15.3 shows, the mother's educational attainment has little relationship to the outcomes for adopted children. This confirms findings from a study in Norway on the effect of introducing compulsory schooling: additional years of education for parents do not in themselves predict more years of schooling for their children.[9] Similarly, a study in Sweden has shown that for adopted children, years of education can be

[8] It is two times the correlation between genetically related siblings minus the correlation between genetically unrelated siblings.

[9] Black, Devereux, and Salvanes 2005.

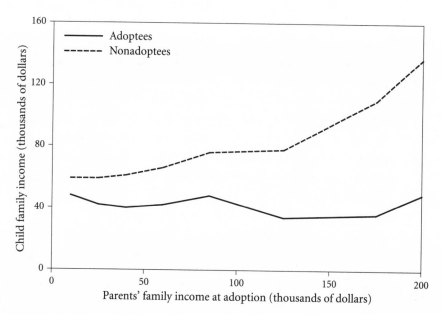

FIGURE 15.2. Income for Korean adoptees versus parents' income.

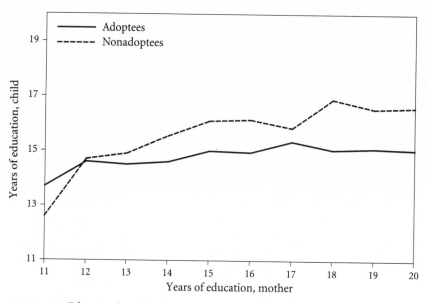

FIGURE 15.3. Education level for Korean adoptees and their mothers.

predicted from the educational attainment of both the biological parents and the adoptive parents. The effects of the adoptive parents are stronger in the Swedish case than in the case of the Korean adoptees. But the variation in biological parents' education still explains twice as much variation in children's educational attainment as that of the adoptive parents.[10]

In the Korean adoptions study, families did play a substantial role in educational achievement in one respect: getting adopted children into more selective colleges (table 15.1). Here the correlations between unrelated sibling adoptees were substantial, and genetics played a subsidiary role. But the earnings outcomes suggest that getting into selective colleges had little effect on the future incomes of adoptees, for which the correlations were much lower.

These adoption studies suggest that even if we could make the familial environment of every child in the United States identical, we would reduce the intergenerational correlation of social outcomes by only modest amounts, perhaps one-quarter of existing values. Moreover, it is not clear that public policies can do much to change family environments in the ways that matter to the social outcomes for children. Public policy can change the amounts of income available to families and even the amounts of education parents receive. But the causal role that family income and parental education play in child outcomes is itself highly uncertain. Other elements of parental behavior that cannot be compensated for by public policy may be the crucial ones. And these other parental behaviors may well be associated with the genetics of parents. It may be impossible to reduce the influence of inheritance in determining social outcomes through government actions.

Confirming the idea that genetics potentially plays a substantial role in outcomes are the correlations in earnings reported in an interesting recent study of siblings of different types in Sweden. Assume that the correlation in earnings between siblings has separable contributions from shared environments and shared genetics. Assume also that the environment contribution to correlation for all siblings raised together is s, and for siblings raised apart it is zero. The genetic connection produces a correlation of g for those sharing all genes. Assume, finally, that mating is not assortative for the genes that matter to earnings.

This model has two strong simplifying assumptions. The assumption of zero environment correlation for siblings raised apart is unrealistic, but it turns

[10] Björklund, Lindahl, and Plug 2006.

out that this is not what mainly determines the fit of the model. The assumption of no assortative mating is more important. In this case it implies the correlation of adopted siblings should be s, half siblings reared together $s + 0.25g$, half siblings living apart $0.25g$, full siblings and fraternal twins reared together $s + 0.5g$, full siblings reared apart $0.5g$, and identical twins reared together $s + g$. Table 15.2 shows the predicted pattern of correlations under these assumptions, as well as the observed pattern. The authors report that the best fit under this model would be a family-environment contribution to correlation of only 0.02 and a genetic contribution of 0.26. Table 15.2 shows why these values come close to explaining the patterns observed. This would make genetics more than ten times as important as environment in explaining earnings outcomes.

The authors report that in statistical terms, this simple model fails to explain the observed correlations: the correct model of the correlations has to be different. But although it fails, what is interesting is how close it comes to succeeding. The effects of family environment are more important than this simple model implies, but any explanation of these various sibling correlations requires a much larger genetic component than has typically been assumed.

If social status is largely transmitted through inherited genes or familial cultures, then shocks to wealth should have a much smaller effect on social status over generations than wealth that is gained through some inborn higher level of social competence. It is difficult, however, to find instances of random shocks to wealth that are uncorrelated with the characteristics of recipients for which we can observe the effects on the next generation. In an interesting and ingenious study, Hoyt Bleakley of the University of Chicago and Joe Ferrie of

TABLE 15.2. Earnings correlations between siblings of different types, Sweden, 1987–93

Sibling type	Reared together, predicted	Reared together, observed	Reared apart, predicted	Reared apart, observed
Identical twins (monozygotic)	$g + s$	0.34	—	—
Fraternal twins (dizygotic)	$0.5g + s$	0.14	—	—
Full siblings	$0.5g + s$	0.15	$0.5g$	0.14
Half siblings	$0.25g + s$	0.10	$0.25g$	0.08
Adoptive siblings	s	0.07	—	—

Northwestern University document one such random shock to wealth and its generational consequences. The removal of the Cherokee from the eastern part of the United States, following the passage of the Indian Removal Act of 1830, opened up for distribution large parcels of land in northwest Georgia. The state of Georgia organized a lottery to distribute eighteen thousand 160-acre parcels of land in Cherokee County in 1832.[11]

Adult males resident for at least three years in Georgia were eligible to one draw in this lottery, and almost all eligible men entered. The winners constituted just under one-fifth of the adult male population. The parcels of land had an average value equal to the median wealth in Georgia by 1850. Further, the land could be immediately sold: the winners did not need to take possession themselves or to homestead their property. So the lottery prize was equivalent to a large cash transfer (equivalent to nearly $150,000 today) to a random selection of adult males in Georgia.[12]

Tracking winners and their sons through the United States censuses of 1850, 1870, and 1880, Bleakley and Ferrie show, first, that by 1850, winners were indeed richer on average than losers. The value of the allotted land by then averaged $900, and the average wealth of winners was $700 higher than that of losers. So the winners were able to retain much of the benefit of winning for at least some years.

However, when we look at the children of the winners in 1870 and 1880, we see little sign that the good fortune of their fathers significantly changed their life chances. They were no more literate than the children of losers. Their occupational status was no higher. Their own children in 1880 (the grandchildren of the 1832 winners) were again no more literate. Worse, they were significantly less likely to be enrolled in school than the grandchildren of the losers.[13]

The comparative wealth of the children of lottery winners and losers is harder to estimate precisely; data on children's wealth are available only for 1870. Wealth is not statistically significantly higher for lottery winners' children, but the variance is so great that we cannot rule out the possibility that the wealth gains from the lottery were indeed transferred to the children. What we do observe is that a substantial shock to wealth alone did little to change the social status of families in nineteenth-century Georgia.

[11] The winners, however, did not obtain possession of the land until the removal of the Cherokee in 1838.

[12] Bleakley and Ferrie 2013a.

[13] Bleakley and Ferrie 2013b, table 6.

In an ironic reversal of the Georgia lottery, another set of windfalls has been created recently by Indian gaming profits. A recent study of child mental health in rural North Carolina, by design, oversampled children from the Eastern Band of Cherokee Indians. A casino opened on the Eastern Cherokee reservation in 1997, midway through the study. From 1998 on, parents of Cherokee children in the study received annual lump-sum disbursements of casino profits. Relative to the average incomes of these families, typically less than $30,000 per year, these annual payments of $4,000–$8,000 were large and were expected to be ongoing. Since households did not reduce labor-force participation in response to the payments, these families became substantially better off. Indeed, their anticipated lifetime gains were of a similar relative magnitude to those of Georgia land lottery winners.

The youngest children in the study experienced these family-income gains from age 14 onward, and there was information on their outcomes up to age 21. At age 18, conditional on their graduation from high school, they became eligible for their own annual payment of $4,000 from the casino proceeds.[14] What effect did these payments have on the lives of these Cherokee children?

The study concludes that for those not living in poverty, the effects were limited. There was no measurable change in any educational outcomes, including high-school graduation rates, by age 21—despite the immediate cash gains that the children got for three years just for completing high school. Beneficiaries were less likely to commit minor crimes (but not major crimes) or sell drugs. Among those who were living in poverty before the income supplement, children in the youngest cohort were much more likely to graduate from high school, and they completed one to two more years of education by age 21. As with children from the more prosperous families, there were fewer minor crimes and less drug selling.[15]

In one respect these results confirm the "large effects" of exogenous shocks to income, as the authors describe them. But in another respect, they show that the influence of wealth on outcomes is limited. Children of families above the poverty line—78 percent of U.S. children—seem to gain little from a significant exogenous boost in family income or a cash incentive to complete high school. And while for the poorer children the combination of gains in family income

[14] Akee et al. 2010. All Cherokee children became eligible for the annual payment at age 21, regardless of educational status.
[15] Akee et al. 2010, tables 5 and 9.

and the extra cash inducement to complete high school did lead to more education, it is not certain that this will yield gains in living conditions for these children later in life. At age 21, we are still observing outcomes early in the life cycle.

The absence of such effects at most levels of income is confirmed by a study of the effects of the Norwegian oil boom on educational outcomes for children. Incomes for all families in some regions of Norway increased during the 1970s as the result of increased demand for labor, driven by the exploitation of North Sea oil. The study compared children born between 1967 and 1969 in Rogaland, a county on the southern coast of Norway with extensive connection to oil extraction, with those born in counties unaffected by the boom. The income gains in Rogaland had no effect on the years of education achieved by children there.[16]

The author of the study, Katrine Løken, wonders if this lack of difference is a result of Nordic social-welfare programs: "Norway has very high public investment in children. All students in higher education are eligible for grants and subsidies from the government to finance their education. . . . It is possible that family income would have an impact on children's educational attainment if all of these government interventions were removed."[17] But if this were the case, then social mobility rates in countries with similarly extensive educational and social-welfare programs, such as modern Sweden, should be much higher than elsewhere. We have seen, however, that underlying social mobility rates in Sweden are just as low as in more laissez-faire economies.

At least one study, however, found much stronger effects of income shocks on children's outcomes. Phil Oreopoulos and my colleagues Marianne Page and Ann Stevens looked at the effects on children's income after fathers lost their jobs when a firm closed in Canada. Such job losses have permanent effects on workers' future earnings, and can be regarded as random negative shocks to income that affect individual workers. Each of the male workers chosen for the study had a son between twelve and fourteen years old at the time of the closing.

The study found that six years after the firm closed, the family income was still an average of 9 percent lower than before the closure. Thus the sons experienced a period of lower income in their youth, relative to a control group. By

[16] Løken 2010.
[17] Løken 2010, 128.

age 28, the sons affected by the closure had incomes 8 percent lower than those of sons in the control families. The income shock propagated across generations with an intergenerational correlation close to one.

This is a very puzzling result. Income differences associated with differences in parents' education, personality, drive, and capabilities were, as would be expected, weakly inherited by these sons. A doubling of a father's income from these sources would be associated with a rise of less than half in a child's earnings. But income changes from the random shock of a firm closing, which are transmitted to children only through limited pathways, such as reduced financing for education, are almost fully inherited.[18] This is not a demonstration of the independent effects of income changes on children's prospects: there must be some mechanism other than income at work here to cause such significant effects.

On balance, for the bulk of families in the middle of the status distribution, feasible social interventions, such as income transfers or boosts to education, appear unlikely to significantly change child outcomes. James Heckman and others show evidence that among the most disadvantaged families, early brain development can be substantially influenced by childhood environment.[19] Supporters of social interventions, such as Heckman, point to two well-known randomized trials of the effects of preschool programs: the Perry Pre-School Program and the Abecedarian Project. Both demonstrated statistically and quantitatively significant effects on the subsequent adult lives of the participants. The economic gains to the participants and society as a whole per dollar spent were substantial.[20]

But no matter how efficacious these programs were, there is no strong evidence that the widespread adoption of early interventions such as these would substantially improve outcomes at the bottom end of the status distribution. A recent evaluation of the large U.S. Head Start Program, which incorporates aspects of these two preschool programs, found that at the end of the third grade, randomly chosen Head Start participants showed no better cognitive or noncognitive performance than the randomly chosen nonparticipants.[21] The

---

[18] Oreopoulos, Page, and Stevens 2008.

[19] Heckman 2012.

[20] Heckman et al. 2010a,b. However, the two programs enrolled, respectively, 58 and 57 treated children, and 65 and 54 controls. This constitutes only a modest evidential basis for the effects of early interventions (Campbell et al. 2012).

[21] Puma et al. 2012.

$10 billion or so annually spent trying to improve outcomes for one million poorer children in the United States appears to have no measurable lasting benefits. The programs may still have effects on adult outcomes, but in the Perry and Abecedarian programs that did have successful adult outcomes, program effects were always evident at younger ages. So although some interventions may be shown to be beneficial, the ones actually in place in the United States are of dubious value.

Suppose that in the "good society," a society that looked more like Sweden than the United States, we equalized the social environment for all children. This would produce a period of increased social mobility and a general gain in social and economic outcomes for children at the lower end of the status distribution. Inequalities in education, income, wealth, and health would all narrow.

However, in the new equilibrium, after this transition, what would happen to rates of social mobility? The upper and lower classes would now be sorted purely based on their genetic heritage. Would social mobility rates be higher or lower in this good society than in our current, imperfect one? It is impossible to say. It would all depend on how strongly the genes that determine social success are inherited compared to family ethos and behaviors. But we cannot predict that in the good society, inheritance of status would be any weaker than it is now. Thus in the good society, it is quite possible that social and economic outcomes would be just as predictable as they are in the imperfect and unjust societies that we observe. Low rates of social mobility are not in themselves indicators of social failure or misallocation of potential talent.

Inequality Given Slow Mobility

This book shows time and again that social mobility is slow, is strongly inherited within families, and that there is little evidence of our ability, using feasible social programs, to increase it. Facing such a reality, the emphasis for societies should be on reducing the effects of inherited abilities and family ethos and aspirations on the rewards society generates for those of different abilities. If so much of social outcomes are determined at birth, then we can appeal to people's sense of justice in other circumstances to argue for more redistribution. For example, there is widespread support for the resource transfers necessary to ensure that people born with physical limitations are not thereby impoverished. If social success and failure are strongly ordained at birth, then, by analogy, why not provide more aid for those who are unlucky in the familial random draw?

If we cannot change the heritable advantages and disadvantages of families in the economic and social world, we should at least mitigate the consequences of these differences. For although there is no evidence that we can change social mobility rates, there is plenty of evidence that societies can reduce inequality in earnings, wealth, health, and relative social status. If low social mobility rates really are a law of nature, as incontrovertible as the gravitational constant, then we should spend less time worrying about them and instead worry about the institutions that determine the degree of inequality in social and economic outcomes.

Some of the inequalities of income and wealth are, of course, the product of economic forces beyond the control of social institutions. But the tax system can mitigate the effect of these market forces on the distribution of rewards, and societies can control the degree of inequality they create in various social institutions.

Some societies have used public interventions to compensate, to some degree, for the inherited disadvantages of poorer families. Sweden, for example, has much more extensive and effective educational and health interventions for poorer families than the United States does. Years of education are correlated with life expectancy in both societies, but to different degrees. In Sweden, the difference in life expectancy between high-school graduates and those with some postsecondary education was less than three years at age 30 in 2010.[22] In the United States this gap, just looking at the white population, was seven years at age 25 in 2008.[23] This difference is consistent with the idea that Sweden has narrowed the disparity in living conditions between rich and poor through universal access to health care and other social benefits.

Such interventions to equalize life chances, of course, demand resources raised through the tax system. The average tax burden on wages, for example, is much higher in Nordic countries than in the more laissez-faire states of the Anglo-Saxon economic model. The OECD reports the average tax burden, counting all taxes and assessments on wages, to be 39 percent in Denmark and 43 percent in Sweden in 2012, compared to 30 percent in the United States and 32 percent in the United Kingdom.[24]

We also see above that earnings are more equal in Nordic countries, though how much that is due to differences in labor supply as opposed to institutional

[22] Statistics Sweden 2011a.
[23] Olchansky et al. 2012.
[24] OECD 2013a, 15, table o.1.

choices is unclear. Unionization, however, is much more extensive in Nordic countries. The OECD reports a unionization rate of 68 percent of employees in Sweden in 2010 and 69 percent in Denmark, compared to 26 percent in the United Kingdom and 11 percent in the United States.[25] While there is no official minimum wage in either Denmark or Sweden, union contracts typically set relatively high minimum wages for their respective economic sectors.

Most economists, who value the free market as an economic regulator, would fear that such union and tax interventions would impose significant losses of output by creating disincentives to work and constraints on productive economic arrangements. It is indeed the case that output per person in the United States in 2010, at $42,000 (in 2005 dollars), was greater than in Sweden ($35,000) or Denmark ($36,000). However, the more free-market United Kingdom had an output of only $32,000, so there is no evidence that output is substantially affected by the much more equalizing Nordic social institutions.[26] And work hours per adult are higher in the United States, so if output were measured per worker hour, the differences between the United States and Nordic countries would be even lower.

Societies make other institutional choices that magnify or diminish inequalities in status. Consider university education, the path to careers and status for many of the next generation. Some societies—including the United States, the United Kingdom, China, and Japan—engage in extreme sorting of undergraduates into educational institutions. The most prestigious universities—Harvard, Princeton, Oxford, Cambridge, Peking, Tsinghua, Tokyo—select their students largely on merit, as defined within each society. They recruit a group of students from the apex of the ability distribution—a group that, as we saw, is concentrated in persistently elite families. In the United States, such universities may also have "legacy" admissions policies that favor students whose parents attended the same university.

In the United States, the advantages of these elite universities are reinforced by a flow of private donations from alumni and others. In a perverse form of philanthropy, those who have get more, and those who have not get nothing.[27]

[25] OECD 2013b.

[26] Feenstra, Inklaar, and Timmer 2013. Expenditure-side real GDP at chained purchasing-power parities.

[27] In 2012 Stanford University received gifts of $1.04 billion, $157,000 per undergraduate (Stanford University 2012). Only a modest share of this money was earmarked for undergradu-

Oxford and Cambridge have been working hard in recent years to emulate this successful U.S. funding strategy of obtaining alms for the rich.

There is no evidence that this extreme sorting by ability is necessary to the operation of a productive university system. In other very successful societies, such as the Netherlands or Germany, universities are much less differentiated in their undergraduate composition. Thus in Germany, there is little distinction in status or student quality across the top ten or twenty German universities. Famous institutions, such as Heidelberg, do not have particularly selective undergraduate admissions. Less-popular undergraduate majors at Heidelberg, such as classics or ancient history, are still open to anyone with the university qualification, the *Abitur*. Other courses of study, such as medicine or law, are highly selective in their admissions, but this is equally true for many other German universities. In the Netherlands, under even greater egalitarian impulses, medical-school places since 1972 have been awarded not purely on merit criteria, such as high-school grades, but through a weighted lottery that was open to all students meeting minimum eligibility criteria.

In the U.S. social model, extreme differentiation of status and outcomes has been permitted, and even encouraged, on the basis that it fosters and increases social mobility. We have seen that in all societies with intermarriage across social groups, social mobility will eventually equalize all social groups and expected outcomes for all families. But the pace of this mobility is very slow. Thus the Nordic model of using social institutions to reduce status differences and outcomes between elites and underclasses may look more attractive.

Inequality across Countries

We have seen in case after case that intergenerational mobility is slow. In particular, social groups converge on similar levels of social and economic success only after many generations, even in the most open societies. The case of the United States shows that strong forces of both positive and negative selection have operated on some of the groups arriving on its shores. Its elites now include a host of subpopulations from societies around the world: Coptic Egyptians, Indian Hindus, Iranians, Maronites, black Africans, and so on. These groups may represent

---

ate education, but undergraduates also benefit from the prestige conferred by the faculty hired and the research accomplished with this money.

as much as 5 percent of the population. Two percent of the population is Jewish, which, as we argue above, is an elite stemming from earlier selection processes. The underclasses of the United States include groups in which negative selection from the mother population is likely: New France descendants, Mexican Americans, and likely also the Hmong. Such groups may account for up to 18 percent of the U.S. population.

This situation implies that the United States has, and will have for generations into the future, a much higher intrinsic level of social inequality than more homogeneous societies such as Germany, Poland, or Italy. Thus it will experience a greater variance of social outcomes for generations to come. Given the historic disparities in its constituent populations and the likelihood that immigration policies will sustain them, the United States needs to consider whether its commitment to social institutions that tolerate and even foster huge social inequalities is appropriate.

SIXTEEN

Escaping Downward
Social Mobility

MOST PARENTS, particularly upper-class parents, attach enormous importance to the social and economic success of their children. They spare
no expenditure of time or money in the pursuit of these goals. In these efforts,
they seek only to secure the best for their children, not to harm the chances of
others. But the social world only has so many positions of status, influence, and
wealth. Inevitably it seems that in pushing their own children up the social ladder,
parents are stamping on the fingers of those climbing up from below. As a character in an Iris Murdoch novel says, "It is not enough to succeed; others must fail."[1]

Competition to enter the best private schools in Manhattan, for example, is
so intense that it begins with kindergarten. The Dalton School on the wealthy
Upper East Side, one of Manhattan's Ivy League feeder schools, has such fierce
demand for places in its kindergarten that four-year-olds undergo IQ tests and
admission interviews. The selection process is so onerous that the deadline for
applications for admission in all of 2013 was November 9, 2012. Thus recent
moves to diversify the school and admit more students "of color" were greeted
with a marked lack of enthusiasm by the parents of nonminority applicants
who would thus face even more competition.[2] Admission gained parents the
privilege of paying annual fees of $38,710 for students in grades K–12 (though
that does include school lunch).

The common entrance exam for Manhattan private elementary schools,
known as the ERB, costs $500 just to attempt. But an ancillary army of advisors

[1] Murdoch 1973, 98.
[2] "She's Warm, Easy to Talk To" 2011.

and tutors is available for hire to ensure that your child has every advantage in getting into the right school and onto the right path in life. This preparation industry has become so expert that most of the private schools in Manhattan are expected soon to end their reliance on the ERB "because of concerns that the popularity of test-preparation programs and coaching had rendered its results meaningless."[3]

When it comes time for college admissions, another army of advisors awaits the call to arms to boost SAT scores, shape college admissions essays, and guide students in selecting from the appropriate armamentarium of extracurricular activities. Since sports provides an avenue of entry to elite universities for those with less than compelling SAT scores and GPAs, battalions of high schoolers are drilled in sports such as field hockey and lacrosse, which exist mainly as an adjunct to the college admission process.[4]

For a long period, from at least 1880 to 1980, the rich and socially successful sharply limited their fertility. Their fewer children would thus each inherit more parental assets and gain a larger share of parental time and resources, than the abundant children of the poor. Yet despite a willingness to spend big in terms of time and treasure, we know that the law of social mobility exercised an inexorable pull, drawing families toward the mean. There is strong persistence of status, but those at the top of the social hierarchy in societies such as the United Kingdom, the United States, and Sweden will inevitably see their children, on average, move down.

Further, the rate of regression downward to the mean is the same for the upper echelons of society, despite their considerable investments in their children, as is the rate of upward mobility for the lower echelons, even the ones who don't bother to turn up for the PTA meetings.

The forces of regression to the mean may seem glacially slow from the point of view of those at the bottom of the social ladder. But for the elites of Manhattan, Greenwich, or Silicon Valley, these forces exercise a death grip on dynastic ambitions. These are people used to getting what they want. Why should they

---

[3] "Private Schools Are Expected to Drop a Dreaded Entrance Test" 2013.

[4] In my second year as an assistant professor at Stanford University, I was assigned the task of mentoring six freshmen. Each appeared on paper to have an incredible range of interests for an eighteen-year-old: chess club, debate club, history club, running team, volunteering with homeless shelters. I soon discovered that these supposed interests were just an artifact of the U.S. college admission process, adopted to flesh out the application forms and discarded as soon as they had worked their magic.

be frustrated in this one primal ambition, for their children to enjoy the same rewards in life as their parents?

The empirical evidence that middle- and upper-class parents can significantly boost their children's human capital and economic outcomes through expenditure on children is weak, as Bryan Caplan recently emphasized in his book *Selfish Reasons to Have More Kids*.[5] Even the pampered progeny of the lords of finance in Manhattan remain subject to the law of social mobility.

This is all consistent with the idea that once parental inputs to children reach a certain basic level, which does not include Baby Einstein toys, playing Mozart to babies in the womb, or sending them to the Dalton School, parents can do nothing to improve outcomes for children. Beyond this point, social outcomes are potentially all in the genes, determined at the point of conception—or driven by a set of aspirations and values already embedded in parents and transmitted automatically to the children, who drink in their social class with their mother's milk. Most likely, given the evidence above, the majority of status is actually genetically determined. You can hit the jackpot in the great genetic casino or go bust.

Is there anything that this book can say to people who want the best possible income, wealth, education, and health outcomes for their children? The one scientific contribution we can make is to point out that with the appropriate choice of mates, a family can avoid downward mobility forever.

The chapters above emphasize that one of the things that slows social mobility is the assortative nature of marriage. People in all societies tend to marry others of similar social status. Recently Charles Murray has argued that marriage has become even more assortative and that this trend will slow social mobility further.[6] The reasoning behind Murray's claim is that in earlier generations, women did not get much education, and thus potential male partners had less information about their abilities, energy, and drive. But the rise of women's education is permitting a much better matching of marital partners on these observed characteristics, thus slowing rates of social mobility. Even white society in America, on this view, is increasingly being segregated into lineages of prosperity and deprivation.[7]

---

[5] Caplan 2011.

[6] Murray 2012.

[7] The empirical evidence for increased sorting is actually weak. See, for example, Kremer 1997, 126, which reports a modest decline in the correlation of years of education of spouses between 1940 and 1990.

But no matter how assortative mating may become, downward mobility will continue. For downward mobility is driven by the fact that people typically select mates who resemble them on the basis of observed social characteristics —their achieved education, income, occupational status, wealth, height, weight, and health.[8] This is their social phenotype, the sum of their observed characteristics. However, as we have seen above, we can usefully think of individuals as also having a social genotype, or underlying social status.[9] Their social genotype produces the observed phenotype, but with random components in each dimension.

This means that the people currently occupying the upper tails of the distribution of education, wealth, and occupational prestige tend to include disproportionately the lucky, the ones who benefited from happy accidents. Systematically, at the top, the phenotype is better than the genotype. Symmetrically, concentrated at the bottom are people who have experienced bad luck and unhappy accidents. There, the social genotype is much better than the observed phenotype. The curse of the elite is that they are surrounded by imposters, possibly including themselves, and thus the marriage market for the upper classes is full of prospects likely to underperform as carriers of a lineage. In contrast, the bottom of the marriage market is full of potential overperformers. Bad luck dominates, rather than bad social genotypes. So outcomes for the next generation tend to be better.

When marriage is endogamous within an elite group, however, high status can be maintained forever. Witness the Brahmin class in Bengal, or the Copts of Egypt. Conversely, endogamous marriage can condemn low-status groups such as the Muslims of West Bengal to perpetual deprivation.

These findings imply that to maximize mobility in a society, we want assortment in marriage to be based just on observed current status. If religious or ethnic background, or skin color, is correlated with social status at the group level, and marriage rates are much higher within religious, ethnic, and skin-color groups, social mobility will be slowed.

Countering Charles Murray's concerns about marriage becoming more assortative in modern America, endogamous marriage is clearly in decline. Thus

---

[8] Love of course plays its part, but the wisdom of the ages is that reciprocal love flourishes best between socially matched partners.

[9] This does not imply that the social genotype is actually derived from genetics, just that it behaves in a way that mimics genetic transmission of characteristics.

the National Jewish Population Survey of 2001 found increasing rates of inter-marriage for Jews in the United States. Before 1970 only 13 percent of Jews married non-Jews. By 1991–2001 the rate was 45 percent.[10] Rates of exogamy for Jews in the United States have risen to very high levels. In a strange irony, the achievement in the United States, finally, of a society largely free of discrimination against the Jewish population will eventually end a near two-thousand-year tradition of unusual Jewish social and intellectual achievement through the mechanism of greater intermarriage between the Jewish and gentile communities. Across U.S. society as a whole between 1980 and 2008, using the U.S. Census Bureau definitions of race and ethnicity, rates of exogamous marriage rose from 7 percent to 15 percent.[11]

If the way to produce children of the highest possible social phenotype is to find a partner of the highest possible social genotype, the path is clear for those whose aim in life is to produce the highest-achieving progeny possible. To discover the likely underlying social genotype of your potential partner, you need to observe not just their characteristics but also the characteristics of all their relatives. What is the social phenotype of their siblings and their parents? And what is the observed status of their grandparents and cousins?

The point here is not that any of these relatives will contribute anything directly to the social and economic success of your child. As far as can be observed, they will not. But the social status of the relatives indicates the likely underlying social status of your potential mate. This social genotype, rather than the observed social phenotype, is what your children will inherit.

These observations of the status of relatives can be formed into an aggregate with predictable weightings. If social status turns out to be mainly genetically determined, as for heights, we can also determine the weights to attach to each relative for the best prediction. If mating is not assortative, for example, then, in line with the simple model of table 15.2, the potential partner gets a weight of one. Their siblings and parents thus get a weight of one-half.[12] Grandparents and aunts and uncles get one-quarter. Great-grandparents and cousins get a weight of one-eighth. However, since mating is highly assortative, the shared genetics of siblings, parents, grandparents, aunts, uncles, cousins, and so on is correspond-

<hr />

[10] United Jewish Communities 2003, table 14.

[11] Passel, Wang, and Taylor 2010.

[12] Because of dominance effects, genetically transmitted traits are slightly more highly correlated between siblings than between parents and children, so the weighting should be somewhat greater.

ingly much greater than suggested here. The entire lineage becomes strongly predictive of the underlying status of a potential marriage partner.

In line with this reasoning, a recent study in Japan examined the effects of the educational attainment of grandparents, aunts, and uncles on both sides of a family on children's probability of going to university. Controlling for the parents' education, there was a positive correlation between the education level of all four sets of relatives and the child's probability of attending university.[13]

As noted in chapter 6, for a group of more than four thousand people in England with rare surnames, we know their wealth at death as well as all their familial connections over more than four generations (1858–2012). These data allow for the estimation of the correlation of wealth at death not just for parent and child but also for great-grandparent and child, cousins, and even second cousins. What is remarkable about this wealth information is the persistence of wealth connections with increasingly distant relatives. The parent-child correlation in wealth averages 0.43 and the sibling correlation 0.56. But the correlation for cousins, who in genetic terms are only one-quarter as related by descent as siblings, is still 0.34. And second cousins, one-sixteenth as related by descent, still have a correlation of 0.22. If genetics underlies social status, then mating must be highly assortative, so that second cousins are much more closely connected than might be expected.[14]

This implies that even very distant relatives are surprisingly closely related in terms of social status. That information can be used to predict the likely outcomes for the children of anyone in this lineage. It is this fact that underlies cases such as that of the Darwin family, mentioned in chapter 7, in which the twenty-seven adult great-great-grandchildren of Charles Darwin still form a surprisingly distinguished cohort.

All this implies that if the weighted score for the relatives is as high as for your potential mate, who is of high status, his or her underlying social genotype is as high as the observed phenotype. For the purpose of producing high-quality children—and for this purpose alone—this potential partner is a bargain on the marriage market. If the weighted score of the relatives is even higher than that of the potential partner, then he or she is a marital fire sale. Conversely, if the relatives are, on average, of lower status, this marriage is unlikely

[13] Aramaki 2013.
[14] Cummins and Clark 2013.

to produce children with social potential as high as the partner's, because the partner's social phenotype is better than the genotype.

Additional information about the likely outcomes for your offspring can be drawn from factors such as the potential mate's ethnic or social group. The more the individual deviates positively from the average social phenotype of that group, the more likely their current status is to be the product of accident, higher than their underlying social genotype. The more they fall below the average for the group, the more likely it is that this status is the result of chance: the person's underlying social genotype is likely to be better adapted for success.[15]

Suppose you are faced with a choice of two marriage partners, both of whom have a high-status phenotype. They are both graduates from elite colleges and have PhD's in philosophy, for example, or both are board certified in rhinoplasty. But one partner is of Ashkenazi Jewish background and the other of New France descent. Then the predicted status of your children will be higher if you select the Jewish partner.

Since Coptic surnames are those that stand out in figure 13.10 as the highest-status group in the United States, all else being equal, if you want high-status offspring, find yourself a partner named *Girgis, Boutros,* or *Shenouda.* Chinese and black African surnames also stand out as particularly high status. So again, all else being equal, choose *Chen* over *Churchill, Okafer* over *Olson.*

In *Selfish Reasons to Have More Kids,* Caplan points out correctly that upper-class parents pointlessly invest too much time in the rearing of their children. In his view, genetics is what matters, so you might as well have more children, invest less in each, and enjoy being a parent more. That all seems sensible and humane.

Caplan does, however, address the stark corollary outlined above. If genetics determines child outcomes, then we can determine just from lineage which potential partners have (on average) the best genes. So the current competition

[15] Given the findings above suggesting the importance of genetics in predicting outcomes for upper-class children, the same considerations would apply for those seeking donors or eggs or sperm for in-vitro fertilization. A recent study of the implicit market for human eggs found that despite guidelines from the American Society of Reproductive Medicine that recommend a fixed level of compensation for donors "to avoid putting a price on human gametes or selectively valuing particular human traits," compensation for donation was strongly correlated with the average SAT scores for admission to the colleges that the potential donors attended (Levine 2010, 28–31).

to produce high-status offspring will be displaced by competition to mate with someone of the highest genetic potential. A better, more humane, less competitive, social world than ours may exist, but it is not obvious how we will attain it in a world where people have such strong aspirations for the social success of their own children.

APPENDIX 1: MEASURING SOCIAL MOBILITY

INTERGENERATIONAL SOCIAL MOBILITY is a staple of sociology and economics. The preferred tool of sociologists in the study of mobility, because social classes are not easily assigned a numerical status value, is the *transition matrix*. Parents and children are divided into ranked groups according to social class, occupation, income, or wealth. The standard occupational classification used in the United Kingdom until recently, for example, placed people into six categories:

A. Higher managerial, administrative, or professional workers
B. Intermediate managerial, administrative, or professional workers
C1. Supervisory or clerical and junior managerial, administrative, or professional workers
C2. Skilled manual workers
D. Semiskilled and unskilled manual workers
E. Casual or lowest-grade workers, pensioners, and others who depend on the state for their income

To measure father-son mobility, for example, each father and each son is assigned a status. The transition matrix shows the fractional distribution of outcomes for fathers of each status category, as in table A1.1 (where the numbers are hypothetical, chosen purely to illustrate the appearance of a typical transition matrix). Each row shows the probability of a son achieving a certain status given the father's status. The numbers in each row add up to one. The table shows

TABLE A1.1. Sample transition matrix

	Sons			
Fathers	A	B	C	D
A	0.5	0.2	0.2	0.1
B	0.1	0.6	0.2	0.1
C	0.1	0.3	0.4	0.2
D	0.0	0.1	0.3	0.7

that in this example the chances of a son of a father of the lowest class ending up in the highest class, and vice versa, are low.

Table A1.2 shows the case of complete immobility, in which occupational status of all sons is the same status as the fathers.' In contrast, table A1.3 shows complete mobility. The distribution of sons' occupational status is the same for all ranks of fathers, and thus the fathers' status provides no information about the sons.'

TABLE A1.2. Sample transition matrix showing no mobility

	Sons			
Fathers	A	B	C	D
A	1	0	0	0
B	0	1	0	0
C	0	0	1	0
D	0	0	0	1

TABLE A1.3. Sample transition matrix showing complete mobility

	Sons			
Fathers	A	B	C	D
A	0.1	0.4	0.4	0.1
B	0.1	0.4	0.4	0.1
C	0.1	0.4	0.4	0.1
D	0.1	0.4	0.4	0.1

Although such transition matrices offer the most complete description of social mobility in any society, they can be hard to interpret and compare. How much mobility does table A1.1 imply, for example? Is it closer to table A1.2, showing no mobility, or table A1.3, showing complete mobility? Another approach to measuring mobility, typically favored by economists and psychologists, is to rank aspects of social status—such as income, wealth, years of education, cognitive skills, and longevity—on a numerical scale. Even occupations can be represented in this way by assigning to each occupation a status score corresponding, for example, to the average earnings of each occupation or the average years of schooling required for each occupation.

If we are measuring mobility by comparing the earnings of fathers and their sons, we might observe the pattern pictured in figure A1.1. The line that best fits this pattern of data will be of the form

$$y_{t+1} = a + by_t + v_t,$$

(A1.1)

where y is the measure of status, v_t is some random component, and t indexes the initial generation. Then b measures the persistence of status over a generation. For a given sample of fathers and sons, b could potentially have any value. A b of 0 indicates no persistence of status: no prediction can be made about

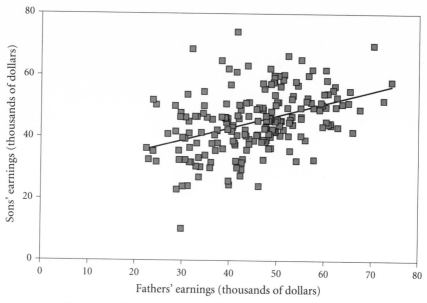

FIGURE A1.1. Earnings of fathers versus earnings of sons.

sons' status from the fathers'. The larger is b, the greater the predictive power of fathers' status for sons' status.

However, if the status measure has constant variance across generations, as is typically the case for societies as a whole, then b has special properties. In this case, b is also the intergenerational correlation of y and has a value between –1 and 1. In figure A1.1, which is drawn with constant variance, the slope of the line that best fits these observations, b, describes the intergenerational persistence rate of earnings. In this case it is 0.4. $(1 - b)$ is thus the obverse, the rate of social mobility. As can be seen, with a b of 0.4, sons' earnings can vary substantially from the fathers'. For fathers with mean earnings of \$45,000, sons' earnings range from \$24,000 to \$63,000. Here b describes just the systematic components of inheritance. The lower is b, the more important are the random components.

When a measure of status has constant variance across generations, b^2 measures the share of variance predictable at birth. The reason for this is that if σ^2 measures the variance of the status measure y, and σ_v^2 measures the variance of the random component in status, then, from equation A1.1,

$$\sigma^2 = b^2\sigma^2 + \sigma_v^2.$$

Thus random components explain a share of the current variance of status of $(1 - b^2)$ and inheritance the other share of variance, b^2. That is also why b has to lie between –1 and 1 in this case. Figure A1.2 shows what happens as b approaches 1. In this case, for a stable variance of status, it has to be the case that the random component in status becomes zero. Child status is perfectly predictable from parent status.

This intergenerational correlation is the simplified measure of mobility employed throughout this book. This simplification is not appropriate if social mobility rates vary at different points on the social scale, as some have argued. But one of the arguments of the book is that social mobility rates seem to be constant across the whole range of social status. This measure also requires that we assign a cardinal measure to social status at all social ranks.[1]

Because of data limitations, standard measures of social mobility often focus only on fathers and sons. But people, of course, have two parents. Women's earnings, education, and wealth have become increasingly important to the social

---

[1] Long and Ferrie (2013b) propose more complex measures to deal with cases in which such a cardinal measure of social status is impossible.

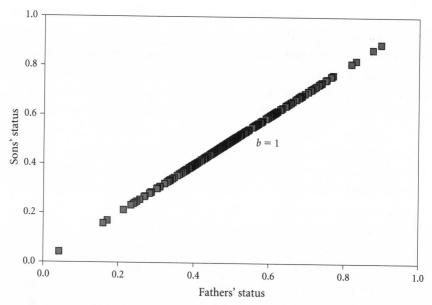

FIGURE A1.2. Social mobility when $b = 1$.

status of families in recent generations, and mothers' status also contributes to their children's outcomes, independently of fathers' status on these measures. Does the traditional focus on fathers produce distorted estimates of intergenerational correlations?

Suppose mating were completely assortative with respect to social position. Then the intergenerational correlation of fathers and sons, or fathers and daughters, with respect to earnings, wealth, or education would be the same as if we took the average of fathers' and mothers' status as the measure for the earlier generation. So the conventional b measures would still summarize overall social mobility. Because mating is not completely assortative, these individual b measures tend to overestimate overall social mobility. However, even if mating were completely random, the correlation of children's characteristics with the average of the parents' characteristics would still just be 1.4 times the individual correlation.[2] Assuming a correlation of 0.5 in the characteristics of the parents on

[2] Assuming the correlation of the child with each parent individually is the same and is ρ, the correlation with the average of both parents is $\dfrac{\rho}{\sqrt{0.5(1 + \rho_{fm})}}$, where ρ_{fm} is the correlation of the parent characteristics.

any measure, the correlation between children's characteristics and the average of parent characteristics is 1.15 times the single correlation. This is only a little higher than the single-parent correlations typically measured.

The simplified measure b used in this book, the intergenerational correlation of characteristics, makes it very easy to compare mobility rates across societies and across different measures of social status. It also has a simple natural interpretation. Conventional estimates of these intergenerational correlations suggest that modern societies exhibit high rates of social mobility for any particular measure of status. Thus the intergenerational correlation for such attributes, including features that we think of as largely biologically inherited in high-income societies (such as height), is typically in the range 0.13–0.54 for a single parent. Even when this figure is increased to account for inheritance from both parents, the typical correlation between parents and children in income, education, wealth, IQ, height, body mass index, and longevity is only 0.25–0.75.[3] This implies that typically only 6–50 percent of all variation in these characteristics among children is predictable from the characteristics of parents. Parents of extreme characteristics typically see their children revert toward the mean by substantial amounts.

Mobility across Multiple Generations

What happens to the intergenerational correlations of status as we consider grandchildren, great-grandchildren, and later generations? To answer this question, a further simplification is helpful: to normalize y, the measure of status, in each generation to have zero mean, so that equation A1.1 simplifies to

$$y_{t+1} = by_t + v_t. \tag{A1.1}*$$

If y is income, for example, just defining income as the difference between the individuals' income and average income creates this normalization.

Suppose all the information useful to predict the outcomes for children is provided by the status of the parents, so that the status of grandparents and even

---

[3] On height, see Pearson and Lee 1903; Silventoinen et al. 2003a; Galton 1886. On body mass index: Silventoinen et al. 2003b. On cognitive and social abilities: Grönqvist, Öckert, and Vlachos 2010. On longevity: Beeton and Pearson 1899; Cohen 1964. On earnings: Corak 2013. On wealth: Harbury and Hitchens 1979. On education: Hertz et al. 2007. On occupational status: Francesconi and Nicoletti 2006; Ermisch, Francesconi, and Siedler 2005; Long 2013.

earlier generations provides no independent information on the likely outcomes for their descendants. In this case the mobility process is said to be first-order Markov, or AR(1). Then equation A1.1* implies that over n generations, the characteristics of the link in status is

$$y_t = by_{t-1} + v_t = b^2 y_{t-2} + bv_{t-1} + v_t = b^n y_{t-n} + v_n^*, \qquad \text{(A1.2)}$$

where $v_n^* = b^{n-1} v_{t-n+1} + \ldots + bv_{t-1} + v_t$. The correlation between grandparents and grandchildren is b^2, and between great-grandparents and great-grandchildren b^3.

In this case, given the conventional estimates of the intergenerational correlations of parents and children, long-run social mobility is rapid. Even when $b = 0.5$, b^n rapidly approaches zero as n increases. Thus the intergenerational correlation between one generation and their great-grandchildren is only 0.12. This in turn implies that only 2 percent of the variation in outcomes for great-grandchildren is explained by the characteristics of the first generation. The share of variance of status explained by the status of the current generation after n generations goes even more quickly toward zero, since it is b^{2n}. Figure A1.3 illustrates how rapidly the expected status of two families, with initial wealth twelve times and one-twelfth of the mean respectively, converges on the mean

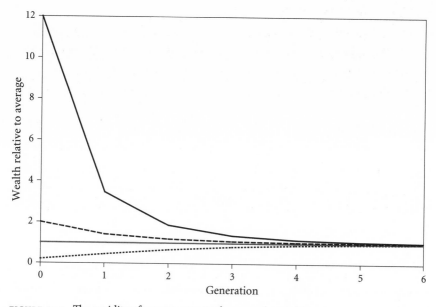

FIGURE A1.3. The rapidity of convergence to the mean for wealth.

if b is 0.5.[4] Within five generations, the descendants of these two families, whose initial wealth differed by a factor of 144, will both have an expected wealth within 10 percent of the social average.

Recent studies of social mobility that look at outcomes over three or even four generations suggest, however, that grandparents seem to have an independent influence on grandchild outcomes. In this book, the hypothesis of the nature of intergenerational mobility and persistence assumes that the underlying process is actually first-order Markov. Grandparents inherently do not influence grandchild outcomes once we have full information on their parents. Thus, if measured status is y_t and underlying status x_t, the social mobility model assumed in this book (see chapter 6) is

$$y_t = x_t + u_t,$$

$$x_t = bx_{t-1} + e_t$$

with x and y both distributed normally with zero mean and constant variance, and u and e random components. Suppose also that the ordinary least squares (OLS) estimate of β in the fitted expression

$$y_t = \beta y_{t-1} + v_t$$

is $\hat{\beta}$. Then if $\theta = \dfrac{\sigma_x^2}{\sigma_x^2 + \sigma_u^2}$, where σ_u^2 is the variance of the random component and σ_x^2 the variance of underlying social competence, the expected value of $\hat{\beta}$ will be

$$E(\hat{\beta}) = \theta b.$$

Also the expected value of the OLS estimate of β_n, the observed correlation in y across n generations,

$$y_t = \beta_n y_{t-n} + v_{nt},$$

will be $E(\hat{\beta}_n) = \theta b^n$.

If we estimate by OLS the parameters in

$$y_t = \beta_{t-1} y_{t-1} + \beta_{t-2} y_{t-2} + v_t,$$

which looks at the effect of grandparent status controlling for parent status, then

---

[4] As is usual for these estimates, b is calculated for the logarithm of wealth.

$$E(\hat{\beta}_{t-1}) = \theta b \left(\frac{1 - \theta b^2}{1 - \theta^2 b^2} \right)$$

$$E(\hat{\beta}_{t-2}) = \theta b^2 \left(\frac{1 - \theta}{1 - \theta^2 b^2} \right) > 0.$$

Even though grandparents have no independent role in child outcomes, they appear to have such an influence according to these estimates. If we estimate by OLS the parameters in

$$y_t = \beta_{t-1} y_{t-1} + \beta_{t-2} y_{t-2} + \beta_{t-3} y_{t-3} + v_t,$$

which looks at the independent effects of both grandparents and great-grandparents, controlling for parent status, then

$$E(\hat{\beta}_{t-1}) = \theta b \, \frac{1 - \theta^2 b^2 - \theta b^2 + 2\theta^2 b^4 - \theta b^4}{1 - 2\theta^2 b^2 + 2\theta^3 b^4 - \theta^2 b^4}$$

$$E(\hat{\beta}_{t-2}) = \theta b \, \frac{b(1 - \theta)(1 - \theta b^2)}{1 - 2\theta^2 b^2 + 2\theta^3 b^4 - \theta^2 b^4} > 0$$

$$E(\hat{\beta}_{t-3}) = \theta b \, \frac{b^2 (1 - \theta)^2}{1 - 2\theta^2 b^2 + 2\theta^3 b^4 - \theta^2 b^4} > 0.$$

If $b > 0$, then both $\hat{\beta}_{t-2}$ and $\hat{\beta}_{t-3}$ have positive value. Even great-grandparents, generally dead before the great-grandchild is born, will appear to exert some independent influence on great-grandchild outcomes.

APPENDIX 2: DERIVING MOBILITY RATES
FROM SURNAME FREQUENCIES

WHERE THERE IS INFORMATION ON wealth or occupations by surname, the procedures for estimating the intergenerational correlation of status are analogous to those used in conventional mobility studies. The social mobility rate is measured just by how much closer to the mean status surnames of each type move with each generation.

The persistence parameter estimated for surname groupings, however, is potentially biased toward zero compared to the underlying persistence parameter for families (if it were observable). This is because in surname cohorts, when we estimate

$$\bar{y}_{kt+1} = b\bar{y}_{kt} + u_{kt+1},$$

$\bar{y}_{kt}$ measures average social status on some measure across a group of people with the surname k in the initial generation. But some of these people have no children and are not included in the within-family estimates. And in any generation, those with one child are weighted as much as those with ten children. This introduces noise into the estimates and biases estimated intergenerational elasticity toward zero.

However, for most of the studies in this book, the measurement of the status of surname groupings in any generation is based on the share of that surname among elites (or underclasses) compared to its share in the general population. These elites can be groups such as wealth holders, university graduates, authors, physicians, attorneys, or members of Parliament.

To extract implied persistence rates, the procedure is as follows. Define the *relative representation* of each surname or surname type, z, in an elite group such as physicians as

$$\text{Relative representation of } z = \frac{\text{Share of } z \text{ in elite group}}{\text{Share of } z \text{ in general population}}.$$

With social mobility, any surname that initially has a relative representation differing from one should tend toward one, and the rate at which it does so is determined by the rate of social mobility.

However, assuming that all social mobility is governed by

$$x_{t+1} = bx_t + e_t$$

implies that even social elites tend to have the same variance of status as the population as a whole, as long as they have been present in the society for a number of generations. For even if they start with a zero variance of social status, then n generations later, based on the above law of mobility, the variance of that underlying status will be

$$\sigma_n^2 = (1 - b^{2n})\sigma^2,$$

where σ^2 is the status variance of the population as a whole. Even at a high underlying persistence rate of 0.75, after just one generation the variance of this elite will be 44 percent of the population variance. After four generations it will be 90 percent. Thus in estimating the persistence rate, b, from the shares of surnames observed among elites, it is assumed that the variance of the elite group is the same as for the general population, but the mean is shifted to the right, as in figure A2.1. Similarly, the underclass groups are assumed to have the same variance as the population, but with the mean shifted to the left.

This assumption of equal variance for elite and underclass surname groups is validated by measuring the distribution of their outcomes on status measures. We see in chapter 2 that this holds true for the income of people with aristocratic surnames in Sweden. In chapter 3 it holds true for educational status among Jews and blacks in the United States. And it holds true for the distribution of wealth among elite rare-surname groups in England for the period 1858–2011 (see chapter 5). In all cases, there is considerable variance of outcomes within elite and underclass surname groups.

This assumption also fits the data well when initial elites or underclasses are observed over many generations, as in England or Sweden. In case after case, the model fits the evolution of elite and lower-class surname groups well, with the estimated persistence rates falling within a relatively narrow range, 0.7–0.9. Assumptions that the initial elite group has a more compressed distri-

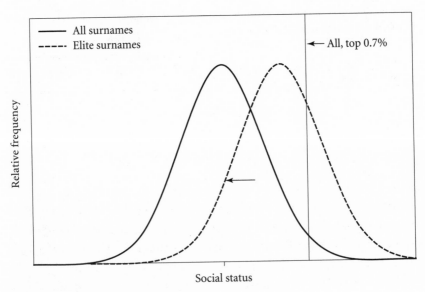

FIGURE A2.1. Initial position of an elite.

bution of status than the population as a whole lead to predicted paths of relative representation that do not fit with the observed data, unless persistence rates are very different for the initial generations than for later generations.

With the assumptions above, when the relative representation of an elite surname group z is observed in some upper part of the distribution of status, such as the top 2 percent, then we can fix the initial mean status of this group, $\bar{x}_{z0}$. That mean status will evolve according to the equation

$$\bar{x}_{zt} = \bar{x}_{z0}b^t,$$

where t is the number of generations. For only two generations, this procedure yields an exact estimation of b. For multiple generations, we could either estimate a b for each generation or fit one b to the whole series by minimizing the deviations in relative representation implied by each choice of b. Studies of long series of relative representation of elites and underclasses in England, Sweden, and China show that often one fitted b fits the observed patterns of relative representation even across five to ten generations.

The value of b that best fits this data does not change much if the assumed cutoff point in the status distribution for the elite population is altered. Thus in chapter 5 (figure 5.8) we estimate the persistence of educational status from rare-surname groups at Oxford and Cambridge for 1830–2012 as 0.73. In arriving at

TABLE A2.1. Intergenerational correlations under different assumptions for rare surnames at Oxford and Cambridge, 1830–2012

Assumed initial educational variance for elites	Cutoff for elite status (% of population)			
	0.1	0.7	2	5
Population variance	0.74	0.73	0.72	0.69
One-quarter of population variance	0.65	0.70	0.70	0.71
One-tenth of population variance	0.63	0.69	0.70	0.71

this estimate, the assumed cutoff for the university elite in each period is changed to correspond to the student share in each cohort, which ranges from 0.5 to 1.2 percent. Suppose instead a uniform cutoff of 0.1 percent, 0.7 percent, 2 percent, or 5 percent was assumed (the extremes here being quite unrealistic). How much would that change the estimated value of b? The first row of table A2.1 shows the results. Adopting one of these fixed cutoffs across generations yields a best-fitting persistence rate of 0.69–0.74, little different from the preferred estimate.

What would happen if the assumption that the variance of educational outcomes in the elite group was always the same as for the general population was dropped? Suppose the variance was only one-quarter that of the general population initially. The implied values of b for different elite shares are shown in the second row of table A2.1: they range from 0.65 to 0.71.

The last row of the table shows the estimated b under the even more extreme assumption that the variance of the elite surname group was only one-tenth that of the general population when first observed in 1800–1829. Now b is in the range 0.63–0.71. So the conclusion that educational mobility measured using surname groupings is slow relative to conventional estimates is robust to variations in assumptions about the population share of the elite groups observed and the variance of status within the elite population.

Upward Mobility

For elite groups that arise just by the processes of random chance in any economy, such as the rare-surname groups at Oxford and Cambridge in the years 1800–1829, the social law of mobility suggested in chapter 6 also has implication about the way in which they rose to elite status. The major implication is that the path of upward mobility is symmetrical with that of downward mobility. Chapter 12 shows empirical evidence that this prediction is correct in both England and China. Here is shown the reasoning behind this prediction.

If underlying mobility is governed by the expression $x_{t+1} = bx_t + e_t$, we would estimate, empirically, the value of b, minimizing the sum of squared errors, as

$$\hat{b} = \frac{\Sigma x_{t+1} x_t}{\Sigma x_t^2}.$$

Suppose, however, we instead wanted to estimate the connection going backward from x_{t+1} to x_t. That is, if $x_{t+1} = bx_t + e_t$ holds, what is the value of γ that would be estimated for the expression

$$x_t = \gamma x_{t+1} + v_t?$$

You might expect that we could just rewrite $x_{t+1} = bx_t + e_t$ with x_t on the left-hand side, and the result would be $(1/b)$. But this is not the case. The minimum squared deviation empirical estimate of γ in fact would be

$$\hat{\gamma} = \frac{\Sigma x_t x_{t+1}}{\Sigma x_{t+1}^2} = \frac{\Sigma x_{t+1} x_t}{\Sigma x_t^2} = \hat{b}$$

since x_t and x_{t+1}, by construction, have the same variance. Going back in time, the average status of an elite or underclass again regresses toward the mean. The movement of families at the extremes of the distribution—extremes of wealth or poverty, education or ignorance—toward the center will be symmetrical with their earlier movement from the mean to the extremes. Any group observed at the extreme will not only regress to the mean in future generations, but it will also diverge from the mean to reach its extreme position at the same rate at which it returns. Notice, however, that this prediction only applies to families that reach the extremes of the distribution through random shocks.

APPENDIX 3: DISCOVERING THE STATUS OF YOUR SURNAME LINEAGE

F OR THOSE OF US WITH A COMMON SURNAME like *Clark*, there is a limit to the interesting exploration of the history and geography of the surname (though the geographic distribution of the spelling variants *Clark* and *Clarke* is striking). But a variety of sources allow a diverting exploration of the history and geography of rarer surnames. Below we show how to find out how common any surname is, where it is concentrated, and what its average social status has been over time for countries such as England, the United States, Australia, and Sweden.

As we have seen, common surnames may start with high, medium, or low status, but all eventually converge on mean status. Rarer surnames, however, can follow a variety of paths. They may, for example, spend periods at high status, regress to the mean, and then fall to low status before converging on the mean once more; or they may, like the surname *Pepys*, spend hundreds of years at high status.

Surname Frequencies and Distribution

A useful tool for establishing the frequency of surnames in various countries is the Public Profiler World Family Names database, the result of a project at University College London.[1] This website provides estimates of the frequency of surnames per million of the population in Argentina, Australia, Austria, Belgium, Canada, China, Denmark, France, Germany, Hungary, India (partial), Ireland,

---

[1] Public Profiler, n.d.

Italy, Japan, Luxembourg, the Netherlands, New Zealand, Norway, Poland, Serbia, Slovenia, Spain, Sweden, Switzerland, the United Kingdom, and the United States. For each country the information is also given by subunits, which vary in size: in the United States, they are counties. Figure A3.1 shows, for example, the distribution of the surname *Levy,* which is Sephardic Jewish in origin, across Europe. The wide distribution of the surname reflects the great geographic mobility of the Jewish population.

In contrast, figure A3.2 shows the distribution within Europe of the rare surname *Boscawen.* It originated in Cornwall in southwest England and has dispersed little since. Figure A3.3 shows the distribution of the New France surname *Bergeron* in North America, illustrating its spread by migration to Louisiana and New England. At even closer perspective, we can see the distribution of surnames by counties within states in the United States. Figure A3.4, for example, shows the distribution in New York State of the Jewish surname *Teitelbaum,* a prominent surname among the leaders of the Satmar Hasidim sects and the surname of the current rebbe of both major factions of the Satmar.

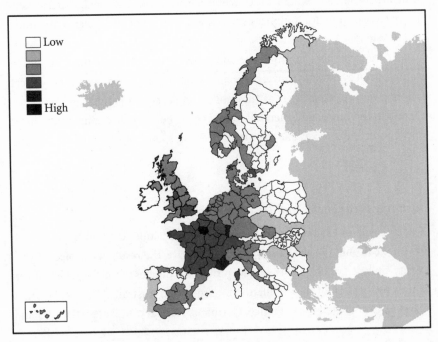

FIGURE A3.1. Distribution of *Levy* in Western Europe, 2012.

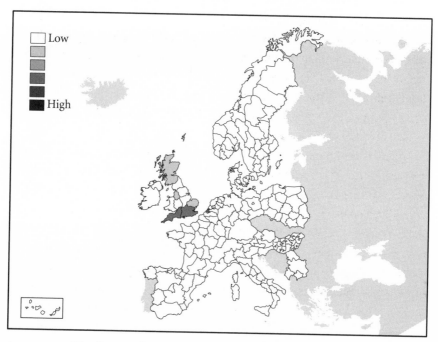

FIGURE A3.2. Distribution of *Boscawen* in Western Europe, 2012.

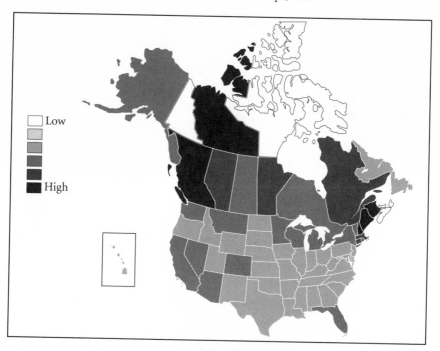

FIGURE A3.3. Distribution of *Bergeron* in North America, 2012.

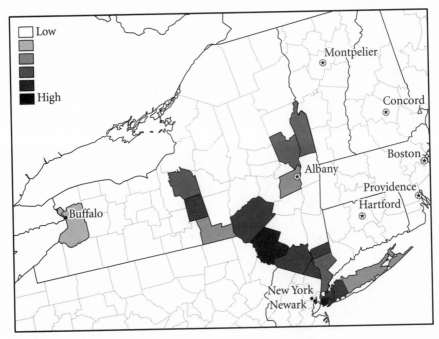

FIGURE A3.4. Distribution of *Teitelbaum* in the state of New York, 2012.

A limitation of this data set, however, is that in some countries, such as the United States, the surname counts are based on telephone directory listings, so that it overrepresents the frequency of high-status surnames and undercounts low-status surnames. More accurate current surname counts for individual countries include the following sources:

United States: The US Census Bureau's *Demographic Aspects of Surnames from Census 2000.* This source lists all surnames in the U.S. census of 2000 with one hundred or more occurrences. It also gives the census-reported racial composition (white, black, Asian–Pacific Islander, Native American, and Hispanic) for each surname. The information is available only as a large Excel file.[2]

United Kingdom: The Office of National Statistics produced a list of surname frequencies for England and Wales in 2002. This source gives all surnames held by at least five people in England and Wales and their fre-

[2] Ward et al. 2012.

quency. The stock of surnames here represents all surnames in 1998, including any births occurring between 1998 and 2002 but not subtracting deaths in those years. It thus overestimates the total size of the population in 2002.[3]

Australia: The Intellectual Property Agency of the Australian Government maintains a searchable database of surname frequencies in Australia, based on the electoral register.[4] In 2012 there were 14.3 million enrolled electors in Australia, representing 90 percent of all adults. Because of the enrollment requirement, there is a tendency for this site to undercount lower-status surnames. This site can be searched for any string of letters in a surname.

Canada, Quebec: The Institut de la Statistique Québec reports the frequencies of the five thousand most common surnames in Quebec.[5] Statistics Canada, however, has not produced any surname frequency listings for Canada as a whole.

Sweden: Statistics Sweden has a searchable database giving the frequency of every surname in Sweden at the end of the preceding calendar year, updated annually, from the population register (maintained by the Swedish tax agency).[6] Statistics Sweden also reports the list of the one hundred most common surnames and their frequency in the previous two years, again updated annually.[7]

Another resource, maintained by the Public Profiler team at University College London, is the Great Britain Family Names website.[8] This shows the surname distribution in Britain by county in 1881 (from the census) and 1998 (electoral register). However, this data set includes only surnames with one hundred or more holders in the 1998 electoral register.

---

[3] U.K., Office of National Statistics 2002.

[4] Australian Government, "Search for Australian Surnames," http://pericles.ipaustralia.gov
.au/atmoss/falcon_search_tools.Main?pSearch=Surname.

[5] Institut de la Statistique Québec, "Les noms de famille," www.stat.gouv.qc.ca/donstat/
societe/demographie/noms_famille/index.htm.

[6] Statistics Sweden, "Namnsök," www.scb.se/Pages/NameSearch.aspx?id=259432.

[7] Statistics Sweden, "Namnstatistik," www.scb.se/Pages/ProductTables____30919.aspx.

[8] Public Profiler, "Great Britain Family Names," http://gbnames.publicprofiler.org/Surnames
.aspx.

Surname Status

We have seen that status tends to be persistent across many generations for surnames. There are a number of ways of inferring the current statuses of surnames.

ENGLAND AND WALES

For England and Wales, one means of ascertaining surname status is to look at the probate rate for a surname relative to the average probate rate for all surnames in a given period. For surnames associated with wealthier groups, the probate rate is higher than the average, and for poorer surname groups it is lower. The website Ancestry.com lists all probates in England and Wales for 1858–1966. (Information for subsequent years can be obtained only by going in person to the Probate Registry in London.) Using this source to look for infrequent surnames in the probate records for 1926–66 and comparing them to data for 1996–2012 gives the results shown in table A3.1.

The average probate rate for all surnames in England and Wales in the earlier period was 39 percent. The surname *Smith* had a 37 percent probate rate, implying a slightly lower-than-average status. However, the probate rate for *Smyths* was 74 percent, implying much higher status. The even more elite-

TABLE A3.1. Probate rates, England and Wales, 1926–66 and 1996–2012

Surname	Deaths, 1926–66	Probates, 1926–66	Probate rate (%) 1926–66	Probate rate (%) 1996–2012
All	21,129,751	8,228,575	39	42
Smith	299,866	110,929	37	—
Smyth	2,371	1,754	74	—
Cave-Brown-Cave	27	23	85	—
Goodhart	39	43	100	58
Boscawen	30	21	70	—
Traveller surnames				
Brazil	271	88	32	30
Gritt	111	14	13	—
Loveridge	1,365	422	31	28
Lowbridge	168	33	20	—
Scarrott	299	80	27	—

sounding *Cave-Brown-Cave* had an 84 percent probate rate. *Goodhart,* an elite surname from the early nineteenth century, topped the charts at 100 percent. (There were in fact thirty-nine recorded *Goodhart* deaths and forty-three probates; some of the *Goodharts* presumably died outside England and Wales.) The Cornish *Boscawen* was also elite, with a 70 percent probate rate.

In contrast, the table includes other surnames associated with the English Traveller/Gypsy community (though only a fraction of the holders of these surnames would identify as Travellers). These all have lower-than-average probate rates.

As noted, to get the current probate rates for these surnames after 1966 requires a visit to the Probate Registry (one of the least welcoming data repositories I have ever encountered—visit there at your peril). Even though the current data are hard to obtain, the probate test for surname status is the most accurate available, because nearly half of British wills are probated. Thus the records reveal status differences even for relatively rare surnames. However, they tell us people's status only at the time of death. Since the average age of death for people in England and Wales is now in the late seventies, these data show the status of people one or two generations before the current one.

Another convenient way to check for the status of surnames is to compare their frequency in high-status occupations with their frequency in the population as a whole. Medical professionals are a good source of this type of information because they now represent both a substantial fraction of the population and a high-status occupation. Moreover, most countries maintain publicly accessible medical registers.

In the United Kingdom, the General Medical Council maintains a register of licensed physicians.[9] But because there are only 2.8 domestically registered physicians per thousand of population, this test can measure only the status of more common surnames, or groups of surnames, with five thousand or more holders. Table A3.2 shows the number of physicians per thousand population, as measured by the 2002 Office of National Statistics surname list, for a standard average surname, *Clarke.* In comparison, we can see that physicians with a high-status surname like *Smyth* are much more numerous, occurring at a rate of 8.6 per thousand. For surnames common in the English Traveller community, such as *Loveridge,* physicians are less than half as frequent as in the general population. So for surnames held by five thousand or more people, or surname

---

[9] General Medical Council 2012.

TABLE A3.2. Numbers of physicians and nurses by surname types, United Kingdom

Surname	Population 2002 (England and Wales)	Physicians 2012 (U.K.)	Physicians per thousand	Nurses and midwives (U.K.)	Nurses per thousand
Clarke	139,654	385	2.76	1,443	10.3
Smyth	11,050	95	8.60	269	24.3
Cohen	9,495	134	14.11	48	5.1
Traveller surnames					
Beaney/Beeney/Beeny	2,544	3	1.18	18	7.1
Brazil/Braziel	1,605	2	1.25	6	3.7
Gritt	404	0	0.00	4	9.9
Loveridge/Leveridge	5,699	6	1.05	36	6.3
Lowbridge	587	1	1.70	6	10.2
Scarrett/Scarrott	1,508	3	1.99	15	9.9
All Traveller	12,347	15	1.21	85	6.9

groups of equivalent size, the Medical Register generally enables a realistic assessment of the current average status of the surname.

One anomaly of these data is that because large numbers of physicians of foreign origin work in the United Kingdom, any foreign physician's surname that is common outside the United Kingdom may incorrectly appear elite on this measure. The surname *Schmidt*, for example, shows up at a rate of nearly thirty per thousand population, suggesting that *Schmidt* represents an elite in Britain. An examination of the first names of these physicians, however, shows they are mostly of German nationality, and we can infer that *Schmidt* is not an elite German surname.[10] However, the heavy overrepresentation of *Cohens* shown in table A3.2 indeed comes mainly from *Cohens* of British origin.

Nursing and midwifery is another field commonly subject to registration. The Nursing and Midwifery Council in the United Kingdom also maintains a register.[11] The advantage of this data set for determining the status of surnames is that it is larger: there are 10.3 registered nurses per thousand population for common domestic surnames, compared to only 2.8 for physicians. Thus for rarer

[10] The register also shows where physicians trained.
[11] Nursing and Midwifery Council, "Search the Register," www.nmc-uk.org/Search-the-register.

surnames this group is less subject to random fluctuations as a measure of status. The disadvantage is that because nursing is not such a high-status occupation, it does not delineate high- and low-status surnames as clearly. Thus we see in table A3.2 that physicians are 3.1 times as frequent among the high-status *Smyths,* but nurses are only 2.4 times as frequent. Also nurses are about two-thirds as common as average among the lower-status Traveller surnames, compared with physicians, who are less than half as common.

Another profession that provides public registration information is attorneys, a category that in the United Kingdom includes both solicitors and the smaller group of barristers. The U.K. Law Society maintains a directory of solicitors.[12] For common surnames, there are about 1.8 solicitors per thousand surname holders. Barristers are listed in a commercial directory, but there are only about 0.3 barristers per thousand people.[13] In both categories, *Smyth* shows up as a higher status surname with 3.7 solicitors per thousand, and 0.54 barristers. The Traveller surnames listed in table A3.2 appear among solicitors at a rate of 0.9 per thousand, half the expected rate. However, their frequency among barristers is 0.4 per thousand, higher than the average rate. This finding emphasizes the importance of random elements when looking at small numbers.

UNITED STATES

In the United States, estimating the current status of surnames is more difficult than in the United Kingdom because the fifty states, rather than the federal government, have jurisdiction over many aspects of life. Thus the United States has no national probate index, and typically professions, such as attorneys, are licensed at the state rather than the national level. The American Medical Association does maintain a national register of physicians that has a million names on it. But the publicly available website listing these names is cumbersome and essentially unusable for systematic research into surname status.[14] The AMA does sell printed and CD versions of its directory that contain much more useful information about individual physicians, such as medical school attended and date of medical school graduation. It is thus a useful, but expensive, source for examining status differences among U.S. surnames.

[12] Law Society, "Find a Solicitor," www.lawsociety.org.uk/find-a-solicitor/?view=solsearch.
[13] Legal Hub, "Law, Expert Witness, and Bar Directory," www.legalhub.co.uk/legalhub/app/main.
[14] American Medical Association, "Doctor Finder," https://extapps.ama-assn.org/doctorfinder/recaptcha.jsp.

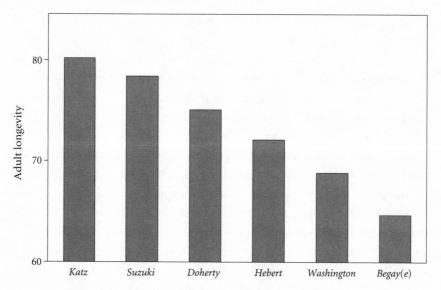

FIGURE A3.5. Longevity versus surname, United States, 2012.

Because social status differences are strongly associated with longevity, one quick way to estimate status levels of surnames in the United States is by calculating average adult ages at death for different surnames. Ancestry.com offers the Social Security Death Index, with information on 92.5 million deaths, available online, though completely free versions are also available.[15] This records the dates of birth and death of most of the U.S. population with a Social Security number who died between 1962 and 2012. Thus it records a very large share of all adult deaths in recent decades.

Figure A3.5 shows the average longevity of those age 21 and older dying circa 2007, calculated from the Social Security Death Index in the United States and holding the surnames *Katz, Suzuki, Doherty, Hebert, Washington,* and *Begay(e).*[16] These are characteristic surnames held by people of Ashkenazi Jewish, Japanese, Irish, New France, black, and Native American ancestry, respectively. Note the great differences in average longevity. The average lifespan of adults with the surname *Katz* was 80.2 years, compared to 64.6 years for those

[15] See, for example, "Social Security Death Master File," on the privately run website http://ssdmf.info/. The Ancestry.com site, however, offers much greater ease of use.

[16] Longevity is calculated for those dying at age 21 and older to limit the effects of differential fertility rates across populations on measured longevity. With higher fertility, proportionately more young people are at risk of death, and hence estimated average longevity is biased downward.

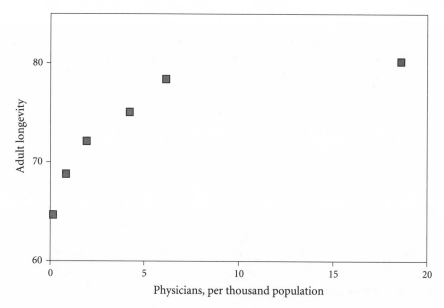

FIGURE A3.6. Longevity versus occupational status for surname groups, United States, 2012.

with the surname *Begay(e)*—a difference of 15.6 years. *Heberts,* whites of New France descent, still live three years less than *Dohertys,* whites of Irish descent.

These longevity differences correlate strongly with general differences in social status. Figure A3.6 shows, for example, the numbers of physicians in the AMA register per thousand holders of these surnames, versus adult longevity.[17] The longevity calculation is less susceptible than occupational measures of status to biases caused by migration of the highly skilled.

AUSTRALIA

The Australian Health Practitioner Regulatory Agency maintains a website that lists all registered medical practitioners: physicians, nurses, midwives, dentists, optometrists, chiropractors, pharmacists, osteopaths, physiotherapists, psychologists, and podiatrists, among others.[18] As in England and the United States, sur-

---

[17] It is also easy to calculate longevity in the United Kingdom for the years up to 2005 from databases available on Ancestry.com, as another way of estimating surname average social status.

[18] Australian Health Practitioner Registration Agency, "Registers of Practitioners," www .ahpra.gov.au/Registration/Registers-of-Practitioners.aspx?m=Search. This database can be searched for surnames beginning with any string but returns only fifty results per search.

name types show wide variations in representation among physicians. For common surnames of English origin, there are 3.5 physicians per thousand people on the voter roll. But for exclusively indigenous Australian surnames, the rate is zero. For the Jewish surnames *Cohen, Katz,* and *Levy,* the rate averages 22 per thousand.

The History of Social Status Using Surnames

ENGLAND AND WALES

For England it is easy to assess the status of surnames back to 1858, and indeed back as far as 1538, using probate records, though the accuracy of the assessment depends on how rare the surname is. The simplest way to measure status is to compare the probate rate of a surname with that of the average surname. This can be done on Ancestry.com for any surname back to 1858, using the national probate and death records.

Figure A3.7, for example, shows the relative probate rates compared to the average for the surnames *Loveridge* and *Doherty/Dougherty. Loveridge,* as noted above, is a surname held by many in the Traveller community. As the figure shows, since about 1900, *Loveridge* has had a probate rate no higher than 80 per-

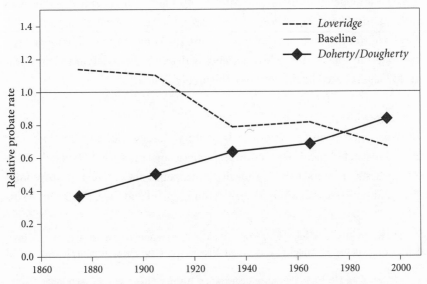

FIGURE A3.7. Probate rates of *Loveridge* and *Doherty/Dougherty,* 1860–2012.

cent of the average, reflecting the low education, earnings, and wealth of many *Loveridges*. But interestingly, before this period, *Loveridge* had a higher-than-average probate rate. Thus *Loveridge* cannot always have been a surname with a large Traveller share of holders. The steady downward movement in the measured social status of the surname presumably reflects an increasing share of *Loveridges* who are Travellers. Traveller families have many more children than the average family in England, and the *Loveridge* surname experienced unusual growth between 1881 and 2002. For the average native surname in England, there were 90 percent more holders in 2002 than in 1881; for *Loveridge* this gain was 382 percent!

In contrast with the decline in status of *Loveridge,* we see a steady rise in the status of the surname *Doherty/Dougherty,* of Irish Catholic origin. Initially this surname appears in probate records at only 27 percent the rate of the average name, but by 1980–2009 the frequency had risen to 84 percent.

The main source for earlier probate records, from 1538–1857, as noted above, is the Prerogative Court of the Archbishop of Canterbury (PCC). Since the wills provided in this court represent a much smaller fraction of the population before 1858, this measure is useful only for common surnames or larger surname groups. An index to these probate records is available online at the Public Record Office.[19] It contains 980,000 probates from England and Wales for the period 1394–1858.

For the surname *Boscawen,* discussed above, we see twenty-five probates in this index. To discover whether that is a large or small fraction of all *Boscawens,* we need an idea of the number of holders of the surname in these years. One convenient source of data for this purpose is the free FamilySearch website, run by the Church of Jesus Christ of Latter-Day Saints.[20] A rich source for demographic information before 1837, when national registration of births, deaths, and marriages was instituted, is parish church records of baptisms, burials, and marriages. Volunteers from the Mormon church have transcribed large numbers of these records, particularly those of baptisms and marriages, for England in the years 1538–1837. The site includes records for eighty-three million baptisms in England and twenty-five million marriages, though these include many duplicate entries. The data imply that the average ratio of probates to marriages was .039.

---

[19] National Archives, n.d.
[20] FamilySearch, n.d.

For the surname *Boscawen,* there are only twenty marriage records in the FamilySearch index. This implies a ratio of probates to marriages of 1.25, thirty-two times the average rate. Thus *Boscawen* was once a very high-status surname. In contrast, *Loveridge* has nineteen probates and 649 marriages, for a ratio of 0.029. Thus *Loveridge* in its early history was a modestly low-status surname.

If we take a famous family from the Middle Ages, such as the Berkeley family, progenitors of the famous philosopher Bishop George Berkeley (1685–1753) and thus the namesake of the University of California, Berkeley, we find the surname overrepresented in these records. There are 122 *Berkeley* probates and 142 *Berkeley* marriages, for a ratio of probates to marriages twenty-two times the average. Surnames derived from *Berkeley,* such as *Barclay* (now of course embodied by the giant Barclays banking corporation), are also overrepresented: for *Barclay* we find 145 probates and 568 marriages, producing a probate rate that is 6.5 times the expected rate.

Other surnames that still show up as high status in the period 1394–1858 on this test are those of the Norman conquerors of 1066. Thus, for example, the surname *Mandeville* appears in the Domesday Book of 1086 as belonging to a substantial landowner. For this surname the PCC index shows 120 probates, compared to 157 marriages, a rate twenty times higher than expected.

The kinds of surnames that tend to be revealed as lower status before 1858 include patronyms and toponyms. *Williamson,* for example, shows 688 probates but 23,400 marriages for a ratio of 0.029, only three-quarters that for the average surname. Toponyms are names such as *Meadow(e)(s)* that indicate the location of the holder's dwelling in the community. *Meadow(s)/Meadowe(s)* had 128 probates, 4,826 marriages, and thus a ratio of probates to marriages of .026, or just over two-thirds of the average.

A second way to estimate the average social status of surnames in the past, which can be done for England and Wales for deaths from 1866 and later, is to calculate the average adult longevity of those dying with the surname (see n. 16). In all periods, longevity is closely linked to social status. From 1866 on, the death records in England and Wales indicate age at death. Another means of estimating surname status in earlier years in England and Wales is to examine the occupations reported in the census from 1841 to 1911. These data, however, have typically not been digitized by sites such as Ancestry.com (because occupational status is peripheral to the primary interests of genealogists), so using them can be extremely time consuming.

TABLE A3.3. Surname types and characteristics, Ireland, 1911

Surname type	Literate (%)	Skilled (%)	Catholic (%)
Indigenous (e.g., *Doherty/Dougherty*)	89	6	87
Scottish (e.g., *Buchanan*)	94	14	11

IRELAND

Ireland has generally poor records of historical surname distributions and status. The original returns of the censuses of 1821 through 1851 were largely destroyed by an explosion at the Public Record Office in 1922 during the Irish civil war. The original census returns for 1861–91 had earlier been destroyed by administrative action. The censuses of the Irish Free State from 1926 on still have not been publicly released.

However, the National Archives of Ireland has digitized the household census returns in their entirety for all of Ireland from the censuses of 1901 and 1911, and these are freely available on the Internet.[21] These censuses reveal for each person indications of literacy and occupations, from which it is possible to infer average surname status. They also reveal the religious affiliation of each person. Thus if we compare classically Gaelic and indigenous Irish surnames, such as *Doherty/Dougherty,* and surnames that arrived with the settlement from Scotland in the seventeenth century, such as *Buchanan,* we observe a large difference in status between such surnames in 1911. Table A3.3 shows results for men age 18 and older. Interestingly, in Ireland, the fraction of the holders of a surname in 1911 who were Catholic is a good indicator of its average social status.

UNITED STATES

Finding useful sources for the history of surname status is again more challenging for the United States than for England. There is no equivalent to the probate registries for England, the evidence on age at death, or the national counts of marriages, births, and deaths from parish records and the national registry. There is, however, copious material from the censuses of the period 1850–1940. This generally supplies information on occupations, and sometimes, as in 1860 and 1870, on the value of real and personal property. However, again Ancestry .com has not generally digitized occupations and other material considered ancillary to its customers' interests in genealogy.

[21] Census of Ireland 1911.

The Origins of Surnames

The etymology of surnames is another field of interest. The origin of surnames is often not transparent. Some surnames come from other languages: English surnames may be originally Cornish, Welsh, Gaelic, Latin, or French. Some pertain to occupations that have disappeared in the modern era. And some have mutated from their original form into variants, especially when their meanings have become opaque.

Smith has remained firmly *Smith,* with few variants, in part because everyone knows what a smith is and how to spell it. But another medieval occupational surname, *Arbalistarius,* recorded as a surname in the Domesday Book of 1086 and derived from the Latin *arcus* (bow) and *ballista* (catapult), has no meaning to the untrained modern ear. Thus it has mutated into the forms *Arblaster* (held by 450 people in England and Wales in 2002), and *Alabaster* (held by 468 people).

Similarly the medieval surname *Cholmondeley,* derived from a place-name in Cheshire, England, came to be pronounced as either *Chomley* or *Chumley.* As the name spread farther from its namesake locality, several variants developed, with the following numbers of holders in 2002:

Cholmondeley	141
Cholmondley	11
Cholmeley	18
Chomley	8
Chumley	94
Chamley	335
Champley	60

This ramification stems in part from these originally elite surnames' being carried down the social ladder by social mobility over generations, to be held by people who were illiterate and had no knowledge of the history or meaning of the surname.

Surnames ending in *-ville* constitute a set of high-status English surnames. Most of them date from the Domesday Book, and they indicate that the bearer's home estate was in Normandy. Thus we have *Baskerville, Mandeville, Sackville, Somerville,* and *Turberville,* to name a few. Many of these have also ramified into variants ending in *-field* instead of *-ville.* Since *field* is not a synonym for the French *ville,* this transformation again presumably reflects the downward social mobility of the surname, to the point where it was held by people who had no idea what a *ville* was. This shift, of course, is a central plot element in Thomas Hardy's *Tess of the d'Urbervilles*. Tess Durbeyfield is the daughter of uneducated rural smallholders who learn that they are descended from the d'Urbervilles, a now-extinct Norman noble family. Variants of the original surname *Turberville* were held by the following numbers of people in 2002:

Turberville	203
Turberfield	209
Turbervill	22
Turbefield	48
Turburville	67
Turburfield	22
Turbyfield	12

For the years 1394–1858, we can compare the average status of the *-ville* and *-field* variants. There are 74 probates for the *-ville* variants, compared to 254 marriages before 1837, a rate 7.5 times the average. In contrast, there were three probates of the *-field* variants, compared to 93 marriages, a rate only about four-fifths of the average before 1858. Interestingly, there were two probates for another version of the surname, *Turbervylde,* which perhaps represents a step in the transition from *-ville* to *-field*.

Many books have been published on surname etymology. A comprehensive source for England is Reaney and Wilson's *Dictionary of English Surnames,* with sixteen thousand entries. There are also some online dictionaries of etymology, but these are of very questionable reliability. One is the Internet Surname Database. This is quite extensive in the number of surnames it covers and the history it provides. But for the surname *Smith* it confidently asserts: "Of pre 7th century Anglo-Saxon origins, it derives from the word 'smitan' meaning 'to smite' and as such is believed to have described not a worker in iron, but a soldier, one who smote."[22] The tax rolls for the poll tax of 1381 include, for many taxpayers, not only the surname but also the occupation. A large number of men called *Smith* are also described as having the occupation of smith, suggesting that for these individuals the name must have had a more recent origin and was descriptive of their occupation.

---

[22] Internet Surname Database, "Last Name Origins," www.surnamedb.com.

To avoid cluttering the text with references and citations, this section details the data sources for the figures and tables.

Chapter 1

Figure 1.1. Jeff J. Mitchell / Getty Images.

Figure 1.2. Gregory Clark.

Figure 1.3. Corak 2013, figure 2. For Canada: Miles Corak, personal communication, July 27, 2012. For India: Hnatkovska, Lahiri, and Paul 2013. For South Korea: Ueda 2013. Gini for income: World Bank, n.d.

Figure 1.4. Hertz et al. 2007, table 2; World Bank, n.d.

Figure 1.5. © National Portrait Gallery, London.

Figure 1.6. The conventional estimates are the average of those shown in figures 1.3 and 1.4. The surname-group estimates are described in subsequent chapters.

Chapter 2

Figure 2.1. Photo by Tage Olsin / Wikimedia Commons.

Figure 2.2. Almenberg and Dreber 2009, 178.

Figure 2.3. List of noble surnames from Riddarhuset 2012. The stock of different types of surnames as of December 31, 2011, was derived from Statistics Sweden, Surname Search, www.scb.se/namesearch. The population share of the aristocratic surnames was then 0.6 percent. The share of aristocratic surnames over time was calculated from the trend in the share of surnames beginning with *Adler-, Af-, Ankar-, Ehren-, Gripen-, Gyllen-, Leijon-, Lillie-, Munck-, Oxen-, Reuter-, Ridder-, Silfver-, Stiern-,* and *von* for men born in the years 1810–2009 and those dying in the years 1901–2009. Federation of Swedish Genealogical Societies 2011.

Figures 2.4–2.6. Federation of Swedish Genealogical Societies 2011.

Figures 2.7 and 2.8. Kalenderförlaget 2008a,b,c; all 2008 tax returns for the *kommuns* of Botkyrka, Huddinge, Haninge, Nacka, Täby, and Stockholm.

Figures 2.9 and 2.10. Swedish Bar Association 2013. Attorneys were divided into two birth cohorts, 1930–59 and 1960–88. The intergenerational correlations of status in figure 2.10 are based on the assumption that attorneys represent the top 1 percent of the status distribution. In figure 2.10 the relative representation is shown on a logarithmic scale.

Figure 2.11. Physicians in 2011: Sverige, Socialstyrelsen 2011.

Figures 2.12 and 2.13. Physicians registering 1972–2010: Sverige, Socialstyrelsen 2011. 1939–71: Sverige, Socialstyrelsen 1972. 1890–1938: Widstrand 1939. Population share of different surname types estimated from Federation of Swedish Genealogical Societies 2011. In both figures the relative representation is shown on a logarithmic scale.

Figure 2.14. Uppsala University, masters' theses, 2000–2012: http://uu.diva-portal.org/smash/searchadthe.jsf.

Figure 2.15. Matriculating students, 1942–62: Elvin 1956; Uppsala Universitet 1954; Göteborgs nation 1967.

Figures 2.16 and 2.17. Brenner and Thimon 1971; Odén 1902; Elvin 1956; Uppsala Universitet, 1954; Edlund 1979; Karlberg 1908; Lundin 1882; Sjöström 1897, 1901, 1904, 1907, 1908. In both figures the relative representation is shown on a logarithmic scale.

Figure 2.18. Royal Academy of Sciences: for 1739–2012, Wikipedia, "Lista över ledamöter av Kungliga Vetenskapsakademien," http://sv.wikipedia.org. For 2012, Maria Asp Dahlbäck, archivist of the Royal Academy, personal communication, June 25, 2012. Royal Academy, 1779–2012: Wikipedia, "List of Members of the Swedish Academy," http://en.wikipedia.org. Royal Academy of Music (1771–2012): Wikipedia, "Lista över Musikaliska Akademiens ledamöter," http://sv.wikipedia.org. The relative representation is shown on a logarithmic scale.

Figure 2.20. Statistics Sweden 2009, table 6, 20; Kalenderförlaget 2008a,b,c.

Chapter 3

Figure 3.1. The rarer surnames of the rich in 1923–24 were identified from "Taxpayer Listings" 1924, 1925. The rarer surnames of the Ivy League students in 1850 and earlier were identified from Chapman 1867; College of William and Mary 1941; Columbia College 1865; Harvard University 1915; Maxwell 1917; Princeton University 1908; Raven 1909; Yale University 1910.

The physician frequencies are all derived from the listings of physicians in American Medical Association 2012. Only physicians graduating from U.S. and Caribbean medical schools are included. Ward et al. (2012) give surname frequencies in 2000 for surnames held by a hundred or more people. Surname frequencies for rarer surnames, such as those of the rich and the Ivy League students, were estimated from Public Profiler's World Family Names database, whose data for the United States are based on a recent sample of surnames. The implied numbers of surnames in 2000 were estimated from their frequency per million in this source by looking at the relationship for the same class of surnames for those held by 100–120 people in the 2000 census.

Figure 3.2. Public Profiler, n.d.

Figure 3.3. See sources for figure 3.1.

Figure 3.4. Physicians were allocated to thirty-year cohorts by year of medical school graduation listed in American Medical Association 2012. To estimate the relative representation of surname types among doctors in each generation, we need to know the numbers of people bearing each surname type in the corresponding birth cohort. The average age of medical school graduation is assumed to be 25.

Starting from surname stocks in 2000, the cohort size of the black surnames in earlier years was estimated by assuming that this follows the same trend as the black population as a whole. To estimate this trend we use the share of blacks in the total population age 0–9 at the time of each census to obtain a measure of the black share in each cohort of doctors. If the black surnames used here are representative of the black population, the share of each cohort increased over time 1950–2010.

For the New France group, we check the cohort surname frequency by looking at the share of deaths in the Social Security Death Index for these surnames (Social Security Death Index, n.d). For a group of average social status, the Death Index should indicate the relative frequency of births for a surname all the way from the nineteenth century until recently. The Death Index indicates that New France surnames were a constant share of births for the period 1900–1979. Thus for these surnames, we assume the shares for all cohorts to be equivalent to the 2000 census share.

However, because elite groups have lower mortality rates, the Death Index overestimates the population share of these groups in earlier birth cohorts and underestimates it for more recent. In order for a birth in 1900, for example, to be recorded in the Death Index, the person would have to have died in 1962 or later. And for a birth in 1980 to have been recorded, the person would have to have died at age 32 or younger. Thus it is potentially misleading to use this source to measure the cohort frequency of Jewish surnames, the surnames of the rich of 1923–24, and the Ivy League students.

Instead, for the Jewish surname group, we assume that their share of the population changed in a manner consistent with general changes in the representation of Jews in different age groups, as measured in 2004 (Tighe, Saxe, and Kadushin, 2011). This shows the U.S. Jewish population age 20–29 substantially declining by decade from the 1950s but rising again in the past decade.

For the other two rare surname groups we have no source other than the Death Index, but we must be aware that this source may not yield an accurate estimate of the stock of 25-year-olds in these groups for earlier years. The Death Index suggests that the relative frequency of each surname group was declining over time.

Figures 3.5 and 3.6. Crissey 2009, table 1; Pew Forum 2008, 56.

Figure 3.7. The figure is drawn assuming that the Jewish mean status is an estimated 0.62 standard deviations above the mean and the black mean status 0.27 standard deviations below the mean, with each group having the same variance in status.

Figure 3.8. See sources for figure 3.4.

Figures 3.9 and 3.10. We assume that attorneys and physicians are distributed proportionately across states. We then use the ratio of physicians to the general population for these states to estimate for each group the fraction of their population we are observing.

Attorney stocks in 2012 from listings of the state bar associations of Alabama, Arizona, California, Colorado, Connecticut, Florida, Georgia, Illinois, Louisiana, Maine, Maryland, Massachusetts, Michigan, Minnesota, Mississippi, New York, North Carolina, Ohio, Oregon, Pennsylvania, Texas, Utah, Vermont, Washington, and Wisconsin. Surname stocks as for table 3.1 and figure 3.4.

The relative representation here of a surname like *Katz* is defined as the number of attorneys with the surname *Katz* compared to the number of *Katzes* in the 2000 U.S. census, divided by the number of attorneys with the surname *Olson* or *Olsen* compared to the number of *Olsons* and *Olsens* in the census.

Figure 3.11. American Medical Association 2012; Ward et al. 2012. Surnames used were those whose holders were 95 percent or more white.

Figure 3.12. Intermarriage rates all obtained from Ancestry.com, based on the following sources. Connecticut: Marriage index, 1959–2001. Maine: Marriages, 1892–1996. Massachusetts: Town and vital records, 1620–1988. Oregon: Marriage indexes, 1946–2008. Vermont: Marriage records, 1909–2008. State Franco-American population shares are from US Census Bureau 2010.

Figure 3.13. See sources for figure 3.4. The relative representation of Japanese surnames among physicians is measured using all Japanese surnames held by at least a thousand people in the United States in 2000.

Tables 3.1 and 3.2. See sources for figure 3.4.

Table 3.4. Suzuki 2002, table 3, 265.

Chapter 4

Figures 4.1 and 4.2. For this chapter and the next, two main sources are a database of the surnames of those attending Oxford and Cambridge in the period 1170–2012 and a database of those whose estates were probated at the Prerogative Court of the Archbishop of Canterbury, 1384–1858. For the latter, the index of the court wills in series PROB 11 at the National Archives was used to construct a database recording the name, status (from titles such as *Sir, Lord,* and *Gentleman*), and the date of probate. The database contains 903,438 such probates for England. The Oxford and Cambridge database contains the name and year of arrival at the universities of all known students (and faculty in earlier years) from 1170 to 1889, and thereafter a large sample of known attendees. Brasenose College 1909; Cambridge University 1954, 1976, 1998, 1999–2010; Elliott 1934; Emden 1957–59, 1963, 1974; Foster 1887, 1891, 1893; Venn and Venn 1922–27, 1940–54; and Oxford University 1924–2010. For the years 2010–12, student surnames were derived from the e-mail directories for Oxford and Cambridge (www.ox.ac.uk/applications/contact_search; http://jackdaw.cam.ac.uk/mailsearch/). Women students at Cambridge for 1860–1900 were identified from the Cambridge Alumni Database (http://venn.lib .cam.ac.uk/acad/search.html), which contains records for 781,474 persons.

Figure 4.3. British Library, MS. Harley 4866.

Figure 4.4. Locative surnames were defined as those ending in -*ton(n)(e)*, -*tu(n)(e)*, -*don(n)(e)*, -*dun(n)(e)*, -*dg(e)*, -*ham(m)(e)*, -*land(d)(e)*, -*bur(r)(y)(e)*, -*ber(r)(y)(e)*, -*bur(r)i(e)*, and *ber(r)i(e)*. Their share at Oxford and Cambridge was calculated as in figure 4.1. Their share in the population for each period from 1538 to 1837, before national registration of births, deaths and marriages, was estimated from marriages recorded in parish registers and other sources as transcribed for the FamilySearch website.

This approach was preferred to counting births, since infant and child mortality differs by social class. It assumes the same marriage rate for high- and low-status groups. For the years 1837–2012, surname frequencies were estimated from three sources: *England and Wales, Register of Marriages, 1837–2005;* the 1881 census of England and Wales (Schurer and Woollard 2000); and the Office of National Statistics database of surname frequencies in England and Wales in 2002 (U.K., Office of National Statistics 2002). For the years 1200–1837, surname frequencies were estimated by projecting backward the trends observed in marriage records for the period 1538–1600.

Figure 4.5. A list of the surnames of all those in the *Inquisitions Post Mortem* of 1236–99 was formed from Public Record Office 1904, 1906. From these, a sample of names with clearly discernible modern equivalents was selected. In forming this list, a few surnames (*Bruce, Preston,* and *Sutton*) were omitted as they were judged so common that their appearance in the *Inquisitions Post Mortem* was not informative.

Figure 4.6. The Domesday Book surnames were derived from Keats-Rohan 1999. All those with discernible modern equivalents were used, using Reaney and Wilson 2005 as a guide.

Figure 4.7. Photo Austin Osuide / Wikipedia Commons.

Table 4.1. See sources for figure 4.5; Reaney and Wilson 2005.

Table 4.2. See sources for figure 4.6; U.K., Office of National Statistics 2002.

Chapter 5

Figure 5.1. Surname frequencies: U.K., Office of National Statistics 2002. Oxford and Cambridge surnames, 1980–2012: see sources for figure 4.1.

Figure 5.2. Photo Andy Miles.

Figure 5.3. Photo Dennis Novy.

Figure 5.4. Clark and Cummins 2013, table 5.

Figure 5.5. Clark and Cummins 2013, figure 8.

Figure 5.6. Clark and Cummins 2013, figure 3.

Figure 5.7. Oxford and Cambridge surname frequencies: see sources for figure 4.1. Population frequencies by generations of eighteen-year-olds: estimated from the *England and Wales Marriage Register, 1837–2005.*

Figure 5.8. The set of surnames used here is all those with five hundred or fewer occurrences in the 1881 census (Schurer and Woollard 2000) that appear at Oxford and Cambridge in the years 1800–1829 (see sources for figure 4.1). Population frequencies by generations of eighteen-year-olds were estimated from the *England and Wales Marriage Register, 1837–2005,* to establish the overall population trends for these surname groups. A surname count for 2002 from U.K., Office of National Statistics 2002 is used as the surname-frequency benchmark.

Figure 5.9. List of MPs for English and Welsh constituencies from Rayment, n.d. Each election was counted in measuring the relative frequency of surnames, even when the same MP was returned to Parliament. Surname frequencies are estimated as for figure 5.8 but adjusted to an assumed average age for MPs of 50. Surname frequencies for marriages for 1810–37 are estimated from parish records of marriages.

Table 5.1. Clark and Cummins 2013, table 2. All the rare surnames used in this estimate of modern social mobility rates are listed in the appendix of this source. Sample A is the rich, B the poor, and C the prosperous.

Table 5.2. Clark and Cummins 2013, tables 6 and 7.

Table 5.3. Clark and Cummins 2013, table 8.

Chapter 6

Figure 6.2. State employee salaries from Sacramento Bee, n.d.

Figure 6.3. Bureau of Labor Statistics 2010; Statistics Sweden 2011b.

Figure 6.4. Rare-surname samples derived as in chapter 5. Average age of death by surname type from United Kingdom, Civil Registration, Death Index 1866–2005.

Figure 6.5. Rare-surname frequencies by generation from same sources as in figure 5.8. Probate rates for 1858–1966 from *England and Wales, Index to Wills and Administrations, 1858–2013*.

Figure 6.7. Linkages between the twenty-five thousand rare-surname individuals dying between 1858 and 2012, as described in chapter 5, were established using census records, birth and baptism records, marriage records, probate records, passenger ship lists, and university attendance records, as well as genealogies collected from a variety of sources. See Cummins and Clark 2013.

Figure 6.8. See sources for figure 5.8. The surnames were divided into two groups depending on whether the surname appeared at Oxford or Cambridge in the years 1770–99. The outcomes for the years 1770–1829 are not shown because of error introduced for these years by the way the surnames were selected based on their occurrence.

Table 6.1. Pairwise correlations from the following sources. Cognitive ability and education: Husén and Tuijnman 1991; Scarr and Weinberg 1978; Zagorsky 2007. Cognitive ability and occupational status: Cagney and Lauderdale 2002; Griliches and Mason 1972; Hauser 2002. Cognitive ability and earnings: Griliches and Mason 1972; Zagorsky 2007; Zax and Rees 2002. Cognitive ability and wealth: Zagorsky 2007. Education and occupational status: Hauser and Warren 2008; Pfeffer 2011; Scarr 1981. Education and earnings: Cagney and Lauderdale 2002; Griliches and Mason 1972; Pfeffer 2011. Education and wealth: Cagney and Lauderdale 2002; Pfeffer 2011. Occupational status and earnings: Griliches and Mason 1972; Hauser and Warren 2008 (wages). Occupational status and wealth: Pfeffer 2011. Earnings and wealth: Budria et al. 2002; Hendricks 2007.

Table 6.2. See sources for figure 6.4.

Table 6.3. See sources for figure 6.5.

Chapter 7

Figure 7.2. Clark and Cummins 2014, figure 4.

Figure 7.3. Births for 1880–1999 were obtained from *England and Wales, Register of Births, 1837–2005*.

Figure 7.4. Photograph by Herbert Rose Barraud / Wikimedia Commons.

Figure 7.5. This height study was reported in Galton 1886. The data used here are from Hanley 2004.

Figure 7.6. Data kindly supplied by Simon Boserup, Wojceich Kopczuk, and Claus Kreiner. The nature and construction of the data are detailed in Boserup, Kopczuk, and Kreiner 2013.

Chapter 8

Figure 8.1. University Grants Commission 2008, 105.

Figure 8.2. Doctor totals for each surname group were derived from the listings of Medical Council of India, n.d., for physicians in West Bengal registered between 1950 and 2011. Attorney surname distributions were based on a list of judges sitting in the High Court and district courts of West Bengal, obtained from the Calcutta High Court website (http://calcuttahighcourt.nic.in/).

Figure 8.3. Surname shares among doctors were derived from a database of all registered doctors in Bengal for 1860–1947 and West Bengal for 1948–2011. For the period 1915–2009, we compiled a list of 57,407 doctors registered in Bengal and West Bengal between 1915 and 2009 from Indian Medical Registry, n.d. These listings include doctors who graduated from medical school as early as the 1880s. For 1860–1909, doctor registrations were calculated from four sources: Government of Bengal, Bengal Medical Department 1903, which includes 1,507 doctors in Bengal licensed in 1903 or earlier; Government of Bihar and Orissa 1930; Burma Medical Council 1930; and a list of doctors registered in Bengal in 1915 who graduated from medical school between 1900 and 1914.

Population shares by period were estimated as below. The imperial censuses give Muslim shares of population in Bengal for 1871–1941. Muslims constituted 48 percent of the population for 1871–91, 53 percent for 1891–1921, and 55 percent for 1921–31 (Clark and Landes 2013, population appendix). For 1951–2001 we take the relevant Muslim population share as being that for the 20–29 age group in the censuses of India. This is larger than the overall Muslim population share because of the faster growth rate of the Muslim population. The Muslim shares were thus 21 percent for 1950–80 and 29 percent for 1980–2010 (Clark and Landes, 2013, population appendix).

We take the Hindu population share to be the rest of the population, omitting the small Christian and Buddhist populations.

To estimate the share over time of the seven Kulin Brahmin surnames, we proceed as follows. We start by analyzing the data from imperial censuses, which show the Brahmin share of the Hindu population for all of India. For the censuses conducted from 1871 to 1931, the population shares were 6.79, 7.31, 7.14, 7.19, 6.71, 6.58, and 6.34 percent (Clark and Landes 2013, population appendix). Thus before 1931 the Brahmin share was declining despite the elite status of Brahmins. This trend is consistent with the finding of Kingsley Davis that in 1931 the Brahmins had a ratio of children 0–6 to women 14–43 that was only 88 percent of other Hindu groups on average. This was mainly a consequence of the social taboo on Brahmin widows' remarrying (Davis 1946, table 3, 248). Presuming that Brahmins, a group with higher incomes than other Hindus, had better child survival rates would explain the only modestly lower net fertility of Brahmins. Brahmins in Bengal represented the same share among Hindus as for all of India in 1921–31. We thus assume this same population trend for Bengali Brahmins relative to other Hindus for the period 1871–1931.

Since Independence there has been no formal count of Brahmins. However, electoral surveys for 2004–07 estimated Brahmins as 5 percent of the entire Indian population, or 6.2 percent of the Hindu population (Center for the Study of Developing Societies 2009). This implies a modest decline in the Hindu share of Brahmins between 1931 and 2004. However, the Kolkata electoral register suggests that Brahmins had much greater life expectancy than the Hindu population as a whole (Chief Electoral Office, West Bengal 2010). Whereas the seven Kulin Brahmin surnames constituted 4.1 percent of the Hindu electorate in the 20–29 age group, they constituted 9.9 percent of the Hindu electorate in the 70–79 age group. If this distribution is representative of national population, it would imply that Brahmins accounted for only 5 percent of the Hindu population age 20–29 in 2004. We assume the same to be true for Brahmins in West Bengal in the period 2000–2009.

Not all Kulin Brahmins had one of the seven surnames we track. But a list of prominent Bengali Brahmins consists almost entirely of people with these surnames, so we take the seven Kulin surnames as comprising 5 percent of the West Bengal population age 20–29 in 2001, acknowledging that this method modestly overestimates their population share.

Other high-status Hindu groups are assumed to follow the same population trends as Brahmins. The three other Hindu surname groups—poor, scheduled caste, and mixed—are assumed to follow the population trend of the remainder of the Hindu population in Bengal.

Figure 8.4. Kolkata Police Recruitment Board 2010.

Figures 8.5 and 8.6. See sources for figures 8.2 and 8.3.

Figure 8.7. The fraction of each surname group admitted through the reservation system was estimated from Bankura Medical College 2009; Kar Medical College 2010, 2011.

Figure 8.8. For West Bengal: see the sources for figures 8.2 and 8.3 (counting doctors registered in 1960 and later). For West Bengali doctors in the United States: American Medical Association 2012.

Table 8.1. Totals derived from the posted admissions list of the All India Institute of Medical Sciences, Delhi, 2012, www.aiims.edu/aiims/examsection/MBBS12_RESULT_MERIT_WISE.pdf.

Table 8.2. On population shares in 2010, see Clark and Landes 2013, population appendix.

Table 8.3. See sources for figure 8.7.

Tables 8.4 and 8.5. Chief Electoral Officer, West Bengal 2010.

Chapter 9

Figure 9.1. Photo Li Zhensheng, Contact Press Images.

Figure 9.2. Wikipedia Commons.

Figure 9.3. The population shares of surnames in China come from a database obtained from the China National Identity Information Center (CNIIC) that gives the population, ethnicity, and educational attainment of the 1,500 most common Chinese surnames and the regional distribution of a selected group of surnames. This information comes from China's system of household registration (*hukou*), which covers the entire population.

The share of *jinshi* with each surname for the period 1820–1905 is from Zhu and Xie 1980. The frequency of surnames among the Republican era elite is from two sources: a list of high-ranking civil and military leaders of the Republican era (Liu 1989) and a list of university faculty for the years 1941–44 (Wu 1971). To construct the list of professors in 2012 (26,429 names), we used the faculty lists of Beihang, Beijing Normal, Fudan, Nanjing, Peking, Shanghai Jiaotong, Tsinghua, University of Science and Technology, Zhejiang, and Wuhan universities. The sample of the rich in 2006 is from the 2006 census of 1.4 million enterprises in China, from which we selected 130,000 chairmen of the boards of companies with assets of one hundred million yuan and above. The list of high government officials in 2010 is from China Government Directory 2010. For more details on these sources, see Hao and Clark 2012.

Table 9.1. The frequency of surnames in the population for each set of counties was estimated from the names of "honored fallen soldiers" of the period 1927–53, recorded in the Chronicle of Zhejiang (1985), and the Chronicle of Jiangsu (1993). The elite in the first period, 1870–1905, were those attaining the *juren* exam pass, as recorded in the chapters on notable local people in these chronicles. The Republican-era elite in these locations were identified from lists of students at the following universities: Central (Nanjing), 1916–36, 1945–47; Datong, 1923–35, 1940–48; Nanyang, 1905–25; Peking, 1905–48; Tsinghua, 1911–37; Wuhan, 1922–35; Yanjing, 1924–28; and Zhejiang, 1918–47. The elites from Zhejiang in the Communist era were derived from the *Chronicle of Zhejiang Jiang* 2005. The elites from Jiangsu were identified from the Nanjing university entrants from these counties for the period 1952–2011 (http://dawww.nju.edu.cn/pub/?id=1).

Table 9.2. Hao 2013, chapter 2.

Chapter 10

Figure 10.1. Photo Felice Beato / Wikimedia Commons.

Figures 10.2 and 10.3. Medical researchers, 1989–90: *Japanese Medical Researchers Directory* 1990. Attorneys, 1987: *Zenkoku bengoshi taikan* 1987. Corporate managers, 1993: *Diamond's Japan Business Directory* 1993. University professors, 2005: Daigaku shokuinroku kankokai 2005. Scholarly authors, 1990–2012: Google Scholar search.

Figure 10.4. Photo Chris Gladis.

Figure 10.5. Sources for Japanese data as for figure 10.2. Japanese surnames among doctors registered in the United States from American Medical Association 2012.

Figure 10.6. Names of scholarly authors from Google Scholar search.

Table 10.1. Lebra 1992, 55.

Table 10.2. Amano 1990, 193.

Table 10.3. Amano 1990, 193; Sonoda 1990, 103.

Table 10.4. Harootunian 1959, 260–61.

Table 10.5. The frequency of surnames was estimated from Public Profiler, n.d. The table assumes a population of Japan of 124 million in 1990. The potential rare samurai surnames are those listed in Takayanagi, Okayama, and Saiki 1964. The *kazoku* surnames were listed in Kasumi kaikan shoka shiryo chosa iinkai 1982–84.

Table 10.6. *Japanese Medical Researchers Directory* 1966, 1990.

Chapter 11

Figure 11.1. Depositphotos, Inc.

Figure 11.2. HDI by community from Chile, Ministry of Planning and Cooperation 2006. Average wage by occupation and location from Servicio Electoral Republica de Chile 2004; Chile, Ministerio del Trabajo y Prevision Social 2008.

Figure 11.3. OFF / AFP / Getty Images.

Figures 11.4 and 11.5. See sources for figure 11.2.

Table 11.1. Servicio Electoral Republica de Chile 2004. The electoral rolls listed 6,246,198 voters age 18 and above.

Table 11.2. Occupational wages were assigned using Chile, Ministerio del Trabajo y Prevision Social 2008. Locational wages were calculated as the average occupational wage from this source in each *comuna* in Chile.

Chapter 12

Figures 12.1 and 12.2. Figures created by a simulation of the status paths of five hundred families over one hundred generations. The average status trajectories for all families observed in any period in the top 0.14 percent of the status distribution are plotted for the ten earlier and later generations.

Figure 12.3. The probate surname data were obtained as described for figure 4.1. The frequency of surnames for 1680–1837 was estimated from parish records of marriages in England and Wales, obtained from the FamilySearch website. Surname frequencies for 1837 and later were estimated from marriages as recorded in *England and Wales, Register of Marriages, 1837–2005.*

Figures 12.4 and 12.5. Elite rare surnames in each of the periods 1710–39, 1740–69, 1770–88, and 1800–1829 were defined as surnames beginning with the letters *A–C* that appeared at low frequency in the parish records of marriage in the previous thirty years. The frequency cutoff depended on the numbers of marriages recorded in each of those periods: it was three in 1680–1709, four in 1710–39, five in 1740–69, and six in 1770–99. For 1800–29 and 1830–59, rare surnames were defined as those beginning with the letters *A–C* occurring at low frequency in *England and Wales, Register of Marriages, 1837–2005,* for 1837–59 and 1860–89, with a cutoff of ten.

Figure 12.6. The rare surnames of the rich are those discussed in chapter 5 that fell into the rich and prosperous groups. The rare surnames of Oxford and Cambridge students for the years 1800–1829 are those that appeared at the universities in these years and had forty or fewer holders in the 1881 census. The population share of these surnames for the years 1530–1837 was estimated from parish records of marriages, and for the years 1837–2005 from *England and Wales, Register of Marriages, 1837–2005*. The Oxford and Cambridge share of the surnames in each period was estimated from the university database as described above.

Figure 12.7. The four rare-surname groups are surnames appearing at Oxford and Cambridge in the periods 1800–1829, 1830–59, 1860–89, and 1890–1919 that had forty or fewer holders in 1881. The share of these surnames in each period in the population and at Oxford and Cambridge was calculated as for figure 12.6.

Figure 12.8. The share of *Pepyses* attending Oxford or Cambridge in each century was calculated as their numbers at the universities relative to the estimated number of *Pepyses* eligible to attend. For the years 1538–1837, the numbers eligible were estimated from parish marriage records by multiplying the estimated numbers of men attaining age 18 in each century by the marriage share of *Pepyses*. For the period 1837–2012 the estimate was made in the same way, except that the number of university-eligible eighteen-year-olds included women. For 1400–1537, the share of *Pepyses* in the population was assumed to be the same as the share in the years 1538–99.

Figures 12.9 and 12.10. Shares for surname–place of origin combinations among *juren* from south Jiangsu and north Zhejiang for 1660–1905 were derived from *Chronicle of Zhejiang Jiang* 1985 and *Chronicle of Jiangsu* 1993. Population shares of surname–place of origin combinations in these counties were estimated from records of twenty-five thousand soldier deaths from these same counties for the years 1927–53, assuming that the population share of these names was constant over the period 1680–2010. Names were classified as elite in the period 1871–1905 if they appeared at a rate four times the average among *juren*. Surname shares among elites 1905–2010 were estimated as in table 9.1.

Table 12.1. See sources for figure 12.3.

Table 12.2. See sources for figure 12.4.

Table 12.3. See sources for figure 12.5.

Chapter 13

Figure 13.1. Coakley 2004, figure 1.

Figures 13.2–13.4. The household returns are from Census of Ireland 1911. For each person, they list age, gender, literacy, religion, and occupation. Only some occupations could be classified by skill: occupations such as farmer are too diffuse in the Irish context to be assigned a skill level. So the ratio of skilled to unskilled is calculated only for more urban, better-defined occupations.

Figure 13.5. *Daily Telegraph*, October 19, 2011. Photo © 2011 The Associated Press / Matt Dunham.

Figure 13.6. The figure shows groups of surnames based on frequency (number of holders in the general population) as shares of the population in general in England and Wales in the census of 1881 (Schurer and Woollard 2000). Also shown are the shares of the Jewish population in each surname group in the 1881 census. The Jewish population is identified as men and women appearing in the *Register of Marriages* in the years 1910–14 with first names *Aaron, Abe, Abraham, Golda, Hyman, Israel, Jacob, Judah, Meir, Meyer, Myer, Mordecai, Solomon,* and *Yetta.*

Figure 13.7. Population shares for 1881 are derived as for figure 13.6. The Traveller population is defined as a set of people in the 1891 England and Wales census identified by such descriptions as "Living in caravan" or "In tent," from Keet-Black 2002.

Figure 13.8. The probate rates for the surname *Loveridge* for the period 1858–2012 are the number of *Loveridge* probates from *England and Wales, Index to Wills and Administrations, 1858–2013,* divided by the numbers of deaths of people named *Loveridge* age 21 and older from *England and Wales, Register of Deaths, 1837–2005.* The probate rate for the population in general was taken as the number of probates for people named *Brown* divided by the number of *Brown* deaths for people age 21 and above.

Figures 13.10 and 13.11. Doctors as a share of each surname group are derived from all doctors listed under the surname in American Medical Association 2012. For surnames held by one hundred or more people, the size of each surname group in 2000 is estimated from Ward et al. 2012. For rarer surnames, the surname-group size is estimated from Public Profiler, n.d.

Surnames were identified for ethnic groups through a variety of means. For most countries, lists of the most common surnames are available. For doctors trained abroad, the American Medical Association directory gives their national origin, allowing a check on these lists. Groups such as the Hmong were identified by the clustering of surnames in the United States seen in Public Profiler, n.d., at locations of known Hmong communities.

Table 13.1. Botticini and Eckstein 2012, figure 1.1, 18. This source records the share of Jews in the total population for Europe, North Africa, Asia Minor, Arabia, and West Asia.

Table 13.2. Parry et al. 2007, table 2.

Chapter 14

Figures 14.1–14.3. Lists of MPs after 1660 are derived from Rayment, n.d. For the period 1295–1659, information comes from the following sources: for 1386–1421, Roskell, Clark, and Rawcliffe 1993; for 1509–1558, Bindoff 1982; for 1558–1603, Hasler 1981; and for 1604–29, Thrush and Ferris 2010. We also draw on a wide variety of sources on individual constituencies.

Table 14.1. Muster rolls of English armies and garrisons, 1369 to 1453, come mainly from the National Archives series E 101 (94,962 service records), available online at "The Soldier in Later Medieval England," www.medievalsoldier.org. See also Bell et al. 2013.

Chapter 15

Figure 15.1. Plomin et. al. 1997.

Figures 15.2 and 15.3. Sacerdote 2007, 138.

Table 15.1. Sacerdote 2007, table 5.

Table 15.2. Björklund, Jäntti, and Solon 2007, table 1.

Appendix 3

Figures A3.1–A3.4. Public Profiler, n.d.

Figure A3.5. Social Security Death Index, n.d.

Figure A3.6. Doctors per thousand population from American Medical Association 2012; Ward et al. 2012.

Figure A3.7. See sources for figure 13.8.

Table A3.1. *England and Wales, Register of Deaths, 1837–2005; England and Wales, Index to Wills and Administrations, 1858–2013.*

Table A3.2. U.K., Office of National Statistics 2002; General Medical Council 2012; Nursing and Midwifery Council, "Search the Register," www.nmc-uk.org/Search-the-register.

Table A3.3. Census of Ireland 1911.

REFERENCES

Abramitzky, Ran, Leah Platt Boustan, and Katherine Eriksson. 2012. "Europe's Tired, Poor, Huddled Masses: Self-Selection and Economic Outcomes in the Age of Mass Migration." *American Economic Review* 102 (5): 1832–56.

Akee, Randall K. Q., William E. Copeland, Gordon Keeler, Adrian Angold, and E. Jane Costello. 2010. "Parents' Incomes and Children's Outcomes: A Quasi-Experiment Using Transfer Payments from Casino Profits." *American Economic Journal: Applied Economics* 2 (1): 86–115.

Almenberg, Johan, and Anna Dreber. 2009. "Lady and the Trump: Status and Wealth in the Marriage Market." *Kyklos* 62 (2): 161–81.

Amano, Ikuo. 1990. *Education and Examination in Modern Japan*. Tokyo: University of Tokyo Press.

American Medical Association. 2012. *Directory of Physicians in the United States*. Washington, DC: American Medical Association.

Amunátegui Solar, Domingo. 1932. *Historia social de Chile*. Santiago: Editorial Nacimiento.

Ando, Nisuke. 1999. *Japan and International Law: Past, Present and Future*. The Hague: Kluwer Law International.

Aramaki, Sohei. 2013. "Effects of Extended Family Members on Children's Educational Attainment: A Focus on the Diverse Effects of Grandparents, Uncles, and Aunts." In *A Quantitative Picture of Contemporary Japanese Families*, ed. Sigeto Tanaka, 299–320. Sendai: Tohoku University Press.

Arcs, Gregory. 2011. "Downward Mobility from the Middle Class: Waking Up from the American Dream." Washington, DC: Pew Charitable Trust.

Atzmon, G., L. Hao, I. Pe'er, C. Velez, A. Pearlman, P. Palamara, B. Morrow, et al. 2010. "Abraham's Children in the Genome Era: Major Jewish Diaspora Populations Comprise Distinct Genetic Clusters with Shared Middle Eastern Ancestry." *American Journal of Human Genetics* 86 (6): 850–9.

Bankura Medical College. 2009. "The Merit Wise List of Students Admitted in the 1st year

MBBS course at B.S. Medical College, Bankura, for the Academic Session 2009–10." Lokepur, West Bengal.

Bayly, Susan. 1999. *Caste, Society and Politics in India from the Eighteenth Century to the Modern Age*. The New Cambridge History of India, IV.3. Cambridge: Cambridge University Press.

Becker, Gary, and Nigel Tomes. 1979. "An Equilibrium Theory of the Distribution of Income and Intergenerational Mobility." *Journal of Political Economy* 87 (6): 1153–1189.

———. 1986. "Human Capital and the Rise and Fall of Families." *Journal of Labor Economics* 4 (3): S1–S39.

Beeton, M., and K. Pearson. 1899. "Data for the Problem of Evolution in Man, II: A First Study of the Inheritance of Longevity and the Selective Death-Rate in Man." *Proceedings of the Royal Society of London* 65: 290–305.

Behar, Doron M., Mark G. Thomas, Karl Skorecki, Michael F. Hammer, Ekaterina Bulygina, Dror Rosengarten, Abigail L. Jones, et al. 2003. "Multiple Origins of Ashkenazi Levites: Y Chromosome Evidence for Both Near Eastern and European Ancestries." *American Journal of Human Genetics* 73 (4): 768–79.

Bell, Adrian, Anne Curry, Andy King, and David Simpkin. 2013. *The Soldier in Later Medieval England*. Oxford: Oxford University Press.

Bengali Matrimony. n.d. Bengalimatrimony.com, accessed May 2012.

Bindoff, S. T. 1982. *The History of Parliament: The House of Commons, 1509–1558*. Vol. 3. London: Secker and Warburg.

Björklund, Anders, M. Jäntti, and G. Solon. 2007. "Nature and Nurture in the Intergenerational Transmission of Socioeconomic Status: Evidence from Swedish Children and Their Biological and Rearing Parents." *B.E. Journal of Economic Analysis & Policy* 7 (2): 1–21. www.bepress.com/bejeap/vol7/iss2/art4.

Björklund, Anders, Mikael Lindahl, and Erik Plug. 2006. "The Origins of Intergenerational Associations: Lessons from Swedish Adoption Data." *Quarterly Journal of Economics* 121 (3): 999–1028.

Björklund, Anders, Jesper Roine, and Daniel Waldenström. 2012. "Intergenerational Top Income Mobility in Sweden: Capitalist Dynasties in the Land of Equal Opportunity?" *Journal of Public Economics* 96: 474–84.

Black, Sandra E., Paul J. Devereux, and Kjell G. Salvanes. 2005. "Why the Apple Doesn't Fall Far: Understanding Intergenerational Transmission of Human Capital." *American Economic Review* 95: 437–49.

Bleakley, Hoyt, and Joseph Ferrie. 2013a. "Shocking Behavior: The Cherokee Land Lottery of 1832 in Georgia and Outcomes across the Generations." Working Paper, Booth School, Chicago University.

———. 2013b. "Up from Poverty? The 1832 Cherokee Land Lottery and the Long-Run Distribution of Wealth." Working Paper, Booth School, Chicago University.

Borjas, George J. 1995. "Ethnicity, Neighborhoods, and Human-Capital Externalities." *American Economic Review* 85 (3): 365–90.

Borst, Charlotte G. 2002. "Choosing the Student Body: Masculinity, Culture, and the Crisis of Medical School Admissions, 1920–1950." *History of Education Quarterly* 42 (2): 181–214.

Boserup, Simon Halphen, Wojciech Kopczuk, and Claus Thustrup Kreiner. 2013. "Intergenerational Wealth Mobility: Evidence from Danish Wealth Records of Three Generations." Working Paper, University of Copenhagen.

Botticini, Maristella, and Zvi Eckstein. 2012. *The Chosen Few: How Education Shaped Jewish History, 70–1492*. Princeton: Princeton University Press.

Bowles, Samuel, and Herbert Gintis. 2002. "Intergenerational Inequality." *Journal of Economic Perspectives* 16 (3): 3–30.

Boyce, Charles. 2005. *Critical Companion to William Shakespeare: A Literary Reference to His Life and Work*. New York: Facts on File.

Brasenose College. 1909. *Brasenose College Register, 1509–1909*. Oxford: Basil Blackwell.

Brenner, S. Otto, and Gösta Thimon. 1971. *Uppsala universitets matrikel 1595–1817: Register*. Uppsala: Almqvist and Wiksell.

Budría, S., J. Díaz-Giménez, V. Quadrini, and J. V. Ríos-Rull. 2002. "New Facts on the Distributions of Earnings, Income and Wealth in the US." *Federal Reserve Bank of Minneapolis Quarterly Review* 26: 2–35.

Bureau of Labor Statistics. 2010. *National Occupational Employment and Wage Estimates*. May. Washington, D.C.

Burma Medical Council. 1930. *Annual List of Registered Medical Practitioners*. Rangoon: Superintendent, Government Printing and Stationery, Burma.

Cagney, Kathleen A., and Diane S. Lauderdale. 2002. "Education, Wealth, and Cognitive Function in Later Life." *Journals of Gerontology, Series B: Psychological Sciences and Social Sciences* 57 (2): P163–P172.

Cambridge University. 1954. *Annual Register of the University of Cambridge, 1954–5*. Cambridge: Cambridge University Press.

———. 1976. *The Cambridge University List of Members, 1976*. Cambridge: Cambridge University Press.

———. 1998. *The Cambridge University List of Members, 1998*. Cambridge: Cambridge University Press.

———. 1999–2010. *Cambridge University Reporter*. Cambridge: Cambridge University Press.

Campbell, Cameron, and James Z. Lee. 2010. "Social, Economic, and Demographic Determinants of Descent Line Growth and Extinction over the Long Term in Historical China." California Center for Population Research Working Paper.

———. 2011. "Kinship and the Long-Term Persistence of Inequality in Liaoning, China, 1749–2005." *Chinese Sociological Review* 44 (1): 71–103.

Campbell, Frances A., E. P. Pungello, M. Burchinal, K. Kainz, Y. Pan, B. H. Wasik, O. A. Barbarin, J. J. Sparling, and C. T. Ramey. 2012. "Adult Outcomes as a Function of an Early Childhood Educational Program: An Abecedarian Project Follow-Up." *Developmental Psychology* 48 (4): 1033–43.

Caplan, Bryan. 2011. *Selfish Reasons to Have More Kids: Why Being a Great Parent Is Less Work and More Fun Than You Think*. New York: Basic Books.

Census of Ireland. 1911. *Household Returns of the Census of Ireland, 1911*. Dublin: National Archives of Ireland. www.census.nationalarchives.ie.

Center for the Study of Developing Societies. Various years (1996, 1998, 1999, 2004, 2009). *National Election Studies*. New Delhi: Center for the Study of Developing Societies.

Chapman, George T. 1867. *Sketches of the Alumni of Dartmouth College, 1771–1867*. Cambridge, MA: Riverside Press.

Chief Electoral Officer, West Bengal. 2010. Kolkata Electoral Roll, 2010. http://www.ceo westbengal.nic.in/Index.aspx. Downloaded and digitized by Lincoln Atkinson.

Chile, Estado que manifiesta la renta agrícola. 1855. *Estado que manifiesta la renta agrícola de los fundos rústicos que comprende el impuesto anual establecido en la sustitución del diezmo por la ley de 25 de Octubre de 1853*. Valparaiso: Imprenta del Diario.

Chile, Ministerio del Trabajo y Prevision Social, 2008. *Empleadores en la 2008, Servicio de Información para Estudios Secundarios and Trabajo*. Santiago.

Chile, Ministry of Planning and Cooperation. 2006. *Las trayectorias del desarrollo humano en las comunas de Chile, 1994–2003*. Santiago.

Chile, Oficina del Censo. 1866. *Censo general de la Republica de Chile, 1865*. Santiago: Imprenta Nacional.

China Government Directory. 2010. *China Government Directory: The Central Government (中国政府机构名录：中央卷)*. Beijing: Zhongyang Wenxian Press.

Chronicle of Jiangsu: Exams (江苏省通志稿：选举志). 1993. Nanjing: Jiangsu Guji Press.

Chronicle of Zhejiang. 1985. *Revised Chronicle of Zhejiang: Exams (重修浙江通志稿：选举)*. Beijing: Chronicles Press.

Chronicle of Zhejiang Jiang. 2005. *Chronicle of Zhejiang Jiang: Famous People (浙江人物志)*. Hangzhou: Zhejiang Renming Press.

Clark, Gregory. 2007. *A Farewell to Alms: A Brief Economic History of the World*. Princeton: Princeton University Press.

———. 2013. "Swedish Social Mobility from Surnames, 1700–2012." Working Paper, University of California, Davis.

Clark, Gregory, and Neil Cummins. 2013. "Intergenerational Mobility in England, 1858–2012: Wealth, Surnames, and Social Mobility." Working Paper, University of California, Davis.

———. 2014. "Malthus to Modernity: Wealth, Status and Fertility in England, 1500–1879." Forthcoming, *Journal of Population Economics*.

Clark, Gregory, and Gillian Hamilton. 2004. "Was Pre-industrial Society Malthusian? Tests from England and New France." Working Paper, University of California, Davis.

———. 2006. "Survival of the Richest: The Malthusian Mechanism in Pre-industrial England." *Journal of Economic History* 66 (3): 707–36.

Clark, Gregory, and Tatsuya Ishii. 2013. "Social Mobility in Japan, 1868–2012: The Surprising Persistence of the Samurai." Working Paper. University of California, Davis.

Clark, Gregory, and Zach Landes. 2013. "Caste versus Class: Social Mobility in India, 1860–2011." Working Paper, University of California, Davis.

Clark, Gregory, Daniel Marcin, Firas Abu-Sneneh, Wilfred Chow, Kuk Mo Jung, Ariel M. Marek, and Kevin M. Williams. 2013. "Social Mobility Rates in the USA, 1920–2012: A Surname Analysis." Working Paper, University of California, Davis.

Coakley, John. 2004. "Ethnic Conflict and the Two-State Solution: The Irish Experience of Partition." University College Dublin, Institute for British-Irish Studies, Ancillary Paper no. 3.

Cochran, Gregory, Jason Hardy, and Henry Harpending. 2006. "Natural History of Ashkenazi Intelligence." *Journal of Biosocial Science* 38 (5): 659–93.

Cohen, H. Bernice. 1964 "Family Patterns of Mortality and Life Span." *Quarterly Review of Biology* 39: 130–81.

College of William and Mary. 1941. *A Provisional List of Alumni, Grammar School Students, Members of the Faculty, and Members of the Board of Visitors of the College of William and Mary in Virginia, from 1693 to 1888: Issued as an Appeal for Additional Information.* Richmond, VA: College of William and Mary.

Columbia College. 1865. *Catalogue of the Governers, etc of Columbia College, 1754–1864.* New York: Van Nostrand.

Corak, Miles. 2013. "Inequality from Generation to Generation: The United States in Comparison." In *The Economics of Inequality, Poverty, and Discrimination in the 21st Century, Vol. 1*, ed. Robert Rycroft. Santa Barbara, CA: Praeger.

Corwin, Lauren A. 1977. "Caste, Class and the Love-Marriage: Social Change in India." *Journal of Marriage and the Family* 39 (4): 823–31.

Crissey, Sarah R. 2009. *Educational Attainment in the United States: 2007.* Washington, D.C.: US Census Bureau.

Cruz-Coke, Ricardo, and Rodrigo S. Moreno. 1994. "Genetic Epidemiology of Single-Gene Defects in Chile." *Journal of Medical Genetics* 31 (9): 702–6.

Cummins, Neil, and Gregory Clark. 2013. "The Inheritance of Wealth and Longevity over Four Generations: England and Wales, 1800–2012." Working Paper, University of California, Davis.

Daigaku shokuinroku kankokai. 2005. *Zenkoku daigaku shokuinroku (shiritsu daigaku hen and koku-koritsu daigaku hen)* (Directory of university faculty). Tokyo: Kojunsha.

Dalmia, Sonia, and Pareena G. Lawrence. 2001. "An Empirical Analysis of Assortative Mating in India and the U.S." *International Advances in Economic Research* 7 (4): 443–58.

Davis, Kingsley. 1946. "Human Fertility in India." *American Journal of Sociology* 52 (3): 243–54.

Diamond's Japan Business Directory. 1993. 27th ed. Tokyo: Diamond Lead Co., 1993.

Eaton, Richard M. 1993. *The Rise of Islam and the Bengal Frontier, 1204–1760.* Berkeley: University of California Press.

Edlund, Barbro. 1979. *Lunds universitets matrikel 1732–1830: Album.* Lund: Academiae Carolinae.

Elhaik, Eran. 2013. "The Missing Link of Jewish European Ancestry: Contrasting the Rhineland and the Khazarian Hypotheses." *Genome Biology and Evolution* 5 (1): 61–74.

Elliott, Ivo, ed. 1934. *Balliol College Register, 2nd edition, 1833–1933.* Oxford: John Johnson.

Elman, B. A. 1992. "Political, Social, and Cultural Reproduction via Civil Service Examination in Late Imperial China." *Journal of Asian Studies* 50 (1): 7–28.

Elvin, Gösta Vilhelm. 1956. *Östgóta Nation i Uppsala 1944–1954, Porträttkatalog med biografiska uppgifter.* Uppsala: Östgöta nation.

Emden, Alfred B. 1957–59. *A Biographical Register of the University of Oxford to AD 1500.* 3 vols. Oxford: Clarendon Press.

———. 1963. *A Biographical Register of the University of Cambridge to 1500.* Cambridge: Cambridge University Press.

———. 1974. *A Biographical Register of the University of Oxford, AD 1501 to 1540.* Oxford: Clarendon Press.

England and Wales, Censuses, 1841–1911. Available online at www.nationalarchives.gov.uk/records/census-records.htm.

England and Wales, Index to Wills and Administrations, 1858–2013. London: Principal Probate Registry. Data for 1858–1966 available online at Ancestry.co.uk.

England and Wales, Register of Births, 1837–2005. Available online at Ancestry.co.uk.

England and Wales, Register of Births, 2006–2011. London Metropolitan Archives.

England and Wales, Register of Deaths, 1837–2005. Available online at Ancestry.co.uk.

England and Wales, Register of Deaths, 2006–2011. London Metropolitan Archives.

England and Wales, Register of Marriages, 1837–2005. Available at Ancestry.co.uk.

Ermisch, John, Marco Francesconi, and Thomas Siedler. 2005. "Intergenerational Mobility and Marital Sorting." *Economic Journal* 116: 659–79.

"Every Other Doctor in Sweden from Abroad." 2009. *The Local.* 30 August. www.thelocal.se/21768/20090830

FamilySearch. n.d. www.familysearch.org.

Federation of Swedish Genealogical Societies. 2011. *Swedish Death Index, 1901–2009* (version 5.00). Stockholm.

Feenstra, Robert C., Robert Inklaar, and Marcel P. Timmer. 2013. "The Next Generation of the Penn World Table." www.ggdc.net/pwt.

Feliciano, Cynthia. 2005. "Educational Selectivity in U.S. Immigration: How Do Immigrants Compare to those Left Behind?" *Demography* 42 (1): 131–52.

Firoozi, Ferydoon. 1974. "Tehran: A Demographic and Economic Analysis." *Middle Eastern Studies* 10 (1): 60–76.

Foroohar, Rana. 2011. "Whatever Happened to Upward Mobility?" *Time.* November 14.

Foster, Joseph. 1887. *Alumni Oxonienses: The Members of the University of Oxford 1715–1886; Their parentage, birthplace and year of birth, with a record of their degrees; Being the Matriculation Register of the University.* 4 vols. Oxford: Parker and Company.

———. 1891. *Alumni Oxonienses: The Members of the University of Oxford 1500–1714: Their parentage, birthplace and year of birth, with a record of their degrees: Being the Matriculation Register of the University.* 2 vols. Oxford: Parker and Company.

———. 1893. *Oxford Men and Their Colleges, 1880–1892.* 2 vols. Oxford: Parker and Co.

Francesconi, Marco, and Cheti Nicoletti. 2006. "Intergenerational Mobility and Sample Selection in Short Panels." *Journal of Applied Econometrics* 21: 1265–93.

Galdames, Osvaldo Silva, and Hugo Amigo y Patricia Bustos, eds. 2008. *Apellidos Mapuche:*

Historia y significado. Departamento de Nutrición, Facultad de Medicina, Universidad de Chile, Santiago.

Galton, Francis. 1886. "Regression towards Mediocrity in Hereditary Stature." *Journal of the Anthropological Institute of Great Britain and Ireland* 15: 246–63.

———. 1889. *Natural Inheritance.* London: Macmillan.

General Council of the Bar / Sweet and Maxwell. 2011. *Bar Directory.* www.legalhub.co.uk.

General Medical Council. 2012. *List of Medical Practitioners.* www.gmc-uk.org/doctors/register/LRMP.asp.

Goberno de Chile, Ministerio de Desarrollo Social. 2011. Encuesta Casen (National Socio-Economic Survey). Santiago. www.ministeriodesarrollosocial.gob.cl/observatorio/casen/.

Goldberger, Arthur S. 1989. "Economic and Mechanical Models of Intergenerational Transmission." *American Economic Review* 79 (3): 504–13.

Gong, C. H., A. Leigh, and X. Meng. 2010. "Intergenerational Income Mobility in Urban China." IZA Discussion Paper no. 4811.

Góngora, Mario. 1970. *Encomenderos y estancieros: Estudios acerca de la constitución social aristocrática de Chile después de la conquista, 1580–1660.* Santiago: Universidad de Chile.

González Pomes, María Isabel. 1966. "La encomienda indígena en Chile durante el siglo xviii." *Historian* 5: 7–103.

Göteborgs nation. 1967. *Göteborgs nation i Uppsala, 1952–1966.* Uppsala.

Government of Bengal, Bengal Medical Department. 1903. *List of Qualified Medical Practitioners in Bengal, 1903.* Calcutta: Government Printing.

Government of Bengal, Political Department. 1930. *Press List of Ancient Documents Relating to the Provincial Council of Revenue at Calcutta, Preserved in the Secretariat Room of the Government of Bengal.* Series 2: Intermediate Revenue Authorities, vol. 3, part 1, 1773–1775.

Government of Bihar and Orissa. 1930. *The Bihar and Orissa Annual Medical List for 1930.* Patna: Superintendent, Government Printing, Bihar and Orissa.

Greenstein, Daniel I. 1994. "The Junior Members, 1900–1990: A Profile." In *The History of the University of Oxford,* vol. 8, ed. Brian Harrison. Oxford: Clarendon Press.

Greif, Avner, Murat F. Iyigun, and Diego Sasson. 2012. "Why England and Not China? Social Norms, Risk-Sharing Institutions and Discoveries." Working Paper, Stanford University.

Griliches, Zvi, and William M. Mason. 1972. "Education, Income, and Ability." *Journal of Political Economy* 80 (3): 74–103.

Grönqvist, Erik, Björn Öckert, and Jonas Vlachos. 2011. "The Intergenerational Transmission of Cognitive and Non-cognitive abilities." IFN Working Paper No. 884. http://dx.doi.org/10.2139/ssrn.2050393.

Guo, C. B., and W. F. Min. 2008. "Education and Intergenerational Income Mobility in Urban China." *Front Education China* 3: 22–24, translated from *Educational Research* (Jiaoyu yanjiu).

Hanley, James A. 2004. "'Transmuting' Women into Men: Galton's Family Data on Human Stature." *American Statistician* 58 (3): 237–43.

Hao, Yu. 2013. "Social Mobility under Three Regimes: China, 1645–2012." PhD diss., University of California, Davis.

Hao, Yu, and Gregory Clark. 2012. "Social Mobility in China, 1645–2012: A Surname Study." Working Paper. University of California, Davis.

Harbury, C. D., and D. M. W. N. Hitchens. 1979. *Inheritance and Wealth Inequality in Britain.* London: Allen and Unwin.

Harootunian, Harry D. 1959. "The Progress of Japan and the Samurai Class, 1868–1882." *Pacific Historical Review* 28 (3): 255–66.

Harvard University. 1915. *Quinquennial Catalogue of the Officers and Graduates of Harvard University, 1636–1915.* Cambridge, MA: Harvard University.

Hashimoto, Masanori. 1974. "Economics of Postwar Fertility in Japan: Differentials and Trends." *Journal of Political Economy* 82 (2): S170–S194.

Hasler, P. W. 1981. *The History of Parliament: The House of Commons, 1558–1603.* Vol. 3. London: TSO.

Hauser, Robert M. 2002. "Meritocracy, Cognitive Ability, and the Sources of Occupational Success." Center for Demography and Ecology, University of Wisconsin.

Hauser, Robert M., and John Robert Warren. 2008. "Socioeconomic Indexes for Occupations: A Review, Update, and Critique." *Sociological Methodology* 27 (1): 177–298.

He, Hu-Sheng, Yao-Dong Li, and Chang-Fu Xiang, eds. 1993. *Government and Party Officials of People's Republic of China* (中华人民共和国职官志). Beijing: China Social Sciences Press.

Heckman, James J. 2012. "Promoting Social Mobility." *Boston Review.* September/October.

Heckman, James J., Seong Hyeok Moon, Rodrigo Pinto, Peter Savelyev, and Adam Yavitz. 2010a. "Analyzing Social Experiments as Implemented: A Reexamination of the Evidence from the HighScope Perry Preschool Program." IZA Discussion Paper no. 5095.

———. 2010b. "The Rate of Return to the HighScope Perry Preschool Program." *Journal of Public Economics,* 94 (1–2): 114–28.

Hendricks, Lutz. 2007. "Retirement Wealth and Lifetime Earnings." *International Economic Review* 48.2 : 421–56.

Hertz, Thomas. 2005. "Rags, Riches and Race: The Intergenerational Mobility of Black and White Families in the United States." In *Unequal Chances: Family Background and Economic Success,* ed. Samuel Bowles, Herbert Gintis, and Melissa Osborne, 165–91. New York: Russell Sage and Princeton University Press.

Hertz, Thomas, Tamara Jayasundera, Patrizio Piraino, Sibel Selcuk, Nicole Smith, and Alina Verashchagina. 2007. "The Inheritance of Educational Inequality: International Comparisons and Fifty-Year Trends." *B.E. Journal of Economic Analysis & Policy* 7.

Hnatkovska, Viktoria, Amartya Lahiri, and Sourabh B. Paul. 2013. "Breaking the Caste Barrier: Intergenerational Mobility in India." *Journal of Human Resources* 48 (2): 435–73.

Ho, Ping-ti. 1964. *The Ladder of Success in Imperial China: Aspects of Social Mobility (1368–1911).* New York: Wiley.

Husén, Torsten, and Albert Tuijnman. 1991. "The Contribution of Formal Schooling to the Increase in Intellectual Capital." *Educational Researcher* 20 (7): 17–25.

Hymes, Robert. 1986. *Statesmen and Gentlemen: The Elites of Fu-chou Chiang-hsi, in Northern and Southern Sung.* Cambridge: Cambridge University Press.

"I'm So Broke I'm Trying to Get a Job as a Lorry Driver: Earl of Cardigan on Moving out His Stately Pile and Why He's Living on Benefits." 2013. *Daily Mail*. February 1.

Inglehart, Ronald, and Christian Welzel. 2010. "Changing Mass Priorities: The Link between Modernization and Democracy." *Perspectives on Politics* 8 (2): 551–67.

Irigoyen, José Francisco de. 1881. *Colección alfabética de apellidos bascongados con su significación en castellano, México, Valdés 1809*. San Sebastian: Biblioteca Euskal Erria.

Jadhav, Praveen. 2008. "Relative Disparity in the Implementation of Reservation Policy in India." In *The Development of Scheduled Castes and Scheduled Tribes in India*, ed. Jagan Karade, 1–10. Newcastle, U.K.: Cambridge Scholars Publishing.

Japanese Medical Researchers Directory: Igaku kenkyusha meibo. Various years (1961–90). Tokyo: Igaku Shoin.

Japan Statistical Yearbook. Various years (1976–2012). Tokyo: Nihon Tokei Kyokai.

Jenkins, Nicholas. 2013. "W. H. Auden: 'Family Ghosts.'" Website devoted to the genealogy of the intellectual classes in England. www.stanford.edu/group/auden/cgi-bin/auden/.

Jones, F. L., Hideo Kojima, and Gary Marks. 1994. "Comparative Social Fluidity: Trends over Time in Father-to-Son Mobility in Japan and Australia, 1965–1985." *Social Forces* 72 (3): 775–98.

Kalenderförlaget. 2008a. *Taxerings- och förmögenhetskalender för Stockholms kommun 2008*. Stockholm.

———. 2008b. *Taxerings- och förmögenhetskalender för Stockholms län Norra 2008*. Stockholm.

———. 2008c. *Taxerings- och förmögenhetskalender för Stockholms län Södra 2008*. Stockholm.

Karlberg, Gustaf. 1908. *Studerande kalmarbor I Lund, 16 68–1907: Biografiska och genealogiska anteckningar*. Lund.

Kar Medical College. 2010. "List of Students Admitted Category-Wise (UG) for the Current Year, 2010." Kolkata: R. G. Kar Medical College.

———. 2011. "List of Students Admitted Category-Wise (UG) for the Current Year 2011." Kolkata: R. G. Kar Medical College.

Kasumi kaikan shoka shiryo chosa iinkai. 1982–84. *Showa shinshu kazoku kakei taisei* (Kazoku genealogy). Tokyo: Yoshikawa Kobunkan.

Keats-Rohan, K. S. B. 1999. *Domesday People: A Prosopography of Persons Occurring in English Documents, 1066–1166*. Woodbridge, Suffolk: Boydell Press.

Keet-Black, Janet. 2002. *Some Travellers in the 1891 Census*, vols. 1–4. South Chailey, U.K.: Romany and Traveller Family History Society.

Kennedy, Liam, Brian Gurrin, and K. A. Miller. 2012. "The Planter and the Gael." In *The Imaginary of the Stranger*, 13–26. ed. Karin White. Donegal Multi-Cultural Project. Letterkenny, Ireland.

Kitaoji, Hironobu. 1971. "The Structure of the Japanese Family." *American Anthropologist* 73: 1036–57.

Kolkata Police Recruitment Board. 2010. *List of Provisionally Selected Candidates for the Appointment to the Post of Sergeant in Kolkata Police Examination 2009*. Kolkata.

Kremer, Michael. 1997. "How Much Does Sorting Increase Inequality?" *Quarterly Journal of Economics* 112 (1): 115–39.

Kumar, Sanjay, Anthony Heath, and Oliver Heath. 2002. "Determinants of Social Mobility in India." *Economics and Political Weekly* 37 (29): 2983–87.

Lebra, Takie Sugiyama. 1989. "Adoption among the Hereditary Elite of Japan: Status Preservation through Mobility." *Ethnology* 28 (3): 185–218.

———. 1992. *Above the Clouds: Status Culture of the Modern Japanese Nobility.* Berkeley: University of California Press.

Leonard, Karen, and Susan Weller. 1980. "Declining Subcaste Endogamy in India: The Hyderabad Kayasths, 1900–75." *American Ethnologist* 1 (3): 504–17.

Levine, Aaron D. 2010. "Self-Regulation, Compensation, and the Ethical Recruitment of Oocyte Donors." *Hastings Center Report* 40 (2): 25–36.

Lew, Byron, and Bruce Cater. 2012. "Canadian Emigration to the US, 1900–1930: Characterizing Movers and Stayers, and the Differential Impact of Immigration Policy on the Mobility of French and English Canadians." Working Paper, Trent University.

Li, Shan. 2012. "Asian Women Command Premium Prices for Egg Donation in U.S." *Los Angeles Times.* May 4.

Lindahl, Mikael, Mårten Palme, Sofia Sandgren Massih, and Anna Sjögren. 2012. "The Intergenerational Persistence of Human Capital: An Empirical Analysis of Four Generations." Working Paper, IFAU, Uppsala University.

Liu, Guo-Ming, ed. 1989. *High Ranked Civil and Military Leaders: Republican Era* (中华民国军政职官志). Beijing: Chunqiu Press.

Liu, Yan, Liujun Chen, Yida Yuan, and Jiawei Chen. 2012. "A Study of Surnames in China through Isonymy." *American Journal of Physical Anthropology* 148 (3): 341–50.

Løken, Katrine V. 2010. "Family Income and Children's Education: Using the Norwegian Oil Boom as a Natural Experiment." *Labour Economics* 17 (1): 118–29.

Long, Jason. 2013. "The Surprising Social Mobility of Victorian Britain." *European Review of Economic History* 17 (1): 1–23.

Long, Jason, and Joseph P. Ferrie. 2013a. "Grandfathers Matter(ed): Occupational Mobility across Three Generations in the U.S. and Britain, 1850–1910." Working Paper, Northwestern University.

———. 2013b. "Intergenerational Occupational Mobility in Britain and the USA since 1850." *American Economic Review* 103(4): 1109–37.

Lundin, A. H. 1882. *Småländska nationen i Lund: Biografiska och genealogiska anteckningar.* Lund.

MacKinnon, Mary, and Daniel Parent. 2012. "Resisting the Melting Pot: The Long Term Impact of Maintaining Identity for Franco-Americans in New England." *Explorations in Economic History* 49 (1): 30–59.

Maxwell, W. J. 1917. *General Alumni Catalogue of the University of Pennsylvania.* Philadelphia: University of Pennsylvania Alumni Association.

Medical Council of India. n.d. Indian Medical Registry search page. www.mciindia.org/InformationDesk/IndianMedicalRegister.aspx.

Mehrotra, Vikras, Randall Morck, Jungwook Shim, and Yupana Wiwattanakantang. 2011. "Adoptive Expectations: Rising Sons in Japanese Family Firms." NBER Working Paper no. 16874.

Moïse, Edwin E. 1983. *Land Reform in China and North Vietnam: Consolidating the Revolution at the Village Level*. Chapel Hill: University of North Carolina Press.

Moore, Ray A. 1970. "Adoption and Samurai Mobility in Tokugawa Japan." *Journal of Asian Studies* 29 (3): 617–32.

Moraga, Jesús Fernández-Huertas. 2011. "New Evidence on Emigrant Selectivity." *Review of Economics and Statistics* 93 (1): 72–96.

Mulligan, Casey B. 1999. "Galton versus the Human Capital Approach to Inheritance." *Journal of Political Economy* 107 (S6): S184–S224.

Murdoch, Iris. 1973. *The Black Prince*. London: Chatto and Windus.

Murray, Charles. 2012. *Coming Apart: The State of White America, 1960–2010*. New York: Crown Forum.

Narbarte, N. 1992. "Critica a las etimologías del 'Diccionario de apellidos vascos.'" *Revista internacional de estudios vascos* 37 (2): 431–77.

National Archives (United Kingdom). n.d. *Index to the Prerogatory Court of Canterbury Wills, 1384–1858*. National Archives, London. www.nationalarchives.gov.uk/records/wills.htm.

Nazer Ahumada, Ricardo. 1993. "José Tomás Urmeneta, 1808–1878: Un empresario minero del siglo xix." In Ricardo Nazer Ahumada, Javier Jofre Rodriguez, and Ignacio Domeyko, *Ignacio Domeyko, José Tomás Urmeneta, Juan Brüggen: tres forjadores de la minería nacional*. Santiago: Claus von Plate. 83–154.

———. 2000. "La fortuna de Agustín Edwards Ossandón, 1815–1878." *Historia* 33: 369–415. Pontificia Universidad Catolica de Chile, Instituto de Historia.

Nebel, Almut, Dvora Filon, Marina Faerman, Himla Soodyall, and Ariella Oppenheim. 2005. "Y Chromosome Evidence for a Founder Effect in Ashkenazi Jews." *European Journal of Human Genetics* 13: 388–91.

Nijhawan, N. K. 1969. "Inter-generational Occupational Mobility." *Economic and Political Weekly* 4 (39): 1553–57.

"Nomencracy: Surnames Offer Depressing Clues to the Extent of Social Mobility over Generations." 2013. *Economist*. February 9.

North, Kari E., Lisa J. Martin, and Michael H. Crawford. 2000. "The Origins of the Irish Travellers and the Genetic Structure of Ireland." *Annals of Human Biology* 27 (5): 453–65.

Núñez, Javier, and Leslie Miranda. 2007. "Recent Findings on Intergenerational Income and Educational Mobility in Chile." Working Paper no. 244, Department of Economics, Universidad de Chile.

Nuñez, Javier, and Cristina Risco. 2004. "Movilidad intergeneracional del Ingreso en un Pais en desarrollo: El caso de Chile." Working Paper no. 210, Department of Economics, Universidad de Chile.

Odén, Klas Gustav. 1902. *Östgötars minne: Biografiska anteckningar om studerande Östgötar i Uppsala, 15 95–1900*. Stockholm.

OECD (Organisation for Economic Co-operation and Development). 2013a. *Taxing Wages 2013*. OECD Publishing. http://dx.doi.org/10.1787/tax_wages-2013-en.

———. 2013b. *Trade Union Density*. OECD Statextracts. October 12. http://stats.oecd.org/Index.aspx?QueryId=20167.

OECD/WHO (Organisation for Economic Co-operation and Development/World Health Organization). 2010. *Policy Brief on the International Migration of Health Workforce*. February. www.oecd.org/health/workforce.

Olivetti, Claudia, and M. Daniele Paserman. 2013. "In the Name of the Son (and the Daughter): Intergenerational Mobility in the United States, 1850–1930." NBER Working Paper no. 18822.

Olchansky, S., Toni Antonucci, Lisa Berkman, Robert H. Binstock, Axel Boersch-Supan, John T. Cacioppo, Bruce A. Carnes, et al. 2012. "Differences in Life Expectancy due to Race and Educational Differences Are Widening, and Many May Not Catch Up." *Health Affairs* 31 (8): 1803–13.

Oreopoulos, Philip, Marianne E. Page, and Ann H. Stevens. 2008. "The Intergenerational Effects of Worker Displacement." *Journal of Labor Economics* 26: 455–83.

Ostrer, Harry, and Karl Skorecki. 2013. "The Population Genetics of the Jewish People." *Human Genetics* 132 (2): 119–27.

Oxford University. Various years (1924–2010). *Oxford University Calendar*. Oxford: Clarendon Press.

Paik, Christopher. 2013. "Does Lineage Matter? A Study of Ancestral Influence on Educational Attainment in Korea." Working Paper, New York University Abu Dhabi.

Parry, Glenys, Patrice van Cleemput, Jean Peters, Stephen Walters, Kate Thomas, and Cindy Cooper. 2007. "Health Status of Gypsies and Travellers in England." *Journal of Epidemiology and Community Health* 61: 198–204.

Passel, Jeffrey S., Wendy Wang, and Paul Taylor. 2010. "Marrying Out: One in Seven New U.S. Marriages Is Interracial or Interethnic." Washington, DC: Pew Research Center.

Pearson, Karl, and Alice Lee. 1903. "On the Laws of Inheritance in Man, I: Inheritance of Physical Characters." *Biometrika* 2: 357–462.

Pellegrino, Aprile. 1927. *El censo comercial industrial de la colonia italiana en Chile, 1926–1927: Resumen general de las actividades de la colonia*. Santiago.

Pew Forum on Religion and Public Life. 2008. *U.S. Religious Landscape Survey*. Washington, DC: Pew Research Center.

Pfeffer, Fabian T. 2011. "Status Attainment and Wealth in the United States and Germany." In *Persistence, Privilege, and Parenting. The Comparative Study of Intergenerational Mobility*, ed. Timothy Smeeding, Robert Erikson, and Markus Jäntti, 109–37. New York: Russell Sage Foundation.

Plomin, R., D. W. Fulker, R. Corley, and J. C. DeFries. 1997. "Nature, Nurture, and Cognitive Development from 1–16 years: A Parent-Offspring Adoption Study." *Psychological Science* 8: 442–47.

Princeton University. 1908. *General Catalogue of Princeton University, 1745–1906*. Princeton, N.J.: Princeton University.

"Private Schools Are Expected to Drop a Dreaded Entrance Test." 2013. *New York Times.* September 19.

Public Profiler. n.d. World Family Names. http://worldnames.publicprofiler.org/Default .aspx.

Public Record Office. 1904. *Calendar of Inquisitions Post Mortem and Other Analogous Documents Preserved in the Public Record Office,* vol. 1, *Henry III.* London: Public Record Office.

———. 1906. *Calendar of Inquisitions Post Mortem and Other Analogous Documents Preserved in the Public Record Office,* vol. 2, *Edward I.* London: Public Record Office.

Puma, Michael, Stephen Bell, Ronna Cook, Camilla Held, Pam Broene, Frank Jenkins, Andrew Mashburn, and Jason Downer. 2012. *Third Grade Follow-up to the Head Start Impact Study Final Report.* U.S. Department of Health and Human Services, Administration for Children and Families. Washington, DC: Office of Planning, Research and Evaluation.

Raven, John Howard. 1909. *Catalogue of the Officers and Alumni of Rutgers College, 1766–1909.* Trenton, NJ: State Gazette Publishing Co.

Rayment, Leigh. n.d. "House of Commons." www.leighrayment.com/commons.htm, accessed October 6, 2013.

Reaney, Percy Hide, and Richard Middlewood Wilson. 2005. *A Dictionary of English Surnames.* Oxford: Oxford University Press.

Reich, David, Kumarasamy Thangaraj, Nick Patterson, Alkes L. Price, and Lalji Singh. 2009. "Reconstructing Indian Population History." *Nature* 461: 489–94.

Richardson, Ken, and Sarah H. Norgate. 2006. "A Critical Analysis of IQ Studies of Adopted Children." *Human Development* 49: 319–35.

Riddarhuset. 2012. *Ätter I vapendatabasen* (Arms lineage database). www.riddarhuset.se/ jsp/admin/archive/sbdocarchive/atter_i_AK07_vapendatabasen.pdf.

Romany and Traveller Family History Society. n.d. "Was Your Ancestor a Gypsy?" http:// website.lineone.net/~rtfhs/gypsy.html, accessed September 30, 2013.

Roskell, J. S., L. Clark, and C. Rawcliffe. 1993. *The History of Parliament: The House of Commons, 1386–1421,* vol. 4. London: Sutton.

Sacerdote, Bruce. 2007. "How Large Are the Effects from Changes in Family Environment? A Study of Korean American Adoptees." *Quarterly Journal of Economics* 122 (1): 119–57.

Sacramento Bee. n.d. State Worker Salary Search. www.sacbee.com/statepay.

Saleh, Mohamed. 2013. "On the Road to Heaven: Self-Selection, Religion, and Socio-Economic Status." Working Paper no. 13–428, Toulouse School of Economics.

Scarr, Sandra. 1981. *Race, Social Class, and Individual Differences in IQ.* Hillsdale, NJ: Lawrence Erlbaum.

Scarr, Sandra, and Weinberg, R. A. 1978. "The Influence of 'Family Background' on Intellectual Attainment." *American Sociological Review* 43: 674–92.

Schaffer, Johan Karlsson. 2012. "The Forgotten Revolution: Debunking Conventional Wisdom on Sweden's Transition to Democracy." Working Paper, Norwegian Centre for Human Rights. http://dx.doi.org/10.2139/ssrn.2189354

"Scholars Debate the Roots of Yiddish, Migration of Jews." 1996. *New York Times.* October 29.

Schurer, Kevin and Matthew Woollard. 2000. *1881 Census for England and Wales, the Channel Islands and the Isle of Man* (enhanced version). Computer file. Produced by Genealogical Society of Utah, Federation of Family History Societies. Distributed by U.K. Data Archive, Colchester, Essex. http://dx.doi.org/10.5255/UKDA-SN-417 7-1.

Scriver, Charles R. 2001. "Human Genetics: Lessons from Quebec Populations." *Annual Review of Genomics and Human Genetics* 2: 69–101.

Servicio Electoral Republica de Chile. 2004. *Electoral Register, Municipal Elections of 2004.* Santiago: Servicio Electoral Republica de Chile.

"She's Warm, Easy to Talk To, and a Source of Terror for Private-School Parents." 2011. *New York Times.* December 19.

Silventoinen, Karri, S. Sammalisto, M. Perola, D. I. Boomsma, B. K. Cornes, C. Davis, L. Dunkel, et al. 2003a. "Heritability of Adult Body Height: A Comparative Study of Twin Cohorts in Eight Countries." *Twin Research* 6: 399–408.

Silventoinen, Karri, J. Kaprio, E. Lahelma, R. J. Viken, and R. J. Rose. 2003b. "Assortative Mating by Body Height and BMI: Finnish Twins and Their Spouses." *American Journal of Human Biology* 15: 620–27.

Sjöström, Carl. 1897. *Skånska nationen före afdelningars tid (1682–1833): Biografiska och Genealogiska Anteckningar.* Lund.

———. 1901. *Blekingska nationen, 1697–1900.* Lund.

———. 1904. *Skånska nationen, 1833–1889: Biografiska och genealogiska anteckningar.* Lund.

———. 1907. *Göteborgs nation i Lund, 1669–1906.* Lund.

———. 1908. *Vermlands nation i Lund 1682–1907.* Lund.

Sloan, Josette. n.d. *Archivos diplomáticos de Nantes—Consulado de Chile. Algunos empresarios franceses residentes en Chile.* www.genfrancesa.com/inmigrantes/Nantes/emprfranchile.html.

Social Security Death Index. n.d. Available online at Ancestry.com.

Solicitors Regulation Authority. 2012. *UK Roll of Solicitors.* www.lawsociety.org.uk.

Solon, Gary. 2013. "Theoretical Models of Inequality Transmission across Multiple Generations." Working Paper, Michigan State University.

Sonoda, Hidehiro. 1990. "The Decline of the Japanese Warrior Class, 1840–1880." *Japan Review* 1: 73–111.

Stanford University. 2012. "Stanford Releases Fiscal Year Fundraising Results." *Stanford Report.* October 17.

Statistics Sweden. 2009. *Prices of Real Estate in 2008.* Stockholm.

———. 2011a. "Life Expectancy in Sweden, 2001–2010." Press release. October 20. Stockholm.

———. 2011b. *Wage and Salary Structures, Private Sector (SLP), 2011.* http://www.scb.se/Statistik/AM/AM0103/2011A01/AM0103_2011A01_SM_AM62SM1201.pdf.

Stavis, Ben. 1978. "China and the Comparative Analysis of Land Reform." *Modern China* 4 (1): 63–78.

Suzuki, Masao. 2002. "Selective Immigration and Ethnic Economic Achievement: Japanese Americans before World War II." *Explorations in Economic History* 39 (3): 254–81.

Sverige, Socialstyrelsen. 1972. *Legitimerade läkare, 1972.* Stockholm: Fritze.

———. 2011. *Förteckning över Sveriges legitimerade läkare, 2010/2011.* Stockholm: Fritze.

Swedish Bar Association. 2013. *Online Membership Directory.* www.advokatsamfundet.se/Advokatsamfundet-engelska/Find-a-lawyer/.

Takayanagi, Mitsutoshi, Taiji Okayama, and Kazuma Saiki. 1964. *Shintei kansei choshu shokafu.* Tokyo: Zoku Gunsho Ruiju Kanseikai.

"Taxpayer Listings." 1924. *New York Times.* October 24–November 2, November 4–8, 11–14.

———. 1925. *New York Times.* September 2–6, 8–11, 13.

"The 50 Most Expensive Private High Schools in America." 2013. *Business Insider.* September 4.

Thrush, Andrew, and John P. Ferris. 2010. *The History of Parliament: The House of Commons, 1604–1629,* vol. 6. Cambridge: Cambridge University Press.

Tighe, Elizabeth, Leonard Saxe, and Charles Kadushin. 2011. "Estimating the Jewish Population of the United States: 2000–2010." Cohen Center for Modern Jewish Studies, Brandeis University. http://www.brandeis.edu/ssri/pdfs/EstimatingJewishPopUS.1.pdf.

Ueda, Atsuko. 2009. "Intergenerational Mobility of Earnings and Income in Japan." *B.E. Journal of Economic Analysis & Policy* 9 (1) (Contributions).

———. 2013. "Intergenerational Mobility of Earnings in South Korea." *Journal of Asian Economics* 27: 33–41.

U.K., Equality and Human Rights Commission. 2009. *Gypsies and Travellers: Simple Solutions for Living Together.* Manchester, England.

U.K., Office of National Statistics. 2002. *Surname Database for England and Wales.* Available at www.taliesin-arlein.net/names/search.php.

———. 2007. "Variations Persist in Life Expectancy by Social Class." www.statistics.gov.uk/pdfdir/le1007.pdf.

United Jewish Communities. 2003. *National Jewish Population Survey, 2000–2001.* http://www.jewishfederations.org/local_includes/downloads/4606.pdf.

United Nations Development Program. 1999. *Indice desarrollo humano en Chile 1990–1998.* Temas de Desarrollo Humano Sustentable, no. 3. Washington, DC: UNDP. http://mirror.undp.org/chile/desarrollo/textos/otraspub/Pub03/1indeshu.pdf.

University Grants Commission. 2008. *Higher Education in India.* New Delhi.

Uppsala Universitet. 1954. *Västmanlands-Dala Nation i Uppsala, 1942–1952.* Uppsala: Västmanlands-Dala Nation.

US Census Bureau. 2010. *2006–2010 American Community Survey.* Washington, DC: US Census Bureau.

Valenzuela O., Juvenal, ed. 1920. *Album de la zona austral de Chile.* Santiago: Universitaria.

———, ed. 1923. *Album zona central de Chile: Informaciones agricolas.* Santiago: Universitaria.

Van Straten, Jits. 2007. "Early Modern Polish Jewry: The Rhineland Hypothesis Revisited." *Historical Methods* 40 (1): 39–50.

Van Straten, Jits, and Harmen Snel. 2006. "The Jewish 'Demographic Miracle' in Nineteenth-Century Europe: Fact or Fiction?" *Historical Methods* 39 (3): 123–31.

Venn, John, and John A. Venn. 1922–27. *Alumni Cantabrigienses: A Biographical List of All Known Students, Graduates and Holders of Office at the University of Cambridge, from the Earliest Times to 1751.* 4 vols. Cambridge: Cambridge University Press.

———. 1940–54. *Alumni Cantabrigienses: A Biographical List of All Known Students, Graduates and Holders of Office at the University of Cambridge, 1752–1900.* 6 vols. Cambridge: Cambridge University Press.

Villalobos, Sergio. 1990. *Origen y ascenso de la burguesía capitulo: Extranjeros en la etapa republican.* Santiago: Universitaria.

Walder, Andrew G., and Songhua Hu. 2009. "Revolution, Reform, and Status Inheritance: Urban China, 1949–1996." *American Journal of Sociology* 114 (5): 1395–1427.

Walter, H., D. D. Farhud, Heidi Danker-Hopfe, and Pariwash Amirshahi. 1991. "Investigations on the Ethnic Variability of the ABO Blood Group Polymorphism in Iran." *Zeitschrift für Morphologie und Anthropologie* 78 (3): 289–306.

Ward, David L., Charles D. Coleman, Robert Nunziata, and Robert Kominski. 2012. *Demographic Aspects of Surnames from Census 2000.* Washington, DC: US Census Bureau. www.census.gov/genealogy/www/data/2000surnames/.

Watson, Henry William, and Francis Galton. 1875. "On the Probability of the Extinction of Families." *Journal of the Anthropological Institute of Great Britain* 4: 138–44.

Weyl, Nathaniel. 1989. *The Geography of American Achievement.* Washington, DC: Scott-Townsend.

Widstrand, A., ed. 1939. *Sveriges läkare i ord och bild 1939* (Swedish doctors in words and pictures). Stockholm.

Winstanley, D. A. 1940. *Early Victorian Cambridge.* Cambridge: Cambridge University Press.

World Bank. n.d. "Gini Index." http://data.worldbank.org/indicator/SI.POV.GINI.

Wu, X., and D. J. Treiman. 2007. "Inequality and Equality under Chinese Socialism: The Hukou System and Intergenerational Occupational Mobility." *American Journal of Sociology* 103 (2): 415–45.

Wu, Zu-Xiang (ed.). 1971. "Name List of Chinese College Faculty (1941–1944) (专科以上学校教员名册(民国30年-33年)." Taipei: Zhuanji Wenxue Press.

Yale University. 1910. *Catalogue of the Officers and Graduates of Yale University, 1701–1910.* New Haven: Tuttle, Morehouse and Taylor.

Zagorsky, Jay L. 2007. "Do You Have to Be Smart to Be Rich? The Impact of IQ on Wealth, Income and Financial Distress." *Intelligence* 35 (5): 489–501.

Zax, Jeffrey S., and Daniel I. Rees. 2002. "IQ, Academic Performance, Environment, and Earnings." *Review of Economics and Statistics* 84 (4): 600–616.

Zenkoku bengoshi taikan. 1987. Tokyo: Horitsu Shinbunsha. Internet resource.

Zhu, Bao-Jiong, and Pei-Ling Xie, eds. 1980. *Jinshi Roster of the Ming and Qing Dynasties* (明清进士题名录). Shanghai: Shanghai Guji Press.

Page numbers for entries occurring in figures are followed by an *f;* those for entries in notes, by an *n;* and those for entries in tables, by a *t.*

Carnegie, Andrew, 213, 213n

castes, Indian: classifications of, 144; "creamy layer," 144; educational attainment and, 144–45, 145f; endogamy within, 160–64, 166; genetic distinctions of, 144, 144n; scheduled castes, 144, 149, 150, 151, 156–57, 156f, 158; surnames of, 147–51; untouchables, 144, 157. *See also* Brahmins; reservation system

Cater, Bruce, 66

Catholics, in Ireland, 231–32, 233–35, 233f, 234f, 235n, 315

Celsius, Anders, 24

Census Bureau. *See* U.S. Census Bureau

Chaucer, Geoffrey, 75, 75n, 76f

Cherokee: gaming profits of, 271; removal of, 270

Chiang Kai-shek, 168

children. *See* adopted children; education; families

Chile: coup d'état (1973), 209, 209f, 211; electoral register (2004), 201–2, 205; elites in, 203–5, 208; *encomenderos* in, 203, 210; immigrants to, 204–5; income inequality in, 199; incomes in, 201–2, 202f, 206–8, 207t; indigenous groups in, 202–3; landowners in, 204, 206; Pinochet dictatorship in, 209, 210, 211; poverty in, 199, 200f; social mobility in, 200, 207–11; Spanish settlement of, 203

Chilean surnames: Basque, 203–4; in census (2004), 206, 206t; of elites, 203–5, 206t, 207t, 208, 210; French, 205; German, 205; Italian, 204–5; Mapuche, 202–3, 206, 207–8, 210; occupational incomes by group, 206–8, 207t, 210, 210f, 211f; rare, 203, 204–5, 205; of underclass, 202–3, 206–8, 206t, 207t

China: Cultural Revolution in, 168–70, 169f; education in, 169–70, 173–74, 177; emigration from, 177; kin networks in, 180–81, 180–81n; land reform in, 168;

modern elites in, 172–75, 173f; Republican era in, 168, 173, 175, 176, 177; revolution in, 168; war casualties in, 175. *See also* Qing China

China, social mobility in: Cultural Revolution effects, 168–70; evidence from Qing elite surnames, 171–75, 173f, 180; evidence from surname–place of origin identifiers, 175–78, 177t; geographic limitations on, 172; in lower Yangzi River valley, 175–78, 177t, 226–27, 227f; low rates of, 180, 181; persistence rates, 226; in postreform era, 170; in Qing era, 171–75, 180, 225–27, 227f; studies of, 180

Chinese Communist Party, 168, 176, 180

Chinese surnames: common, 170, 170n, 172, 175, 175n; from lower Yangzi River valley, 172–74, 175–78, 175n; place of origin identifiers and, 175–78, 225–27, 226f; of Qing elites, 171–75, 173f, 176, 180, 181, 225–27; rare, 171–75, 173f; relative representation among modern elites, 172–75, 173f, 176–78, 180; relative representation over time, 226–27, 226f, 227f; in Taiwan, 178

Cholmondeley, 316

Christians: Catholics, 231–32, 233–35, 233f, 234f, 235n, 315; Coptic, 10, 238, 247, 249, 282, 285; early, 230–31; first names in India, 161, 161t, 162; from India, 248; intermarriage in India, 162; Jewish converts, 230–31; Maronites, 247, 248; in Muslim societies, 238–39; Protestants, 229, 231–35

Church of Jesus Christ of Latter-Day Saints, FamilySearch website, 313–14

Clark(e), 71, 89, 218, 307

cognitive ability (IQ), 110n, 112, 112n, 116–17, 264, 264n, 265f

Cohen, 47, 308, 312

Colorado Adoption Project, 264

Coming Apart: The State of White America, 1960–2010 (Murray), 69, 263–64
Communist Party, Chinese, 168, 176, 180
Coptic Church, 248
Copts: conversions to Islam, 238; elite status of, 238, 249; physicians, 247; status persistence of, 10, 282, 285; surnames of, 247, 285; in United States, 247, 249
Corak, Miles, 146n, 292n, 319
Cornwallis, Charles, 91
cultural capital, 63

Dalton School, 279
Darwin, 132–33, 134–35, 135n, 284
Darwin, Charles, 132–33, 134, 135f, 284
Defoe, 93–94
Defoe, Daniel, 93–94
Denmark: noble surnames in, 22–23; wealth inheritance in, 136–37, 138f. See also Nordic countries
Dickens, Charles, 213, 213n
Directory of Physicians in the United States, 45–46, 51, 52, 54, 68, 164, 194–95, 309
doctors. See physicians
Doherty/Dougherty, 310–11, 312–13, 312f, 315
Domesday Book, 7, 51, 81, 85, 107, 314, 316
downward mobility: avoiding, 14–15, 281–86; of elites, 13–14, 212–15, 214f, 216, 280–82; in England, 13–14, 76–78, 79–80, 85, 86–87; fertility rates and, 246–47, 246f; of samurai, 185–86, 195, 196; surname variants and, 316–17; in Sweden, 41. See also regression to mean; social mobility

earnings. See incomes
Eastern Europe, Jews in, 235, 236–37, 237n
East India Company, 147
Eckstein, Zvi, 228–30
education: in China, 169–70, 173–74, 177; economic outcomes of, 273; in England,
73, 130–31, 131n; in India, 144–46; intergenerational correlations in, 3–5, 4f, 100–103; in Japan, 183, 185, 185t, 284; preschool, 273–74; private schools, 130–31, 131n, 279–80; public support for, 129–31, 272, 273–74; in Sweden, 19, 129–30, 266–68, 275; in United States, 111, 131, 131n, 279–80. See also medical schools; universities
educational attainment: of adopted children, 266–68, 267f; of African Americans, 55, 56f; family influences on, 284; of Gypsies and Travellers, 240; of immigrants to United States, 249, 251, 251n; of Indian castes, 144–45, 145f; of Japanese Americans, 67; of Jews in United States, 55, 55f; life expectancies and, 275; of women, 281
educational mobility: in England, 99–103, 117, 221–24; in Japan, 185–86, 186t, 284; in Korea, 197–98; measuring with surname frequencies, 298–99, 299t; persistence rates of, 117, 223–24; in Sweden, 35–39; symmetrical movements in, 221–23; in United States, 54
Edward I, King, 253
Egypt. See Copts
elites: downward mobility of, 13–14, 212–15, 214f, 216, 280–82; emergence of, 140, 228–31, 239, 251–52, 299–300; endogamy among, 135n, 163, 239, 282; fertility rates of, 192, 236, 237n, 280; initial mean status of, 298, 298f; investments in children by, 279–81, 285; status persistence of, 10, 216, 229, 239, 251, 252; in United States, 45, 247–51, 263–64, 277–78, 279–81. See also nobility; individual countries and groups
elite surnames: bimodal distributions of, 41, 42f; regression to mean by, 107; relative representation of, 20; in United States, 45, 47–49, 54–55, 247–51, 248f. See also nobility; rare surnames

endogamy: among elites, 135n, 163, 239, 282; as explanation of status persistence, 160, 252, 282; genetic transmission and, 139–40; in India, 160–64, 166; of Jews, 237; of minorities in Muslim societies, 239; of New France descendants, 64–65, 64f; status persistence and, 13, 239; in United States, 282–83

England: Glorious Revolution in, 167; Industrial Revolution in, 6, 75, 87, 218, 219; Jews in, 102, 240–41, 242f; nobility of, 91. *See also* Parliament members

England, medieval: artisans in, 71–73, 74; class structure of, 74; downward mobility of elites, 76–78, 79–80, 85, 86–87; education in, 73; elites in, 72–73, 76–87, 236; Norman conquerors in, 76, 79, 81–84; Parliament members in, 72, 253–55; persistence rates in, 74, 74f, 84; poll taxes in, 71–72; probate records in, 84–86, 86f, 216–18; social mobility in, 70, 72–80, 83–84, 86–87, 105–6. *See also* English surnames, medieval

England, modern: church records in, 313; educational mobility in, 99–103; education in, 130–31, 131n; fertility and status in, 132–35, 133f, 134f; immigrants to, 90, 240–41; inheritance tax rates in, 96, 97f; life expectancies in, 114, 115–16, 116f, 116t, 314; military of, 256–57, 257f; minority groups in, 240; persistence rates in, 84, 95, 117, 219–20; probate rates in, 96–98, 97f, 117, 117f, 138, 244–45, 306–7, 306t, 312–14; probate records in, 91–98, 216–20, 306, 307, 313; Reform Acts, 105; social mobility in, 88, 95, 105–6; underclass in, 240; wealth inheritance in, 94–98, 95f, 95t. *See also* English surnames, modern; Parliament members

England, social mobility in: consistent rates of, 135, 138; downward mobility of elites, 13–14, 76–78, 79–80, 85, 86–87; educational mobility, 99–103, 117, 221–24; in Industrial Revolution, 218, 219; low rates of, 6–8, 95–96, 100, 102, 105–6; in medieval era, 70, 72–80, 83–84, 86–87, 105–6; in modern era, 88, 95, 105–6; persistence rates, 84, 86t, 98, 219–20, 219t, 221t; regression to mean, 83–84, 87, 88, 216–19; rich as share of population, 10–11

English surnames, medieval: artisan, 71–73, 73f, 75, 85, 87, 254, 254f; changes in, 75–76, 80; inheritance of, 71–72; noble, 91; occupational, 71–72, 89–90; patronyms, 314; persistence rates, 85, 86–87, 86t, 217; of property owners, 78–80, 79t; rare, 216–18, 217t, 222f; regression to mean by, 79–80, 83–84; toponyms, 314; variants of, 316–17. *See also* locative surnames; Norman surnames

English surnames, modern: of African Americans, 50–51; of barristers, 88–89, 309; changes in, 93, 93–94n; common, 88, 89–90, 89f, 242, 244–46; data sources for, 304–5, 312–14; hyphenated, 90; of Irish origin, 312–13; longevity rates by groups, 115–16, 116f, 116t; of medical professionals, 307–9, 308t; origins of, 316–17; of Parliament members, 103–4, 104f; persistence rates, 217, 219–20, 221t; rare, 6–7, 88–89, 90–102, 91t, 103–4, 216–23, 217t; status of, 88, 306–9, 312–14; wealth inheritance and, 94–95, 95f, 95t

entropy, social, 3, 5, 107

equality. *See* inequality

ethnic capital, 124

ethnic groups. *See* minority groups; *individual groups*

exogamy. *See* intermarriage

families: incomes of, 126–29; kin networks, 180–81, 180–81n; underlying

families (*continued*)
status of, 283–86; windfall gains of, 128, 271–73. *See also* adopted children; genetic transmission; grandparents; lineages; surnames
FamilySearch website, 313–14
family sizes: of elites, 10–11, 236, 280; of English upper classes, 14, 132–35, 133f, 134f, 236; of Gypsies and Travellers, 240, 241t, 245–46; investments in children, 279–81; regression to mean and, 128, 280; social mobility and, 13, 132–35, 246–47. *See also* fertility
Feliciano, Cynthia, 249
Ferrie, Joe, 118n, 269–70, 290n
fertility: correlation to status, 132–35, 133f, 134f, 237n; of elites, 192, 236, 237n, 280; regression to mean and, 246–47, 246f
fertility rates, of underclasses, 246–47
Finland. *See* Nordic countries
first names: of Gypsies / Travellers, 243–44; in India, 161–63, 161t, 162t
Franco-Americans. *See* New France settlers
Frei, Eduardo, 209, 210
French Canadians, 49, 65–66. *See also* New France settlers
French immigrants to Chile, 205
French surnames, 49, 205. *See also* New France settlers

Gagnon, 49, 50, 50f, 63, 65
Galton, Francis, 25n, 90, 136, 137f, 223, 292n, 325
Gates, Bill, 11
generations, length between, 20n. *See also* intergenerational correlations
genetic transmission: of biological traits, 136, 137f, 266; endogamy and, 139–40; importance of, 6, 12–14, 268–69, 274, 281; of intelligence, 264, 264n; as primary source of status persistence, 13,

14–15, 126–27, 136–37; regression to mean, 136, 139; of underlying abilities, 14–15, 126–27, 128, 263. *See also* inheritance; nature vs. nurture
genotype: definition, 11–12; social, 12, 14–15, 282, 283–86
Georgia, land lottery in, 270
German immigrants to Chile, 205
German surnames, 50–51, 205, 308
German universities, 277
Gini coefficient, 5
Gintis, Herb, 112n
Glasgow, 1, 2f
good society, 1, 5, 274
Google Scholar, 193–94, 195–96
grandparents: influence of, 118–22, 119f, 294–95; intergenerational correlations with, 5, 119–21, 120t, 292–95. *See also* families; lineages
Great Britain. *See* England; Wales
Great Britain Family Names website, 305
Gu, 172
Gypsies/Travellers: children of, 240, 241f, 243–44; in England, 10, 89n, 240–46, 241t; fertility rates of, 240, 241t, 245–46; first names of, 243–44; in Ireland, 240, 243n; origins of, 240–44; probate rates of, 307, 312–13, 312f; social mobility of, 244–46; status persistence of, 10, 240, 247; surnames of, 89n, 240–42, 243f, 244–46, 244n, 309, 312–13; as underclass, 240

Haitians, 248
Hamlet (Shakespeare), 22–23
Hao, Yu, 178, 179
Hardy, Thomas, *Tess of the d'Urbervilles*, 317
Harootunian, Harry D., 186
Hayls, John, 7f
HDI. *See* Human Development Index
Head Start Program, 273–74

Hebert, 50, 310–11

Heckman, James, 261, 262, 264, 273

heights, genetic transmission of, 136, 137f, 266

Hertz, Tom, 123, 123n, 124, 146n, 292n, 319

higher education. *See* education; universities

Hindus: endogamy of, 161–63; first names of women, 161–63, 161t. *See also* castes

Hindu surnames: elite, 147–48, 150; mixed, 149, 150, 157, 158, 165; of physicians in India, 147–50; of physicians in United States, 247, 251; of poor, 149, 150, 155, 158, 163

Hispanics. *See* Latino Americans

Hmong, 250–51

Ho, Ping-ti, 180

Homer, 107

Hu, Songhua, 180

Huguenots, 90, 91, 92

human-capital theory, 126–35. *See also* education

Human Development Index (HDI), 201–2

Iceland. *See* Nordic countries

immigrants: to Canada, 179; to Chile, 204–5; to England, 90; to Sweden, 26n

immigrants to United States: assimilation of, 63; educational attainment of, 249, 251, 251n; Hmong, 250–51; illegal, 251; incomes of, 251n; Japanese, 67–68, 68t, 124; Latin American, 251; restrictions on, 67, 68; selectivity, 249; skilled, 249; social mobility of, 124, 277–78; Taiwanese, 179; Vietnamese, 249. *See also* New France settlers

income inequality. *See* inequality

income mobility: in Chile, 200; in Japan, 184; in Korea, 196; in Taiwan, 178. *See also* social mobility

incomes: of adopted children, 266, 267f; in Chile, 201–2, 202f, 206–8, 207t; correla-

tions among siblings, 268–69, 269t; education and, 273; exogenous shocks to, 128, 271–73; of immigrants to United States, 251n; intergenerational correlations of, 3, 4f, 5, 109, 126–28, 127f, 127n, 146; of parents, 126–28, 289–92, 289f; random component of, 108; as status measure, 108, 109, 111–12, 112t; Swedish surnames and, 27–28, 29f

India: British rule of, 144, 147, 154–55, 157; elites in, 143, 147–48, 150; independence of, 144, 154, 155, 156, 167; Muslims in, 144, 149–50, 151–52, 154, 239n; prime ministers of, 167. *See also* Brahmins; castes

India, social mobility in: in Bengal, 147–57, 158–60; of Christians, 143; endogamy and, 160–64, 166; at family level, 164; of Hindu groups, 143; intergenerational correlation in income, 146; low rates of, 143, 150, 159–60, 166; of Muslims, 151–52; persistence rates, 150–51, 151t, 154–55; of scheduled castes, 156–57; studies of, 146, 146n. *See also* reservation system

Indians. *See* Native Americans

Indian surnames: Christian, 162; common, 147; of elites, 147–48, 148f, 150, 152–55, 153f, 157, 158; first names from another religious group, 161–63, 162t; mixed Hindu, 149, 150, 157, 158, 165; Muslim, 148, 149–50, 151–52, 162; of poor Hindus, 149, 150, 155, 158, 163; relative representation among physicians and judges, 147–50, 148f, 150f, 151, 152–57, 153f, 158; of scheduled castes, 149, 150, 151, 156–57, 158

indigenous groups. *See* Mapuche; Native Americans

Industrial Revolution, 6, 75, 87, 218, 219

inequality: in Chile, 199; criticism of, 1; Gini coefficient, 5; in Nordic countries, 19, 275–76; reducing, 15, 274–77; status

inequality (*continued*)

persistence and, 9–10, 126–28, 199–200; in Sweden, 113–14, 114f; in United States, 113–14, 114f, 261, 263–64, 277–78. *See also* elites; social mobility; underclasses

inheritance: of cognitive abilities, 110n, 112n, 116–17; of cultural traits, 126, 136, 137f, 139–40; economic models of, 126–28, 127f, 127n; of longevity, 114–16; matrilineal vs. patrilineal lines of, 15–16; of underlying status, 108–13, 126; of wealth, 94–98, 95f, 95t, 136–37, 138f. *See also* genetic transmission

Inquisitions Post Mortem (IPM), 78–80, 79t, 80f, 85–86, 85f, 86f, 87

intelligence. *See* cognitive ability

intergenerational correlations: in China, 173–75; in education, 3–5, 4f, 100–103; estimates of, 109; of fathers and children, 289–92; with grandparents, 5, 119–21, 120t, 292–95; in incomes, 3, 4f, 5, 109, 126–28, 127f, 127n, 146; in Japan, 185; of mother's status, 290–92; with multiple generations, 5, 292–95, 293f; for rare English surnames, 94–98, 95t, 98t, 106, 120–21, 284; as social mobility measure, 1–3, 290; in Sweden, 20, 30, 32, 36, 37, 41; in Taiwan, 178; universal rate of, 12; of wealth in England, 94–98, 106, 120–21, 120t, 121f, 284. *See also* persistence rates

intergenerational elasticity, 296

intermarriage: across class lines, 14; of Christians in India, 162; of Irish Americans, 64–65; of Jews in United States, 282–83; mobility effects of, 140; of New France settlers in United States, 64–65, 64f; of samurai descendants, 190–91. *See also* marriages

Internet Surname Database, 317

in-vitro fertilization, 285n

IPM. See *Inquisitions Post Mortem*

IQ. *See* cognitive ability

Iran: emigration from, 249; religious minorities in, 238–39; revolution (1979), 249

Iranian surnames of U.S. physicians, 247

Ireland: Catholics in, 231–32, 233–35, 233f, 234f, 235n, 315; censuses of, 315; Gypsies / Travellers in, 240, 243n; Protestants in, 231–35, 232f, 234f

Irish Americans: assimilation of, 63; intermarriage of, 64–65; physicians, 63–64, 63f

Irish surnames: in England, 312–13; in Ireland, 231–35, 315; religious affiliations and, 231–35, 233f; of Scottish origin, 231–32, 232n, 233, 315; social differentiation and, 233–35, 234f; status of, 315, 315t; in United States, 63–65, 310–11

Islam. *See* Muslims

Italian surnames, 64, 204–5

Japan: commoners in, 191–92; constitution (1947), 184; cultural homogeneity of, 182, 183, 184; education in, 183, 185, 185t, 284; elites in, 182–84, 188–94, 195–96; Gentleman's Agreement, 67, 68; Meiji restoration in, 182–83; minority groups in, 184; occupational distribution in, 67–68, 68t. *See also* samurai

Japan, social mobility in: educational mobility, 185–86, 186t, 284; evidence from rare surnames, 187–91, 189f, 190f, 192–94, 193f, 195–96; low rates of, 194, 195, 198; of samurai, 185–86, 195, 196; studies of, 182, 184, 186

Japanese Americans: educational attainment of, 67; immigrants, 67–68, 68t, 124; internments of, 67n; physicians, 67f, 68, 192, 194–95; regression to mean by, 66–68; social mobility of, 66–68, 123, 124; surnames of, 45, 48, 66–68, 192, 194–95, 310–11

Japanese surnames: changes in, 187–88; common, 191–92, 192f, 193–95, 193f;

lineage effects, 118–22, 123f, 140
lineages: Chinese, 180–81; Japanese, 187; Korean clans, 196–98; underlying status of, 285–86. *See also* families; grandparents; intergenerational correlations; surnames
Linnaeus, Carolus, 23–24
locative surnames: downward mobility of, 76–78, 77f, 87; of Norman origin, 76–77, 78–79; of Parliament members, 254, 255, 255f, 256f; in probate records, 85–86, 85f, 86f; social mobility rates of, 255, 256f; of university students, 77–78, 77f
Løken, Katrine V., 272
longevity: educational attainment and, 275; of Gypsies and Travellers, 240; increase in modern societies, 98; inheritance of, 114–16; of parents, 115; status and, 114–16, 310, 314; by surname, 310
Loveridge, 244–46, 245f, 245n, 247, 307, 312–13, 312f, 314
luck, 3, 11, 108, 181, 224–25, 282
Lund University, 36–39, 38f

Mandeville, 76, 314, 316
Mao Zedong, 170, 170n, 180
Mapuche, 202–3, 206, 207–8, 210
Markov process, 12, 113, 140
Maronite Christian surnames, of U.S. physicians, 247, 248
marriages: advertisements in West Bengal, 147n, 163, 166; assortative mating, 14, 139, 163, 281, 285–86; records of, 6, 313–14; selecting partners, 14–15, 282, 285–86; wife's surname adopted by husband, 75, 80. *See also* endogamy; intermarriage
measures of social mobility. *See* social mobility measures
medical professionals: in Australia, 311–12; nurses, 308–9, 308t; relative representation of surname groups among, 307–9, 308t. *See also* physicians

medical researchers, Japanese, 194, 194t
medical schools: for African Americans, 54; in India, 145–46, 151–52, 154, 156–57, 157, 157n, 159t; quotas for Jews, 53–54, 54n, 57
medieval England. *See* England, medieval
meritocracies, 262
Mexican immigrants, 251. *See also* Latino Americans
minority groups: in England, 240; in Japan, 184; in Muslim societies, 238–39; social mobility rates of, 5–6, 62, 111, 113, 123–25; social phenotypes of, 285. *See also individual groups*
Miranda, Leslie, 207
Mizrahi Jews, 235–36
mobility. *See* social mobility
Murdoch, Iris, 279
Murray, Charles, 69, 263–64, 281, 282
Muslims: converts, 238; first names in India, 161, 161t, 162; in India, 144, 149–50, 151–52, 154, 239n; social mobility of, 151–52
Muslim societies: head taxes in, 238; religious minorities in, 238–39. *See also* Iran

names. *See* first names; surnames
Nanjing University, 177
National Archives of Ireland, 315
Nationalist Party, Chinese, 168, 172, 173, 174. *See also* Taiwan
National Jewish Population Survey, 283
National Taiwanese University, 178, 179
Native Americans: gaming profits of, 271; physicians, 52n, 250; removal of, 270; social mobility of, 5–6; surnames of, 45, 51, 310–11
nature vs. nurture: adoption studies, 264–69; dominance of nature, 13, 14–15, 126, 131–32, 136–37; nurture seen as dominant, 6. *See also* genetic transmission

Qian, 172

Qing China: collapse of, 168; elite surnames in, 171–75, 173f, 176, 180, 181,
225–27; examination system of, 171–72,
171f, 173, 174, 176, 180–81, 226; kin networks in, 180–81; social mobility in,
171–75, 180, 225–27, 227f

Quebec, 65–66, 305. *See also* New France
settlers

racial groups. *See* African Americans;
minority groups; whites

rare surnames: Chilean, 203, 204–5, 205;
Chinese, 171–75, 173f; Japanese, 187–91,
189f, 190f, 192–94, 193f, 195–96; lack of
status association, 90, 301; origins of,
90. *See also* English surnames; United
States, surnames in

regression to mean: definition, 3; evidence
of, 5, 11, 107; explanations of, 14; from
extreme positions, 212–16, 214f, 280–82,
300; fertility effects on, 246–47, 246f; of
genetic traits, 136, 139; of heights, 136;
underlying status and, 108–9, 112–13,
212, 282. *See also* downward mobility

relative representation: changes in, 20;
of elite surnames, 20; by occupational
status, 307–9; researching, 307; of
surnames in elite groups, 28–30, 46,
296–300, 298f

religions: converts, 230–31, 232–36, 235n,
238; influence of, 229–31; Zoroastrian-
ism, 239. *See also* Christians; Jews;
Muslims

reservation system, India: beneficiaries
of, 164–65; in education, 145–46, 146t,
151–52, 154, 154n, 156–57, 157n; effects on
mobility, 143, 145, 150, 154, 155, 156–60,
159f, 159t, 166; Muslims excluded from,
151–52; quota levels of, 145n

Rhineland hypothesis, 236, 237

Riddarhuset (House of Nobility), Sweden,
21–22, 21f, 22f. *See also* Swedish nobility

Roine, Jesper, 41

Roma. *See* Gypsies/Travellers

Rothschild, Alfred de, 102

Royal Academy, Swedish, 20, 21t, 39–41,
40f

Rudbeckius, Olaus, 24

Rusbridger, 8

Rusbridger, Alan, 8

Sacerdote, Bruce, 265, 330

Saleh, Mohamed, 238

samurai: adult male adoption by, 187;
downward mobility of, 185–86, 195, 196;
government officials, 182, 185, 186, 186t;
intermarriage of descendants of, 190–91;
Meiji restoration and, 182–83; population share of, 185–86; of Satsuma clan,
183f; social status of, 182, 185; surnames
of, 187–91, 189f, 189t, 190f, 193–94, 193f,
194t, 195; university graduates, 185, 185t

scheduled castes, 144, 149, 150, 151, 156–57,
156f, 158. *See also* castes, Indian; reservation system

scholarly authors, 193–94, 195–96

Scotland. *See* Glasgow

Scottish surnames, in Ireland, 232–35,
232n, 234f

Selfish Reasons to Have More Kids
(Caplan), 281, 285

Sephardic Jews, 45, 48, 235–36. *See also*
Jews

Shakespeare, William: *Hamlet,* 22–23; *A
Midsummer Night's Dream,* 93–94n

Shen, 172

siblings, income correlations among, 268–
69, 269t. *See also* adopted children;
families

Sinclair, 81

Smalls, 51

Smith/Smyth/Smythe, 71, 80, 89, 89n, 242,
244n, 306, 316, 317

social competence: of parents, 13; underlying, 8, 108–13, 125, 282

social entropy, 3, 5, 107
social genotype, 12, 14–15, 282, 283–86
social mobility: desirability of, 1, 5, 274; as Markov process, 140; policies promoting, 268, 274; popular perceptions of, 6, 8; predictability of, 3, 10, 117, 212, 262–63; standard estimates of modern, 3–6, 4f, 8–9, 9f, 11, 12; symmetrical movements, 213–15, 214f, 218, 220; unpredictable outcomes for individuals, 262–63; variations in, 5–6. *See also* downward mobility; educational mobility; regression to mean; status persistence; *individual countries and groups*
social mobility measures: across multiple generations, 292–95; correlations among, 112, 112t, 118; earnings comparisons, 289–90, 289f; of intergenerational mobility, 287–92; one-generation studies, 11; partial, 8, 11, 107, 108, 109, 110, 111–12, 112t, 116–18; standard, 107, 109, 110, 113, 116–17, 290; surname frequencies, 8–9, 9f, 11, 12, 107, 296–300, 298f; transition matrices, 287–89, 288t; underlying status and, 112–13; wealth persistence as, 98, 107. *See also* intergenerational correlations
social mobility rates: consistency of, 9–10, 12, 136–39; increase in modern societies, 6, 9–10; independence of social institutions, 125, 198, 208; low, 3, 9–10, 12, 107, 212–16, 261–62, 274; of minority groups, 5–6, 111, 113, 123–25; in Nordic countries, 5, 19; relative representation changes and, 20; underlying, 8, 108–13, 117, 125, 212, 282; variations across societies, 112, 113–14
social mobility theory: anomalies, 213, 228, 229–35, 238–47, 253–57, 257; assumptions of, 108–9, 228; concerns about, 261–63; deterministic component of, 215; estimates of underlying social mobility, 110–11; explanations of status

persistence, 228–29; family dynamics and, 212, 223–25; law of motion, 109, 212–16; persistence rates, 108–10; predictions of, 112–13, 117, 212, 262–63; random component of, 113–14, 117, 215, 216, 290; simple law, 125, 212, 263; surface vs. underlying status, 108–13, 110f, 117, 125, 282; symmetrical movements, 213–15, 214f, 218; tests of, 120–21, 216–27
social phenotype, 12, 14–15, 282, 283–86
Social Security Death Index, 46, 48, 310
Solon, Gary, 127n, 128n, 330
South Jiangsu, China, 175–76, 176f, 177–78
South Korea. *See* Korea
Stanford University, 276–77n, 280n
Stanley, 80
status: intergenerational transmission of, 109–11, 110f; random component of, 108, 125. *See also* elites; inequality; social entropy; social mobility; underclasses
status measures. *See* education; occupational status; wealth
status persistence: of Brahmins, 10, 154, 282; in Chile, 208; in China, 174–75, 177–78, 177t, 181; of Copts, 10, 282, 285; of elites, 10, 216, 229, 239, 251, 252; in England, 6–8; explanations of, 12–13, 160, 247, 252, 282; genetic transmission and, 13, 14–15, 126–27, 136–37; of Gypsies/Travellers, 10, 240, 247; inequality and, 126–28, 199–200; of Jews, 229, 231; in Sweden, 20, 21t, 30, 41–44, 138; of underclasses, 11, 247, 251, 252. *See also* intergenerational correlations; persistence rates
Stevens, Ann H., 272–73
students. *See* education; university students
surnames: common, 301; frequencies, 301–5; occupational, 71–72, 89–90, 316, 317; origins of, 316–17; patrilineal, 15; researching, 301–15; status related to, 88, 306–12; toponyms, 27, 314. *See also* rela-

tive representation; *individual countries and groups*

Suzuki, 310–11

Suzuki, Masao, 67

Sweden: adopted children in, 266–68; cognitive abilities in, 116–17; democratic transition in, 167; education in, 19, 129–30, 266–68, 275; house prices in, 42f, 43; immigrants in, 26n; income correlations among siblings in, 268–69, 269t; income inequality in, 113–14, 114f; physicians in, 20, 21t, 26–27, 32–35, 32f, 33f, 34f; social programs of, 275; social segregation in, 43; taxation in, 19; tax records of, 27–28, 29f

Sweden, social mobility in: current, 20, 41; educational mobility, 35–39; evidence from surname frequencies, 20, 34–35, 41–44; perceived as high, 19; status persistence, 20, 21t, 30, 41–44, 138; studies of, 19

Swedish Academy of Music, 39–41

Swedish Academy of Sciences, 39–41

Swedish Bar Association, 30

Swedish National Agency for Higher Education, 129

Swedish nobility: current members of, 23; history of ennoblement, 22, 22f; ranks, 22; Riddarhuset, 21–22, 21f; surnames of, 20, 22–23, 24f, 28, 29f, 30, 33–34, 35–36, 40, 41–43

Swedish surnames: of attorneys, 30–32, 31f; changes, 24–25, 26–27, 30–32, 38–39; data sources for, 305; of elites, 20; incomes and wealth and, 27–28, 29f; latinized, 23–25, 25f, 28, 30, 33–34, 38–39, 39f, 40, 41; noble, 20, 22–23, 24f, 28, 29f, 30, 33–34, 35–36, 40, 41–43; patronyms, 25–27, 26f, 27f, 28, 30, 33–34, 35–36, 37, 40–41; of physicians, 26–27, 32–35, 32f, 33f; regulation of, 23, 24–25; topographical, 26f, 27, 27f; of university students, 35–39, 35f, 37f, 38f

Taiwan: elites in, 178–79, 179t; emigration from, 179; refugees from China in, 168, 178; social mobility in, 178–79, 179t; surnames in, 178

taxes: head, 238; inheritance, 96, 97f; in Nordic countries, 19, 275; poll, 71–72; redistributive, 9–10, 275; in United States, 48, 275

Teitelbaum, 302, 304f

Tess of the d'Urbervilles (Hardy), 317

toponyms, 27, 314

Tottenham House, 91–92, 92f

transition matrices, 287–89, 288t

Travellers. *See* Gypsies/Travellers

Tsinghua University, 173–74

underclasses: in England, 240; fertility rates of, 246–47; formation of, 140, 239, 251–52; rare surnames of English, 93–94; regression to mean by, 212–13, 214f; relative representation of surnames, 20; status persistence of, 11, 247, 251, 252; surnames of, 297; underlying status of, 282; in United States, 45, 49–51, 54–55, 249–51, 250f, 263–64, 278

underlying status, 8, 108–13, 117, 125, 126, 212, 282, 283–86

unionization rates, 276

United Kingdom. *See* England; Wales

UK Equality and Human Rights Commission, 240

United Nations Development Program, 201

United States: education in, 111, 131, 131n, 279–80; elites in, 45, 247–51, 263–64, 277–78, 279–81; Head Start Program, 273–74; income inequality in, 113–14, 114f, 261, 263–64, 277–78; Korean adoptees in, 265–66, 266t, 267f, 268; poverty in, 262; taxes in, 48, 275; underclass in, 45, 49–51, 54–55, 249–51, 250f, 263–64, 278. *See also* immigrants to United States

THE PRINCETON ECONOMIC HISTORY
OF THE WESTERN WORLD

Joel Mokyr, Series Editor

(continued next page)